Learn Excel 2011 for Mac

Guy Hart-Davis

Apress®

Learn Excel 2011 for Mac

ISBN-13 (pbk): 978-1-4302-3521-7

ISBN-13 (electronic): 978-1-4302-3522-4

Printed and bound in the United States of America (POD)

Trademarked names, logos, and images may appear in this book. Rather than use a trademark symbol with every occurrence of a trademarked name, logo, or image we use the names, logos, and images only in an editorial fashion and to the benefit of the trademark owner, with no intention of infringement of the trademark.

The use in this publication of trade names, trademarks, service marks, and similar terms, even if they are not identified as such, is not to be taken as an expression of opinion as to whether or not they are subject to proprietary rights.

President and Publisher: Paul Manning
Lead Editor: Michelle Lowman
Development Editor: Douglas Pundick
Technical Reviewer: Jennifer Kettell
Editorial Board: Steve Anglin, Mark Beckner, Ewan Buckingham, Gary Cornell, Jonathan Gennick, Jonathan Hassell, Michelle Lowman, Matthew Moodie, Jeff Olson, Jeffrey Pepper, Frank Pohlmann, Douglas Pundick, Ben Renow-Clarke, Dominic Shakeshaft, Matt Wade, Tom Welsh
Coordinating Editor: Adam Heath
Copy Editor: Sharon Terdeman
Compositor: MacPS, LLC
Indexer: BIM Indexing & Proofreading Sevices
Artist: April Milne
Cover Designer: Anna Ishchenko

Distributed to the book trade worldwide by Springer Science+Business Media, LLC., 233 Spring Street, 6th Floor, New York, NY 10013. Phone 1-800-SPRINGER, fax (201) 348-4505, e-mail orders-ny@springer-sbm.com, or visit www.springeronline.com.

For information on translations, please e-mail rights@apress.com, or visit www.apress.com.

Apress and friends of ED books may be purchased in bulk for academic, corporate, or promotional use. eBook versions and licenses are also available for most titles. For more information, reference our Special Bulk Sales–eBook Licensing web page at www.apress.com/info/bulksales.

This book is dedicated to Rhonda and Teddy.

Contents at a Glance

Contents

■ Chapter 2: Configuring Excel:Mac to Suit the Way You Work 53

■ Chapter 3: Creating Effective Workbooks and Templates 83

About the Author

 **Guy Hart-Davis** is the author of more than 60 computer books including *Learn Microsoft Office 2011 for Mac OS X* and *Beginning Microsoft Office 2010*.

About the Technical Reviewer

Jennifer Ackerman Kettell has written and contributed to dozens of books about software applications, web design, and digital photography. She has worked for Microsoft and other top companies, and has done freelance web design and online community management. Jenn has lived all over the United States, but currently calls upstate New York home.

Acknowledgments

My thanks go to the many people who helped create this book:

- Dominic Shakeshaft for signing me to write the book
- Michelle Lowman and Tom Welsh for developing the manuscript.
- Jenn Kettell for reviewing the manuscript for technical accuracy and contributing helpful suggestions.
- Sharon Terdeman for editing the manuscript with care.
- Adam Heath for coordinating the book project and keeping things running.
- MacPS, LLC for laying out the chapters of the book.
- BIM Indexing & Proofreading Services for creating the index.

Introduction

Do you need to get your work done with Excel—smoothly, confidently, and as quickly as possible?

If so, you've picked up the right book.

Who Is This Book For?

This book is designed to help beginning and intermediate users get up to speed quickly with Excel 2011 for Mac and immediately become productive with it.

If you need to learn to use Excel to accomplish everyday tasks, at work or at home, you'll benefit from this book's focused approach and detailed advice. You can either start from the beginning of the book and work through the chapters in sequence, or use the Table of Contents or the Index to find the topic you need immediately, and then jump right in there.

What Does This Book Cover?

This book contains three parts that cover everything you need to know to use Excel 2011 effectively.

Part 1, "Becoming Proficient with Excel:Mac," makes sure you know essential moves for using Excel:

- Chapter 1, "Learning the Secrets of the Excel:Mac Interface," teaches you the ins and outs of the four main means of controlling Excel: the Ribbon, the toolbars, the menus, and keyboard shortcuts. You grasp how to navigate through worksheets and workbooks; learn about quick ways of entering text in workbooks; and use splitting, freezing, and custom views to display exactly the items you need.

- Chapter 2, "Configuring Excel:Mac to Suit the Way You Work," shows you how to make Excel work you way by setting the most important preferences and by customizing the keyboard shortcuts, toolbars, menus, menu bars, and Ribbon. You also learn how to open workbooks automatically when you launch Excel and how you can save the layout of multiple open workbooks as a workspace that you can instantly restore.

- Chapter 3, "Creating Effective Workbooks and Templates," explains how to create workbooks in which you can enter, edit, and manipulate data quickly and effectively. You learn which file formats to save the workbooks in, how to how to add property information to help you identify workbooks when searching, and how to make the most of templates—including creating templates of your own. You also learn how to organize worksheets, lay data out effectively, define named ranges to make navigation easier, and create a collapsible worksheet.

- Chapter 4, "Formatting Your Worksheets Quickly and Efficiently," shows you how to format worksheets quickly and efficiently using the various tools that Excel provides. We start with formatting rows and columns— everything from changing column width and row height to inserting and deleting rows and columns and hiding sensitive data. Then we go through how to apply straightforward formatting, how to apply conditional formatting to quickly flag values that need attention, and how to use data validation to check for invalid entries. Finally, we cover how to save time by using table formatting or Excel's styles, and how to add headers and footers to worksheets.

Part 2, "Performing Calculations and Presenting Data," gets you up to speed with formulas, functions, charts, and graphical elements such as pictures and sparklines:

- Chapter 5, "Performing Custom Calculations with Formulas," makes sure you know what formulas and functions are, and what the difference between the two is. This chapter then teaches you how to create your own formulas using Excel's calculation operators, starting with straightforward formulas that use a single calculation operator each, and then moving on to more complex formulas that use multiple calculation operators. You also learn how to override Excel's default order for evaluating operators and how to troubleshoot common problems that occur with formulas.

- Chapter 6, "Using Excel's Built-In Functions," explains how to insert functions in your worksheets using the various tools that Excel provides, find the functions you want, and point the functions to the data they need for the calculations. The second part of the chapter reviews Excel's different categories of functions, such as database functions, logical functions, and math and trigonometric functions, and gives examples of how to use widely used functions.

- Chapter 7, "Creating Clear and Persuasive Charts," teaches you how to present data clearly and persuasively using Excel's wide range of charts. You learn the different ways you can place charts in worksheets, the components of charts, and the types of charts you can use. We then dig into how you create a chart from your data, lay it out the way you want, and then give it the look it needs. We also look at ways of reusing the custom charts you create and ways of using Excel charts in Word documents or PowerPoint presentations.

- Chapter 8, "Using Data Bars, Color Scales, Icon Sets, and Sparklines," shows you how to add visual appeal to your worksheets by using those four types of single-cell graphical elements. You quickly get the hang of using data bars to compare the values in a range of cells, adding color scales to adjust the background colors of cells to provide a visual reference to their values, and using icon sets to provide quick visual reference to performance. And you learn to create single-cell charts using sparklines.

- Chapter 9, "Illustrating Your Worksheets with Pictures, SmartArt, and More," explains ways of giving your workbooks visual interest by adding graphics, shapes, SmartArt diagrams, and WordArt items. You learn how to make a picture look the way you want it, how to position graphical objects wherever you need them, and how to position graphical items relative to cells and how to arrange graphical objects to control which ones are visible.

Part 3, "Analyzing Data and Sharing and Automating Your Workbooks," shows you how to analyze, manipulate, and share the workbooks you've built:

- Chapter 10, "Creating Tables with Databases," covers using Excel's tables to create databases for storing information, sorting it, and filtering it to find the records you need. You also learn how to put Excel's database functions to work with tables.

- Chapter 11, "Solving Business Questions with What-If Analysis, Goal Seek, and Solver," teaches you how to analyze your data using four powerful tools. You learn to use data tables to assess the impact of one or two variables on a calculation and how to use scenarios to experiment with different sets of values without changing your core data. You also learn to use Goal Seek to solve single-variable problems and Solver to crack multivariable problems.

- Chapter 12, "Analyzing Data with PivotTables," explains what PivotTables are and how you can use them to examine the data in your worksheets and find the secrets it contains. You learn how to create PivotTables either using Excel's automated tool or by placing fields manually where you need them, how to change the PivotTable once you've created it, and how to sort and filter the data it contains.

- Chapter 13, "Collaborating and Sharing with Macs and Windows PCs," takes you through ways of sharing your workbooks with others. We start by covering how to print worksheets, create PDF files from them, and export data to comma-separated values files. We then move on to sharing workbooks so that multiple people can work on them at the same time, tracking the changes if necessary so that you can review them. We finish by looking at how to merge changes from separate copies of the same workbook into one workbook and how to consolidate multiple worksheets into a single worksheet.

- Chapter 14, "Automating Tasks with Macros and VBA," shows you how to record macros to eliminate the drudgery of performing the same task over and over again. You learn how to run macros using the menus or toolbars, using keyboard shortcuts, or even by assigning them to worksheet objects such as command buttons. I also introduce you to the Visual Basic Editor and show you how to edit a macro to change what it does.

Conventions Used in This Book

This book uses several conventions to make its meaning clear without wasting words:

- *Ribbon commands.* The ~TRA arrow shows the sequence for choosing an item from the Ribbon. For example, "choose Layout ~TRA Print ~TRA Preview" means that you click the Layout tab of the Ribbon (displaying the tab's contents), go to the Print group, and then click the Preview button.

- *Menu commands.* The ~TRA arrow shows the sequence of commands for choosing an item from the menu bar. For example, "choose Data ~TRA Data Table" means that you open the Data menu and then click the Data Table item on it.

- *Special paragraphs.* Special paragraphs present information that you may want to pay extra attention to. Note paragraphs contain information you may want to know; Tip paragraphs present techniques you may benefit from using; and Caution paragraphs warn you of potential problems.

- *Check boxes.* Excel uses many check boxes—the square boxes that can either have a check mark in them (indicate that the option is turned on) or not (indicating that the option is turned off). This book tells you to "select" a check box when you need to put a check mark in the check box, and to "clear" a check box when you need to remove the check mark from it. If the check box is already selected or cleared, you don't need to change it—just make sure it's set the right way.

- *Keyboard shortcuts.* In Excel, you can often save time and effort by using a keyboard shortcut rather than a Ribbon command or a menu command. This book uses + signs to represent keyboard shortcuts. For example, "press Cmd+S" means that you hold down the Cmd key, press the S key, and then release the Cmd key. "Press Cmd+Option+T" means that you hold down the Cmd key and the Option key, press the T key, and then release the Cmd key and the Option key.

Part I

Becoming Proficient with Excel:Mac

In this part of the book, you become proficient at the essentials of Excel:Mac.

In Chapter 1, you learn the ins and outs of the four main means of controlling Excel: the Ribbon, the toolbars, the menus, and keyboard shortcuts. You grasp how to navigate through worksheets and workbooks; learn about quick ways to enter text in workbooks; and use splitting, freezing, and custom views to display exactly the items you need.

In Chapter 2, we cover how to make Excel work your way by setting the most important preferences and by customizing the keyboard shortcuts, toolbars, menus, menu bars, and Ribbon. You also learn how to open workbooks automatically when you launch Excel and how you can save the layout of multiple open workbooks as a workspace that you can instantly restore.

In Chapter 3, you study how to create workbooks in which you can enter, edit, and manipulate data quickly and effectively. You learn which file formats to save the workbooks in, how to add property information to help you identify workbooks when searching, and how to make the most of templates—including creating templates of your own. You also learn how to organize worksheets, lay out data effectively, define named ranges to make navigation easier, and create a collapsible worksheet.

In Chapter 4, we go through how to format worksheets quickly and efficiently using the various tools that Excel provides. We start with formatting rows and columns—everything from changing column width and row height to inserting and deleting rows and columns and hiding sensitive data. Then we see how to apply straightforward formatting, how to apply conditional formatting to quickly flag values that need attention, and how to use data validation to check for invalid entries. Finally, we cover how to save time by using table formatting and Excel's styles, and how to add headers and footers to worksheets.

Chapter 1

Learning the Secrets of the Excel:Mac Interface

In this chapter, you'll learn the ins and outs of the Excel:Mac interface and the many secrets it holds.

We'll start by looking at the four main ways to control Excel: the Ribbon, the toolbars, the menus on the menu bar, and keyboard shortcuts. These give you great flexibility in the way you control Excel, especially when you set them up as you prefer.

From there, we'll discuss how to navigate through worksheets and workbooks. We'll then go through the various ways in which you can get data into your Excel workbooks—from importing existing data to entering it more quickly using AutoCorrect, AutoFill, and the Scrapbook.

Toward the end of the chapter, I'll show you the smart ways to view your workbooks so you can work quickly and efficiently. These include splitting the window to show different parts of the worksheet at the same time, opening extra windows, and freezing key rows and columns so that they stay onscreen when you scroll to other parts of the worksheet. You can even create custom views to keep your data laid out exactly as you need it.

Getting Ready to Learn Excel's Secrets

You'll probably want to have Excel running as you go through this chapter so you can try out the modifications and techniques that interest you. So launch Excel if it's not already running: either click the Excel icon on the Dock or (if there isn't one) click the desktop to activate the Finder, choose Go ➤ Applications, and then double-click the Excel icon in the Microsoft Office 2011 folder.

Excel may display the Excel Workbook Gallery dialog box. If so, click the Excel Workbook icon in the All category and then click the Choose button. This makes Excel create a blank workbook rather than one based on a content template. We'll look at how to use the Excel Workbook Gallery to create workbooks in Chapter 3.

Four Ways to Control Excel

To control Excel, you give commands. For example, when you need a new workbook, you give the command to create a new workbook.

In Excel 2011 (see Figure 1–1), you can give commands in the four main ways we noted:

- *Menus.* Like most Mac applications, Excel provides a set of menus that appear on the Mac OS X menu bar when Excel is the active application. To give a command, you click the menu, and then click the command.

- *Ribbon.* The Ribbon is the new control strip introduced in Excel 2011. To give a command, you click its button or control.

- *Toolbars.* Excel includes the Standard toolbar and the Formatting toolbar. The Standard toolbar appears across the top of the Excel window by default, as in Figure 1.1. To give a command, you click its button or control.

- *Keyboard shortcuts.* To give a command, you press the associated key combination.

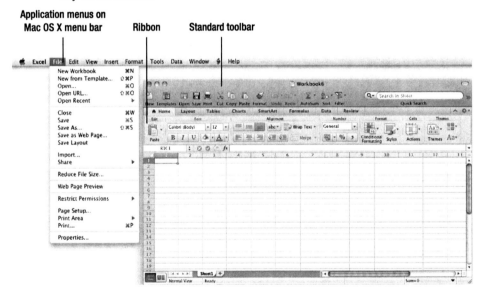

Figure 1–1. *You can control Excel using the Ribbon, the toolbars, the menus on the menu bar, or keyboard shortcuts.*

Let's dig into each of these in turn, starting with the Ribbon.

Secrets of the Ribbon

The Ribbon is the control strip that runs across the top of the Excel window below the window's title bar and any toolbars you've chosen to display. The Ribbon is a control bar that contains multiple tabs, each containing several groups of controls. At any time, the Ribbon displays one tab's contents; to switch to the contents of another tab, you click that tab. As you can see in Figure 1–2, the active tab is a different color than the other tabs, so you can easily pick it out.

NOTE: To make clear where you find the controls, I give Ribbon instructions in the sequence tab–group–control. For example, "choose **Formulas ➤ Audit Formulas ➤ Trace Precedents**" means that you click the Formulas tab to display its contents, go to the Audit Formulas group (without clicking it), and then click the Trace Precedents button.

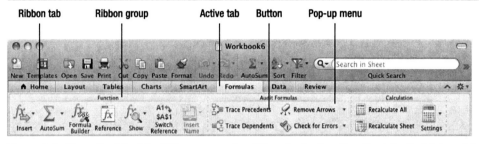

Figure 1–2. *The active tab of the Ribbon appears in a different color than the other tabs. Each tab contains groups of controls, such as buttons and pop-up menus.*

Understanding How the Ribbon's Tabs Work

Most of the time, the Ribbon displays eight tabs that contain controls for most normal operations in Excel:

- *Home.* This tab contains controls for cut, copy, and paste; font, alignment, and number formatting; conditional formatting and styles; inserting and deleting rows, columns, and cells; and applying themes.

- *Layout.* This tab contains controls for manipulating page setup, changing the view, choosing which items to print, and arranging workbook windows.

- *Tables.* This tab contains controls for working with data tables, which you use for creating databases in Excel.

- *Charts.* This tab contains controls for inserting charts and sparklines (miniature charts that fit in a single cell), choosing the layout for charts and sparklines, and applying layouts and styles to charts.

- *SmartArt.* This tab contains controls for inserting and formatting SmartArt graphics.

- *Formulas.* This tab contains controls for inserting functions, auditing formulas, and controlling how Excel performs calculations.

- *Data.* This tab contains controls for sorting and filtering data, creating PivotTables and performing what-if analysis, connecting to external data source, validating data, and grouping and outlining worksheets. (Chapter 3 discusses grouping and outlining.)

- *Review.* This tab contains controls for checking spelling, working with comments, applying protection to a worksheet or workbook, and sharing a workbook.

As well as these standard tabs, the Ribbon contains other tabs that it displays only when you need them. These are sometimes called *context-sensitive tabs*. For example, when you select a chart, Excel automatically displays the Chart Layout tab and the Format tab (see Figure 1–3).

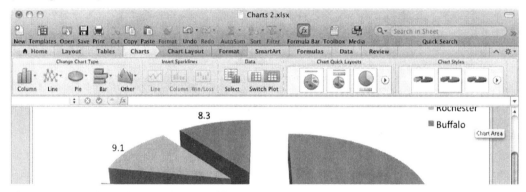

Figure 1–3. *The Ribbon displays context-sensitive tabs when you select an object for which tabs are available. Here, the Chart Layout tab and Format tab appear on the Ribbon because a chart is active.*

NOTE: Office:Mac got the Ribbon late compared to Office for Windows, but in many ways Office:Mac has lucked out—its Ribbon is the better of the two. In Office for Windows, the Ribbon replaces the menu bar and the toolbars, so you have to use it unless you set up myriad keyboard shortcuts. In Office:Mac, the Ribbon supplements the menu bar and the toolbars, and you can choose how much to use it. Normally, you'll want to leave the Ribbon on so you can access the extra features it provides; but if you find the menus and toolbars contain all the commands you need, you can turn the Ribbon off.

Understanding How the Ribbon's Groups and Controls Work

Chances are you got the hang of using the Ribbon's tabs the first time you used Excel. The groups and controls are a little trickier because they change depending on whether the Excel window is wide enough to display the entire Ribbon.

When the Excel window *is* wide enough, all the groups appear, and they display their controls—the buttons, pop-up menus, check boxes, and so on—in their most spacious arrangement. For example, the top part of Figure 1–4 shows the rightmost sections of the Layout tab of the Ribbon. All the controls in the Print group and the Window group appear with labels, so you can easily identify each control.

But when there's less space, Excel gradually collapses parts of the Ribbon so as to display as much as possible in the available space. For example, the middle part of Figure 1–4 shows the rightmost sections of the Layout tab again, but this time the labels have disappeared from the Split button, Arrange pop-up menu, Save Layout button, and Freeze Panes pop-up menu. In the Print group, the Fit To label still appears, but Excel has removed the "page(s) wide" and "page(s) tall" labels to save space.

When the window is even narrower, Excel collapses the groups and controls further. In the lower part of Figure 1–4, you can see that the Print group now contains only the Preview button and the Setup button. But you can click the Setup button to display the Print Setup dialog box, in which you can configure all the Print group settings the Ribbon has hidden, not to mention other settings.

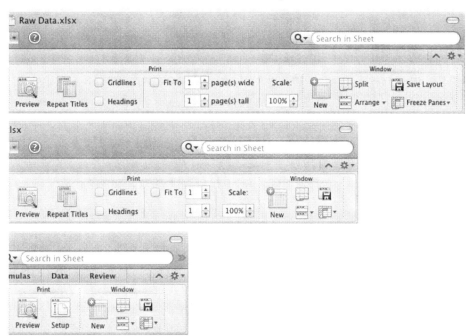

Figure 1–4. *As the Excel window becomes narrower, Excel hides first the labels for the less important controls and then the controls themselves, as you can see here with the controls in the Print group and Window group of the Layout tab.*

By automatically changing the Ribbon to suit the window width, Excel keeps as many controls as possible at the tip of your mouse. But because labels may not appear, you will sometimes need to display the ScreenTip to identify a control; to display the ScreenTip, hold the mouse pointer over the control for a moment (see Figure 1–5).

Figure 1–5. *When a control's label doesn't appear on the Ribbon, hold the mouse pointer over the control to display a ScreenTip explaining what it does.*

Further, because some controls may appear in different places when the Ribbon's whole width isn't displayed, you may sometimes need to hunt for the controls you need. This book assumes that the window is displayed wide enough for you to see all the controls on the Ribbon, but it notes some of the disappearing controls that can cause confusion.

If you can't see a command that's supposed to be there, have a poke around the remaining controls in the group to find where Excel has hidden the control, or to see if one of the controls opens a dialog box that contains the controls. (Or use the menu alternative if there is one.)

Collapsing the Ribbon

When you need more space to work on a worksheet, collapse the Ribbon to just its tab bar (see Figure 1–6) in one of these ways:

- Click the tab that's currently active.
- Click the Collapse Ribbon button (the ^ button) at the right end of the Ribbon.
- Choose **View ➤ Ribbon** from the menu bar (removing the check mark next to the Ribbon item).
- Press Cmd+Option+I.

Expand Ribbon

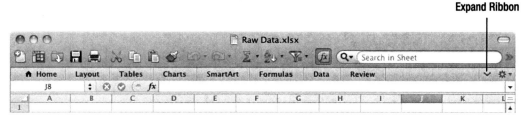

Figure 1–6. *Click the Collapse Ribbon button to collapse the Ribbon to just its tabs. Click the Expand Ribbon button (which replaces the Collapse Ribbon button) to expand the Ribbon again.*

As you'd guess, you use almost the same moves to display the Ribbon again:

- Click the tab you want to see.
- Click the Expand Ribbon button (the ∨ button) at the right end of the Ribbon.
- Choose **View ➤ Ribbon** from the menu bar.
- Press Cmd+Option+I.

> **TIP:** If you don't want to use the Ribbon, you can turn it off completely. And if you do want to use it, you can choose which tabs appear and the order they appear in. See the section "Customizing the Ribbon" in Chapter 2 for details.

Secrets of the Toolbars

Excel comes with two built-in toolbars—Standard and Formatting—but you can create as many others as you need. You can choose which toolbars to display and how to display them. And you can customize both the built-in toolbars and your own toolbars, as you'll see in Chapter 2.

Choosing Which Toolbars to Display

First, decide which toolbars you want to display. The easiest way to do this is to Ctrl+click or right-click a toolbar that's displayed, click or highlight the Toolbars item on the context menu, and then click the toolbar you want to display or hide. Excel puts a check mark next to a displayed toolbar on the Toolbars submenu. If the toolbar is displayed, you click to remove the check mark and hide the toolbar.

If no toolbar is displayed, choose **View ➤ Toolbars** to display the Toolbars submenu on the View menu, and then click the toolbar you want to display.

Switching the Standard Toolbar Between Icons and Text and Icons Only

Next, choose whether to display the buttons on the Standard toolbar as icons with text labels or as icons only. If you find the text labels make the icons easier to identify, they're worth the small amount of extra space they take up.

To switch between icons and labels and icons only, Ctrl+click or right-click the Standard toolbar and then click the Icon and Text item or the Icon Only item on the context menu, as appropriate.

NOTE: The Formatting toolbar displays only icons—you don't have the option of displaying text labels for its buttons.

Undocking and Docking the Formatting Toolbar

At first, Excel displays the Standard toolbar at the top of the window, between the title bar and the Ribbon (unless you've turned off the Ribbon). The same goes for the Formatting toolbar if you display it.

The Standard toolbar remains docked all the time, but you can undock the Formatting toolbar if you prefer to have it floating, so you can position it freely on your Desktop.

To undock the Formatting toolbar, Ctrl+click or right-click the toolbar and then click Dock Toolbar in Window on the context menu to remove the check mark. Excel undocks the toolbar and displays it as a floating toolbar that you can reposition as needed (see Figure 1–7).

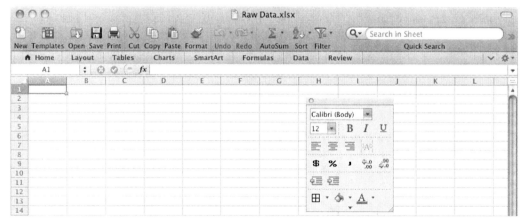

Figure 1–7. *You can undock the Formatting toolbar to position it anywhere on the screen. To free up the Excel window, position the toolbar outside the window. When you need the formatting controls close to your data, position the toolbar over the Excel window like this.*

> **TIP:** You can toggle the display of the docked toolbars on and off by clicking the jellybean button (the gray rounded-rectangle button) at the right end of the title bar.

Secrets of the Menu Bar

If you've used other Mac applications, you probably know how to use the menu bar:

1. If the application for which you want to issue a command isn't active, click one of the application's windows to make it active. Mac OS X then displays the application's menus on the menu bar. For example, when Excel is active, you see its menus, with Excel's own menu appearing at the left end of the menu bar.

2. Click the menu you want to open.

3. Click the command you want to give. Or, if the command is on a submenu, click or highlight the submenu item to display the submenu, then click the item.

> **NOTE:** An ellipsis (...) at the end of a menu command's name usually indicates that the command displays a dialog box rather than taking an action. For example, the Close command on the File menu closes the active document, while the Save As... command displays the Save As dialog box. (The Save command also displays the Save As dialog box—but only if you've never saved this workbook before.) But with the move to the Ribbon, some menu commands with ellipses display the tab of the Ribbon that contains the command you need to complete the action.

Giving a command via the menu bar could hardly be easier. But the menu bar also has two secrets. You can:

- *Close all open workbooks at once.* Hold down Shift and click the File menu, then click the Close All command that replaces the regular Close command. If any of the workbooks contains unsaved changes, Excel prompts you to save them, just like when you close a single workbook.

- *Customize the menus and menu bar.* You can customize the menus and menu bar to put the commands you need where you find them most useful. See the section "Customizing the Menus and the Menu Bar" in Chapter 2 for details.

Driving Excel with Keyboard Shortcuts

If you like to work with the keyboard, spend some time learning Excel's built-in keyboard shortcuts and creating custom shortcuts for other commands you want to be able to give from the keyboard.

For the commands you use often from the menu bar, you can quickly learn the keyboard shortcuts by opening the menus and looking at the shortcut keys shown to the right of the commands. The File menu (shown on the left in Figure 1–8) and the Edit menu (shown on the right in Figure 1–8) have the most keyboard shortcuts assigned at first.

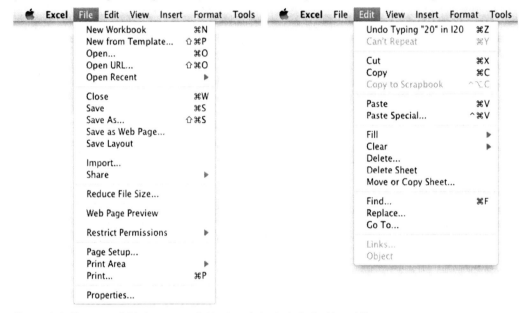

Figure 1–8. *You can quickly learn essential keyboard shortcuts by looking at the menus.*

To find other keyboard shortcuts, click the Help menu on the menu bar to open it, type **excel keyboard shortcuts** in the Search box, and then click the Excel Keyboard Shortcuts topic that Excel offers.

> **NOTE:** Throughout the book, I'll teach you the most widely useful keyboard shortcuts alongside the Ribbon, toolbar, and menu methods of giving commands.

If you find that Excel doesn't have a keyboard shortcut for a command, or that the existing keyboard shortcut is awkward to press or hard to remember, you can create your own. See the section "Creating Custom Keyboard Shortcuts" in Chapter 2 for instructions.

TIP: You can also use the Customize Toolbars and Menus dialog box to learn the keyboard shortcuts assigned to existing commands. This is useful when you know which command you want but can't easily locate its keyboard shortcut either on the menus or in the Help files.

Making the Toolbox Work Your Way

Like the other Office applications, Excel has a tool palette called the Toolbox. The Toolbox floats freely rather than being docked to the application window, so you can position it wherever is best for you.

In Excel, the Toolbox contains four palettes:

- *Scrapbook.* The Scrapbook is a storage area for collecting items you want to be able to paste easily into your workbooks. We'll look at the Scrapbook later in this chapter.

- *Reference Tools.* The References Tools palette gives you quick access to an online thesaurus, dictionary, bilingual dictionary, translation engine, and Web search.

- *Formula Builder.* The Formula Builder is a tool for inserting functions and formulas. I'll show you how to use the Formula Builder in Chapter 5.

- *Compatibility Report.* You use the Compatibility Report palette to review possible problems when saving Excel workbooks in older file formats (for example, so that people with older versions of Excel can use them). Chapter 3 shows you how to use the Compatibility Report palette.

To display the Toolbox's palettes, choose View ➤ Formula Builder, View ➤ Scrapbook, View ➤ Reference Tools, or View ➤ Compatibility Report from the menu bar. The Toobox opens, showing the palette you chose. You can also click the Toolbox button on the Standard toolbar, go to the tab bar to the top of the Toolbox, and then click the tab button for the tab you want.

TIP: Press Shift+F3 to display the Formula Builder or Cmd+Option+R to display the Reference Tools palette

To hide the Toolbox, you can click its Close button (the red button in its title bar) or give the View menu command again—for example, when the Scrapbook palette is displayed, choose View ➤ Scrapbook to hide the Toolbox. Or you may want to make the Toolbox collapse, fade, or close after you've left it unused for a number of seconds. To set it to take one of these actions, follow these steps:

1. Click the Toolbox Settings button, the curling-arrow button in the upper-right corner of the Toolbox. The Toolbox flips over and displays the Toolbox Settings palette (see Figure 1–9).

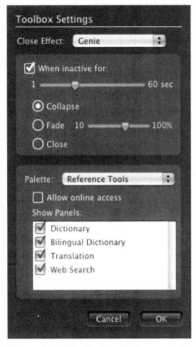

Figure 1–9. *The Toolbox Settings palette on the back of the Toolbox lets you make the Toolbox collapse, fade, or close automatically after a period of inactivity.*

2. In the Close Effect pop-up menu, choose the effect you want to use for closing the Toolbox: Genie, Scale, or None. (Genie and Scale are the same effects used for minimizing applications to the Dock.)

3. Select the When inactive for check box.

4. Drag the slider to set the number of seconds of inactivity—from 1 to 60.

5. Select the appropriate option button:

    ▪ *Collapse.* Select this option button to make the Toolbox collapse to just its title bar and the tab bar. The Toolbox expands again when you click a tab button.

    ▪ *Fade.* Select this option button to make the Toolbox fade. Drag the slider to set the fade percentage—from 10 percent (almost invisible) to 100 percent (fully there). The Toolbox reappears when you move the mouse pointer over it.

    ▪ *Close.* Select this option button to make the Toolbox actually close.

NOTE: In the lower part of the Toolbox Settings palette, you can choose which items appear in the Reference Tools palette. Make sure that Reference Tools is selected in the Palette pop-up menu, and then select or clear the check boxes in the Show Panels list box as needed. Select the Allow online access check box if you want the reference tools to be able to look up material on the Internet.

6. Click the OK button to close the Toolbox Settings palette. The Toolbox flips over and displays the palette that was displayed before.

ODDITIES OF THE TOOLBOX

The Toolbox is designed to look like just another floating window but it apparently involves particularly fiendish coding challenges, with multiple different windows being displayed in the same frame. Because of these, you may see the Toolbox behave oddly in three ways:

- If your Mac has multiple monitors, you may find that Excel displays the Toolbox on a different monitor than the active workbook window.

- If you're using Leopard (Mac OS X 10.5) rather than Snow Leopard (Mac OS X 10.6), you may find that the Toolbox moves to a different Space when you switch from one Space to another using the Spaces feature.

- When you switch panes in the Toolbox, you may notice a delay—especially when you're switching to the Scrapbook. This delay happens because Excel is actually conjuring up a new window on the fly rather than displaying a pane that's already there.

All these odd behaviors are normal, if annoying. But at this writing the Toolbox also seems to cause memory problems on some Macs. If you find your Mac suddenly starts running much more slowly when the Toolbox is open, close the Toolbox and then reopen it.

Navigating Quickly Through Worksheets and Workbooks

To work swiftly and easily in Excel, you need to know the best ways of navigating through worksheets and workbooks. We'll look at these in this section—after we check that we're using the same terms to refer to the elements in the Excel user interface.

Elements of the Excel User Interface

When you've created a new workbook or opened an existing one, Excel displays the workbook's worksheets. Figure 1–10 shows Excel with a workbook open and the main elements of the user interface labeled.

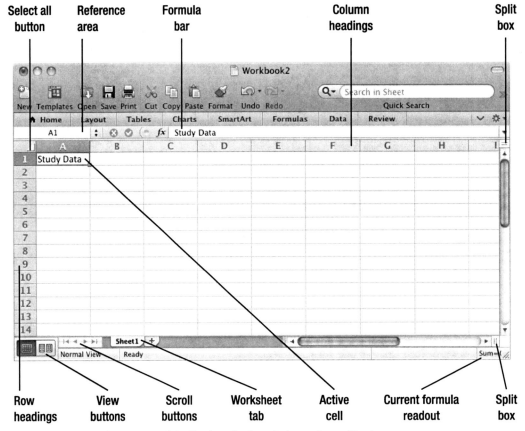

Figure 1–10. *The main elements of the Excel application window and a workbook*

▓ *Formula bar.* This is the bar below the Ribbon. This area shows the data or formula in the active cell and gives you an easy place to enter and edit data.

▓ *Reference area.* This area appears at the left end of the formula bar. It shows the active cell's address (for example, A1) or the name you've given the cell so as to refer to it easily.

▓ *Row headings.* These are the numbers at the left side of the screen that identify each row. The first row is 1, the second row 2, and so on, up to the last row, 1048576.

▓ *Column headings.* These are the letters at the top of the worksheet grid that identify the columns.

    ▓ The first column is A, the second column B, and so on up to Z.

    ▓ Excel then uses two letters: AA to AZ, BA to BZ, and so forth until ZZ.

    ▓ After that, Excel uses three letters: AAA, AAB, and so on up to the last column, XFD.

- *Cells.* These are the boxes formed by the intersections of the rows and columns. Each cell is identified by its column letter and row number. For example, the first cell in column A is cell A1 and the second cell in column B is cell B2. The last cell in the worksheet is XFD1048576.

- *Active cell.* This is the cell you're working in—the cell that receives the input from the keyboard. Excel displays a blue rectangle around the active cell.

- *Select All button.* Click this button at the intersection of the row headings and column headings to select all the cells in the worksheet.

- *Worksheet tabs.* Each worksheet has a tab at the bottom that bears its name. To display a worksheet, you click its tab in the worksheet tabs area.

- *Scroll buttons.* Click these buttons to scroll the worksheet tabs so you can see the ones you need. Click the leftmost button to scroll all the way back to the first tab, or click the rightmost button to scroll to the last tab. Click the two middle buttons to scroll back or forward by one tab.

- *View buttons.* Click these buttons to switch between Normal view and Page Layout view. You'll learn how to use these views later in this chapter.

- *Split boxes.* You use these boxes when you need to split the worksheet window into two or four areas. You'll learn how to do this in the section "Splitting the Window to View Separate Parts of a Worksheet" later in this chapter.

- *Current formula readout.* This readout shows you the result of any of six common formulas—AVERAGE, COUNT, COUNTNUMS, MIN, MAX, or SUM—as applied to the current cell or range. You can click the readout to switch formulas, or choose the None item to display no formula result. For example, if you select cells B1:B4 and choose the SUM formula, you'll see the total produced by the values in these cells.

Navigating Among Worksheets

Each workbook consists of one or more worksheets or other sheets, such as chart sheets or macro sheets. You can use as many worksheets as you need to separate your data conveniently within a single workbook file. For example, you can have a separate budget-planning worksheet for each department in a single workbook file rather than having a separate workbook for each department.

To display the worksheet you want to use, click its tab in the worksheet tab bar (see Figure 1–11). If the worksheet's tab isn't visible in the worksheet tab bar, click the scroll buttons to display it (unless you've hidden the worksheet).

> **TIP:** If you want to make the worksheet tab bar wider so you can see more tabs at once, drag the divider bar to the right. Excel makes the horizontal scroll bar smaller to compensate.

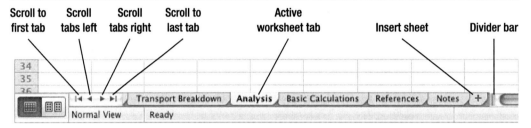

Figure 1–11. *Use the worksheet tab bar to display the worksheet you want or to insert a new worksheet. You can drag the divider bar to change the length of the tab bar.*

> **TIP:** You can quickly move to the next worksheet by pressing Cmd+Page Down or to the previous worksheet by pressing Cmd+Page Up.

Changing the Active Cell

In Excel, you usually work in a single cell at a time. That cell is called the *active cell* and it receives the input from the keyboard.

You can move the active cell easily using either the mouse or the keyboard:

- *Mouse.* Click the cell you want to make active.

- *Keyboard.* Press the arrow keys to move the active cell up or down by one row or left or right by one column at a time. You can also press the keyboard shortcuts shown in Table 1–1 to move the active cell further.

> **TIP:** If your Mac's keyboard doesn't have the Home key, End key, Page Up key, and Page Down key, you'll need to use function-key shortcuts. Press Fn+left arrow for Home, Fn+right arrow for End, Fn+up arrow for PageUp, and Fn+down arrow for PageDown. Use these keys as needed with the keyboard shortcuts in Table 1–1—for example, press Cmd+Fn+left arrow to move to the first cell in the active worksheet.

Table 1–1. *Keyboard Shortcuts for Changing the Active Cell*

To Change the Active Cell	Press This Keyboard Shortcut
To the first cell in the row	Home
To the first cell in the active worksheet	Cmd+Home
To the last cell used in the worksheet	Cmd+End
Down one screen	Page Down
Up one screen	Page Up
Right one screen	Option+Page Down
Left one screen	Option+Page Up
To the last row in the worksheet	Cmd+down arrow
To the last column in the worksheet	Cmd+right arrow
To the first row in the worksheet	Cmd+up arrow
To the first column in the worksheet	Cmd+left arrow or Home
To the next corner cell clockwise in a selected range	Ctrl+. (Ctrl and the period key)

Selecting and Manipulating Cells

To work with a single cell, you need only click it or use the keyboard to make it the active cell. When you need to affect multiple cells at once, you select the cells using the mouse or keyboard.

Excel calls a selection of cells a *range*. A range can consist of either a rectangle of contiguous cells or two or more cells that aren't next to each other. The left illustration in Figure 1–12 shows a range of contiguous cells, while the right illustration shows a range of separate cells.

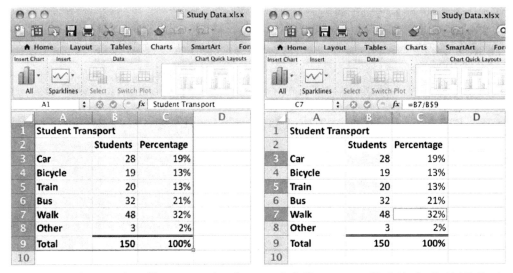

Figure 1–12. *You can select either a range of contiguous cells (left) or a range of individual cells (right). Excel darkens the headers of the rows and columns that contain the range to make the range easier to see.*

You can select a range of contiguous cells in any of these three ways:

- *Click and drag.* Click the first cell in the range, then drag to select all the others. For example, if you click cell B2 and then drag to cell E7, you select a range that's four columns wide and six rows deep. Excel uses the notation B2:E7 to describe this range—the starting cell address, a colon, and then the ending cell address.

- *Click and then Shift+click.* Click the first cell in the range, then Shift+click the last cell. Excel selects all the cells in between. You can use this technique anytime, but it's most useful when the first cell and last cell are widely separated; for example, when the first cell and last cell don't appear in the Excel window at the same time.

- *Hold down Shift and use the arrow keys.* Use the arrow keys to move the active cell to where you want to start the range; then hold down Shift and use the arrow keys to extend the selection for the rest of the range. This method is good if you prefer using the keyboard to the mouse.

You can select a range of noncontiguous cells by clicking the first cell (or dragging through a range of contiguous cells) and then holding down Cmd while you click other individual cells or drag through ranges of contiguous cells. Excel uses commas to separate the individual cells in this type of range. For example, the range D3,E5,F7,G1:G13 consists of three individual cells (D3, E5, and F7) and one range of contiguous cells (G1 through G13).

NOTE: You can quickly select a row by clicking its row heading or pressing Shift+spacebar when the active cell is in that row. Likewise, you can select a column by clicking its column heading or pressing Ctrl+spacebar. To select all the cells in the active worksheet, click the Select All button (where the row headings and column headings meet). You can also either press Cmd+A or press Shift+spacebar followed by Ctrl+spacebar (or vice versa).

To deselect a range you've selected, click anywhere outside the range.

Tools for Entering Text and Formulas Quickly

The most straightforward way of entering text and formulas in your workbooks is to type it in. But no matter how fast you type, it pays to know all the alternative ways of getting data and formulas into your workbooks. These range from importing the data from an existing file, connecting to an external data source, speeding up data entry by maxing out AutoCorrect, taking advantage of the powerful AutoFill feature, and using copy and paste in all its flavors. You can even using the Replace feature to enter text.

Importing Data

If you have the data you need in an existing file, you can usually import it into Excel. Excel can import files in these five formats:

- *Comma-separated values (CSV).* A CSV file uses a comma to separate the contents of cells.

- *Tab-separated values (TSV).* A TSV file uses a tab to separate the contents of cells.

NOTE: Most spreadsheet applications and database applications can export data in CSV format or TSV format. You can also create these files manually if necessary. For example, if you need to create some data on a mobile device that doesn't have a spreadsheet application, you can create it as a text file with a comma separating each field.

- *Space-separated values.* A space-separated values file (not usually referred to as SSV) uses a space to separate the contents of cells.

- *FileMaker Pro database.* FileMaker Pro is a heavy-duty database application that runs on both Mac OS X and Windows. FileMaker Pro files use the .fp7 file extension.

- *HTML.* HTML (HyperText Markup Language) is the markup language used for Web pages.

NOTE: Importing works best when you need all the data from a file. When you need only some of the data, copy and paste is usually more effective. Alternatively, you can import all the data and then delete what you don't need.

To import data from an existing file, follow these steps:

1. Open the workbook you want to import the data into. If you want to put the data in a new workbook, press Cmd+N to create one.

2. Choose **File ➤ Import** to display the Import dialog box (see Figure 1–13).

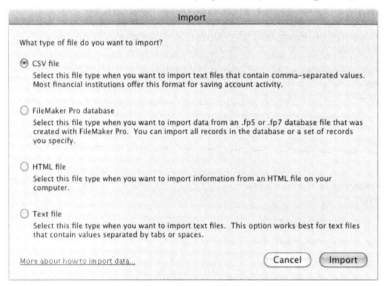

Figure 1–13. *In the Import dialog box, select the appropriate option button based on the type of file you want to import.*

3. Select the CSV file option button, the FileMaker Pro database option button, the HTML file option button, or the Text File option button (for tab-separated files or space-separated files).

NOTE: To import data from a FileMaker Pro database, you must have FileMaker Pro installed on your Mac. Without FileMaker Pro, Excel can't read a FileMaker Pro database.

4. Click the Import button to display the dialog box for identifying the file. The name of this dialog box varies depending on your choice in step 3: it's the Choose a File dialog box for CSV files or text files, the Choose a Database dialog box for FileMaker Pro, and the Open: Microsoft Excel dialog box for HTML files.

5. Choose the file that contains the data and then click the Get Data button, the Choose button, or the Open button (depending on the dialog box).

6. Follow the steps of the Import Wizard that opens. The following sections explain the main considerations.

Importing Data from a Comma-Separated Values File or a Text File

When you import data from a comma-separated values file or a text file, the Text Import Wizard walks you through the import process.

On the wizard's first screen (see Figure 1–14), start by making sure that Excel has selected the Delimited option button if your file is delimited with commas, tabs, or another character. If it's a text file that uses spaces to create fixed-width columns, select the Fixed width option button.

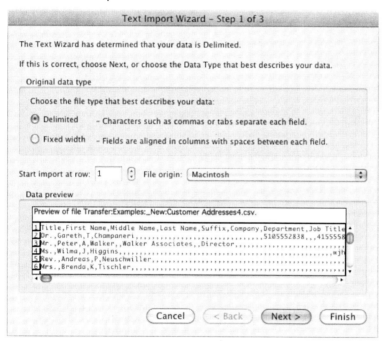

Figure 1–14. *Make sure that the Text Import Wizard has made the right choice between the Delimited option button and the Fixed width option button. You can also decide at which row to start importing.*

If you need to skip some rows at the beginning of the file, increase the value in the Start import at row box. To start from the beginning, make sure this box is set to 1.

If the preview in the Data preview box looks wrong, open the File origin pop-up menu, and choose the encoding the file uses. For example, if the file was created on a Windows PC, you may need to choose the Windows (ANSI) item to make the text display correctly. If the file was created on a Mac, choosing Macintosh in the File origin pop-up menu should do the trick.

When the preview looks okay, click the Next button to move to the second screen (see Figure 1–15).

Figure 1–15. *On the second screen of the Text Import Wizard for a CSV or TSV file, make sure that Excel has identified the correct delimiters.*

> **NOTE:** For a text file laid out with fixed-with columns, the second screen of the Text Import Wizard lets you create, delete, and move break lines to make the fields the right widths. The options on the third screen of the Text Import Wizard are the same for a text file laid out with fixed-width columns as for a delimited text file.

In the Delimiters box, make sure Excel has selected the check box for the delimiter the file uses—for example, the Tab check box.

Select the Treat consecutive delimiters as one check box if you want Excel to treat two or more consecutive delimiters as a single delimiter. Using this setting has the effect of collapsing blank fields in the data. Normally, you won't need to use this setting.

If your data file uses single quotes or double quotes to mark strings of text, make sure that Excel has selected the right type of quotes in the Text qualifier pop-up menu. If not, select it yourself.

Check that the data in the Data preview box looks okay, and then click the Next button to display the third and final screen of the Text Import Wizard (see Figure 1–16). On this screen, you can set the data format of any column by clicking the column in the Data preview box and then selecting the appropriate option button in the Column data format box:

- *General.* The Text Import Wizard suggests this format for most columns. The General format makes Excel convert numeric values to numbers, convert date values to dates, and treat any other type of data as text. This works pretty well for most fields, so you may want to simply leave this setting. Otherwise, you can set each field to the type needed.

- *Text.* Select this format for any data you want Excel to treat as text. Sometimes you may want to set this format for data that Excel would otherwise convert to numbers.

- *Date.* Select this format to make sure Excel knows that a column contains dates. In the pop-up menu, choose the order in which the month (M), day (D), and year (Y) appear: MDY, DMY, YMD, MYD, DYM, or YDM. If you're using the U.S. localization, Excel uses the MDY format by default so you won't need to change it unless the file has come from somewhere that treats dates differently.

- *Do not import column (Skip).* Select this button for any column you want to skip. This option can be great for data you're sure you don't need, though you may find it easier to import all of the columns and delete those you don't need after the import.

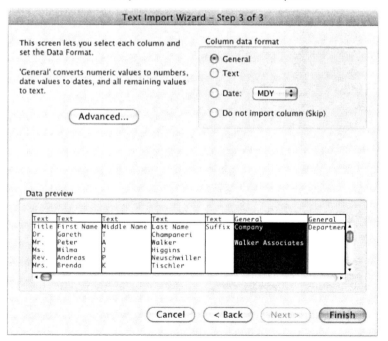

Figure 1–16. *On the third screen of the Text Import Wizard for a CSV or TSV file, you can set the data format for each column. You can also tell Excel not to import particular columns you don't need.*

NOTE: If you need to set Excel to use a different character than the period as the decimal separator or the comma as the thousands separator, click the Advanced button on the third screen of the Text Import Wizard. In the Advanced Text Import Settings dialog box that opens, choose the appropriate setting in the Decimal separator pop-up menu and the Thousands separator pop-up menu, and then click the OK button.

When you finish choosing text-import settings, click the Finish button. The Text Import Wizard imports the data into the active worksheet.

Importing Data from a FileMaker Pro Database

When you import data from a FileMaker Pro database, the FileMaker Pro Import Wizard (see Figure 1–17) walks you through the process of choosing the right fields.

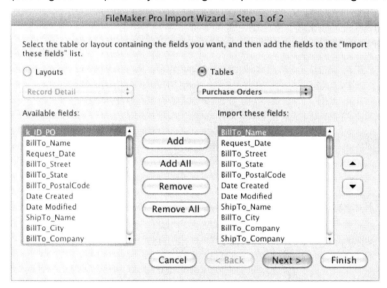

Figure 1–17. *On the first screen of the FileMaker Pro Import Wizard, choose the layout or table you want to import, pick the fields, and then arrange them into your preferred order.*

On the first screen of the FileMaker Pro Import Wizard, follow these steps:

1. Click the Layouts option button if you want to use a layout. Click the Tables option button if you want to use a table.

2. Open the pop-up menu below the Layouts option button or Tables option button (whichever you chose), and then click the layout or table you want to use. Excel displays the fields from the layout or table in the Available fields list box.

3.   Add the fields you need to the Import these fields list box:

   ▓   **Add a single field.** Click the field in the Available fields list box and then click the Add button. Repeat as needed.

   ▓   **Add all the fields.** Click the Add All button. Often, you'll want to add all the fields and then remove a few of them.

   ▓   **Remove a field.** Click the field in the Import these fields list box and then click the Remove button.

   ▓   **Remove all fields.** Click the Remove All button.

4.   In the Import these fields list box, put the fields in your preferred order. To move a field up or down, click it and then click the Move Up button (the button with the up arrow) or the Move Down button (the button with the down arrow).

When you've chosen the fields you want and arranged them into your preferred order, click the Next button to display the second and final screen of the FileMaker Pro Import Wizard (see Figure 1–18). On this screen, you can set the criteria to pick only the records you want from the table or layout you chose.

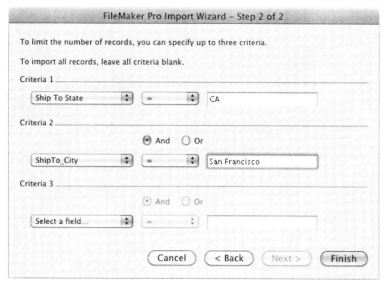

Figure 1–18. *On the second screen of the FileMaker Pro Import Wizard, set up the criteria needed to limit the import to only the records you want.*

If you want all the records in the table or layout, you can simply click the Finish button. But if you want to strip the table or layout down to only records that match particular criteria, follow these steps:

1.   In the Criteria 1 area, set up your first criterion:

   ▓   Open the left pop-up menu and click the field to use for the criterion.

- Open the middle pop-up menu and click the comparison: =, <=, >=, <, >, begins with, ends with, or contains.

- In the text box, specify the value for the comparison.

2. If you need a second criterion, select the appropriate option button:

  - Select the And option button to make the records match the first criterion and the second criterion—for example, Ship To State = CA and Ship To City = San Francisco.

  - Select the Or option button to make the records match either the first criterion or the second criterion—for example, Ship To State = CA or Ship To State = AZ.

3. Set up the second criterion in the Criterion 2 box using the same technique as for the first.

4. If you need a third criterion, select the And option button or the Or option button (as appropriate), and then use the third line of controls to specify the criterion.

When you've nailed down your criteria, click the Finish button to close the FileMaker Pro Import Wizard. The Wizard displays the Returning External Data to Microsoft Excel dialog box (see Figure 1–19).

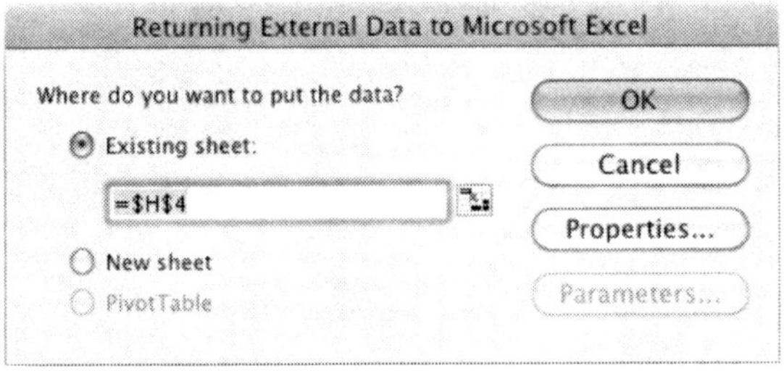

Returning External Data to Microsoft Excel

Where do you want to put the data?

⊙ Existing sheet:

`=$H$4`

○ New sheet

○ PivotTable

[OK]
[Cancel]
[Properties...]
[Parameters...]

Figure 1–19. *In this dialog box, choose the Existing sheet option button or the New sheet option button as appropriate. Then click the OK button.*

In the Where do you want to put the data area, select the Existing sheet option button if you want to put the incoming data on the worksheet you've selected. Usually, this is the best bet. The text box shows the active cell; if you need to change it, you can type a different address, or click in the workbook and then click the cell you want to use as the upper-left corner of the range. Otherwise, if you want to create a new worksheet and put the data on it, select the New sheet option button.

Click the OK button to close the Returning External Data to Microsoft Excel dialog box. The Wizard queries the database, returns the records that match your criteria, and then enters them in the worksheet you specified.

Importing Data from an HTML File

When you import data from an HTML file, Excel simply opens the file without displaying any Import Wizard screens. You can then manipulate the contents of the file as needed.

Connecting a Worksheet to External Data Sources

If you have an external data source that contains data you need to use in your Excel worksheet, you can connect the worksheet to the data source and pull in the data so you can work with it in Excel.

To get the data into the worksheet, you use the same tools we just discussed for importing data—for example, you use the FileMaker Pro Import Wizard to import data from a FileMaker Pro database. After importing the data, you can refresh some or all of it as needed, updating the worksheet with the latest data from the data source.

Chapter 11 explains how to work with external data.

Entering Text Using AutoCorrect

As you work in a worksheet, the AutoCorrect feature analyzes the characters you type and springs into action if it detects a mistake it can fix or some formatting it can apply. This feature can save you a lot of time and effort and can substantially speed up your typing, so it's well worth using—but you need to set it up to meet your needs. AutoCorrect also has some features that can cause surprises, so you'll want to choose settings that suit the way you work.

Opening the AutoCorrect Preferences Pane

To set up AutoCorrect, choose Tools ➤ AutoCorrect from the menu bar to display the AutoCorrect preferences pane in the Excel Preferences dialog box (see Figure 1–20).

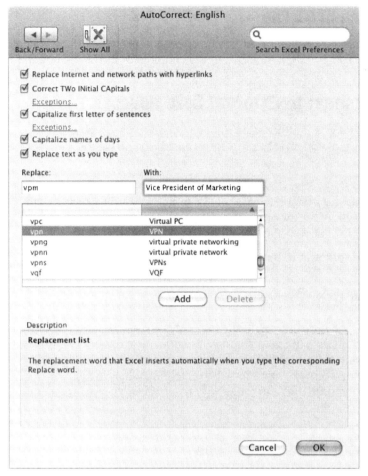

Figure 1–20. *You can use AutoCorrect to enter text quickly in your worksheets as well as to correct typos and create hyperlinks.*

Choosing Options to Make AutoCorrect Work Your Way

With the AutoCorrect preferences pane displayed, select the check box for each option you want to use:

- *Replace Internet and network paths with hyperlinks.* Select this check box to have AutoCorrect insert a hyperlink when you type a URL (for example, www.apress.com) or a network path (such as \\server1\users). This option is helpful if you want live hyperlinks in your workbooks—for example, if you're making a list of products with URLs, and you want to be able to click a link to open the web page in your browser.

- *Correct TWo INitial CApitals.* Select this check box to have AutoCorrect apply lowercase to a second initial capital—for example, changing "THree" to "Three."

- *Capitalize first letter of sentences.* Select this check box if you want AutoCorrect to automatically start each new sentence in a cell with a capital letter. AutoCorrect doesn't capitalize the first sentence in the cell, as this option only kicks in once you've typed some text followed by a period. Clear this check box if you want to control capitalization yourself.

- *Capitalize names of days.* Select this check box to have AutoCorrect automatically capitalize the first letter of the day names (for example, Sunday). This option is usually helpful unless you're writing minimalist poetry in Excel.

- *Replace text as you type.* Select this check box to use AutoCorrect's main feature, replacing misspellings and abbreviations with their designated replacement text. You will want to use this feature to make the most of AutoCorrect.

Creating AutoCorrect Exceptions

If you select the Correct TWo INitial CApitals check box or the Capitalize first letter of sentences check box, you can create exceptions that tell AutoCorrect not to fix particular instances of two initial capitals or sentences.

To create exceptions, click the Exceptions link under either the Correct TWo INitial CApitals check box or the Capitalize first letter of sentences check box. Excel displays the AutoCorrect Exceptions dialog box; the left screen in Figure 1–21 shows the First Letter tab, and the right screen in Figure 1–21 shows the INitial CAps tab.

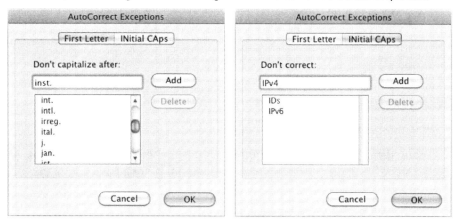

Figure 1–21. *Use the First Letter tab and INitial CAps tab of the AutoCorrect Exceptions dialog box to set up exceptions to the rules for capitalizing the first letter of sentences or lowercasing the second letter of a word.*

On the First Letter tab, list the terms that end with periods but after which you don't want the next word to start with a capital letter. Office starts you off with a list of built-in terms, such as vol. and wk. To add a term, type it in the Don't capitalize after text box, and then click the Add button.

On the INitial CAps tab, list the terms that start with two initial capital letters that you don't want AutoCorrect to reduce to a single capital—for example, IPv6. Type a term in the Don't correct text box, and then click the Add button to add it to the list.

On either tab, you can remove an existing term by clicking it in the list box, and then clicking the Delete button.

When you've finished setting up the exceptions, click the OK button to close the AutoCorrect Exceptions dialog box.

Creating Replace-As-You-Type Entries

Inserting missed capitals and creating hyperlinks automatically helps a bit, but the main point of AutoCorrect is to correct typing errors.

AutoCorrect comes with a list of standard errors, such as "abbout" for "about," that you'll probably want it to correct automatically. But where you can really take advantage of AutoCorrect is by creating entries that aren't errors but rather abbreviations that you type deliberately and have AutoCorrect expand for you. For example, you can create an entry that changes "vpm" to "Vice President of Marketing" or one that changes "ssf" to "Second Storage Facility, Virginia (Security Grade II)".

> **NOTE:** Excel shares its AutoCorrect entries with Word, PowerPoint, and Outlook, so no matter which application you create an entry in, you can use it in the others as well. Each entry must be unique—you can't use "vpm" for "Vice President of Marketing" in Word and "virtual processor module" in Excel. In Word, you can also create formatted AutoCorrect entries that contain formatting, paragraph marks, and other objects (such as graphics or tables); these entries work only in Word.

Creating AutoCorrect Entries

To create an AutoCorrect entry, follow these steps:

1. Type the entry name (the text that triggers the replacement) in the Replace box. The name can be up to 32 characters long, but shorter entries save you more time.

> **TIP:** When naming an AutoCorrect entry, you'll usually want to avoid using any words or names you may need to type in your workbooks. The exception is when you always want to change a particular word. For example, if your boss has a pet hate of the word "purchase," you could set up AutoCorrect entries to change "purchase" to "buy," "purchased" to "bought," and so on.

2.   Type or paste the replacement text in the With box. The replacement can be up to 255 characters long (including spaces and punctuation).

> **NOTE:** You can enter AutoCorrect entries only into a single cell. Even if you select multiple cells and paste them into the With box in the AutoCorrect pane, AutoCorrect strips out the cell divisions.

3.   Click the Add button.

If you need to delete an existing entry, select it either by clicking in the Replace box and typing its name or by scrolling down to it and clicking it. Then click the Delete button.

Using Your AutoCorrect Entries

Once you've set up your AutoCorrect entries, Excel automatically replaces an entry after you type it and then press the spacebar or a punctuation key or move to another cell.

Entering Text with AutoFill and Custom Lists

In many workbooks, you'll need to enter a series of data, such as a list of months or years, a sequence of numbers, or a progression of dates (such as every Monday). In many cases, you can save time and effort by using Excel's AutoFill feature.

AutoFill works by analyzing the contents of one or more cells you select, and then entering the relevant series of data in the cells to which you extend the selection by dragging. AutoFill figures out mathematical sequences or date sequences on the fly and uses built-in custom lists to fill in the days of the week or the months of the year. You can also create your own custom lists for data you want to teach Excel to fill in.

Using AutoFill's Built-in Capabilities

The best way to grasp what you can do with AutoFill is to try it. So open a workbook you're comfortable experimenting with and try the examples in this section.

First, have AutoFill fill in the days of the week. Follow these steps:

1. Type Monday in cell A1 and click the Enter button on the Formula bar to enter the data. (If you prefer to press Return to enter the data, click cell A1 again to select it once more.)

2. Drag the AutoFill handle—the blue square that appears at the lower-right corner of the selection—down to cell A7. As you drag past each cell, AutoFill displays a ScreenTip showing the data it will fill in that cell (see Figure 1–22).

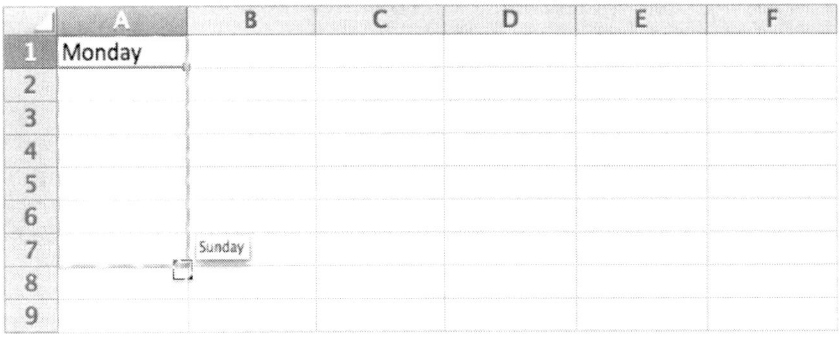

Figure 1–22. *Drag the AutoFill handle down or across to fill in a series of data derived from one or more existing entries. In this case, AutoFill fills in the days of the week and repeats the series if you drag farther.*

3. Release the mouse button on cell A7. AutoFill fills in the days Tuesday through Sunday.

> **NOTE:** If AutoFill doesn't work, you need to turn it on. Choose **Excel ➤ Preferences** to display the Excel Preferences dialog box, and then click the Edit icon in the Authoring area to display the Edit pane. Select the Enable fill handle and cell drag-and-drop check box, and then click the OK button to close the Excel Preferences dialog box.

Now drag through the range to select it, then press Delete to clear the data. Then follow these steps to enter a sequence of months:

4. Click cell B2, and type a date such as **5-15-11** in it.

5. Click the Enter button on the Formula bar. Excel changes the date value to a full date—for example, 5/15/2011.

6. Ctrl+click or right-click the AutoFill handle and drag it to cell G2. As you drag, AutoFill displays dates incremented by one day for each column (5/16/2011, 5/17/2011, and so on), but when you release the mouse button, AutoFill displays a context menu (see Figure 1–23).

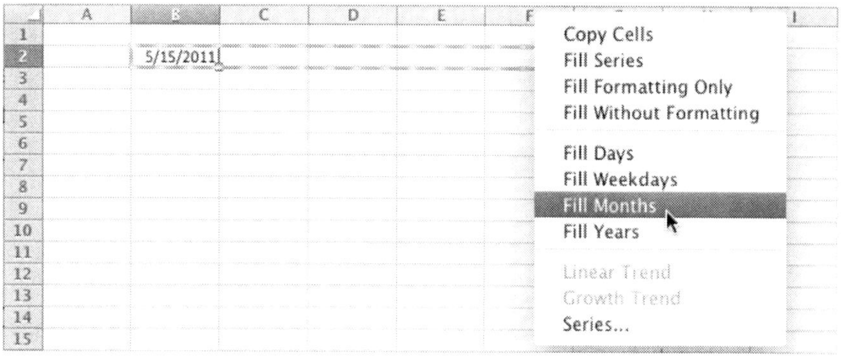

Figure 1–23. *To reach more AutoFill options, Ctrl+drag or right-drag the AutoFill handle, and then click the fill option you want on the context menu.*

7. Click the Fill Months item, and Excel fills in a separate month for each column: 6/15/2011, 7/15/2011, and so on.

Now clear your data again and then create a sequence of numbers. Follow these steps:

1. Click cell A1 and type **5** in it.

2. Press Return to move to cell A2, type **25** in it, and press the up arrow to move back to cell A1.

3. Press Shift+down arrow to select cells A1 and A2.

4. Click the AutoFill handle and drag downward. AutoFill fills in a series with intervals of 20—cell A3 gets 45, cell A4 gets 65, and so on—using a linear trend.

Delete the data that AutoFill entered, leaving 5 in cell A1 and 25 in cell A2. Then follow these steps:

1. Select cells A1 and A2.

2. Ctrl+click or right-click the AutoFill handle and drag downward. As you drag, you'll see ScreenTips for the same values as in the previous list.

3. Release the mouse button and then click Growth Trend on the context menu. AutoFill enters a growth trend instead of the linear trend: because the second value (25) is 5 times the first value (5), Excel multiplies each value by 5, giving the sequence 5, 25, 125, 625, 3125, and so on.

> **NOTE:** The AutoFill context menu also contains items for filling the cells with formatting only (copying the formatting from the first cell), filling the cells without formatting (ignoring the first cell's formatting), and filling in days, weekdays, months, and years.

Those are the basics of AutoFill. But you can also create custom AutoFill lists to quickly enter exactly the data you need.

Creating Your Own Custom AutoFill Lists

If you need to enter the same series of data frequently, follow these steps to create your own AutoFill lists:

1. If the data for the series already appears in a worksheet, select the cells that contain it.

2. Choose Excel ➤ Preferences or press Cmd+, (Cmd and the comma key) to display the Excel Preferences dialog box.

3. In the Formulas and Lists area, click the Custom Lists item to display the Custom Lists pane (shown in Figure 1–24 with settings chosen). If you selected cells in step 1, the references appear in the Import list from cells text box; move ahead to step 6.

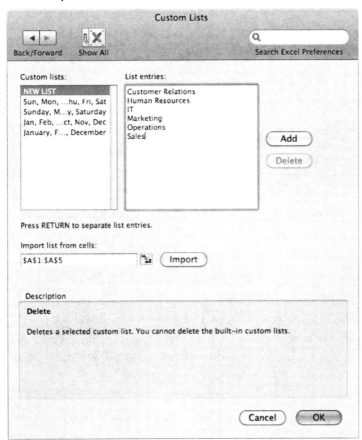

Figure 1–24. *You can supplement Excel's built-in AutoFill lists by creating your own data series.*

4. In the Custom lists box, click the NEW LIST item.

5. Click in the List entries box, and then type your list, putting one item on each line.

6. If you've just entered a list, click the Add button to add the list to the Custom lists box. If you imported a list from a worksheet, click the Import button.

> **TIP:** If you need to create another list from worksheet data at this point, you don't need to close the Excel Preferences dialog box. Instead, click the Collapse Dialog button to the left of the Import button to collapse the Custom Lists dialog box to a shallow dialog box, then drag through the list on the worksheet. Click the Collapse Dialog button to restore the Excel Preferences dialog box, where the range appears in the Import list from cells text box. Then click the Import button to bring in the data.

7. Click the OK button to close the Excel Preferences dialog box.

Entering Text Using Paste and Paste Options

Often, you can enter text more quickly in your workbooks by pasting it in from other sources. For example, if you receive sales figures in an e-mail message, you can copy and paste them into a worksheet. To paste, select the upper-left cell of the range of cells into which you want to paste the data, and then give a Paste command—for example, click the Paste button on the Standard toolbar or press Cmd+V.

Excel lets you paste data in with or without all its formatting. Usually it's easiest to go ahead with a straightforward paste operation and then use the Paste Options action button (see Figure 1–25) to change the result if it's not what you want.

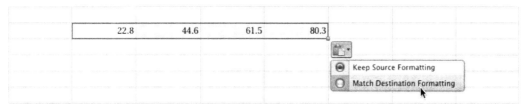

Figure 1–25. *Use the Paste Options action button to switch pasted text from using its original formatting to matching the formatting of the destination.*

When you paste in data you've copied from another application and you know you don't want to paste the formatting, use the Paste Special command like this:

1. Copy the data in the other application.

2. Switch to Excel.

3. Click the cell at the upper-left corner of the range you want to paste the data in.

4. Choose **Edit ➤ Paste Special** from the menu bar or **Home ➤ Edit ➤ Paste ➤ Paste Special** from the Ribbon (clicking the Paste pop-up button rather than the main part of the button) to display the Paste Special dialog box (see Figure 1–26).

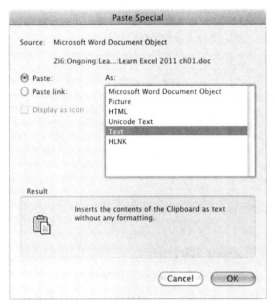

Figure 1–26. *Select the Text item in the As box in the Paste Special dialog box to paste in data from another application without pasting its formatting.*

5. In the As box, click the Text item.

> **TIP:** If pasting using the Text item in the Paste Special dialog box puts all the text in one cell rather than in multiple cells, try using the Unicode Text item instead.

6. Click the OK button.

> **NOTE:** The options in the Paste Special dialog box vary depending on the data you've copied. As you'll see in Chapter 4, when you paste data copied from Excel, the Paste Special dialog box provides many more options.

Switching Data from Rows to Columns

Often when you're laying out a worksheet, the best way to arrange the data isn't obvious at first—so you may find you've laid out your data out in rows when a column arrangement would work better.

Instead of spending hours retyping the data or using drag-and-drop to move it, you can fix the problem in moments using Excel's Transpose command. Follow these steps:

1. Make space for the transposed version of the data. Usually, it's easiest to put it on a separate worksheet; if so, click the Insert Sheet button to add one.

2. Select the data you want to switch from rows to columns.

3. Give a Copy command in any of the usual ways: Press Cmd+C, click the Copy button on the Standard toolbar, or choose Edit ä Copy from the menu bar.

4. Click the cell at the upper-left corner of the area into which you want to paste the transposed data.

5. Choose **Home ➤ Edit ➤ Paste ➤ Transpose** from the Ribbon, clicking the Paste pop-up button rather than the main part of the button. Excel pastes in the data, transposing its rows and columns.

> **NOTE:** If Excel displays the This Selection Is Not Valid dialog box (see Figure 1–27) when you give the Transpose command, make sure you're not trying to paste the data back into its original location. Even though the dialog box implies that you can paste the data back into the original location or an overlapping location as long as you've selected the right number of rows and columns, pasting the data back like this simply doesn't work at this writing.

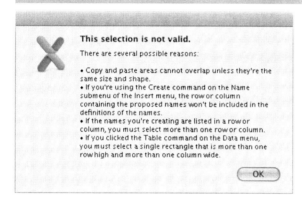

Figure 1–27. *The This Selection Is Not Valid dialog box may indicate that you're trying to paste the transposed data back into its original location, an overlapping location, or a location that's the wrong shape.*

Pasting in a Table from Word

If you have data in a table in Word, you can paste it straight into a worksheet in Excel. Excel places each table cell in a different worksheet cell, as you'd want.

You'll get the best results from a table that has a regular layout, with the same number of cells in each row. If some rows have more cells than other rows, you may need to move some cells in Excel after pasting them. In most cases, it's easiest to make the table regular in Word (for example, by making a copy of it in a spare document and the changing the copy) before pasting it into Excel.

Getting Comma-Separated Data into a Worksheet

If you have data in comma-separated format, you can get it into an Excel worksheet in three ways:

- *Use the Text Import Wizard.* As described earlier in this chapter, choose File ➤ Import, then use the Text Import Wizard to control exactly how Excel imports the text.

- *Open the file in Excel.* You can simply use the File ➤ Open command and the Open dialog box to open a comma-separated file in Excel. Excel automatically puts each comma-separated item in a separate cell. You can then copy and paste the data as needed.

- *Convert the comma-separated data to a Word table, then paste it.* If you have the data in comma-separated format as part of a document or e-mail message, follow these steps:

  1. Paste the data into a Word document.

  2. In Word, select the pasted data.

  3. Choose Table ➤ Convert ➤ Convert Text to Table from the menu bar to display the Convert Text to Table dialog box.

  4. In the Separate text at area, make sure the Commas option button is selected.

  5. Click the OK button. Word converts the text to a table.

  6. Select the table.

  7. Copy the table.

  8. Switch to Excel and paste in the table.

Pasting in Multiple Items with the Scrapbook

As you know, the Mac OS X Clipboard lets you store only one item at a time, so each time you copy something to the Clipboard, you overwrite its previous contents. But often you'll want to store various copied items so you can paste them whenever you need to. For example, you may want to store a graphics file containing your company logo or sections of boilerplate text that you need in many workbooks.

To let you store clippings and files in a single handy location from which you can paste them anywhere, Office:Mac provides the Scrapbook. The Office applications share the Scrapbook, so you can collect items in one application and use them in another.

Opening the Scrapbook

To open the Scrapbook, choose View ➤ Scrapbook from the menu bar or click the Toolbox button on the Standard toolbar and then click the Scrapbook button. Figure 1–28 shows the Scrapbook with several items stored in it. The left screen shows the Scrapbook's List view, the middle screen Detail view, and the right screen Large Preview.

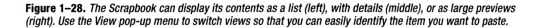

Figure 1–28. *The Scrapbook can display its contents as a list (left), with details (middle), or as large previews (right). Use the View pop-up menu to switch views so that you can easily identify the item you want to paste.*

Adding an Item to the Scrapbook

You can add an item to the Scrapbook in any of these ways:

- *Add a selection.* Select the text or other item you want to add to the Scrapbook. Then click the Add button in the middle of the Scrapbook palette.

- *Add a graphics file.* Click the Add drop-down button, then click Add File to display the Choose a File dialog box. Select the file you want and then click the Choose button.

- *Add whatever you've copied to the Clipboard.* Copy the item to the Clipboard as usual—for example, by selecting it in an application and then pressing Cmd+C. Then click the Add drop-down button in the Scrapbook palette and click Add from Clipboard.

- *Add everything you copy to the Clipboard.* If you use the Scrapbook extensively, you can make Office add a clipping of everything you copy in Mac OS X while the Scrapbook palette is open. To do so, click the Add drop-down button in the Scrapbook palette, then click Always Add Copy, placing a check mark next to this item. The application displays the Always Add Clipping Selected dialog box to warn you that this feature may slow your Mac down or take up disk space. Click the OK button.

> **TIP:** To make your clippings easier to find, you can add keywords to them. Click a clipping, type one or more keywords in the Keywords pane, and then click the Apply button. You can then open the pop-up menu in the upper-left corner of the Scrapbook palette, choose Keyword contains, and type the keyword by which you want to search.

Inserting an Item from the Scrapbook

To insert an item from the Scrapbook, select the cell or range in which you want to paste it. Then click the item in the Scrapbook palette and click the Paste button.

If you want to paste the item as plain text (without formatting) or as a picture, click the item and then click the Paste pop-up button. On the menu, click Paste as Plain Text or Paste as Picture, as needed.

Deleting an Item from the Scrapbook

Chances are you'll want to keep some items permanently in your Scrapbook, but you'll need to get rid of others when you no longer need them. Here's how to get rid of items:

- *Delete a single item.* Click the item, then click the Delete button.

- *Delete all items currently displayed.* Display the items you want to delete, click the Delete drop-down button, and then click Delete Visible.

- *Delete all items from the Scrapbook.* Click the Delete drop-down button, and then click Delete All.

Entering Text with Find and Replace

Excel includes a powerful Replace feature that you can use to replace text items in either the active worksheet or every worksheet in the active workbook. You can limit the search to matching the case you specify or by finding the match only as the entire contents of a cell rather than within a cell's contents.

To work with Replace, follow these steps:

1. Open the Replace dialog box (see Figure 1–29) in one of these ways:

   ■ *Mouse.* Click the pop-up button on the Search field on the Standard toolbar, then click Replace on the pop-up menu.

   ■ *Menus.* Choose **Edit ➤ Replace**.

   ■ *Keyboard.* Press Cmd+F to display the Find dialog box, then click the Replace button.

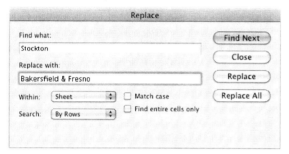

Figure 1–29. *You can use the Replace dialog box to quickly make changes throughout a worksheet or all the worksheets in a workbook.*

2. Type the search term in the Find what box.

3. Type the replacement text in the Replace with box.

4. In the Within pop-up menu, choose Sheet if you want to replace instances of the search term only on the active worksheet. Choose Workbook if you want to replace items on all the sheets in the workbook.

5. In the Search pop-up menu, choose By Rows if you want to search across each row in turn. Choose By Columns if you want to search down each column in turn.

6. Select the Match case check box if you want to locate only instances that match the way you've typed the search term in the Find what box.

7. Select the Find entire cells only check box if you want to find only the cells whose entire contents match the search term. With this check box cleared, Excel also finds matches that form only part of a cell's contents.

8. Click the appropriate command button:

   ■ *Find Next.* Click this button to find the next instance of the search term so that you can decide whether to replace it.

   ■ *Replace.* Click this button to replace the instance that Excel has found and to find the next instance (if there is one). Lather, rinse, and repeat.

   ■ *Replace All.* Click this button to replace all the instances in the worksheet or workbook (depending on the setting you've chosen in the Within pop-up menu).

■ *Close.* Click this button when you've finished using the Replace dialog box.

Inserting Symbols in a Document

Just by typing, you can easily insert any characters that appear on your keyboard—but many documents need other symbols, such as letters with dieresis marks over them (for example, ë) or ligatures that bind two characters (for example, Æ).

You can quickly insert one or more symbols in a workbook by using the Symbol Browser pane in the Media Browser.

> **NOTE:** When you insert a symbol using the Symbol Browser, the application inserts the symbol character in the same font you're currently using—if that font contains that character. If not, the Symbol Browser substitutes a font that does have the character. By contrast, when you use the Symbol dialog box, you can see exactly which symbols are available for a specific font.

You can use the Symbol Browser pane in the Media Browser to insert a symbol in Word, Excel, or PowerPoint. To insert a symbol, follow these steps:

1. In the document, position the insertion point where you want the symbol to appear.

2. Choose Insert ➤ Symbol from the menu bar to display the Symbols pane of the Media Browser (see Figure 1–30).

Figure 1–30. *To insert a symbol in a workbook, click the symbol in the Symbol Browser. Choose the All Symbols item in the pop-up menu to browse all symbols (left), or select only the set you're interested in (right).*

3. Find the symbol you want in one of these ways:

- *Browse all symbols.* Choose All Symbols in the pop-up menu at the top of the Symbol Browser, and then scroll down.

TIP: Drag the slider at the bottom of the Symbol Browser to zoom in to enlarge the symbols, or zoom out to see more symbols at once.

- *Display only a set of symbols.* Open the pop-up menu at the top of the Symbol Browser and click the set you want. For example, click the Greek set to display Greek characters.

4. Click the symbol to insert it in the document.

5. Leave the Symbol Browser open if you need to insert more symbols or other media objects. Otherwise, click the Media Browser's Close button (the button at the left end of the title bar) to close it.

Viewing Your Workbooks

Excel offers two views for working in your workbooks:

- *Normal view.* This is the view in which workbooks normally open and it's the one in which you'll do most of your data entry, formatting, and reviewing. Normal view is the view in which you've seen Excel so far in this chapter.

- *Page Layout view.* This view shows your worksheets as they'll look when laid out on paper. You use it to adjust the page setup. You'll learn how to do this in the section "Formatting Pages" in Chapter 4.

To switch the view, click the Normal View button or the Page Layout View button at the left end of the status bar (see Figure 1–31) or choose View ➤ Normal or View ➤ Page Layout from the menu bar.

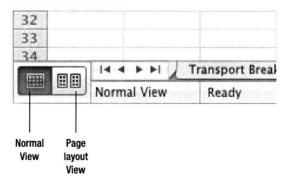

Figure 1–31. *Use the View buttons at the left end of the status bar to change views quickly.*

TIP: When you want to see as much of a worksheet as possible, choose **View ➤ Full Screen** from the menu bar. Excel hides the Ribbon and displays the worksheet full screen but doesn't hide the menu bar or the Dock the way Word's Full Screen view does. You can use Full Screen in either Normal view or Page Layout view. When you want to leave Full Screen view, click the Close Full Screen button on the Close Full Screen toolbar (which Excel displays automatically when you switch to Full Screen view), choose **View ➤ Full Screen** again, or simply press Esc.

Splitting the Window to View Separate Parts of a Worksheet

Often, it's useful to be able to see two parts of a worksheet at the same time—for example, to make sure your notes correctly describe your data or when you're copying information from one part to another.

When you need to see two parts of the worksheet in the same window, you can split the window either horizontally or vertically. To do so, you use the horizontal split box at the right end of the horizontal scroll bar, the vertical split box at the top end of the vertical scroll bar, or the Split button in the Window group of the Layout tab of the Ribbon (see Figure 1–32).

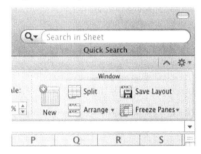

Figure 1–32. *The Window group on the Layout tab of the Ribbon contains several essential commands, but most of the button names appear only when the Excel window is very wide.*

Double-click the horizontal split box to split the window horizontally above the active cell, or double-click the vertical split box to split the window vertically to the left of the active cell. If the active cell isn't in the right place for splitting, click the horizontal split box or the vertical split box, and then drag it until the split bar appears where you want the split.

If you want to split the window into four panes, you can also split it in the other dimension. For example, if you've already split the window horizontally, now split it vertically as well. Figure 1–33 shows the Excel window split into four panes.

NOTE: You can also split the window into four panes by choosing **Layout ➤ Window ➤** Split from the Ribbon or **Window ➤ Split** from the menu bar.

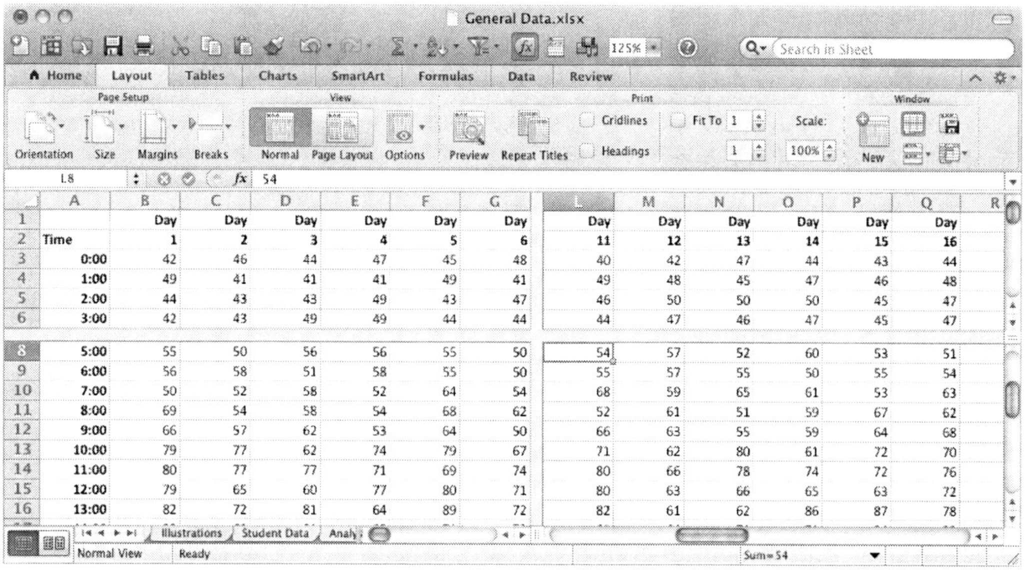

Figure 1–33. *Split the Excel window into two or four panes when you need to work in separate areas of the worksheet at the same time.*

Once you split the window, you get a separate scroll bar in each part, so you can scroll the panes separately to display whichever areas of the worksheet you need.

NOTE: When you split the window, you may find it helpful to freeze certain rows and columns, as discussed later in this chapter, to keep them visible even when you scroll to other areas of the worksheet.

To reposition the split, click the split bar, and drag it to where you want it. If you've split the window into four panes, you can resize all four panes at once by clicking where the split bars cross and then dragging.

To remove the split, either double-click the split bar or click and drag it all the way to the left of the screen or all the way to the top. You can also choose **Layout ➤ Window ➤ Split** from the Ribbon or **Window ➤ Remove Split** from the menu bar.

Opening Extra Windows to Show Other Parts of a Workbook

Instead of splitting a window, you can open one or more extra windows to show other parts of the workbook.

Choose **Layout ➤ Window ➤ New** from the Ribbon or **Window ➤ New Window** from the menu bar to open a new window in the active workbook. Excel distinguishes the windows by adding :1 to the name of the first and :2 to the name of the second—for example, General Data.xlsx:1 and General Data.xlsx:2.

> **NOTE:** Opening extra windows has two advantages over splitting a window. First, you can display other worksheets in the windows if you want, rather than just other parts of the same worksheet. Second, you can zoom each window by a different amount as needed or use a different view in each window.

Changing the Window and Arranging Open Windows

The easiest way to change the window you're working in is to click the window you want to use—either click the window itself (if you can see it) or click its button on the Taskbar. You can also choose to open the Window menu on the menu bar and then click the window in the list at the bottom.

When you've opened several windows, you can arrange them using standard Mac OS X techniques, such as by dragging them to the size and position you want. You can also use Excel's Arrange Windows dialog box or Arrange pop-up menu to place the windows.

To position windows using the Arrange Windows dialog box, follow these steps:

1. Choose **Window ➤ Arrange** from the menu bar or **Layout ➤ Window ➤ Arrange ➤ Arrange Windows** from the Ribbon to display the Arrange Windows dialog box (see Figure 1–34).

Figure 1–34. *Use the Arrange Windows dialog box to tile or otherwise arrange all Excel windows or only those from the active workbook.*

2. Click the option button for the arrangement you want:

   ▦ *Tiled.* Select this option button to make Excel resize all the non-minimized windows to roughly even sizes so they fit in the Excel window. If you have several windows open, tiling may make them too small to work in, but it's good for seeing which windows are open and closing those you don't need.

   ▦ *Horizontal.* Select this option button to arrange all the windows horizontally in the Excel window. This arrangement works well for two windows in which the data is laid out in rows rather than columns.

   ▦ *Vertical.* Select this option button to arrange all the windows vertically in the Excel window. This arrangement works well for two windows in which the data is laid out in columns rather than rows.

   ▦ *Cascade.* Select this option button to arrange the windows in a stack so you can see each one's title bar. This arrangement is useful for picking the window you want out of many open windows.

3. To arrange only the windows of the active workbook, select the Windows of active workbook check box. This option is good for the Horizontal and Vertical arrangements.

4. Click the OK button to close the Arrange Windows dialog box. Excel arranges the windows as you chose.

> **TIP:** When you don't need to see a particular window, you can hide it to get it out of the way. Click the window, and then choose **Window ➤ Hide**. To display the window again, choose **Window ➤ Unhide**, click the window in the Unhide dialog box, and then click the OK button.

To arrange windows quickly using the Arrange pop-up menu, choose **Layout ➤ Window ➤ Arrange,** and then click either Vertical or Cascade on the pop-up menu, as needed. You can also click the Arrange Windows item to display the Arrange Windows dialog box.

Zooming to Show the Data You Need to See

To make a worksheet's data easier to read, you can zoom in. Or if you need to see more of a worksheet at once, you can zoom out.

The easiest way to zoom in or out is by opening the Zoom pop-up menu on the Standard toolbar and then clicking one of the items on it: 200%, 150%, 125%, 100%, 75%, 50%, 25%, Selection, or (in Page Layout view only) One Page.

You can set a custom view percentage by clicking the Zoom box or opening the Zoom pop-up menu, typing the percentage you want, and then pressing Return.

When you need to zoom just the right amount to display a particular area of the worksheet as large as it will fit in the window, select the area, open the Zoom pop-up menu, and then click Selection.

> **NOTE:** If you choose not to display the Standard toolbar, use the other way of setting the Zoom percentage—by using the Zoom dialog box. Choose View ➤ Zoom from the menu bar, choose the appropriate option button, and then click the OK button.

Freezing Rows and Columns So They Stay Onscreen

To keep your data headings onscreen when you scroll down or to the right on a large worksheet, you can freeze the heading rows and columns in place. For example, if you have headings in column A and row 1, you can freeze column A and row 1 so they remain onscreen.

You can quickly freeze the first column, the top row, or your choice of rows and columns:

- *Freeze the first column.* Choose Layout ➤ Window ➤ Freeze Panes ➤ Freeze First Column from the Ribbon.

- *Freeze the first row.* Choose Layout ➤ Window ➤ Freeze Panes ➤ Freeze Top Row from the Ribbon.

- *Freeze your choice of rows and columns.* Click the cell below the row and to the right of the column you want to freeze. For example, to freeze the top two rows and column A, select cell B3. Then choose Layout ➤ Window ➤ Freeze Panes ➤ Freeze Panes from the Ribbon or Window ➤ Freeze Panes from the menu bar.

Excel displays a gray line along the gridlines of the frozen cells. Once you've applied the freeze, the frozen columns and rows don't move when you scroll down or to the right. Figure 1–35 shows a worksheet with rows 1 and 2 and column A frozen.

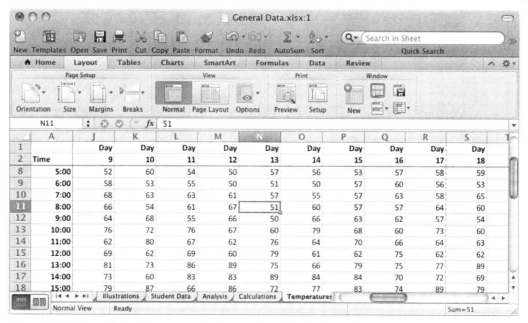

Figure 1–35. *Freeze the heading rows and columns to keep them in place when you scroll down or across the worksheet.*

When you no longer need the freezing, choose **Layout ➤ Window ➤ Freeze Panes ➤ Unfreeze** from the Ribbon or **Window ➤ Unfreeze Panes** from the menu bar to remove it.

Using Custom Views

When you need to keep your data laid out in a particular way, you can create a custom view. To do so, follow these steps:

1. Set up the workbook exactly the way you want it. For example:

   ▪ Display the worksheet you want to see.

   ▪ Hide any columns and rows you don't want to view. You'll learn how to hide columns and rows in Chapter 4.

   ▪ Switch to the view you want.

   ▪ Zoom the view as needed.

   ▪ Set the print area.

   ▪ Apply any filtering needed (see Chapter 10).

2. Choose **View ➤ Custom Views** from the menu bar to display the Custom Views dialog box (shown on the left in Figure 1–36 with two views already added).

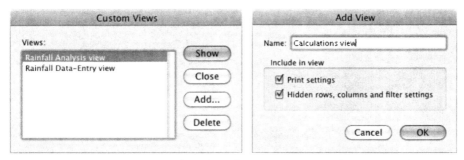

Figure 1–36. *Use the Custom Views dialog box (left) to add, delete, and display custom views. Use the Add View dialog box (right) to create a new custom view.*

3. Click the Add button to display the Add View dialog box (shown on the right in Figure 1–36). Excel closes the Custom Views dialog box.

4. Type the name for the view in the Name text box.

5. Select the Print Settings check box if you want the view to include the current print settings.

6. Select the "Hidden rows, columns and filter settings" check box if you want the view to include hidden rows, hidden columns, and any filtering you've applied.

7. Click the OK button to close the Add View dialog box. Excel creates the view.

You can now switch to the view by choosing **View ➤ Custom Views** from the menu bar to display the Custom Views dialog box, clicking the view in the Views list, and then clicking the Show button.

Summary

In this chapter, you learned the secrets of the Excel:Mac interface and how to navigate it. You know how to control Excel using the Ribbon, the toolbars, the menus on the menu bar, and keyboard shortcuts; how to get around worksheets and workbooks; and how to enter data in your workbooks by importing it or using tools such as AutoCorrect, AutoFill, and the Scrapbook. You also learned how to work more quickly and efficiently by splitting the window, freezing panes, opening extra windows, and using custom views.

In the next chapter, I'll show you how to customize Excel to suit the way you work.

Chapter 2

Configuring Excel:Mac to Suit the Way You Work

In this chapter, we look at how to configure Excel:Mac to suit the way you work. You can change Excel's appearance and behavior in many ways, and by setting it up as you prefer, you can save yourself plenty of time and effort.

The main way of configuring Excel is by setting its preferences in the Excel Preferences dialog box. This dialog box contains more settings than we can sensibly cover all at once, so let's concentrate on the ones that will make most difference in the way you use Excel most of the time—General, View, Edit, Save, and Compatibility. We cover other preferences elsewhere in the book when we reach their topics. For example, Chapter 1 covers AutoCorrect and Custom Lists preferences; Chapter 7 covers Chart preferences; Chapter 10 covers Tables preferences and Filter preferences; and Chapter 13 covers Security preferences.

Our first move is to open the Excel Preferences dialog box. We look next at how to control how the Excel window appears, then move on to choose editing options and default settings for saving your workbooks.

Besides setting preferences, you can also change the Excel user interface. In the second half of the chapter, I show you how to create custom keyboard shortcuts; how to customize the toolbars, menus, and menu bar; and how to make the fairly limited changes that Excel allows to the Ribbon.

Finally, you learn how to open one or more workbooks automatically when you launch Excel, and how you can save the layout of multiple open workbooks as a workspace you can instantly restore when needed.

Opening the Excel Preferences Dialog Box

To work through this chapter, open the Excel Preferences dialog box by choosing Excel ➤ Preferences from the menu bar or by pressing Cmd+, (Cmd and the comma key).

As you can see in Figure 2–1, the Excel Preferences dialog box contains three main categories of preferences—Authoring, Formulas and Lists, and Sharing and Privacy. Each category contains five or six icons that you click to display the corresponding preferences pane.

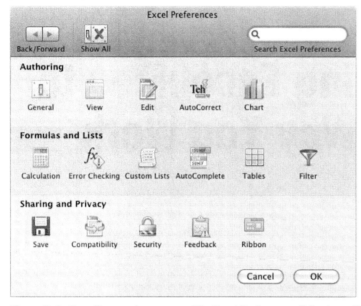

Figure 2–1. *From the overview screen of the Excel Preferences dialog box, click the icon for the preferences pane you want to display.*

You navigate the Excel Preferences dialog box much as you do Mac OS X's System Preferences window:

- Click the icon for the preferences pane you want to display. For example, click the General icon to display the General preferences pane.

- Click the Show All icon to return to the overview screen so you can display another category of preferences.

- Click the Back button to return to the previous screen. The previous screen is almost always the overview screen, so clicking the Back button tends to have the same effect as clicking the Show All button.

- Don't click the Forward button—at this writing, it never becomes enabled so it doesn't do anything.

- To search for a preference, click in the Search box, then type a keyword. In the list of matching preferences that Excel displays, click the preference you want. Excel highlights the relevant icon for a moment so you can identify it, then displays the preferences pane.

Controlling How the Excel Window Appears

In this section, I show you where to find the options that control how the Excel window appears.

Start by displaying the General preferences (see Figure 2–2) and then set the following preferences:

- *Use R1C1 reference style.* Make sure this check box is cleared unless you want to use R1C1 references, in which both the columns and the rows are identified by number. For example, the reference for cell A1 is R1C1 (row 1, column 1), and the reference for cell E2 is R2C5.

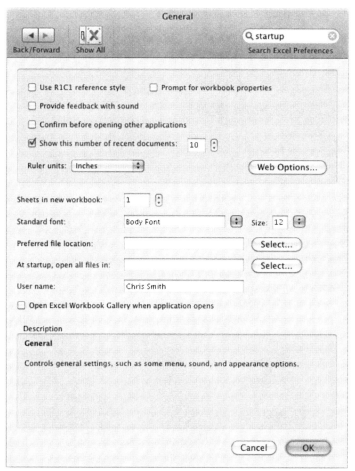

Figure 2–2. *In the General preferences pane, you can choose essential settings including the number of recent documents to show in the File menu, the number of sheets in a workbook, your standard font and font size, and your preferred file location.*

- *Standard font.* In this pop-up menu, choose the font you want to use as the default, the one that Excel uses until you apply a different font. If you choose the Body Font item, Excel uses the font that's set as the Body Font in the workbook's theme.

- *Size.* In this pop-up menu, choose the default font size.

- *User name.* Use this box to make sure Excel shows your name the way you want it.

- *Open Excel Workbook Gallery when application opens.* Select this check box if you want Excel to display the Excel Workbook Gallery dialog box on launch. Clear this check box if you don't need the Excel Workbook Gallery displayed at first.

Now click the Show All button to go back to the Overview screen, then click the View icon to display the View preferences pane (see Figure 2–3).

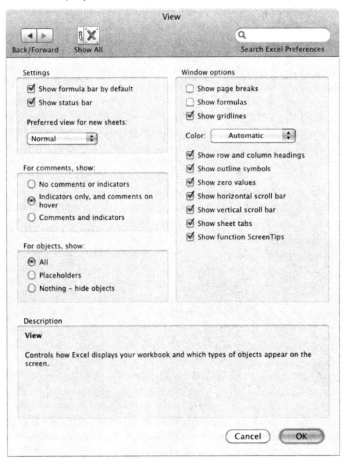

Figure 2–3. *The settings in the View preferences pane let you control the display of the formula bar and status bar, choose your preferred view, control how comments and objects appear, and decide which options to display in windows.*

You can now choose settings as described in the following subsections.

Choosing Options in the Settings Area of View Preferences

The Settings area of the View preferences pane contains three preferences you'll want to make sure are set the way you like:

- *Show formula bar by default.* Select this check box to make Excel show the formula bar, which is typically useful.

- *Show status bar.* Select this check box to make Excel show the status bar. This too is usually helpful.

- *Preferred view for new sheets.* In this pop-up menu, click Normal if you want to use Normal view for each new sheet you add to a workbook. Click Page Layout if you want Excel to use Page Layout view for new sheets.

Choosing How to Display Comments

In the "For comments, show" area of the View preferences pane, select the option button that describes how you want to display comments attached to cells:

- *No comments or indicators.* Select this option button when you need to simplify a worksheet's look by hiding the comments.

- *Indicators only, and comments on hover.* Select this option button to display a comment indicator (a red triangle in the upper-right corner of the cell) for each comment, and to display the comment in a balloon when the user hovers (holds) the mouse pointer over the cell. This is the default setting and is usually the best choice for regular work.

- *Comments and indicators.* Select this option button to display both comment indicators and comment balloons all the time. Use this setting when you want to make certain you see all the comments in a worksheet.

Choosing How to Display Objects

In the "For objects, show" area of the View preferences pane, select the appropriate option button to control how objects such as pictures and command buttons appear in the worksheets:

- *All.* Select this option button to display all graphical objects in the workbook. This setting lets you see where everything in the workbook is, but it may make Excel display or scroll worksheets with many graphical objects more slowly.

■ *Placeholders.* Select this option button to display empty-rectangle placeholders instead of pictures, but show command buttons.

■ *Nothing – hide objects.* Select this option button to hide all objects so you can see the data without distractions.

NOTE: The "For objects, show" setting applies only to the active workbook, not to all workbooks.

Choosing Window Options

In the Window options area of the View preferences pane, choose which of the window options to display and which to hide. Here are the details:

■ *Show page breaks.* Select this check box to make Excel display where page breaks fall. Usually, you need to see page breaks only right before printing, so you'll probably want to clear this check box.

■ *Show formulas.* Select this check box to make Excel display the formulas rather than the values they produce. Showing the formulas is helpful when you're troubleshooting calculations, but there's an easier way to show them, as you'll see in Chapter 4. Normally, you want to keep this check box cleared.

■ *Show gridlines.* Select this check box to make Excel display the gridlines around the cells. These are usually helpful, but you may sometimes want to switch them off for special effects.

■ *Color.* In this pop-up palette, click the color you want to use for the gridlines (when you're displaying them). The Automatic setting is usually the best choice unless you need a specific color (for example, red or blue).

■ *Show row and column headings.* Select this check box to display the row and column headings. You almost always want to display these, except when you're sharing a worksheet in which you've hidden some rows and columns but you don't want the missing row numbers or column letters to alert your audience to what you've hidden.

■ *Show outline symbols.* Select this check box to display the symbols that indicate you've created an outline in the worksheet (as discussed in Chapter 3). Normally, you want to display these symbols so that users can expand and collapse the outline as needed—but you may sometimes need to hide the outlining.

■ *Show zero values.* Select this check box to display a 0 (zero) in each cell whose value is zero. Showing zero values is usually helpful; if you need to suppress zero values, clear this check box.

- *Show horizontal scroll bar.* Select this check box to display the horizontal scroll bar. This too is usually helpful.

- *Show vertical scroll bar.* Select this check box to display the vertical scroll bar. Normally you need this UI feature.

- *Show sheet tabs.* Select this check box to display the bar of sheet tabs at the bottom of the window to enable you and your colleagues to navigate easily from one worksheet to another.

- *Show function ScreenTips.* Select this check box to have Excel display a ScreenTip showing the arguments of a function you're typing into a cell. These ScreenTips are usually helpful, but you can clear this check box if they bug you.

Choosing Editing Options

To control how Excel behaves when you're editing your worksheets, display the Edit preferences pane (see Figure 2–4) and choose options like this:

- *Double-click allows editing directly in the cell.* Select this check box if you want to be able to double-click a cell to open it up for editing. This is usually helpful—but if you clear this check box, double-clicking a cell makes Excel select the first cell referenced by the formula in that cell. This capability can be great when you're checking through formulas, so you need to decide which of the two double-click behaviors will be most helpful to you.

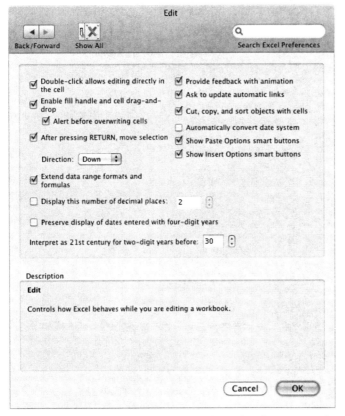

Figure 2–4. *The Edit preferences pane contains various important settings you should understand, even if you choose not to change them.*

- *Enable fill handle and cell drag-and-drop.* Select this check box if you want to be able to use the AutoFill feature (explained in Chapter 1) for entering custom lists and text sequences, and to be able to use drag-and-drop to move the contents of one cell to another cell. If you select this check box, you can select the Alert before overwriting cells check box to have Excel display a warning dialog box when an AutoFill or drag-and-drop operation will overwrite the existing contents of cells.

- *After pressing RETURN, move selection.* Select this check box if you want Excel to automatically select another cell after you press Return to enter the contents of the active cell. This movement is usually helpful. In the Direction pop-up menu, choose the direction: Down, Up, Right, or Left. The default direction is Down.

- *Extend data range formats and formulas.* Select this check box to make Excel automatically extend formatting and formulas when you get to the end of the current data range and add another row or column. This behavior usually saves time and effort.

- *Display this number of decimal places.* If you want Excel to automatically insert a decimal point in numbers you enter in cells, select this check box, and use the spin buttons to set the number of decimal points. For example, if your standard format for numbers uses two decimal places, select this check box, and then enter 2 in the box. Then, when you type 123 in a cell, Excel automatically converts it to 1.23 without you having to type in the decimal point. You can set a negative number if you want Excel to multiply the number by that power of 10—for example, if you set -3, Excel multiplies each number by 1000, so if you enter 9, you get 9000. (You can set any value from -300 to 300, but you'll seldom need to go near these limits.)

- *Preserve display of dates entered with four-digit years.* Select this check box if you want Excel to maintain four-digit years (such as 2011 or 2012) that you type in your worksheets rather than converting the dates to two-digit years (for example, 10/2/11 for the date 10/2/2011 that you entered).

- *Provide feedback with animation.* Select this check box if you want Excel to animate the insertion or deletion of cells, rows, or columns in the worksheet. The animation makes each change easier to see, but it may make Excel run slowly on an underpowered Mac; if so, clear this check box.

- *Ask to update automatic links.* Select this check box if you want Excel to display a dialog box asking you for permission to update automatic links. Having this confirmation is good if you need to maintain control of automatic links rather than have Excel update them without consulting you.

- *Cut, copy, and sort objects with cells.* Select this check box if you want Excel to include objects (such as graphics and buttons) with cells you cut, copy, or sort. This is normal behavior.

- *Automatically convert date system.* Select this check box if you want Excel to automatically convert dates between the 1900 date system used by Excel for Windows and current versions of Excel:Mac and the 1904 date system used by most versions of Excel:Mac up till recently.

NOTE: The 1900 date system uses the serial number 1 to represent 1 January 1900; the 1904 date system uses the serial number 1 to represent 1 January 1904. Unless you have a compelling reason to use the 1904 date system, stick with the 1900 date system for clarity. Excel stores dates and times as serial numbers so that it can perform math operations with them easily.

- *Show Paste Options smart buttons.* Select this check box if you want Excel to display a Paste Options action button after you paste in an item. You can click the Paste Options action button to display a pop-up menu of other ways of pasting in the data. This is usually helpful.

- *Show Insert Options smart buttons.* Select this check box if you want Excel to display an Insert Options action button when you insert cells, rows, or columns. You can click the Insert Options action button to display choices for formatting the items you've inserted. This too is usually helpful.

Setting Preferences for Creating and Saving Your Workbooks

One thing you're pretty much certain to do in Excel is create workbooks and save them. So it's worth spending a minute or two to set Excel to create workbooks with the right number of worksheets, using the folder and workbook format you prefer. You'll also want to choose where to save your workbooks and whether to keep automatic backups as you work. You can also have Excel prompt you to enter property information in your workbooks to make them easier to identify.

Creating Workbooks with the Number of Worksheets You Need

When you create a new workbook, Excel gives it a single worksheet by default. You can add as many other worksheets as you need by clicking the Insert Sheet button, but if you usually need multiple worksheets in each workbook, you can have Excel add them for you.

To control how many worksheets Excel gives each workbook, set the number in the Sheets in new workbook box in the General preferences pane.

Choosing the Default Folder for Opening and Saving Workbooks

Next, set the default folder to save workbooks in. This is the folder that Excel displays each time you open the Open dialog box and the first time you open the Save As dialog box in an Excel session. (After that, if you've saved a workbook, the Save As dialog box displays the workbook's folder.)

To set the default folder, go to the General preferences pane and click the Select button to the right of the Preferred file location box. In the Choose a Folder: Microsoft Excel dialog box that opens, click the folder and then click the Choose button. The folder name appears in the Preferred file location box.

Choosing the Default Format for Saving Workbooks

Next, make sure Excel is set to save workbooks in the format you prefer. To do this, go to the Compatibility preferences pane (see Figure 2–5), open the Save files in this format pop-up menu, and then click the format.

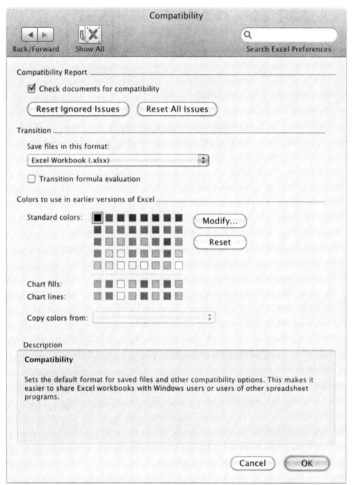

Figure 2–5. *In the Compatibility pane, select the Check documents for compatibility check box to make sure Excel alerts you to compatibility issues. In the Save files in this format pop-up menu, pick your default format for saving workbooks.*

Excel typically provides more than two dozen formats, but you're likely to use one of these four formats as your standard format:

- *Excel Workbook*. This is Excel's default format. Use it if you will be the only person to use the workbooks or if your colleagues have Office 2011, Office 2008 for Mac, Office 2010 for Windows, or Office 2007 for Windows. Anyone with Office 2004 for Mac or Office 2003 for

Windows will need to install filters (file converters) to be able to open the workbooks.

- *Excel Macro-Enabled Workbook*. Use this format if you need to include macros in your workbooks to perform custom actions. Again, your colleagues will need to have Office 2011, Office 2008, Office 2010, Office 2007, or either Office 2004 or Office 2003 with filters installed to open these workbooks.

NOTE: Office 2008 for Mac doesn't include VBA. So although you can include macros in an Excel Macro-Enabled Workbook file, Excel 2008 users won't be able to run them.

- *Excel Binary Workbook*. Use this format if you create large and complex workbooks and need to improve performance. Once more, your colleagues will need to have Office 2011, Office 2008, Office 2010, Office 2007, or either Office 2004 or Office 2003 with filters installed to work with these workbooks.

- *Excel 97–2003 Workbook*. Use this format if your colleagues have Office 2004 for Mac, Office 2003 for Windows, or an earlier version of Office. You can also use this format for greater compatibility with other spreadsheet applications, such as older versions of OpenOffice.org Calc (the latest version can handle the Excel Workbook format).

While you're in the Compatibility preferences pane, make sure that the Check documents for compatibility check box at the top of the pane is selected. This setting ensures that when you save a workbook in Excel 97–2003 or another format with fewer capabilities than the Excel Workbook format, Excel warns you about information that may not appear correctly in that format.

NOTE: In the Compatibility Report area at the top of the Compatibility preferences pane, you can click the Reset Ignored Issues button to reset the warnings for any compatibility issues you've ignored when performing a compatibility check. You can click the Reset All Issues button if you want to force Excel to recheck all aspects of a workbook's compatibility.

Setting AutoRecover to Keep Backups of Your Workbooks for Safety

Next, decide whether to keep AutoRecover files of your workbooks. AutoRecover is a safety net that automatically saves a copy of each open workbook every few minutes in case Excel or your Mac crashes and loses the changes you've made. After such a crash, when Excel restarts automatically or you restart it manually, it opens the latest AutoRecover files for you so you can choose which versions to keep. If you save your workbooks and then quit Excel normally (for example, by choosing **Excel ➤ Quit**), Excel gets rid of the saved AutoRecover files.

> **CAUTION:** Never rely on AutoRecover as protection against disasters. When AutoRecover works as it should, it can save your bacon, but sometimes it doesn't save everything, especially if Excel or your Mac crashes shortly before an AutoRecover save is due. So, you should always save your workbooks frequently while working on them and use AutoRecover only if disaster strikes. You can save a workbook at any time by pressing Cmd+S, clicking the Save button on the Standard toolbar, or choosing **File ➤ Save** from the menu bar.

To choose AutoRecover settings, follow these steps:

1. Display the Save preferences pane.

2. Select or clear the Save AutoRecover information after this number of minutes check box.

3. If you select the check box, enter the number of minutes in the text box.

   - You can set any interval from 1 minute to 120 minutes.

   - An interval of around 3 minutes usually works well, because it saves information frequently enough to avoid disaster but doesn't overly interrupt your work by saving constantly.

   - If you edit workbooks that contain many worksheets and lots of data, saving the AutoRecover files may take long enough to interrupt your work. In this case, either increase the AutoRecover interval to make the interruptions less frequent or turn AutoRecover off and save the workbook manually whenever is convenient.

Making Excel Prompt You to Enter Workbook Properties

In each workbook you save, you can store extra information to help yourself and your colleagues identify the workbook, its purpose, and its status. Excel provides slots called *properties* to contain such information.

Excel fills in some properties for you—for example, it enters your user name in the Author property, fills in the Created property with the time you first saved the workbook, and updates the Modified property each time you save the document. But filling in the rest of the properties is up to you. The best time to get started filling in the properties is when you save the workbook for the first time.

To make Excel automatically display the Properties dialog box when you save a workbook for the first time, select the Prompt for workbook properties check box at the top of the General preferences pneral preferences pane.

NOTE: You can open the Properties dialog box at any point by choosing File ➤ Properties. We look at the Properties dialog box in Chapter 3.

Creating Custom Keyboard Shortcuts

When you find that a command you need to run from the keyboard has no predefined keyboard shortcut, you can create a custom keyboard shortcut. You can also create one to replace or supplement an existing keyboard shortcut or to run a macro you create (Chapter 14 covers creating macros).

To create a custom keyboard shortcut, follow these steps:

1. Choose Tools ➤ Customize Keyboard to display the Customize Keyboard dialog box (shown in Figure 2–6 with settings already chosen for creating a shortcut).

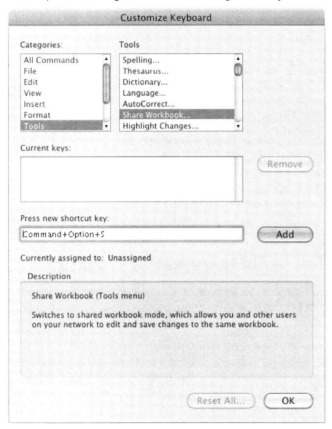

Figure 2–6. *Use the Customize Keyboard dialog box to set up custom keyboard shortcuts for the commands you need to give frequently from the keyboard.*

2. In the Categories list box, click the category of command for which you want to create a keyboard shortcut.

    ▩ The All Commands item at the top gives you access to all of the commands in alphabetical order. Use this category when you're looking for a command that doesn't appear on a menu (or whose menu you've forgotten).

    ▩ Click one of the regular menu items—the File menu, the Edit menu, the View menu, and so on—to display the items that appear on that menu and related commands that don't appear on the menu.

    ▩ Click the Charting category to display the charting commands.

TIP: If you find you use the same charting commands frequently, create keyboard shortcuts for them using the Charting category in the Customize Keyboard dialog box. That way, you can give essential commands quickly from the keyboard without having to use the Ribbon.

3. In the Commands list box, click the command you want to create a keyboard shortcut for. Excel displays information about the command:

    ▩ *Current keyboard shortcuts*. The Current keys list box shows any keyboard shortcuts currently assigned to the command (some commands have several shortcuts). If this command has any shortcuts, check that you know them and decide whether you need to create another.

    ▩ *Description*. This area shows the description of the command. Read it to make sure you've picked the command you intended. Some command names are clear, but others can be confusing. (If in doubt, close the Customize Keyboard dialog box and try the command from the Ribbon or the menu to make sure it does what you think it does.)

4. Click in the Press new shortcut key text box.

5. Press the keyboard shortcut you want to assign:

    ▩ You can create keyboard shortcuts that start with the Cmd and Ctrl keys: Cmd, Cmd+Option, Cmd+Ctrl, Cmd+Option+Shift, Cmd+Option+Ctrl, Cmd+Option+Ctrl+Shift, Cmd+Ctrl+Shift, Ctrl, Ctrl+Option, Ctrl+Shift, Ctrl+Option+Shift are all possible.

    ▩ You can use pretty much any key on the keyboard—letters, numbers, function keys, and so on.

6. Check the Currently assigned to readout to see whether the keyboard shortcut is currently used. If so, press another keyboard shortcut if you don't want to overwrite it.

7. Click the Assign button. Excel assigns the keyboard shortcut to the command.

8. When you've finished assigning keyboard shortcuts, click the Close button to close the Customize Keyboard dialog box.

Customizing the Toolbars with the Commands You Need

To make the toolbars work the way you prefer, you can customize them. You can either change the buttons that appear on the Standard toolbar and Formatting toolbar, or you can create custom toolbars of your own and give them only the buttons they need.

> **NOTE:** You can also customize both the menus and the menu bar, as you'll see later in this chapter. For example, you can add extra commands to the menus, remove commands you don't use, or create custom menus of your own. To customize the menus and the menu bar, you use the same techniques as for the toolbar, because the menu bar is technically the same type of object (a "command bar") as the toolbars, even though it looks and acts differently.

Getting Ready to Customize the Toolbars

To prepare to customize the toolbars, open the Customize Toolbars and Menus dialog box and display the toolbar you will customize. Follow these steps:

1. Open Excel, or activate Excel if it's already running.

2. Right-click the Standard toolbar or the Formatting toolbar, and then click the Customize Toolbars and Menus item on the context menu to display the dialog box. You can also choose View ➤ Toolbars ➤ Customize Toolbars and Menus.

3. If the Toolbars and Menus tab isn't already at the front, click it to bring it to the front. Figure 2–7 shows the Customize Toolbars and Menus dialog box with the Toolbars and Menus tab at the front. The Formatting toolbar is undocked and appears above the dialog box.

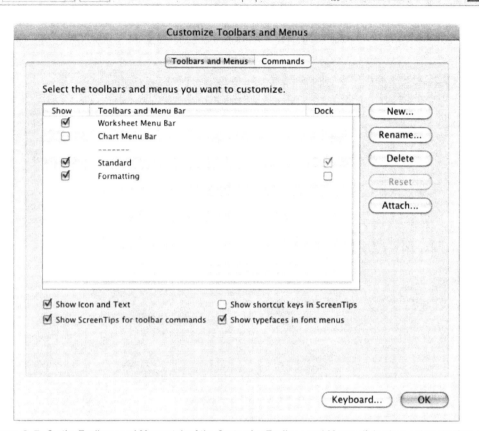

Figure 2–7. *On the Toolbars and Menus tab of the Customize Toolbars and Menus dialog box, select the Show check box for each toolbar or menu you want to display so that you can customize it. The toolbar above the dialog box here is the Formatting toolbar, undocked from the window.*

4. In the Show column, select the check box for each toolbar or menu bar you want to customize. For example, if you want to customize the Formatting toolbar, select the Show check box in the Formatting row to make the Formatting toolbar appear.

5. In the Dock column, select the Dock check box if you want to dock the toolbar; clear this check box if you want the toolbar to float. The Dock check box appears only for the Standard toolbar and the Formatting toolbar, not for custom toolbars you create. But because the Dock check box for the Standard toolbar is selected and unavailable, the Formatting toolbar is the only toolbar for which you can use this setting.

You're now ready to create a new toolbar or customize the toolbars as discussed in the following sections.

Creating a New Toolbar

To create a new toolbar, click the New button on the Toolbars and Menus tab of the Customize Toolbars and Menus dialog box. In the Add a Toolbar dialog box that opens, type the name you want to give the toolbar, and then click the OK button.

The new toolbar appears as a small floating window (it's small because it doesn't yet contain any buttons or other controls). You can then add commands to the new toolbar as described in the section after next.

Finding the Commands to Add to the Toolbars or Menus

To find the commands you want to add to the toolbars or menus, follow these steps:

1. Click the Commands tab of the Customize Toolbars and Menus dialog box to display its contents (see Figure 2–8).

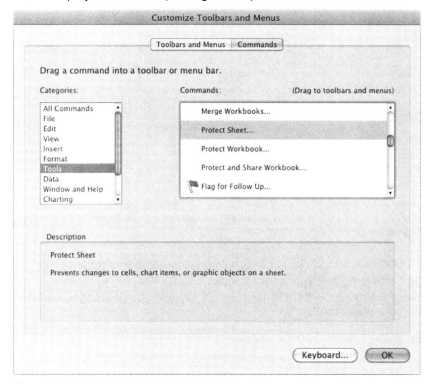

Figure 2–8. *On the Commands tab of the Customize Toolbars and Menus dialog box, click the category that contains the command you want to add to a toolbar or menu.*

2. In the Categories list box, click the category of commands you want. For example, click the File category to see the commands associated with the application's File menu.

NOTE: Each category contains more commands than appear on the associated menu. For example, if you click the File category in the Categories list box, you see not only the commands that actually appear on the File menu but also those that don't appear but perform operations related to files.

3. In the Commands box, locate the command you want to add to the toolbar or menu.

You're now ready to add the command to a toolbar, as described in the following sections.

Adding an Item to a Toolbar

To add a command to a toolbar, drag the command from the Commands list box on the Commands tab of the Customize Toolbars and Menus dialog box to the toolbar. Excel shows a light blue line where the button will appear. If the toolbar is positioned horizontally, the blue line is vertical; if the toolbar is positioned vertically, the blue line is horizontal.

Removing an Item from a Toolbar

To remove an item from a toolbar, drag the item off the toolbar and either into the document area of the window or over the Customize Toolbars and Menus dialog box. The item disappears from the toolbar.

Repositioning Items on a Toolbar

To reposition an item on a toolbar, drag it from its current position to where you want it to appear. You can drag an item from one toolbar to another if you want. For example, you can drag a button from the Standard toolbar to the Formatting toolbar to move it from one to the other, or drag it to a custom toolbar that you create.

Changing How a Toolbar Button Appears

When you add a button to a toolbar, Excel uses the item's regular icon, text, or both. To make the button easier to identify, you can change the icon and text. To do so, follow these steps:

1. Ctrl+click or right-click the toolbar button, and then click Properties on the context menu. Excel displays the Command Properties dialog box (see Figure 2–9).

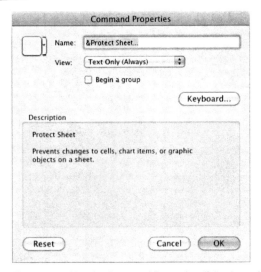

Figure 2–9. *Use the Command Properties dialog box when you want to change the icon, text, or both that appear for a toolbar button. The icon to the left of the Name box shows the current icon for the command (if any).*

2.   In the Name text box, type the name you want to display for the toolbar button.

> **NOTE:** Some commands display an ampersand character (&) in the Name text box—for example, in Figure 2–9, the Protect Sheet command appears as &Protect Sheet. This character is used in Windows to control the letter used as an access key for the command—for instance, when you press Alt+F to display the File menu, F is the access key. The ampersand character doesn't work like this on the Mac, so you don't need to include it in names you type. An ellipsis (…) at the end of a command's name means that the command displays a dialog box, just like on the menus.

3.   In the View pop-up menu, choose how you want the toolbar button or menu item to appear:

- *Default Style.* Choose this item to make a toolbar button appear using the default style you've set for toolbars. (If you've chosen to show icons and text, the button appears as an icon with text beside it; if you've chosen to show only icons, just the icon appears.) A menu item appears as text with an icon if the command has an associated icon.

- *Text Only (Always).* Choose this item to make the toolbar button or menu item appear as text without an icon.

- *Text Only (in Menus).* Choose this item to make a menu item appear only as text.

- *Image and Text.* Choose this item to make the toolbar button or menu item appear as an icon with text beside it.

4. If you want to change the icon, click the arrow button to the left of the Name box, and then click the icon you want on the pop-up menu.

> **TIP:** If you want to use the icon from another toolbar button or menu item, click the Cancel button to close the Command Properties dialog box. Ctrl+click or right-click the item with the icon and click Properties from the context menu to display the Command Properties dialog box for that command. Click the arrow button to the left of the Name box, and then click Copy Button Image on the pop-up menu. Click the Cancel button to close the Command Properties dialog box. Now open the Command Properties dialog box for the other item, click the arrow button to the left of the Name box, and then click Paste Button Image on the pop-up menu. This description is a bit long-winded, but once you know what to do, you can perform the moves in seconds.

5. Select the Begin a group check box if you want to place a divider line before the item. This is useful when you want to put different groups of items in different sections of the menu or toolbar.

6. Click the OK button to close the Command Properties dialog box.

Adding a Built-in Menu to a Toolbar

One customization that can be a great help is adding one or more of the built-in menus to a toolbar. You may find this handy if you like to give commands using the menus but you find moving the mouse all the way up and across to the menu wastes time—on a large monitor, for example, or with a multimonitor setup.

To add a built-in menu to a toolbar, follow these steps:

1. On the Commands tab of the Customize Toolbars and Menus dialog box, scroll down to the bottom of the Categories list box.

2. Click the Built-in Menus item to display the list of menus in the Commands box.

3. Drag the menu to the toolbar and drop it where you want it to appear.

Customizing the Menus and the Menu Bar

The Ribbon is a neat addition to Excel 2011, but you may find the menus are still the most convenient way to give many commands. If so, you probably want to customize the menus to put the commands you need the most within easy reach, add specialized commands you find useful, and strip out the commands you seldom or never use.

To customize the menus and the menu bar, open the Customize Toolbars and Menus dialog box and display the toolbar for the standard menu bar like this:

1. Right-click the Standard toolbar or the Formatting toolbar, then click the Customize Toolbars and Menus item on the context menu to display the Customize Toolbars and Menus dialog box. You can also choose **View ➤ Toolbars ➤ Customize Toolbars and Menus.**

2. If the Toolbars and Menus tab isn't already at the front, click it to bring it to the front.

3. Select the Worksheet Menu Bar check box if it's not already selected. Excel displays the toolbar for the standard menu bar (the one you see when working with worksheets rather than charts) on the screen.

You can now add commands to the menus or to the menu bar, as described next.

Customizing the Menus

To customize the menus, follow these steps with the Customize Toolbars and Menus dialog box open and the Worksheet Menu Bar toolbar displayed:

1. Click the Commands tab to bring it to the front of the Customize Toolbars and Menus dialog box.

2. Using the techniques described earlier in this chapter, find the command you want to add to a menu.

3. Click the command, and then drag it to the appropriate menu on the Worksheet Menu Bar toolbar. Excel displays the menu.

4. Still holding down the mouse button, drag the command to where you want it on the menu. Figure 2–10 shows an example of dragging a command to a menu.

Figure 2–10. *To add a command to a menu, drag the command to the toolbar that represents the menu bar, and then drag the command to where you want it on the menu.*

5. When you drop the command, it appears on the menu. You can then customize the menu item by Ctrl-clicking or right-clicking it and working in the Command Properties dialog box, as discussed for customizing toolbars earlier in this chapter.

Customizing the Menu Bar

To customize the menu bar, open the Customize Toolbars and Menus dialog box and display the Worksheet Menu Bar toolbar. You can then customize the menu bar in these ways:

■ *Add a new menu.* To do so, follow these steps:

Scroll down to the bottom of the Categories list box and click the New Menu item. The Commands list box displays a single item, New Menu.

In the Commands list box, click the New Menu item and then drag it to the menu bar. When Excel displays a vertical blue line between the menus where you want to place the new menu, release the mouse button. Excel adds a new menu named New Menu to the menu bar.

> **NOTE:** If you want to add the new menu as a submenu on an existing menu, drag the New Menu item to the existing menu. Still holding down the mouse button, wait for the menu to open, and then drag to the position you want before releasing the mouse button.

Ctrl-click or right-click the New Menu item, and then click Command Properties to display the Command Properties dialog box.

In the Name box, type a name for the new menu.

Select the Begin a group check box if you want to put a vertical separator line before the menu name. Separator lines tend to be less useful on the menu bar than on the toolbars, but you may like the look.

Click the OK button to close the Command Properties dialog box.

Add commands to the new menu as discussed in the previous section. Figure 2–11 shows a custom menu in place with a new command being added.

Figure 2–11. *After adding a new menu and naming it, drag commands to it from the Customize Toolbars and Menus dialog box.*

- *Change an existing menu.* Ctrl-click or right-click the menu on the Worksheet Menu Bar toolbar, then click Command Properties to display the Command Properties dialog box. You can then change the menu's name or select the Begin a group check box to put a separator line before the menu. Click the OK button.

- *Delete an existing menu.* Ctrl-click or right-click the menu on the Worksheet Menu Bar toolbar, and then click Delete Command on the pop-up menu.

- *Move an existing menu.* Click the menu on the Worksheet Menu Bar toolbar, and then drag the menu to where you want it to appear.

When you've finished customizing the menus and menu bar, click the OK button to close the Customize Toolbars and Menus dialog box. Your changes then appear in Excel's main menu bar.

> **NOTE:** The Workbook Menu Bar toolbar represents the standard Excel menu bar that appears when you're working with anything except a chart. When a chart or chart element is selected, Excel displays the chart menu bar instead. To customize the chart menu bar, select the Chart

Menu Bar check box on the Toolbars and Menus tab of the Customize Toolbars and Menus check box, and then work with the command bar that appears.

Turning Off or Customizing the Ribbon

As you learned in Chapter 1, you can also customize the Ribbon—only a little compared to the full-on changes you can make to the toolbars and the menu bar—but still enough to help. You can control the Ribbon's behavior and appearance, and you can choose which tabs appear and their order.

You can also turn the Ribbon off completely. We start with this topic.

NOTE: While using this book as a reference, you'll probably find it easiest to keep the Ribbon onscreen with all its standard tabs displayed. If you hide or customize the Ribbon, finding the commands you need will be harder.

Turning the Ribbon Off So It Doesn't Appear

Collapsing the Ribbon gives you more screen space, but you may want to try turning the Ribbon off altogether to see if you can do without it. If so, follow these steps:

1. Click the Set Ribbon Preferences or Tab Order button (the cog button) at the right end of the Ribbon, and then click Ribbon Preferences. Excel displays the Ribbon preferences pane (see Figure 2–12).

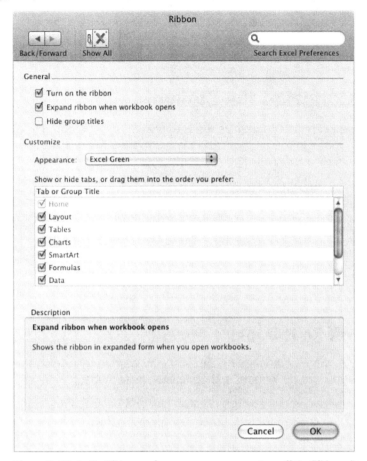

Figure 2–12. *In the Ribbon preferences pane, you can turn off the Ribbon altogether, hide the names of Ribbon groups, or customize the tabs that appear in the Ribbon all the time.*

2. In the General area, clear the Turn on the ribbon check box.

3. Click the OK button to close the Excel Preferences dialog box.

NOTE: When you want to turn the Ribbon on again, choose **Excel ➤ Preferences** or press Cmd+, (Cmd and the comma key) to display the Excel Preferences dialog box, then click the Ribbon icon in the Sharing and Privacy category. Then select the Turn on the ribbon check box, and click the OK button.

Customizing the Ribbon

You can customize the Ribbon by choosing which tabs to display and the order in which to display them. You can't get rid of the Home tab or change its position, but you can suppress or move any of the other tabs.

Customizing the Ribbon the Quick Way

The quick way to customize the Ribbon is to click the Set Ribbon Preferences or Tab Order button (the cog button) at the right end of the Ribbon, and then click Customize Ribbon Tab Order on the pop-up menu. Excel displays a x button and a handle (three vertical bars) on each tab except the Home tab (see Figure 2–13).

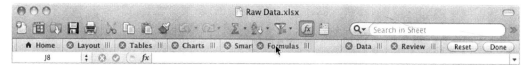

Figure 2–13. *You can customize the Ribbon by dragging its tabs into your preferred order or by removing the tabs you don't need. Click the Done button when you finish.*

You can then click a tab and drag it to where you want it, or click a tab's x button to remove it. When you finish customizing the tabs, click the Done button. And if you mess up, click the Reset button to restore the tabs to their normal setup.

Customizing the Ribbon Using the Ribbon Preferences Pane

The other way to customize the Ribbon is by using the Ribbon preferences pane. Use this method when you want to control whether Excel automatically expands the Ribbon when you open a workbook, when you want to hide the names of Ribbon groups, and when you want to redisplay tabs you've hidden (without having to reset the Ribbon as a whole).

To customize the Ribbon using the Ribbon preferences pane, follow these steps:

1. Click the Set Ribbon Preferences or Tab Order button (the cog button) at the right end of the Ribbon, then click Ribbon Preferences. Excel displays the Ribbon preferences pane (shown in Figure 2–12, earlier in this chapter).

2. In the General area at the top, clear the Expand ribbon when workbook opens check box if you don't want Excel to automatically expand the Ribbon in each workbook you open. Some people find this automatic expansion helpful; others don't.

3.   Also in the General area, select the Hide group titles check box if you want to prevent the names of groups from appearing. Hiding the group titles makes the Ribbon a little shallower, so you may want to try it if you're pushed for space. But it will make following the instructions in this book harder, because they include the groups in Ribbon commands.

4.   In the Appearance pop-up menu, choose Graphite if you want to make the Ribbon tabs gray rather than the default Excel Green.

5.   In the "Show or hide tabs, or drag them into the order you prefer" list box, set up the tabs the way you want them:

   ▪   Clear the check box for any tab you don't want to display.

   ▪   Drag the tabs into the order you want.

6.   Click the OK button to close the Excel Preferences dialog box.

> **NOTE:** At the bottom of the "Show or hide tabs, or drag them into the order you prefer" list box, you find the Developer tab. This tab contains controls for working with Visual Basic for Applications (VBA, the programming language built into the Office applications), running add-ins, and building forms with controls such as check boxes, list boxes, and command buttons.

Opening One or More Workbooks Automatically with Excel

If you want, you can have Excel automatically open one or more workbooks when you launch the application. This is handy when you generally need to work with the same workbook or workbooks each time you use Excel.

To make Excel open one or more workbooks automatically, create a folder that contains only those workbooks. Then go to the General preferences pane, click the Select button to the right of the "At startup, open all files in" box, select the folder in the Choose a Folder: Microsoft Excel dialog box, and then click the Choose button.

> **TIP:** If you want to launch Excel automatically when you log in, Ctrl+click or right-click the Excel icon on the Dock. Click or highlight Options to display the Options submenu and then click the Open at Login item, placing a check mark next to it.

You can also open a workbook at startup by putting it in the Applications/Microsoft Office 2011/Office/Startup/Excel/ folder. Doing this affects all users of Excel on your Mac, though, not just the person who creates the workbook. This capability is occasionally useful, but normally each user will want to be able to choose which workbooks (if any) to open at startup.

Saving the Layout of Open Workbooks as a Workspace

If you need to work with several workbooks at once, you can take advantage of Excel's workspace feature. A *workspace* is a way of saving the layout of open workbooks so you can open them the same way next time.

To save a workspace, follow these steps:

1. Open the workbooks and arrange them however you want them.

2. Choose **File ➤ Save Layout** to display the Save: Microsoft Excel dialog box.

3. Type a name for the workspace.

4. Click the Save button.

To use a workspace you've saved, open it as you would any other file:

- Usually, the quickest way to open a workspace is from the Recent Workbooks list in the Excel Workbook Gallery dialog box or from the **File ➤ Recent Files** submenu.

> **TIP:** You can save a workspace layout file in the Excel startup folder to automatically open all the workbooks in the workspace and arrange them in your saved layout.

- If you haven't used the workspace recently, click the Open button (or press Cmd+O or choose **File ➤ Open** from the menu bar), then use the Open dialog box to open the workspace.

- You can also double-click a workspace file in the Finder to open the workspace, launching Excel if it's not already running. For example, you can put a workspace you use often on the Dock so that it's easy to reach.

Summary

In this chapter, you learned how to configure Excel:Mac to suit the way you work by setting essential preferences, including the General preferences, the View preferences, the Edit preferences, the Save preferences, and the Compatibility preferences. You also now know how to customize the keyboard shortcuts, menus, menu bar, and toolbars; how to change the way the Ribbon appears and works; and how to open workbooks automatically on launching Excel or restore several workbooks to the layout you prefer.

With Excel set up the way you want, you're ready to roll up your sleeves and get to work. We'll start in the next chapter by looking at how to create effective workbooks and templates. Turn the page when you're ready to start.

Chapter 3

Creating Effective Workbooks and Templates

In this chapter, I'll show you how to create workbooks in which you can enter, edit, and manipulate data quickly and effectively. You'll learn how to save the workbooks, which file formats to use when, and how to add property information to help you identify workbooks when searching.

You may need to start some workbooks from scratch, but you'll be able to save time and effort by basing other workbooks on templates. Excel comes with a good variety of templates, and you can download others from the Office web site; but to save the most time, you'll likely want to create your own templates, as discussed at the end of the chapter.

After seeing how to create and save workbooks, you'll learn how to organize the worksheets in a workbook, how to lay out data effectively, and how to enter data quickly on multiple worksheets at the same time. From there, we'll move on to creating named ranges to identify parts of your worksheets easily, and creating a collapsible worksheet by using Excel's outlining feature.

Creating Workbooks from Scratch or from Templates

When you launch Excel, it automatically displays the Excel Workbook Gallery dialog box (see Figure 3–1) so you can create a new workbook or open one you've recently used. In this section, we'll look at how to create a new workbook, either from scratch or based on a template; how to save the workbook in a suitable format; and how to enter information in its properties to make it easier to identify.

NOTE: If you don't want the Excel Workbook Gallery dialog box to open when you launch Excel, select the Don't show this when opening Excel check box at the bottom of the Excel Workbook Gallery dialog box, and then click the Cancel button. To start displaying the Excel Workbook Gallery dialog box again on launch, choose **Excel ➤ Preferences** or press Cmd+, (Cmd and the comma key) to display the Excel Preferences dialog box. In the Authoring area, click the General icon to display the General pane. Select the Open Excel Workbook Gallery when application opens check box, and then click the OK button.

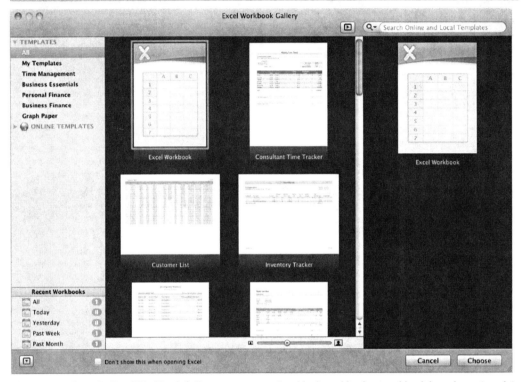

Figure 3–1. *From the Excel Workbook Gallery, you can create a blank workbook, a workbook based on a template on your Mac, or a workbook based on an online template. You can also open a workbook you've used recently.*

Creating a New Blank Workbook

When you need a new workbook with no contents or formatting, create it in one of these ways:

- *Excel Workbook Gallery.* Click the Excel Workbook item, and then click the Choose button.

- *Keyboard.* Press Cmd+N.

- *Menu bar.* Choose File ➤New Workbook.

Creating a New Workbook Based on a Template

To create a new workbook based on a template, you use the Excel Workbook Gallery dialog box (see Figure 3–1). By default, it opens when you launch Excel, but you can also display it at any other time by choosing **File ➤ New from Template** from the menu bar or by pressing Cmd+Shift+P.

From here, you can choose the template you want:

■ *Template on your Mac.* To create a new workbook based on a template that's stored on your Mac, follow these steps:

Click the appropriate category in the Templates list in the left pane—or click the All category if you want to see all the templates.

In the middle pane, click the template you want. A preview appears in the right pane. If the workbook has multiple sheets, you can preview them by clicking the Previous (<) button and Next (>) button in the right pane. For an even quicker but smaller preview, move the mouse over the template image in the middle pane.

> **NOTE:** The Excel Workbook item that appears first in the list of templates produces a blank workbook.

Click the Choose button to create a workbook based on the template.

■ *Online template.* To create a workbook based on a template from Microsoft's Office.com site, follow these steps:

1. In the left pane, click the disclosure triangle to the left of the Online Templates item to expand it.

2. Click the category of templates you want—for example, Budgets. The middle pane displays the available templates.

3. In the middle pane, click the template you want. The right pane displays details about the template.

4. Click the Choose button to download the template and create a workbook based on it.

Creating a New Workbook Based on an Existing Workbook

Templates can save you a lot of time if you set them up right, but often the easiest way to create a new workbook is to base it on an existing workbook. To do this, follow these steps:

1. Choose **File ➤ Open** to display the Open: Microsoft Excel dialog box.

2. Navigate to the existing workbook, and then click it.

3. Click the Open pop-up menu, and then click Copy.

4. Click the Open button. Excel closes the dialog box and opens a new workbook containing the same contents as the existing workbook.

5. Choose File ➤ Save to display the Save As dialog box, and then save the workbook under a name you specify, just as when you create a new workbook.

> **NOTE:** If you don't choose Copy in the Open pop-up menu in the Open: Microsoft Excel dialog box, you open the original workbook. You can then use the File ➤ Save As command to save it under a different name or in a different folder—but it's easy to get distracted, forget to use Save As, and then save changes to the original file by mistake.

Saving a Workbook

To save a workbook for the first time, give the Save command in any of the usual ways—by clicking the Save button on the Standard toolbar, by choosing File ➤ Save from the menu bar, or by pressing Cmd+S. In the Save As dialog box, select the folder in which to save the workbook, type the workbook name, and then click the Save button.

When you save a workbook, Excel selects the file type that's set in the Compatibility preferences pane. If you've chosen the format you want, as discussed in the section "Choosing the Default Format for Saving Workbooks" in Chapter 2, you're all set. If you haven't chosen a different format, Excel uses the format called Excel Workbook, which works well for the four latest versions of Excel—Excel 2011 and Excel 2008 for Mac, and Excel 2010 and Excel 2007 for Windows—but may cause problems with earlier versions..

> **TIP:** If you start recording or writing macros to automate your work in Excel, you'll need to use a workbook format that can contain macros, because the Excel Workbook format can't. Use the Excel Macro-Enabled Workbook format if the workbook is for Excel 2011, Excel 2010 for Windows, or Excel 2007 for Windows; use the Excel 97–2004 format if the workbook is for Excel 2004, Excel 2003, or an earlier version. Excel 2008 for Mac doesn't run macros.

If you need to save the workbook in a different format than the default one, open the Format pop-up menu and click the format you want to use. For example, if you will share the workbook with people who use Excel 2004 for Mac or Excel 2003 for Windows, choose the Excel 97–2004 Workbook format.

NOTE: The latest Excel file format (the one called simply Excel Workbook) is technically superior to the earlier file format (Excel 97–2004 Workbook or Excel 97–2003 Workbook). Using the Excel Workbook format, you can create workbooks containing more worksheets and each worksheet can have many more rows and columns. This file format is also more resistant to data corruption. But for normal-size spreadsheets, such as those most business users and home users create, the earlier file format works just fine.

Protecting a Workbook with Automatic Backups and Passwords

For any workbook that contains valuable data you can't risk losing, it's a good idea to set Excel to create automatic backups.

TIP: Setting Excel to create automatic backups is a good safety measure, but you'll still want to back your valuable workbooks up to media outside your Mac in case the Mac's hard disk crashes. For example, save copies of your workbooks to a USB stick or to an online storage service such as Apple's MobileMe service.

Similarly, you may need to protect important or confidential workbooks with a password. Excel lets you use two different types of passwords:

- *Password to open.* This is a password that anyone who wants to open the workbook must provide. Without the right password, Excel won't open the workbook. Use a password to open when you want to make sure that only authorized people can open the workbook.

- *Password to modify.* This is a password that anyone who wants to open the original copy of the workbook must provide. Without the right password, Excel lets you open a copy of the workbook, but not the original file. Use a password to modify when you need to protect a particular workbook against changes but want to allow free access to the information in the workbook.

The best time to put these safety nets in place is the first time you save the workbook. Follow these steps:

1. In the Save As dialog box, click the Options button to display the Save Options dialog box (see Figure 3–2).

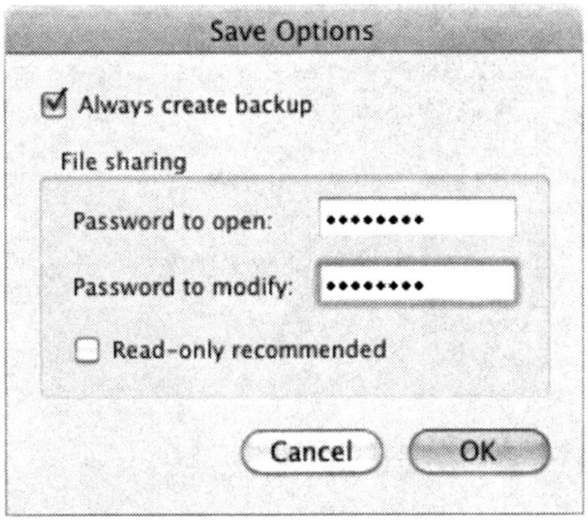

Figure 3–2. *In the Save Options dialog box, you can apply a password to open, a password to modify, or both. You can also set Excel to automatically make a backup of the workbook or to recommend that others open it as read-only.*

2. Select the Always create backup check box if you want Excel to automatically create a backup of this workbook each time you save it.

> **NOTE:** Excel creates the automatic backup by renaming the existing saved version of the workbook with the name "Backup of" and the original filename (for example, "Backup of Office Performance.xlsx"), and then saving the current version of the workbook in a new file. This means the backup is of the previously saved version of the workbook rather than the latest version, but as long as you save frequently, it enables you to recover almost all of your work. Excel keeps the backup file in the same folder as the original file.

3. To apply a password to open, type it in the Password to open text box.

4. To apply a password to modify, type it in the Password to modify text box.

5. If you want to recommend that people open the workbook in a read-only state, so that they can't save changes to it, select the Read-only recommended check box.

> **CAUTION:** Avoid using the Read-only recommended feature. Unless your colleagues are exceptionally amenable, it won't prevent them from editing the workbook. To force them to open the workbook as read-only, give the workbook a password to modify, and don't share it with your colleagues.

6. Click the OK button. If you set either kind of password, Excel displays the Confirm Password dialog box (see Figure 3–3) prompting you to enter it again (to make sure you got it right). Type the password, and then click the OK button.

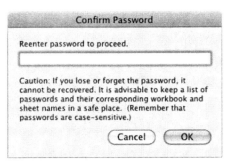

Figure 3–3. *Type the password again in the Confirm Password dialog box. If you set both a password to open and a password to modify, the Confirm Password dialog box opens twice—the first time for the password to open (which it calls the "password to proceed"), the second time for the password to modify.*

7. After Excel returns you to the Save As dialog box, finish saving the workbook as usual.

When you open a workbook protected with a password, Excel displays the Password dialog box. The left screen in Figure 3–4 shows the Password dialog box for a password to open; either you provide the password, or you can't open the workbook. The right screen in Figure 3–4 shows the Password dialog box for a password to modify; here, you can either provide the password and click the OK button to open the workbook for editing, or click the Read Only button without providing the password to open the workbook without being able to save changes to it.

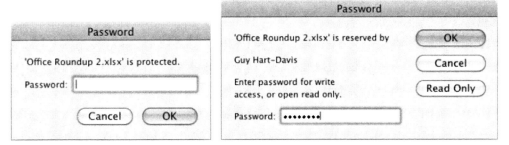

Figure 3–4. *When you try to open a workbook protected with a password to open, the Password dialog box requests the password (left). If the workbook has a password to modify, the Password dialog box includes the Read Only button (right), allowing you to open the workbook without providing the password.*

To remove the password from a workbook, follow these steps:

1. Open the workbook, providing the password when Excel demands it.

2. Choose **File ➤ Save As** to display the Save As dialog box.

3. Click the Options button to display the Save Options dialog box.

4. Delete the password in the Password to open text box or the Password to modify text box, as appropriate.

5. Click the OK button to close the Save Options dialog box. Excel returns you to the Save As dialog box.

6. Click the Save button, saving the workbook with its original name and location. Excel displays a dialog box to confirm that you want to overwrite the file.

7. Click the Replace button. Excel saves the workbook without the password.

Entering Workbook Properties

If you selected the Prompt for workbook properties check box in the General preferences pane, Excel displays the Properties dialog box automatically when you save a workbook for the first time. As you can see in Figure 3–5, the Properties dialog box contains five tabs: General, Summary, Statistics, Contents, and Custom. You can enter data on only the Summary tab and Custom tab, so start by clicking the Summary tab to bring it to the front.

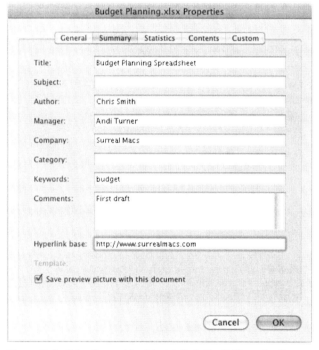

Figure 3–5. *Enter the workbook's details in the fields on the Summary tab of the Properties dialog box.*

NOTE: The General tab of the Properties dialog box contains readouts for the file name, type (for example, Microsoft Excel Workbook), location (the folder that contains the workbook), created date (when you first saved the workbook), and last-modified date (when you last saved the workbook). Excel doesn't compile this information until you first save the workbook, so the fields will be blank when Excel displays the Properties dialog box automatically when you're saving a file for the first time. The General tab also contains a Read-Only check box and a Hidden check box. The Statistics tab contains readouts of when the file was created, last modified, and last printed; the name of the user who last saved it; the revision number; and the total editing time. The Contents tab contains a list of the document's worksheets, chart sheets, macro sheets, and dialog sheets.

Entering Standard Properties on the Summary Tab

Enter the relevant details in the fields on the Summary tab—the workbook's title and subject, your name, your manager's name, and so on. Excel puts your user name in the Author box but leaves the others up to you. Even if Excel enters your name correctly (rather than something like Authorized User, which may be set as your user name), you may want to change the Author field to include coworkers or a business team—or to put the blame for the workbook on your manager.

NOTE: In the Hyperlink base box, you can enter the URL that forms the basis for hyperlinks in the workbook. For example, if all the URLs start with http://www.surrealmacs.com, enter that URL in the Hyperlink base box. You then need enter only the remaining part of each URL in the worksheet. (For URLs that don't use the hyperlink base, enter the full URL in the worksheet.)

Select the Save preview picture with this document check box if you want Excel to include a preview in the workbook. Saving a preview can make the workbook easier to recognize in Quick Look, and it makes the workbook file only a little larger, so it's usually a good idea.

TIP: You can use Spotlight to search using the Title, Subject, Authors, Keywords, and Comments fields—so you'll probably want to fill in these fields in your workbooks.

Entering Extra Data on the Custom Tab

The fields on the Summary tab are enough to store essential metadata, but if you need to manage your workbooks tightly, you'll want to store more property information in them. To do so, click the Custom tab to display it (see Figure 3–6). Here you'll find a list of built-in properties including Client, Department, Date Completed, and Project. You can also create your own properties.

Figure 3–6. *On the Custom tab of the Properties dialog box, you can enter data for a wide range of built-in properties or create extra properties of your own. You can also link a property to content in the workbook.*

To create custom properties, you type their names in the Name text box. You can also assign to a property the contents of the first cell in a named range in the workbook. This capability enables you to store the contents of specific cells automatically in the properties and thus have them indexed along with the other property information.

To add property information, follow these steps:

1. Choose the property:

   ▉ If the property is built-in, click its name in the Name list box.

   ▉ To create a custom property, type a new name in the Name box.

2. In the Type pop-up menu list, select the appropriate type for the property: Text, Date, Number, or Yes or No. This choice isn't relevant if you're linking the property to a range in the workbook.

3. Enter the data for the property as appropriate:

   ▉ *Text, Date, or Number value.* Type the value in the Value text box.

   ▉ *Yes or No.* Select the Yes option button or the No option button.

- *Information contained in a named range in a worksheet.* Select the Link to Content check box. Excel displays a Source pop-up menu that contains the named ranges in the workbook. Select the range from this list.

4. Click the Add button. Excel adds the property and data to the Properties list box.

To delete a field, select it in the Properties list box and click the Delete button.

Your Workbooks by Using Properties

ve entered properties in your workbooks, you can use the property to identify the workbooks more easily when searching with Spotlight. This is you have many workbooks and need to find the right one quickly.

ising property information in Spotlight, follow these steps:

-click or right-click the Finder icon on the Dock, and then click New Finder Jow on the context menu to open a new Finder window. If you don't have any other Finder windows open, you can also simply click the Finder icon on the Dock to open a new window.

2. Navigate to the folder where you want to start the search. For example, if you keep all your workbooks in the same folder, select that folder rather than searching your whole Mac and its connected drives.

3. Choose File ➤ Find or press Cmd+F to switch to Search mode.

4. In the Search bar at the top of the window, click the folder you selected in step 2.

5. Click the + button at the right end of the Search bar to display a line of controls for setting up the search. Figure 3–7 shows a search window with a search underway.

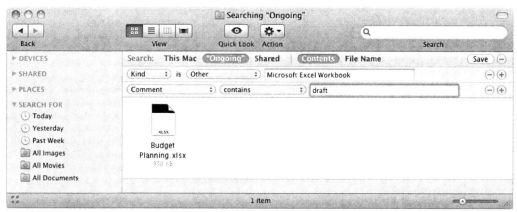

Figure 3–7. *After adding property information to your workbooks, you can locate workbooks using their properties.*

6. On the line of search controls, open the Any pop-up menu, and then click Other.

7. Type Microsoft Excel Workbook in the text box that the Finder displays when you select Other in the pop-up menu.

8. Click the + button at the end of the first line of search controls to display another line.

9. Open the left pop-up menu, and then click Other to display the Select a search attribute dialog box (see Figure 3–8).

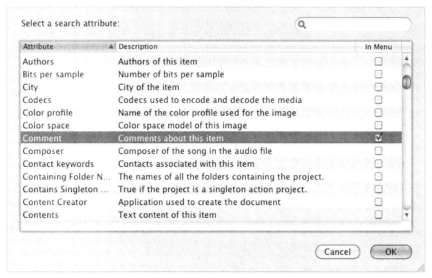

Figure 3–8. *In the Select a search attribute dialog box, click the attribute you want to search by. Select the In Menu check box if you want to make the attribute easier to use in searches.*

10. Click the attribute (in other words, the property) you want to use for the search. Using the Title, Subject, Authors, Keywords, or Comment attributes is usually the best way of finding Excel workbooks for which you've set properties.

> **TIP:** If you will need to search by a particular property frequently, select the In Menu check box on its row to make Mac OS X include the property in the pop-up menu. That way, you won't need to open the Select a search attribute dialog box to reach the property.

11. Click the OK button to close the Select a search attribute dialog box. The attribute you selected appears in the pop-up menu.

12. Use the remaining controls on the line to specify the comparison. For example, use **Title contains budget** to search for workbooks whose Title property includes the word "budget."

13. Add any other search criteria needed. For example, you may want to find only workbooks modified in the past two weeks, or ones whose Authors property includes your boss.

As you complete each condition, the Finder window displays the list of matching workbooks. As soon as you identify the workbook you want, you can open it by double-clicking it. Or if you need to look quickly at its contents without opening it, press Spacebar or click the Quick Look button on the toolbar.

> **TIP:** When you've created a search like this, you can save it as a Smart Folder by clicking the Save button in the upper-right corner of the Search window. A *Smart Folder* is Mac OS X's name for a saved search. In the Save As dialog box that opens, type the name for the Smart Folder and select the folder in which to store it; the default folder, the Saved Searches folder, works well unless you have somewhere better. Select the Add To Sidebar check box if you want to add the Smart Folder to the Search For list in the Sidebar, where you can reach it in moments.

Saving Your Workbooks for Use with Older Versions of Excel

Over the years, Microsoft has added many features to Excel and has changed its file format several times. As a result, two problems occur:

- An older version of Excel may not be able to open a workbook you create in Excel 2011. If the older version can open the workbook, it may not display correctly.

- An older version of Excel can't support the features that have been added to Excel in subsequent versions. For example, Microsoft added sparklines (in-cell charts) in Excel 2011; earlier versions, such as Excel 2008 and Excel 2004, don't have sparklines.

The first essential for sharing a workbook with older versions of Excel is to choose a suitable file format:

- *Excel Workbook format.* Use this format for sharing with Excel 2011, Excel 2008 for Mac, Excel 2010 for Windows, or Excel 2007 for Windows. You can also use it for sharing with Excel 2004 for Mac or Excel 2003 for Windows provided that computer has installed filters that enable it to read this file format (which Microsoft introduced in Excel 2007). This format uses the .xlsx file extension.

NOTE: You can download the filters for free from the Microsoft Web site (www.microsoft.com/downloads/). For Windows, look for the Microsoft Office Compatibility Pack for Word, Excel, and PowerPoint File Formats download. For Mac, look for the Open XML File Format Converter for Mac download.

■ *Excel 97–2004 Workbook format.* Use this format for sharing with Excel 2004 for Mac, Excel 2003 for Windows, or older versions of Excel. This format, which uses the .xls file extension, is also good for sharing with other spreadsheet applications.

To save a workbook file in a format different from the one it currently uses, follow these steps:

1. Choose **File ➤ Save As** from the menu bar or press Cmd+Option+S to display the Save As dialog box.

2. In the Format pop-up menu, choose the format you want to use.

3. Optionally, change the file name in the Save As text box, or choose a different folder. Because the Excel Workbook format and the Excel 97–2004 Workbook format use different file extensions, you usually needn't change the name—but having two workbooks with almost identical names can be confusing.

4. Click the Save button. Excel closes the Save As dialog box and saves the workbook.

The second essential is to make sure the file you save is as compatible as possible with earlier versions of Excel. To help you identify potential problems and (if you want) root them out, Excel's Toolbox includes the Compatibility Report palette. You use it like this:

1. Open the workbook if it's not already open.

2. Choose **View ➤ Compatibility Report** to open the Toolbox with the Compatibility Report palette at the front.

3. Open the Check compatibility with pop-up menu, and then click the version of the application with which you want to make sure the workbook is compatible. The Results box shows a list of possible problems (see Figure 3–9).

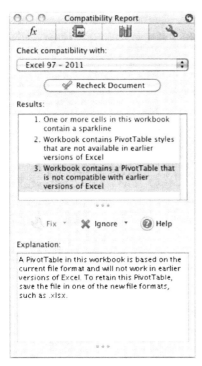

Figure 3–9. *In the Compatibility Report palette, choose the version of Excel with which to check the workbook's compatibility. You can then choose which problems to fix and which to ignore.*

4. To see the details of a problem, click it in the Results box. The Explanation box displays a description of the problem.

5. To fix a problem, click it in the Results box. If the Fix button is available, click it to fix this instance of the problem. To fix all the instances, click the Fix drop-down button, and then click Fix All on the menu.

6. To ignore a problem, click it in the Results box, and then click the Ignore button. To ignore all the instances, click the Ignore drop-down button, and then click Ignore All on the menu. To teach the application not to bother you with this problem again, click the Ignore drop-down button and then click Don't Show Again on the menu.

Organizing the Worksheets in a Workbook

When you create a blank workbook, Excel gives it the number of sheets set in the Sheets in new workbook box in the General preferences pane—by default, a single worksheet. If you need more worksheets, you can easily insert them. And you can get rid of any worksheets you no longer need.

Excel gives each worksheet a default name at first—Sheet1, Sheet2, and so on. Usually, you want to give the worksheets descriptive names so you can easily identify them. You may also need to rearrange the worksheets into a different order.

Inserting a New Worksheet

To insert a new worksheet, take one of these actions:

- *Insert a new worksheet after the last existing worksheet.* Click the Insert Sheet button that appears on the tab bar after the last worksheet tab.

- *Insert a new worksheet after a particular worksheet.* Ctrl+click or right-click the existing worksheet, and then click Insert Sheet on the context menu.

> **TIP:** Excel's default keyboard shortcut for inserting a new worksheet after the active worksheet is Shift+F11. This keyboard shortcut works only if Mac OS X isn't using F11 for a different purpose, such as the Show Desktop feature in Exposé. If Mac OS X is already using F11, you need to map the Insert Sheet command to a different keyboard shortcut using the technique explained in the section "Creating Custom Keyboard Shortcuts" in Chapter 2. Alternatively, you can change the Mac OS X feature that's using F11.

Naming a Worksheet

To make a worksheet easier to identify, give it a descriptive name. Double-click the worksheet's tab to select the default name, type the name you want, and then press Return to apply the name. You can use up to 31 characters in the name—enough for several words.

Changing a Worksheet's Tab Color

If you want to make a worksheet's tab stand out, Ctrl+click or right-click the tab, click Tab Color to display the Tab Color window, and then click the color for the tab. Click the Close button (the button at the left end of the title bar) to close the Tab Color window.

> **NOTE:** If you copy a worksheet, the copy gets the same tab color as the original—so you may want to change the color to make the copy easier to distinguish.

Deleting a Worksheet

To delete a worksheet, Ctrl+click or right-click its tab, and then click Delete on the context menu. Excel displays a dialog box (see Figure 3–10) to double-check that you're prepared to delete it; click the Delete button to go ahead.

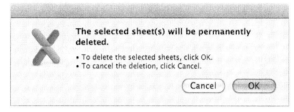

The selected sheet(s) will be permanently deleted.

• To delete the selected sheets, click OK.
• To cancel the deletion, click Cancel.

Cancel　　OK

Figure 3–10. *Click the OK button to confirm that you want to delete the worksheet.*

Rearranging the Worksheets in a Workbook

To get a workbook's worksheets in the order you want, you can rearrange them.

The quick way to move a worksheet is to click its tab, drag it left or right until Excel displays a downward arrow between the worksheets where you want to place it, and then drop it.

> **TIP:** To move two or more worksheets, select them first. To select a range of worksheets that appear next to each other, click the first worksheet's tab, and then Shift+click the tab for the worksheet at the other end of the range. To select worksheets that aren't next to each other, click the first worksheet's tab, and then Cmd+click each other worksheet's tab in turn.

Dragging a worksheet tab is easy for short distances, but when you need to move a worksheet further, use the Move or Copy dialog box instead. You can also use the Move or Copy dialog box to move or copy worksheets to a different workbook. Follow these steps:

1. If you want to move or copy the worksheets to a different workbook, open that workbook.

2. In the source workbook, Ctrl+click or right-click the worksheet's tab to display the context menu. To move multiple worksheets, select them, and then Ctrl+click or right-click one of the selected tabs.

3. On the context menu, click the Move or Copy item to display the Move or Copy dialog box (see Figure 3–11).

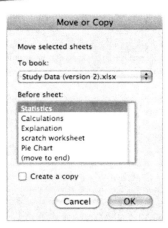

Figure 3–11. *Use the Move or Copy dialog box to move one or more worksheets farther than you can comfortably drag within a workbook, or to move or copy worksheets to another open workbook.*

4. In the To book pop-up menu, make sure the current workbook is selected unless you want to move the worksheet to another workbook—in which case, select that workbook.

5. In the Before sheet list box, click the worksheet before which you want to position the worksheet you're moving. If you want to put the worksheets at the end of the workbook, select the (move to end) item.

6. Select the Create a copy check box if you want to copy the worksheet to the destination rather than move it. Copying tends to be most useful when the destination is another workbook, but you can copy within a workbook as well.

7. Click the OK button to close the dialog box. Excel moves or copies the worksheet to the destination you chose.

Four Easy Rules for Laying Out Your Worksheets

Excel gives you a great deal of flexibility in how you lay out your worksheets. Each worksheet contains more than 16 billion cells, and you can put pretty much as many worksheets in a workbook as you want.

> **NOTE:** If you pack a huge number of worksheets into a workbook and populate them all with data, you may find that Excel slows your Mac down. If this happens, move some of the worksheets into another workbook to improve performance.

Here are four rules to follow when laying out your worksheets to make them as easy as possible to use.

- **Put different topics on different worksheets.** Given that Excel's worksheets can contain a huge amount of information, you may feel tempted to put all your data on a single one. But usually it's better to break the data up and put a different topic on each worksheet.

> **TIP:** Give the worksheet tabs descriptive labels so you can easily pick the worksheet you want. If a workbook has so many worksheets that navigating with worksheet tabs is awkward, create a summary worksheet at the front containing a list of the other worksheets and their contents—and hyperlinks you can click to jump directly to each sheet.

- **Divide up your data by columns.** Lay out the data so that the cells in any given column contain the same type of data. Doing this enables you to sort and filter the range by rows.

- **Put important data above the range rather than beside it.** When you need to include notes or other explanatory data, put that data above the range it's related to. Don't put the data to the left or right of the range, because Excel may hide the data if you filter the range to show only certain values.

- **Separate your data ranges from each other.** If you include several different types of data in the same worksheet, put each type in a separate range, with one or more blank columns and one or more blank rows between the ranges. Having this extra space makes it easier for both Excel and you to identify and select the ranges individually.

Entering Data on Multiple Worksheets at Once

You may sometimes be able to save time by entering data on multiple worksheets at once. For example, if a workbook needs a separate worksheet for each month's sales, you may need to create 12 worksheets with a similar structure.

To enter the data, follow these steps:

1. Select the tab of each worksheet you want to receive the data. For example, click the first tab, and then Shift+click the last tab. The selected tabs appear white rather than gray, as in Figure 3–12. Excel displays [Group] after the workbook's name in the title bar as a reminder.

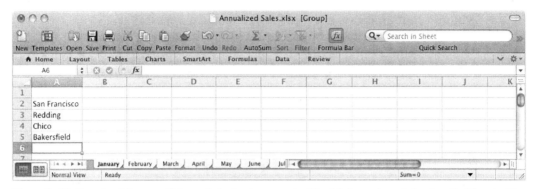

Figure 3–12. *To enter data on multiple worksheets at once, select the tab for each worksheet, so that Excel adds [Group] to the title bar. You can then enter the data as usual in the worksheet that's displayed.*

2.   You can now enter the data in the cells of the worksheet that's displayed. Excel enters the same data in each of the other selected worksheets.

3.   When you've finished working with the group, click an unselected tab to cancel the grouping.

Identifying Parts with Named Ranges

When you're setting up formulas in your workbooks, you'll often need to refer to particular cells and ranges. You can always refer to cells and ranges using their addresses, but these can be hard to remember—especially if you change their location by adding cells, rows, or columns to your worksheet.

To make your references easier to enter and recognize, you can give a name to any cell or range. You can then refer to the cell or range by that name. Excel tracks the current position of each name, so even if you add or delete cells (or rows or columns), you can still use the name without worrying about exactly where it is.

You can also use named ranges to navigate your worksheets easily: To go to a named range, open the pop-up menu in the reference area and click the range's name.

Assigning a Name to a Cell or Range

You can assign a name to a cell or range either quickly using the Reference Area or more formally using the Define Name dialog box. The advantage to using the Define Name dialog box is that you can manage your existing range names from there too.

These are the rules for creating names:

   ▧   The name must start with a letter or an underscore.

   ▧   The name can contain only letters, numbers, and underscores. It can't contain spaces or symbols.

■   The name must be unique in the workbook.

Assigning a Name to a Cell or Range Quickly

To assign a name to a cell or range quickly using the Reference area, follow these steps:

1.   Select the cell or range you want to name.

2.   Click in the Reference area. Excel selects its current contents, which is the reference of the active cell (for example, B5).

3.   Type the name for the cell or range, and then press Return to apply it.

> **NOTE:** If you type an existing name in the Reference area, Excel selects that cell or range when you press Return—just as if you'd opened the pop-up menu in the Reference area and then clicked the name.

Assigning a Name to a Cell or Range with the Define Name Dialog Box

To assign a name to a cell or range using the Define Name dialog box, follow these steps:

1.   Select the cell or range you want to name.

2.   Choose **Insert ➤ Name ➤ Define** from the menu bar to display the Define Name dialog box (shown in Figure 3–13 with settings chosen).

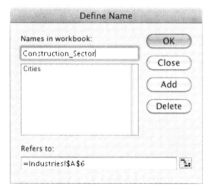

Figure 3–13. *In the Define Name dialog box, type the name you want to assign the cell or range so you can easily refer to it.*

3.   In the Name text box, type the name for the cell or range.

4. Make sure that the Refers to box shows the right cell or range. If not, click the Collapse Dialog button, select the right cell or range in the worksheet, and then click the Collapse Dialog button again to restore the dialog box.

5. If you want to create only this one name, click the OK button to apply the name to the range and close the Define Name dialog box. If you want to create more names before you close the Define Name dialog box, click the Add button.

Creating Range Names Automatically

If your worksheet has headings in the first column or last column or the first row or last row of an area, you can have Excel automatically create range names for you. This feature can save you time and effort.

When Excel creates the named ranges, it makes each an equal-sized section of the range you select. For example, if you create named ranges using the top row of the selection (A1:F5) shown in Figure 3–14, Excel creates a range named Stockton for cells B2:B5, a range called Modesto for cells C2:C5, and so on. Excel replaces spaces, punctuation, symbols and other characters in the headings that aren't allowed in names with underscores—for example, the heading City of Industry produces the name City_of_Industry.

	A	B	C	D	E	F	G
1		Stockton	Modesto	Fresno	Bakersfield	City of Industry	
2	2011						
3	2012						
4	2013						
5	2014						
6							
7							

Figure 3–14. *Creating named ranges using the headings in this selection produces ranges named Stockton for the range B2:B5, Modesto for the range C2:C5, and City_of_Industry for the range F2:F5.*

To create names automatically, follow these steps:

1. Enter the headings in the worksheet.

> **NOTE:** In order to create names, each heading must begin with a letter rather than a number. So if you need to create names for cell containing (say) years, you need to preface the numbers with one or more letters—for example, Year 2011 rather than plain 2011.

2. Select the range that contains the headings. The headings must be in the top row, bottom row, left column, or right column of the selection.

> **NOTE:** When selecting the range from which to create labels, you must select more than one row (if the headings are in a row) or more than one column (if the headings are in a column). Otherwise, Excel displays the The Selection Is Not Valid dialog box. If this happens, click the OK button and change your selection.

3. Choose **Insert ➤ Name ➤ Create** to display the Create Names dialog box (see Figure 3–15).

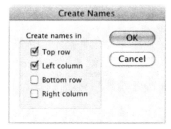

Figure 3–15. *In the Create Names dialog box, select the check box for each column and row that contains the headings you want to turn into range names.*

4. In the Create names in box, select the Top row check box, the Left column check box, the Bottom row check box, and the Right column check box, as appropriate.

5. Click the OK button. Excel closes the Create Names dialog box and creates the names.

Excel doesn't display a dialog box or otherwise confirm that it has created the names. If you want to check that the names are there, open the pop-up menu on the Reference area and you'll see them in alphabetical order.

Using a Range Name in Your Formulas

After you name a range, you can use the name in your formulas instead of the cell reference or range reference. Named ranges can be a great time-saver, because names are much easier to remember and type than the cell references or range references.

For example, if you give a cell the name Interest_Rate, you can use it in a formula like this:

```
=B1*Interest_Rate
```

When your range names are straightforward like this, you may want to just type them in. Other times, you may find it easier to paste a name in like this:

1. Move the active cell to where you want the formula.

2. Start the formula as usual. For example, type =.

3. When you reach the part of the formula that needs the name, choose **Insert ➤ Name ➤ Paste** to display the Paste Name dialog box (see Figure 3–16).

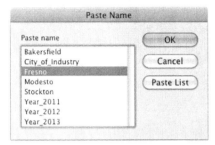

Figure 3–16. *Use the Paste Name dialog box to paste a range name into a formula. You can also paste the whole list of range names and their locations for reference.*

4. In the Paste name list box, click the range name you want to paste.

5. Click the OK button. Excel closes the Paste Name dialog box and pastes in the name.

> **TIP:** If you want to create a list of all the range names in a worksheet along with their locations, position the active cell where you want the list to start, choose **Insert ➤ Name ➤ Paste** to display the Paste Name dialog box, and then click the Paste List button.

Deleting a Range Name

To delete a range name, follow these steps:

1. Choose **Insert ➤ Name ➤ Define** from the menu bar to display the Define Name dialog box.

2. Click the range name in the Names in workbook list box.

3. Click the Delete button.

4. Delete other range names as needed, then click the Close button to close the Define Name dialog box.

Changing the Cell or Range a Name Refers To

If you need to change the cell or range a name refers to, follow these steps:

1. Choose **Insert ➤ Name ➤ Define** from the menu bar to display the Define Name dialog box.

2. Click the existing name in the Names in workbook list box.

3. Triple-click in the Refers to box to select the current reference.

4. In the worksheet, click the cell or select the new range. (You can click the Collapse Dialog button first if you need to reduce the Define Name dialog box, but usually it's easier just to work around it.)

5. Click the OK button if you want to make the change and close the Define Name dialog box. Click the Add button if you want to make the change but keep the Define Name dialog box open.

Creating a Collapsible Worksheet by Outlining It

Worksheets that contain many columns or rows of data can become hard to navigate even if you freeze the headings on screen the way you learned in Chapter 1. To make navigation easier, you can use Excel's outlining feature to create a collapsible worksheet, and then expand only those sections you need to see at any particular time. Figure 3–17 shows a worksheet containing an outline with some rows and columns expanded and others collapsed.

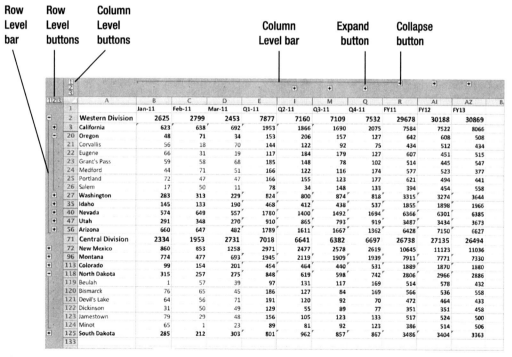

	Jan-11	Feb-11	Mar-11	Q1-11	Q2-11	Q3-11	Q4-11	FY11	FY12	FY13
2 Western Division	2625	2799	2453	7877	7160	7109	7532	29678	30188	30869
3 California	623	638	692	1953	1866	1690	2075	7584	7522	8066
20 Oregon	48	71	34	153	206	157	127	642	608	508
21 Corvallis	56	18	70	144	122	92	75	434	512	434
22 Eugene	66	31	19	117	184	179	127	607	451	515
23 Grant's Pass	59	58	68	185	148	78	102	514	445	547
24 Medford	44	71	51	166	122	116	174	577	523	377
25 Portland	72	47	47	166	155	123	177	621	494	441
26 Salem	17	50	11	78	34	148	133	394	454	558
27 Washington	283	313	229	824	800	874	818	3315	3274	3644
35 Idaho	145	133	190	468	412	438	537	1855	1898	1966
40 Nevada	574	649	557	1780	1400	1492	1694	6366	6301	6385
47 Utah	291	348	270	910	865	793	919	3487	3434	3673
56 Arizona	660	647	482	1789	1611	1667	1362	6428	7150	6627
71 Central Division	2334	1953	2731	7018	6641	6382	6697	26738	27135	26494
72 New Mexico	860	853	1258	2971	2477	2578	2619	10645	11123	11036
96 Montana	774	477	693	1945	2119	1909	1939	7911	7771	7330
113 Colorado	99	154	201	454	464	440	531	1889	1870	1880
118 North Dakota	315	257	275	848	619	598	742	2806	2966	2886
119 Beulah	1	57	39	97	131	117	169	514	578	432
120 Bismarck	76	65	45	186	127	84	169	566	536	558
121 Devil's Lake	64	56	71	191	120	92	70	472	464	433
122 Dickinson	31	50	49	129	55	89	77	351	351	458
123 Jamestown	79	29	48	156	105	123	133	517	524	500
124 Minot	65	1	23	89	81	92	123	386	514	506
125 South Dakota	285	212	303	801	962	857	867	3486	3404	3363

Labels pointing to the figure: Row Level bar, Row Level buttons, Column Level buttons, Column Level bar, Expand button, Collapse button.

Figure 3–17. *Use Excel's outline features to create a worksheet that you can collapse and expand to show only the sections you need.*

Outlining works best for worksheets whose data is arranged in a structure or hierarchy. You can create up to eight levels for rows and eight levels for columns, giving you fine control over the outlines.

You can have Excel create an outline automatically for you from the structure it detects in a worksheet you've laid out with formulas. This is often the best way to start. If you find the automatic outline isn't what you need, you can create an outline manually instead, putting the levels exactly where you want them.

Having Excel Create an Outline Automatically

To have Excel create an outline automatically, you must set up the structure of the worksheet with the formulas in place. Excel uses the formulas to determine the hierarchy of the outline, so if the formulas aren't there, outlining doesn't work. You don't need to enter all the rows and columns of data—just those that contain the formulas and enough of the data rows and columns for the formulas to refer to.

The left screen in Figure 3–18 shows the beginning of a worksheet structured with formulas that will produce an outline. Here's what you can see:

- The leftmost column (column A) contains the divisions, states, and city offices of a large and nefarious organization that we'll allow to remain nameless. You can see the Western Division (which contains California, Oregon, Washington, Idaho, Nevada, Utah, and Arizona) and the Central Division (which includes New Mexico, Montana, Colorado, and various states you can't see).

- Each state contains just a couple of the offices to get the structure right. Once the structure is in place, you can add the extra rows needed.

- Each state's row contains a SUM() formula that adds up the results of the city offices. For example, the California row contains the formula =SUM(B4:B5) in cell B3, adding the rich pickings from Bakersfield and Chico.

- Each division's row contains a SUM() formula that adds up the results of the division's states. For example, the Western Division row contains the formula =SUM(B3,B6,B9,B12,B15,B18,B22) in cell B2, adding the results from California, Oregon, and so on.

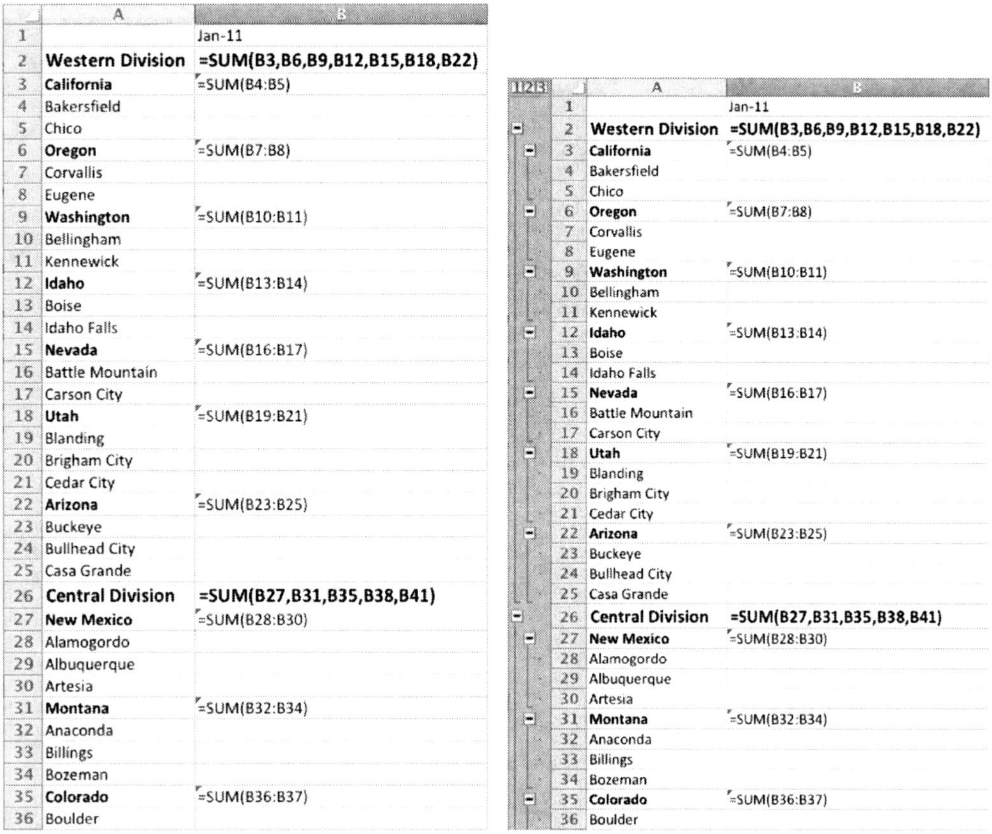

Figure 3–18. *By setting up a worksheet with a hierarchy of formulas (left), you can use Excel's automatic outlining feature to create an outline based on the formulas (right).*

When you've got the formulas in place, choose Data ➤ Group & Outline ➤ Group ➤ Auto Outline from the Ribbon or Data ➤ Group and Outline ➤ Auto Outline from the menu bar to create the outline automatically. The right screen in Figure 3–18 shows the same range of data turned into an outline with three levels. You can click one of the – signs in the outlining bar on the left to collapse a section, and click the + sign that replaces the – sign to expand a section again.

If the outline turns out the way you want it, you can enter the remaining formulas and data. In many cases, you'll be able to use the AutoFill feature (discussed in Chapter 1) to automatically insert the formulas in a row or column based on an existing formula.

If the automatic outline doesn't suit you, try changing the settings for automatic outlining, as discussed next. Alternatively, clear the outline by choosing Data ➤ Group & Outline ➤ Ungroup ➤ Clear Outline from the Ribbon or Data ➤ Group and Outline ➤ Clear Outline from the menu bar. You can then create your outline manually, as discussed in the section after next.

Changing the Settings for Outlining

To change the settings that Excel uses for outlining, follow these steps:

1. Choose the data range:

    - To change an existing outline, click any cell in the outline.

    - To create a new outline, select the data range.

2. Choose Data ➤ Group and Outline ➤ Settings from the menu bar to display the Settings dialog box (see Figure 3–19).

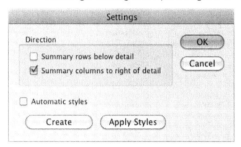

Figure 3–19. *Use the Settings dialog box to control the way Excel creates an automatic outline from your worksheet.*

3. In the Direction box, select the Summary rows below detail check box if the summary rows are below the detail rows. Select the Summary columns to right of detail check box if the worksheet uses summary columns that appear to the right of the columns they summarize.

4. Select the Automatic styles check box if you want Excel to automatically apply styles to the outline to differentiate the different outline levels. Excel applies the RowLevel_1 style to the first level of rows, the RowLevel_2 style to the second level of rows, and so on. For the columns, Excel uses styles named ColLevel_1, ColLevel_2, and so on.

5. Click the command button to close the Settings dialog box and take the action you want:

    - *Create.* Click this button to create a new outline.

    - *Apply Styles.* Click this button to apply styles to an existing outline. You'll need to have selected the Automatic styles check box.

    - *OK.* Click this button to apply the Direction settings you've chosen to an existing outline.

Creating an Outline Manually

Often, it's not convenient to build the structure of a worksheet fully so that Excel can outline it automatically. In these cases, create the outline manually by using the Group command. You can also use the Group command (and its counterpart, Ungroup) to adjust an outline Excel has created for you.

Grouping Rows or Columns

To group rows or columns, follow these steps:

1. Select cells in the rows or columns you want to group. For example:

    - To group rows 4 and 5 under row 3, select cells in rows 4 and 5.

    - To group columns B, C, and D under column E, select cells in columns B, C, and D.

    > **TIP:** You can speed up the process of grouping or ungrouping rows or columns by selecting entire rows or entire columns rather than just cells in them. When you do this, Excel doesn't display the Group dialog box or the Ungroup dialog box, because it can tell from the selection whether it's rows or columns you want to group or ungroup.

2. Choose Data ➤ Group & Outline ➤ Group from the Ribbon (clicking the main part of the Group button rather than its pop-up button) or Data ➤ Group and Outline ➤ Group from the menu bar to display the Group dialog box (shown on the left in Figure 3–20).

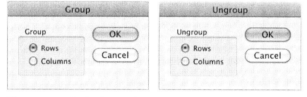

Figure 3–20. *In the Group dialog box (left) or the Ungroup dialog box (right), select the Rows option button or the Columns option button, as appropriate.*

3. Select the Rows option button if you want to group by rows. Select the Columns option button if you want to group by columns.

4. Click the OK button to close the Group dialog box. Excel applies the grouping.

Repeat this procedure to create more groups as needed. For example, in the worksheet I showed you earlier, you would first group the cities under their states, and then group the states under their divisions.

Ungrouping Rows or Columns

To ungroup rows or columns, follow these steps:

1.   Select the range you want to ungroup.

2.   Choose Data ➤ Group & Outline ➤ Ungroup from the Ribbon (clicking the main part of the Ungroup button rather than its pop-up button) or Data ➤ Group and Outline ➤ Ungroup from the menu bar to display the Ungroup dialog box (shown on the right in Figure 3–20).

3.   Select the Rows option button or the Columns option button, as appropriate.

4.   Click the OK button to close the Ungroup dialog box and remove the grouping.

Expanding and Collapsing an Outline

When you have created the outline, you can expand it or collapse it so it shows exactly what you need to see.

Click the Column Level button for the column level you want to see. For example, click the Column Level 2 button to display all the second-level columns.

Click the Row Level button for the row level you want to see. For example, click the Row Level 3 button to display all of the third-level rows.

Click the + button to expand a collapsed section of rows or columns or the – button to collapse an expanded section.

Updating the Outline After Adding or Deleting Rows or Columns

After you add or delete rows or columns within the outlined area of a worksheet, you need to update the outline. Follow these steps:

1.   Place the active cell anywhere in the outlined area.

2.   Choose Data ➤ Group & Outline ➤ Group ➤ Auto Outline from the Ribbon or Data ➤ Group and Outline ➤ Auto Outline from the menu bar. Excel displays the untitled dialog box shown in Figure 3–21.

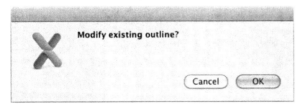

Figure 3–21. *Click the OK button in this dialog box to update the outline with details of the rows or columns you've added or deleted.*

3. Click the OK button. Excel updates the outline.

Remove an Outline

To remove outlining from a worksheet, choose **Data ➤ Group & Outline ➤ Ungroup ➤ Clear Outline**.

Making the Most of Templates

As you know, each workbook you create in Excel is based on a template. If you create a blank workbook, Excel uses a skeleton workbook template that gives you complete freedom of movement but doesn't save you any time. By contrast, if you use a template that comes complete with contents and formatting, you may need to fill in only a small amount of information to produce a complete workbook.

As you saw earlier in this chapter, Excel comes with a good variety of templates, and you can access many more on the Web by opening the Online Templates category in the Excel Workbook Gallery dialog box. But to save the most time, you'll almost certainly need to create your own templates, either from scratch or by customizing existing templates.

To make the most out of templates, follow these suggestions:

- **Assess your needs carefully.** Examine the workbooks that you and your colleagues create most often—sales analysis, project planning, budgets, invoices, timesheets, or whatever it may be. Figure out which of these workbooks you and your colleagues could create more quickly and easily using a template.

- **Base the template on an existing workbook or template.** If you have an existing workbook that contains much (or even some) of the information the template will need, open a copy of that workbook, and then save it as a template. (You'll learn these two moves later in this section.) You may be able to save further time and effort by copying and pasting items from other existing workbooks or templates into your new template.

- **Make the template as complete as possible.** Needs will vary, but you'll normally want to do the following:

  - Insert the number of worksheets most workbooks based on the template will need.

  - Name the worksheets. Color the worksheet tabs if this will help you pick out key tabs quickly.

  - Set up each worksheet with standard text and formulas.

  - Format cells with validation to ensure users enter suitable values.

- Apply conditional formatting to make extreme values stand out.

- Add comments to cells to explain what information is required and what is optional.

- **Automate the template with macros.** To help users enter and manipulate data swiftly and accurately, you may need to add macros to your templates. See Chapter 14 for information on creating and using macros.

Creating a Template Based on an Existing Workbook

To create a template based on an existing workbook, follow these steps:

1. Open Excel if it's not already running.

2. Click the Open button on the Standard toolbar (or press Cmd+O) to display the Open: Microsoft Excel dialog box.

3. Navigate to the folder that contains the existing workbook, and then click the workbook.

4. Click the Open pop-up menu, and then click Copy instead of the default selection, Original.

NOTE: Opening a copy of the existing workbook helps you avoid overwriting it by mistake if you forget to use the Save As command to save it under a different name. Using the Save As command could hardly be easier—but it's equally easy to get distracted before you give the command.

5. Click the Open button to open a copy of the workbook.

You can now save the template as described in the next section.

Saving a Template

To save a template, you use the Save command as usual, but you need to choose the best template format for your needs and pick the right folder to save the template in.

To save the active workbook as a template, follow these steps:

1. Choose File ➤ Save or press Cmd+S to display the Save As dialog box.

2. Open the Format pop-up menu, and then click Excel Template (.xltx).

> **NOTE:** If you need to store macros in the template, choose Excel Macro-Enabled Template (.xltm). If colleagues using Excel 2004 (Mac) or Excel 2003 (Windows) or earlier versions will need to use the template, choose Excel 97–2004 (.xlt) in the Format pop-up menu; this template format can contain macros if necessary.

3. Choose the folder in which to store the template:
    - When you choose one of the Template formats in the Format pop-up menu, Excel automatically changes folder to your My Templates folder.
    - If you plan to share the template with your colleagues, you may want to store it in a folder on the network instead.

4. Click the Save button.

> **NOTE:** To create a workbook based on a template that's stored in a folder other than the template folders that Excel checks, display the Open dialog box and navigate to the folder. Click the template, choose Copy in the Open pop-up menu, and then click the Open button. You can then use the Save command to save the new workbook.

Summary

In this chapter, you learned how to create workbooks and templates in which you can work smoothly and effectively. You now know how to create workbooks based on templates, how to choose the best file formats for saving them, and how to add property information to make the workbooks easier to identify. You can also create your own templates—basing them on existing workbooks or templates if needed.

We also looked at how to organize the worksheets in a workbook, how to lay out data logically, and how to enter data quickly on multiple worksheets at the same time. You saw how to identify parts of your worksheets quickly by creating named ranges and how to make a large worksheet manageable by outlining it.

In the next chapter, I'll show you how to format your workbooks quickly and efficiently.

Chapter 4

Formatting Your Worksheets Quickly and Efficiently

To make your worksheets show the information you need and present it so that it's easy to understand, you'll need to format them. This chapter shows you how to format worksheets quickly and efficiently using the various tools that Excel provides.

The first essential is to format the worksheet's rows and columns. You may need to insert or delete rows, columns, or blocks of cells; you'll often need to hide some rows or columns to get them out of the way or remove them from inquisitive eyes; and you'll almost certainly need to change some column widths and row heights. We'll cover this first.

After that, I'll show you how to format cells and ranges, how to apply conditional formatting to quickly flag values that need attention, and how to use data validation to check for invalid entries.

Toward the end of the chapter, we'll look at how to format worksheets quickly using table formatting or Excel's styles, and how to add headers and footers to worksheets to make them and their contents easy to identify.

Working with Rows and Columns

In this section, you'll learn how to insert and delete rows, columns, and cells; change the width of columns and the height of rows; and hide rows or columns when you don't need to see them.

Inserting and Deleting Rows, Columns, and Cells

When laying out your worksheets, you'll often need to insert or delete entire columns or rows. Sometimes you may also need to delete a block of cells without deleting an entire column or row.

Inserting Columns and Rows

The easiest way to insert a column or row is to Ctrl+click or right-click the heading of the existing column or row before which you want to insert the new one and then click Insert on the context menu.

To insert more than one column or row, select the same number of columns or rows first. For example, to insert three columns before column F, drag through the headings of columns F, G, and H to select those columns; then Ctrl+click or right-click anywhere in the selected headings, and click Insert on the context menu.

You can also insert a column by selecting a cell in the column before which you want to add the new column, and then giving either of these commands:

- *Ribbon.* Choose **Home ➤ Cells ➤ Insert ➤ Insert Columns**.

- *Menu bar.* Choose **Insert ➤ Columns**.

> **NOTE:** If the Excel window isn't wide enough for the Insert button, Delete button, and Format button to appear in the Cells group, an Actions pop-up button appears instead. Click this button to display a pop-up menu with an Insert submenu, a Delete submenu, and a Format submenu. Click the appropriate menu, and then make your choice from it.

Similarly, you can insert a row by selecting a cell in the row before which you want to add the new row and then giving either of these commands:

- *Ribbon.* Choose **Home ➤ Cells ➤ Insert ➤ Insert Rows**.

- *Menu bar.* Choose **Insert ➤ Rows**.

As before, if you want to insert multiple columns or rows, select cells in the corresponding number of columns or rows first.

> **NOTE:** What the Insert button in the Cells group on the Home tab of the Ribbon inserts depends on what you've selected. Select one or more columns to make the Insert button insert columns; select one or more rows to make the Insert button insert rows; or select one or more cells to make the Insert button insert cells. If you haven't selected the appropriate item, click the Insert pop-up button rather than the main Insert button, and then choose the item you want from the pop-up menu.

Inserting Some Cells

To insert just some cells, follow these steps:

1. Select the range before which you want to insert the cells.

2. Choose Home ➤ Cells ➤ Insert ➤ Insert Cells to display the Insert dialog box (see Figure 4–1).

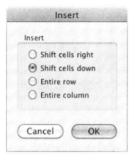

Figure 4–1. *When you insert a block of cells, click the Shift cells right option button or the Shift cells down option button in the Insert dialog box to tell Excel which way to move the existing cells.*

3. Select the Shift cells right option button to move the existing cells to the right. Select the Shift cells down option button to move the existing cells down the worksheet. You can also select the Entire row option button to insert a whole row or select the Entire column option button to insert a whole column, but it's usually easier to insert a row or column by using the methods described earlier.

4. Click the OK button to close the Insert dialog box. Excel inserts the cells.

Deleting Columns or Rows

The easiest way to delete a column or row is to Ctrl+click or right-click its heading, and then click Delete on the context menu. Alternatively, you can select the row or column and then choose Edit ➤ Delete from the menu bar or Home ➤ Cells ➤ Delete (clicking the main part of the Delete button) from the Ribbon.

Instead of selecting the column or row, you can click a cell in it, choose Home ➤ Cells ➤ Delete (clicking the Delete pop-up button), and then click Delete Columns or Delete Rows, as needed. Usually, it's easier to select the row or column first.

Deleting Some Cells

To delete just some cells, select them, and then choose Home ➤ Cells ➤ Delete ➤ Delete Cells. In the Delete dialog box (see Figure 4–2) that Excel displays, select the Shift cells left option button or the Shift cells up option button, as appropriate, and then click the OK button.

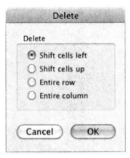

Figure 4–2. *When you delete a block of cells, click the Shift cells left option button or the Shift cells up option button in the Delete dialog box to tell Excel how to fill the gap in the worksheet.*

NOTE: In the Delete dialog box, you can select the Entire row option button to delete the row the selected cell is in, or select the Entire column option button to delete the column. This is useful when you realize you need to delete entire rows or columns rather than just a block of cells. Otherwise, you don't need to open the Delete dialog box to delete rows or columns.

Setting Row Height

Excel normally sets the row height automatically to accommodate the tallest character or object in the row. For example, if you type an entry in a cell, select the cell, and click the Increase Font Size button in the Font group of the Home tab a few times, Excel automatically increases the row height so that there's enough space for the tallest characters.

If Excel doesn't set the row height automatically, choose Home ➤ Cells ➤ Format ➤ AutoFit Row Height to force automatic fitting.

Automatic row height works well for many worksheets, but you may sometimes need to set the row height manually. Use either of these ways:

- *Drag the lower border of the row heading.* Move the mouse pointer over the lower border of the row heading so that the pointer changes to an arrow pointing up and down, and then click and drag the border up (to make the row shallower) or down (to make the row deeper).

- *Use the Row Height dialog box.* Ctrl+click or right-click the row heading, and then click Row Height on the context menu to display the Row Height dialog box (see Figure 4–3). Type the row height you want, and then click the OK button.

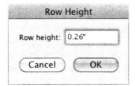

Figure 4–3. *Use the Row Height dialog box when you need to set a row's height precisely.*

NOTE: You can also display the Row Height dialog box by choosing **Home ➤ Cells ➤ Format ➤ Row Height** from the Ribbon or **Format ➤ Row ➤ Height** from the menu bar.

Setting Column Width

Unlike with row height, Excel doesn't automatically adjust column width as you enter data in a worksheet. This is because many worksheets need long entries in cells, so automatic adjustment would make it hard to work.

You can quickly set column width in any of these ways:

- *AutoFit a column.* Double-click the right border of the column heading. Excel automatically changes the column's width so that it's wide enough to contain the widest entry in the column.

- *AutoFit several columns.* Select cells in all the columns you want to affect, and then double-click the right border of any of the selected column headings. Excel automatically fits each column's width to suit its contents. You can also select the cells and then choose **Home ➤ Cells ➤ Format ➤ AutoFormat Column Width** from the Ribbon or **Format ➤ Column ➤ AutoFit Selection**.

TIP: AutoFit is usually the best way to resize a worksheet's columns. But if some cells have such long contents that AutoFit will create huge columns, set the column widths manually and hide parts of the longest contents. You can also wrap the text within a cell so that it occupies as many lines as it needs; you'll learn how to do this in the section "Setting Alignment" later in this chapter.

- *Resize a column by hand.* Drag the right border of the column heading as far as needed.

- *Resize a column precisely.* Ctrl+click or right-click the column heading, and then click Column Width on the context menu to display the Column Width dialog box (see Figure 4–4). Type the cell width, and then click the OK button.

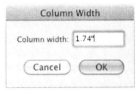

Figure 4–4. *Use the Column Width dialog box when you need to set the column width precisely.*

▓   *Resize several columns precisely to the same width.* Select the columns by dragging through their column headings or by selecting cells in each column. Ctrl+click or right-click in the selected column headings, then click Column Width on the context menu to display the Column Width dialog box. Type the column width and then click the OK button.

Hiding Rows and Columns

Sometimes it's helpful to hide particular columns and rows so that they're not visible in the worksheet. You may want to do this to keep sensitive data from showing or simply to make the part of the worksheet you're actually using fit on the screen all at once.

To hide a column or row, Ctrl+click or right-click its column heading or row heading and then click Hide on the context menu. You can also click a cell in the row or column and choose **Home ➤ Cells ➤ Format ➤ Hide Row** or **Home ➤ Cells ➤ Format ➤ Hide Column** from the Ribbon or **Format ➤ Row ➤ Hide** or **Format ➤ Column ➤ Hide** from the menu bar.

> **TIP:** To quickly hide the active row or selected rows, press Ctrl+9. To hide the active column or selected columns, press Ctrl+0.

To unhide a row or column, select the rows above and below it or the columns on either side of it. Then Ctrl+click or right-click the selected row headings or column headings and click Unhide on the context menu.

> **NOTE:** You can also hide and unhide items by choosing **Home ➤ Cells ➤ Format ➤ Unhide Row** or **Home ➤ Cells ➤ Format ➤ Unhide Column** from the Ribbon or by choosing **Format ➤ Row ➤ Unhide** or **Format ➤ Column ➤ Unhide** from the menu bar.

Formatting Cells and Ranges

In Excel, you can format cells in a wide variety of ways—everything from choosing how to display the borders and background to controlling how Excel represents the text you enter in the cell. This section shows you how the most useful kinds of formatting work and how to apply them.

Each cell comes with basic formatting applied to it—the font and font size to use and usually the General number format, which you'll meet shortly. So when you create a new workbook and start entering data in it, Excel displays the data in a normal-size font.

> **TIP:** To control the font and font size Excel uses for new workbooks, choose **Excel ➤ Preferences** or press Cmd+, (Cmd and the comma key). Click the General icon in the Authoring area of the Excel Preferences dialog box to display the General pane. Open the Standard font menu and click the font you want; the Body Font choice at the top of the list gives you the body font set in the workbook's template; if you change this font, you change the font used in all the styles except the Title style (which uses the Heading font). Then choose the size in the Size pop-up menu. Click the OK button to close the Excel Preferences dialog box.

Understanding the Three Main Tools for Applying Formatting

Excel gives you three main tools for applying formatting to cells and ranges:

- *Formatting Toolbar.* If you display this toolbar (choose **View ➤ Toolbars ➤ Formatting** from the menu bar), you can quickly apply some of the most widely used formatting. Figure 4–5 shows the Formatting toolbar (displayed undocked so you can see it more easily) with its controls labeled.

> **NOTE:** The Home tab of the Ribbon also provides the formatting commands you find on the Formatting toolbar, so you can use whichever is more convenient.

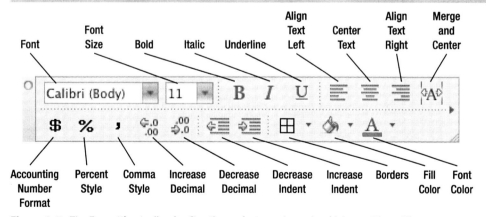

Figure 4–5. *The Formatting toolbar is often the easiest way to apply widely used formatting.*

■ *Home tab of the Ribbon.* The Font group provides widely used font formatting; the Alignment group offers horizontal and vertical alignment, orientation, indentation, wrapping, and merging; and the Number group gives you a quick way to apply essential number formatting. Figure 4–6 shows the Font group with its controls labeled. Figure 4–7 shows the Alignment group and Number group with their controls labeled.

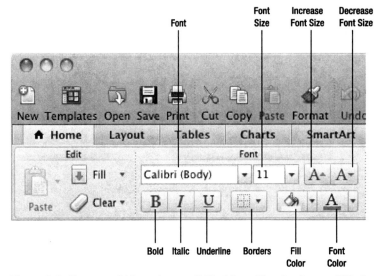

Figure 4–6. *You can quickly apply essential font formatting, borders, and fills from the Font group on the Home tab of the Ribbon.*

NOTE: The Increase Font Size button, Decrease Font Size button, and Borders pop-up menu appear in the Font group on the Home tab of the Ribbon only when the Excel window is wide enough to accommodate them.

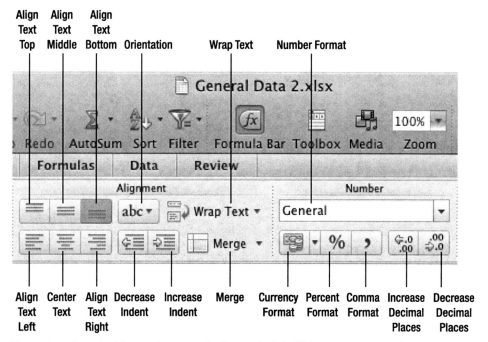

Figure 4–7. *From the Alignment group on the Home tab of the Ribbon, you can set horizontal and vertical alignment, orientation, and wrapping. From the Number group, you can apply number formatting.*

■   *Format Cells dialog box.* When you need to apply formatting types that don't appear on the Standard toolbar or on the Home tab of the Ribbon, open the Format Cells dialog box and work on its six tabs, which you'll meet later in this chapter. The easiest way to display the Format Cells dialog box is to Ctrl+click or right-click a cell or a selection and then click Format Cells on the context menu. You can also open the Format Cells dialog box by pressing Cmd+1 or choosing **Format** ➤ **Cells** from the menu bar.

Controlling How Data Appears by Applying Number Formatting

When you enter a number in a cell, Excel displays it according to the number formatting applied to that cell. For example, if you enter **39250** in a cell formatted with General formatting, Excel displays it as 39250. If the cell has Currency formatting, Excel displays a value such as $39,250.00 (depending on the details of the format). And if the cell has Date formatting, Excel displays a date such as 18 June 2011 (again, depending on the details of the format). In each case, the number stored in the cell remains the same—so if you change the cell's formatting to a different type, the way that Excel displays the data changes to match.

Table 4–1 explains Excel's number formats and tells you the keyboard shortcuts for applying them. You can also apply number formatting by using the buttons on the

Standard toolbar, the Number Format pop-up menu and buttons in the Number group of the Home tab of the Ribbon, and the Number tab of the Format Cells dialog box (see Figure 4–8).

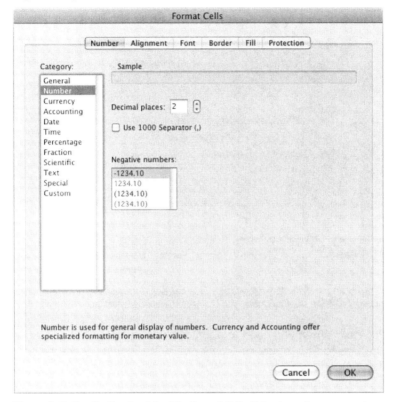

Figure 4–8. *Use the Number tab of the Format Cells dialog box when you need access to the full range of number formatting.*

Table 4–1. *Excel's Number Formats*

Number Format	Explanation	Examples	Keyboard Shortcut
General	Excel's default format for all cells in new worksheets. No specific format, but displays up to 11 digits per cell and uses no thousands separator. For any entry longer than 11 digits, General format uses scientific notation (see the "Scientific" entry later in this table).	1234567 Industry	Ctrl+Shift+~ (tilde)
Number	Displays the number of decimal places you choose. You can choose whether to use the thousands separator and how to display negative numbers.	1000 1,000 1,000.00	Ctrl+Shift+!

Number Format	Explanation	Examples	Keyboard Shortcut
Currency	Displays the number of decimal places you choose, using the thousands separator. You can choose which currency symbol to display (for example, $) and how to display negative numbers.	$2,345.67 −$2,345.67	Ctrl+Shift+$
Accounting	Displays the number of decimal places you choose, using the thousands separator. You can choose which currency symbol to use. The symbol appears aligned at the left edge of the cell. Negative numbers appear with parentheses around them.	$ 1,000,000 $ (99.999.00)	—
Date	Displays any of a variety of date formats.	6/24/2011 Thursday, June 24, 2011	Ctrl+Shift+#
Time	Displays any of a variety of time formats.	11:59:59 PM 23:59:59	Ctrl+Shift+@
Percentage	Displays a percent sign and the number of decimal places you choose.	78.79% 200%	Ctrl+Shift+%
Fraction	Displays the number as a fraction. Fractions tend to be visually confusing, so use them only if you must—for example, for betting charts.	1/2 1 1/4	—
Scientific	Displays the number in exponential form, with E and the power to which to raise the number. You can choose how many decimal places to use.	1.2346E+08 −9.8765E+07	Ctrl+Shift+^
Text	Displays and treats the data as text, even when it appears to be another type of data (for example, a number or date).	Product List 18	—
Special	Displays the data in the format you choose: Zip Code, Zip Code + 4, Phone Number, or Social Security Number.	10013 10013-8295 (212) 555-9753 722-86-8261	—
Custom	Displays the data in the custom format you choose. Excel provides dozens of custom formats, but you can also create your own formats.	[Various]	—

UNDERSTANDING HOW EXCEL STORES DATES AND TIMES

Excel stores dates as serial numbers starting from 1 (Sunday, January 1, 1900) and running way into the future. To give you a couple of points of reference, 40544 represents Saturday, January 1, 2011, while 40909 represents Sunday, January 1, 2012.

You can enter a date by typing the serial number (if you know it or care to work it out), but it's much easier to type a date in a conventional format, because Excel recognizes most of them. For example, if you type **1/1/2011**, Excel converts it to 40544 and displays the date in whichever format you've chosen.

Excel stores times as decimal parts of a day. For example, 40544.25 is 6 a.m. (one quarter of the way through the day) on January 1, 2011.

Older versions of Excel used the starting date January 2, 1904, by default for workbooks. Excel 2011 doesn't do this, but you can set the 1904 starting date manually if necessary (for example, if you're using an older workbook with 1904–based dates). To switch to 1904–based dates, choose **Excel ➤ Preferences** or press Cmd+, (Cmd and the comma key). In the Excel Preferences dialog box, click the Calculation icon in the Formulas and Lists area to display the Calculation pane. In the Workbook options box, select the Use the 1904 date system check box, and then click the OK button.

To create a custom number format of your own, follow these steps:

1. Select a cell that contains the right kind of data. For example, if you want to create a custom date format, select a cell with Date formatting and a date entered in it.

2. Open the Format Cells dialog box by pressing Cmd+1.

3. Click the Number tab if it's not displayed at first.

4. In the Category list box, click the Custom item. Excel displays the controls for creating a custom format (see Figure 4–9). Your sample data appears in the Sample box at the top.

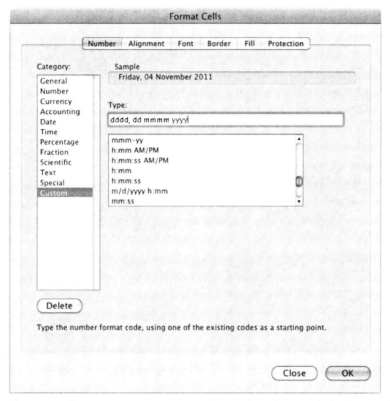

Figure 4–9. *You can create custom number formats by typing them in the Type text box on the Number tab of the Format Cells dialog box. Click the most similar format in the list box to give yourself a head start.*

5. Scroll down the list box until you find the format that's closest to the format you want to create, then click that format. Excel adds the codes for the format to the Type text box and shows the sample data in that format.

6. Edit the format so that the sample data appears the way you want it (see the instructions after this list).

7. Click the OK button to close the Format Cells dialog box.

To create a custom format, you enter format codes telling Excel how to display the information. A custom format can contain a single format, like the date format shown in Figure 4–9, but you can include up to four different formats, separated by semicolons:

- *First format.* How to display positive numbers.

- *Second format.* How to display negative numbers.

- *Third format.* How to display zero values.

- *Fourth format.* How to display text.

Table 4–2 explains the codes for creating custom number formats.

Table 4–2. *Codes for Creating Custom Number Formats*

Code	Effect	Example
[color name]	Display the color named.	Put the appropriate color in brackets as the first item in the section: [Black], [Red], [Blue], [Green], [White], [Cyan], [Magenta], or [Yellow]. For example, **#,##0_);[Red](#,##0)** displays negative numbers in red.

Number Format Codes

Code	Effect	Example
#	Display a significant digit.	###.# displays three significant digits before the decimal point and one significant digit after it. (A significant digit is a nonzero figure.)
0	Display a zero if no digit would otherwise appear in this place.	000 displays a three-digit number, padding it out with leading zeros if necessary. For example, if you enter **7**, Excel displays 007.
%	Display a percentage.	#% displays the number multiplied by 100 and with a percent sign. For example, **8** appears as 800%.
?	Display as a fraction.	# ???/??? displays a number and three-digit fractions—for example, 9 107/112.
.	Display a decimal point.	###.## displays three significant digits before the decimal point and two significant digits after it.
,	Two meanings: display the thousands separator or scale the number down by 1,000.	Thousands separator: $#,###,### displays the dollar sign, seven significant digits, and the thousands separator. Scale by 1,000: €#.##,,, " million" displays the euro symbol, one significant digit before the decimal point and two after, the number scaled down by a million, and the word *million* (after a space). For example, if you enter **12345689**, Excel displays €1.23 million.

Date and Time Format Codes

Code	Effect	Example
d	Display the day in numeric format.	d-mmm-yyyy displays 6/1/11 as 1-Jun-2011.
dd	Display the day in numeric format with a leading zero for single-digit days.	dd/mmm/yy displays 6/1/11 as 01/Jun/11. Leading zeroes can be helpful for standardizing on two-digit dates and for aligning date entries.
ddd	Display the day as a three-letter abbreviation.	ddd dd/mm/yyyy displays 6/1/11 as Wed 01/06/2011.

Code	Effect	Example
dddd	Display the day in full.	dddd, dd/mm/yyyy displays 6/1/11 as Wednesday, 01/06/2011.
m	Display the month in numeric format.	d/m/yy displays 6/1/11 as 6/1/11.
mm	Display the month in numeric format with a leading zero.	mm/dd/yy displays 6/1/11 as 06/01/11.
mmm	Display the month as a three-letter abbreviation.	dd-mmm-yy displays 6/1/11 as 01-Jun-2011.
mmmm	Display the month in full.	dd mmmm, yyyy displays 6/1/11 as 01 June, 2011.
mmmmm	Display the month as a one-letter abbreviation.	January, June, and July appear as J; April and August appear as A; and so on. This code works when you're short of space and include all the months in sequence; if you use only some months, it's confusing.
yy	Display the year as a two-digit number.	m/d/yy displays 6/1/11 as 6/1/11.
yyyy	Display the year in full.	dd-mmm-yyyy displays 6/1/11 as 01-Jun-2011.
h	Display the hour.	h:m displays 2:22 as 2:22.
hh	Display the hour with a leading zero.	hh:mm displays 2:22 as 02:22.
m	Display the minute.	h:m displays 2:01 as 2:1.
mm	Display the minute with a leading zero.	hh:mm displays 2:22 as 02:22. To distinguish mm from the months code (also mm), use it immediately after hh or immediately before ss.
s	Display the second.	h:m:s displays 2:22:01 as 2:22:1.
ss	Display the second with a leading zero.	hh:mm:ss displays 2:22:01 as 02:22:01.
.0, .00, .000	Display tenths, hundredths, or thousandths of seconds.	h:mm:ss.000 displays 2:22:01.11 as 2:22:01.110.
A/P	Display A for A.M. and P for P.M.	h:mm A/P displays 2:22 as 2:22 A. You can use uppercase A/P or lowercase a/p to specify which case to display.

Code	Effect	Example
AM/PM	Display AM for A.M. and PM for P.M.	h:mm am/pm displays 14:22 as 2:22 PM. Excel uses uppercase regardless of which case you use.
[]	Display the elapsed time in the specified unit.	[h]:mm:ss displays the elapsed time in hours, minutes, and seconds—for example, 55:38:43.

Text Format Codes

Code	Effect	Example
_	Display a space as wide as the specified character.	_) makes Excel enter a space the width of a closing parenthesis. You'd use this to align positive numbers with negative numbers that appear in parentheses.
*	Repeat the specified character to fill the cell.	*0 makes Excel fill the cell with 0 (zero) characters. This format is specialized, but you may need it to draw the viewer's attention to particular cells.
\	Display the following character.	[Blue]$#,###.00 *;[Green]$#,###.00 \D displays positive numbers in blue and followed by an asterisk, and negative numbers in green and followed by a D.
"string"	Display the string of text.	$#,##0.00" Net" displays the word Net after the entry. Note the leading space between the " and the word.
@	Concatenate the specified string with the user's text input.	"Value: "@ enters **Value:** and a space before the user's text input. You can use this only in the fourth section (the text section) of a custom format.
N/A	Display the specified character.	$ - + = / ( ) { } : ! ^ & ' ' ~ < > [SPACE]

Setting the Workbook's Overall Look by Applying a Theme

To control the overall look of a workbook, apply a suitable theme to it by choosing Home ➤ Themes ➤ Themes and then clicking the theme you want on the Themes panel.

The theme applies a set of colors and a pair of fonts to the workbook. After applying the theme, you can change the colors or fonts by using the Colors pop-up menu or the Fonts pop-up menu in the Themes group on the Home tab of the Ribbon.

Choosing How to Align Cell Contents

You can quickly align the contents of cells by using the buttons in the Alignment group on the Home tab of the Ribbon or the controls on the Alignment tab of the Format Cells dialog box (see Figure 4–10):

- *Horizontal alignment.* You can align the text Left, Center, Right, or Justify; apply General alignment, which depends on the data type (left for text, right for numbers); choose Center Across Selection to center the text across multiple cells; or choose Distributed (Indent) to distribute the text across the cell (using wider spaces between words).

NOTE: The Fill horizontal alignment fills the cell with the character you specify.

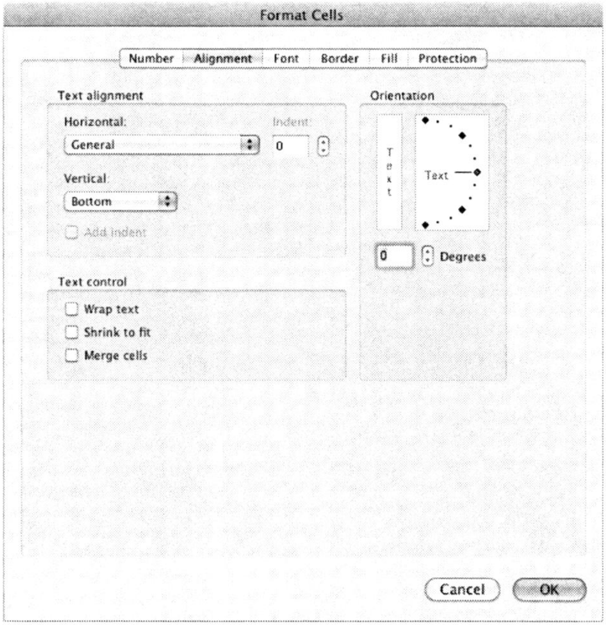

Figure 4–10. *The Alignment tab of the Format Cells dialog box lets you rotate text to precise angles when needed.*

- *Vertical alignment.* You can align text Top, Center, Bottom, or Justify. You can also choose Distributed to distribute the text vertically, which can be useful when you rotate the text so that it runs vertically.

- *Rotate text.* Use the Orientation box on the Alignment tab of the Format Cells dialog box or the Orientation pop-up menu in the Alignment group.

- *Indentation.* You can indent the text as far as is needed.

- *Wrap.* You can wrap the text to make a long entry appear on several lines in a cell rather than disappear where the next cell's contents start. When you wrap text, Excel automatically increases the row height to accommodate the wrapped text. (If you set a specific row height that's less than the height needed to display all the wrapped text, only the text that fits appears in the cell.)

- *Shrink to fit.* Select this check box on the Alignment tab of the Format Cells dialog box to shrink the text so that it fits in the cell. Shrinking works well when the text is only a bit too big for the cell. If the text is much too big, shrinking makes it too small to read.

- *Merge cells.* Use the Merge & Center pop-up menu in the Alignment group to merge selected cells together into a single cell. You can also center an entry across a merged cell. In the Format Cells dialog box, you can merge cells by selecting the Merge cells check box on the Alignment tab.

Choosing Font Formatting

You can quickly format the contents of a cell (or the selected part of a cell's contents) by using the controls on the Standard toolbar, the controls in the Font group on the Home tab, or the Font tab of the Format Cells dialog box (see Figure 4–11).

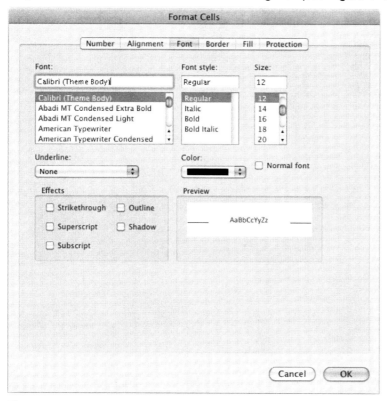

Figure 4–11. *Use the Font tab of the Format Cells dialog box when you need a fuller range of font formatting than the Standard toolbar and the Ribbon's Font group provide.*

Applying Borders and Fills

To apply borders to a cell, open the Borders pop-up menu in the Font group on the Home tab of the Ribbon, and then click the border type you want (see Figure 4–12).

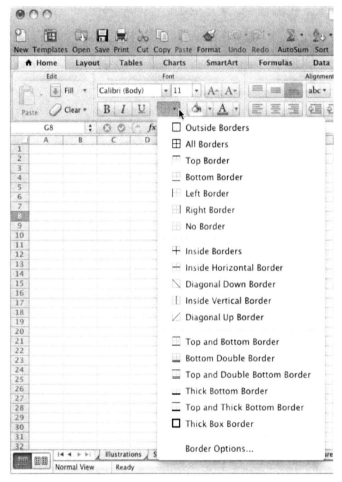

Figure 4–12. *You can quickly apply borders from the Borders pop-up menu in the Font group of the Home tab.*

TIP: If you have displayed the Formatting toolbar, you can apply a border by clicking its Borders pop-up button and then clicking the border type on the panel. After choosing a border type this way, you can apply it quickly to another cell by clicking the main part of the Borders button rather than the pop-up button. You can also tear off the Borders palette to keep it visible so that you don't have to keep opening it. Click the Borders pop-up button, then click the double line at the top of the palette and drag it off the toolbar. When you have finished using the torn-off palette, close it by clicking the Close button at the left end of its title bar.

For more border options, click the Border Options item at the bottom of the Borders pop-up menu to display the Border tab of the Format Cells dialog box (see Figure 4–13). You can also choose Format ➤ Cells from the menu bar (or press Cmd+1) and then click the Border tab. Use the controls on the Border tab to set up the borders you want. For example, to apply a heavy bottom border, click a dark line in the Style box, and then click the Bottom Border button in the Border box. Then click the OK button.

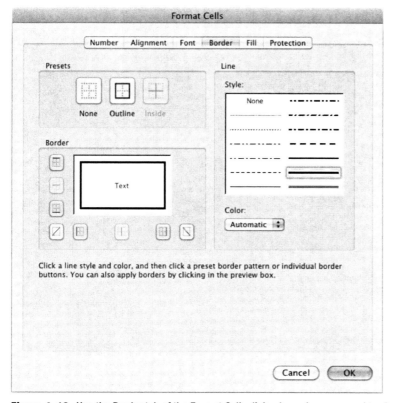

Figure 4–13. *Use the Border tab of the Format Cells dialog box when you need to change the line style or color of borders.*

To apply a fill, use the Fill Colors pop-up menu in the Font group on the Home tab of the Ribbon or the Fill Colors pop-up menu on the Formatting toolbar, or work on the Fill tab of the Format Cells dialog box.

Applying Protection to Cells

The Protection tab of the Format Cells dialog box contains only two controls:

- *Locked.* Select this check box to lock a cell against changes.

- *Hidden.* Select this check box to hide the formula in a cell (the formula's result remains visible).

After selecting either of these check boxes, you must protect the worksheet before the locking or hiding takes effect. You'll learn how to protect a worksheet in the section "Protecting a Worksheet or Workbook" in Chapter 13.

Using Paste Special to Paste Formatting and Perform Actions

If one part of your worksheet contains the type of formatting you need to apply to another part, you can often save time by using the Paste Special command and choosing options in the Paste Special dialog box. For example, you can paste formats or column widths only instead of pasting all the data and formatting from the cells you've copied. The Paste Special command also enables you to transpose data and perform mathematical operations on the cells you're pasting to.

You can access most of the Paste Special options from either the Paste pop-up menu in the Edit group of the Home tab or the Paste Options pop-up menu, but in most cases it's clearest to use the Paste Special dialog box.

To display the Paste Special dialog box (see Figure 4–14), use one of these commands:

- *Ribbon.* Choose **Home ➤ Edit ➤ Paste ➤ Paste Special**.
- *Menu bar.* Choose **Edit ➤ Paste Special**.
- *Context menu.* Ctrl+click or right-click the destination cell, and then click Paste Special.
- *Keyboard.* Press Cmd+Shift+V.

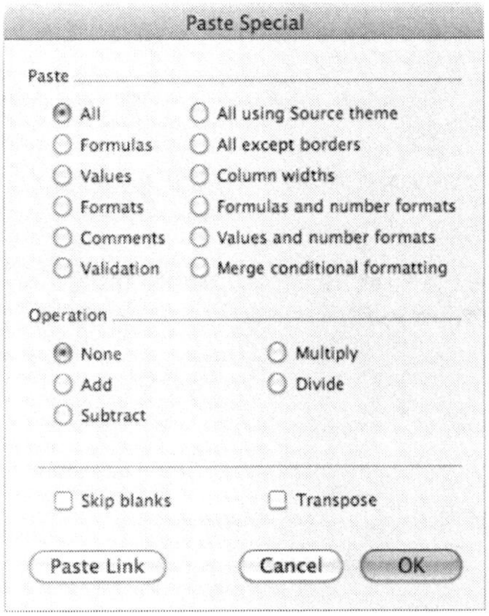

Figure 4–14. *Use the Paste Special dialog box when you need to paste only some of the data, when you need to perform an operation on the data, or when you need to transpose its rows and columns.*

You then choose the option button you want in the Paste area:

- *All.* Select this option button to paste all the data and all its formatting. Normally, you'll want to do this only if you're using the Skip blanks check box, the Transpose check box, or the Paste Link button—otherwise, it's easier to use the Paste command.

- *Formulas.* Select this option button to paste in all the formulas and constants without formatting.

- *Values.* Select this option button to paste in formula values instead of pasting in the formulas themselves. Excel removes the formatting from the values.

- *Formats.* Select this option button to paste in the formatting without the data. This option is great for making one worksheet's formatting similar to another's.

- *Comments.* Select this option button to paste in only comments. This option is handy when you're integrating different colleagues' takes on the same worksheet.

- *Validation.* Select this option button to paste in data-validation criteria.

- *All using Source theme.* Select this option button to paste in all the data using the theme from the workbook the data came from.

- *All except borders.* Select this option button to paste in all the data and formatting but to strip out the cell borders.

- *Column widths.* Select this option button to paste in only the column widths—no data and no other formatting. This option is useful when you need to lay one worksheet out like another existing worksheet but put all different data in it.

- *Formulas and number formats.* Select this option button to paste in formulas and number formatting but no other formatting.

- *Values and number formats.* Select this option button to paste in values (rather than formulas) and number formatting.

- *Merge conditional formatting.* Select this option button to copy all data and formatting and to merge in any conditional formatting. See the next section for details on conditional formatting.

If you need to perform a mathematical operation using the data you're pasting, go to the Operation area of the Paste Special dialog box and select the Add option button, the Subtract option button, the Multiply option button, or the Divide option button, as needed. For example, if you want to multiply the current values in the cells by the values you're pasting, select the Multiply option button. Otherwise, leave the None option button selected to paste the data without performing math with it.

In the bottom section of the Paste Special dialog box, you can select or clear the two check boxes as needed:

- *Skip blanks.* Select this check box to prevent Excel from pasting blank cells.

- *Transpose.* Select this check box to transpose columns to rows and rows to columns. This option is much quicker than retyping data that's laid out the wrong way.

When you've chosen the options you want, click the OK button. Excel closes the Paste Special dialog box and pastes the data or formatting you chose.

NOTE: If you need to link the data you're pasting back to its source, click the Paste Link button in the Paste Special dialog box instead of the OK button. This makes Excel create a link to the source data so that when the source data changes, the linked data changes too. If the source data is in the same workbook, Excel updates the links automatically. If the source data is in another workbook, Excel updates the data when you open the workbook that contains the links.

Identifying Unusual Values with Conditional Formatting

In many worksheets, it's useful to be able to monitor the values in the cells and to pick out values that stand out in particular ways. For example, you may want to see which ten products are bringing in the most revenue, or you may need an easy way to make unusually high values or unusually low values stand out from the others.

To monitor the values in a cell or a range, you can apply *conditional formatting*—formatting that Excel displays only when the condition is met. For example, if you're monitoring temperatures in Fahrenheit, you could apply conditional formatting to highlight low temperatures (say, below 20F) and high temperatures (say, above 100F). Temperatures in the normal range would not receive any conditional formatting, so the low temperatures and high temperatures would jump out on the worksheet.

Understanding Excel's Preset Types of Conditional Formatting

Excel provides five kinds of preset conditional formatting, which you can apply from the Conditional Formatting panel in the Format group of the Home tab of the Ribbon. Figure 4–15 shows the Conditional Formatting panel with the Icon Sets panel displayed.

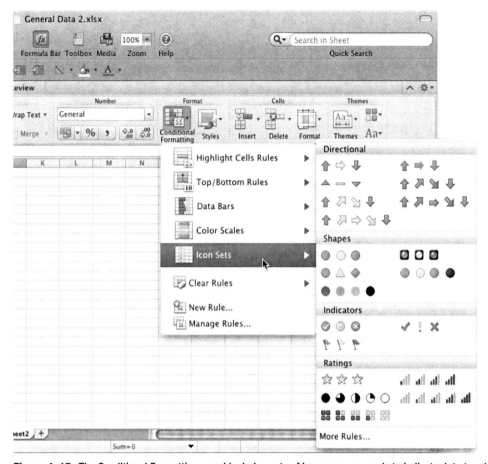

Figure 4–15. *The Conditional Formatting panel includes sets of icons you can apply to indicate data trends.*

- *Highlight Cells Rules.* This panel gives you an easy way to set up conditional formatting using Greater Than, Less That, Between, Equal To, Text that Contains, A Date Occurring, or Duplicate Values criteria.

- *Top/Bottom Rules.* This panel lets you apply conditional formatting for Top 10 Items, Top 10 %, Bottom 10 Items, Bottom 10 %, Above Average, and Below Average criteria.

- *Data Bars.* This panel enables you to apply different gradient fills and solid fills.

- *Color Scales.* This panel lets you set up color scales using two or three colors—for example, using green, amber, and red to indicate different levels of risk associated with activities.

- *Icon Sets.* This panel provides different sets of icons, such as directional arrows (up, sideways, down) or a checkmark–exclamation point–cross set, for indicating data trends.

Applying a Preset Form of Conditional Formatting

To apply one of the preset forms of conditional formatting, open the Conditional Formatting panel, display the appropriate panel from it, click the type of formatting, and then specify the details. For example:

1. Select the cell or range you want to affect.

2. Choose **Home ➤ Format ➤ Conditional Formatting ➤ Highlight Cells Rules ➤ Greater Than** to display the New Formatting Rule dialog box (see Figure 4–16).

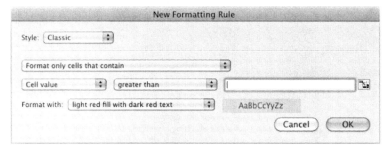

Figure 4–16. *Excel's preset conditional formatting types make it easy to apply conditional formatting to cells quickly.*

3. In the Style pop-up menu, you can choose a different style for the conditional formatting if you want. Excel automatically selects the style that suits the type of conditional formatting you chose—in the example, Classic.

4. The Comparison pop-up menu below the Style pop-up menu shows the comparison for the type of conditional formatting—in the example, Format only cells that contain. You can choose a different comparison if necessary, but you won't normally need to do so.

5. On the next line of controls, set up the comparison. In the example, the first pop-up menu is set to Cell value, and the second pop-up menu is set to "greater than" because this is a Greater Than rule. In the third box, you enter the comparison. You can either type in the value or collapse the dialog box, click the cell that contains the value, and then restore the dialog box.

6. In the Format with pop-up menu, choose the formatting you want. Excel provides various canned options, but you can also create custom formatting by clicking the custom format item at the bottom of the list and working in the Format Cells dialog box that opens. (This is a cut-down version of the Format Cells dialog box you met earlier in the chapter—it has only the Font tab, the Border tab, and the Fill tab.)

7. Click the OK button to close the New Formatting Rule dialog box. Excel applies the conditional formatting.

Creating Custom Conditional Formatting

If none of the preset conditional formatting rules meets your needs, you can define conditional formatting rules of your own. To do so, follow these steps:

1. Select the cell or range you want to affect.

2. Choose **Home ➤ Format ➤ Conditional Formatting ➤ New Rule** to display the New Formatting Rule dialog box.

3. In the Style pop-up menu, choose the type of conditional formatting: 2-Color Scale, 3-Color Scale, Data Bars, Icon Sets, or Classic. The New Formatting Rule dialog box display controls for creating that type of conditional formatting. Figure 4–17 shows the New Formatting Rule dialog box with the controls for creating an icon set displayed.

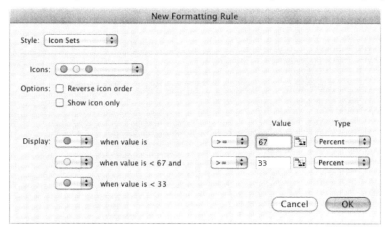

Figure 4–17. *When none of the conditional formatting rules is what you need, use the New Formatting Rule dialog box to create a custom rule.*

4. Use the controls to specify what conditional formatting the rule will apply. For example, for the Icon Sets style shown in Figure 4–17, you could do the following:

   ▪ Open the Icons pop-up menu, and then click the set of icons you want to use as the basis for the formatting.

   ▪ In the Options area, select the Reverse icon order check box if you want to use the icon sequence the other way around—for example, green-yellow-red instead of red-yellow-green. Select the Show icon only check box if you want the icon to appear without the value that produced it; this can be good for simplifying complex worksheets, but it may prompt too many questions about values to be worth using.

- In the Display area, open each pop-up menu, and choose the symbol to use (or simply accept the default symbol). Then use the controls to set up the condition, value, and type.

5. When you've finished creating the rule, click the OK button to close the New Formatting Rule dialog box.

Changing the Order in Which Excel Applies Conditional Formatting Rules

Many cells and ranges need only one type of conditional formatting applied—but others may need two or more types. When you apply multiple types of conditional formatting, you may need to change the order Excel applies the conditional formatting rules in. Or you may simply need an easy way to see which conditional formatting rules you've applied to a particular cell or range.

To see which conditional formatting rules you've applied to cells, and to change the order, follow these steps:

1. Select the cell or range you're interested in.

2. Choose Home ➤ Format ➤ Conditional Formatting ➤ Manage Rules to display the Manage Rules dialog box (see Figure 4–18).

Figure 4–18. *Use the Manage Rules dialog box to check which conditional formatting rules you've applied to a cell or range and to change the order Excel uses the rules.*

3. Verify that the Show formatting rules for pop-up menu shows Current Selection rather than another range. If not, choose Current Selection.

4. In the list box in the center of the Manage Rules dialog box, look through the list of rules. Change the rules or their order as needed.

   ■ *Change the order of the rules.* Click the rule you want to move, go to the Change rule order area, and then click the Move Up button (the up arrow) or the Move Down button (the down arrow), as needed.

   ■ *Delete a rule.* Click the rule, and then click the Remove (–) button.

   ■ *Edit a rule.* Click the rule, click the Edit Rule button, and then work in the Edit Formatting Rule dialog box. This dialog box has the same controls as the New Formatting Rule dialog box.

   ■ *Create a new rule.* Click the Add (+) button, and then work in the New Formatting Rule dialog box, as discussed in the previous section. When you finish creating the rule, move it up the list to where it belongs.

   ■ *Apply the rule to a different range.* In the rule's Applies to column, click the Collapse Dialog button to collapse the Manage Rules dialog box. Select the appropriate range, and then click the Collapse Dialog button again to restore the Manage Rules dialog box.

   ■ *Stop evaluating other rules if a rule is true.* Select the rule's check box in the Stop if true column.

   ■ Click the OK button to close the Manage Rules dialog box. Excel applies your choices to your selection.

Clearing Conditional Formatting from a Cell, Range, or Worksheet

If a cell, range, worksheet, table, or PivotTable no longer needs conditional formatting, clear it as follows:

1. Choose the item:

   ■ Select the cell or range.

   ■ Click in the table or PivotTable.

   ■ Activate the worksheet.

2. Choose Home ➤ Format ➤ Conditional Formatting ➤ Clear Rules, and then click the appropriate item on the submenu: Clear Rules from Selected Cells, Clear Rules from Entire Sheet, Clear Rules from This Table, or Clear Rules from This PivotTable.

Checking Input with Data Validation

When you're entering large amounts of data, it's easy to type an incorrect value by mistake. To help avoid errors in your data, you can use Excel's data validation feature to check entries automatically and flag those that may be wrong. For example, if every entry in a range of cells should be between 250 and 1000 (inclusive), you can validate the data to flag any entry that is not in that range.

> **CAUTION:** Data validation works only when the user types in a value. If the user pastes in a value, Excel doesn't validate it.

To apply validation to cells, follow these steps:

1. Click the cell or select the range you want to validate.

2. Choose **Data ➤ Tools ➤ Validate** (clicking the main part of the Validate button) from the Ribbon or **Data ➤ Validation** from the menu bar to display the Data Validation dialog box.

3. Click the Settings tab (shown in Figure 4–19 with settings chosen) to bring it to the front of the dialog box if it's not already there.

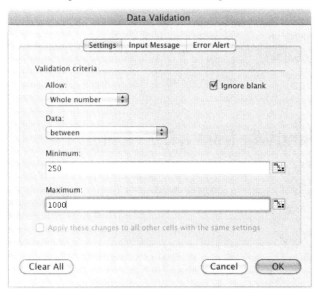

Figure 4–19. *Set up the validation criteria on the Settings tab of the Data Validation dialog box. The controls that appear depend on the data type you choose in the Allow pop-up menu.*

4. In the Allow pop-up menu, choose the type of data you want to validate, and then use the controls that appear to set the details.

▓ *Any value.* Select this item when you want to turn off validation for the cell or range. Even with this setting, you can use the Input Message tab (discussed later in this list) to display a message about the cell or range.

TIP: When setting the criteria for your data validation, you can either type in a value or click the Collapse Dialog button and then click the cell that contains the value. Using a value in a cell enables you to change the value easily without editing the data validation.

▓ *Whole number.* Select this item to set criteria for a whole number—one with no decimal places. For example, in the Data pop-up menu, click the between item and then set the minimum value in the Minimum box and the maximum value in the Maximum box.

▓ *Decimal.* Select this item to set criteria for a number with decimal places. For example, in the Data pop-up menu, click the greater than or equal to item and then set the minimum value in the Minimum box.

▓ *List.* Select this item when you need to restrict the cell to a list of valid entries that you specify. You can enter this list in two ways: either type it in the Source box, separating each entry with a comma, or click the Collapse Dialog button at the right end of the Source box, select the worksheet range that contains the data, and then click the Collapse Dialog button again to restore the dialog box. Select the In-cell drop-down check box to make Excel display a pop-up menu with the valid entries in the cell so that the user can enter them easily.

▓ *Date.* Select this item to set criteria for a date. For example, click the greater than item in the Data pop-up menu and then enter the start date in the Start date box.

▓ *Time.* Select this item to set criteria for a time. For example, click the not between item in the Data pop-up menu, then enter the start time in the Start time box and the end time in the End time box.

▓ *Text length.* Select this item to set criteria for a text entry or formula. For example, click the less than or equal to item in the Data pop-up menu, then enter the maximum length in the Maximum box.

▓ *Custom.* Select this item when you need to enter a formula that returns a logical value of TRUE or FALSE.

5. Select the Ignore blank check box if you want to let the user leave the cell blank. Clear this check box to make the user fill in the cell with valid data.

6. Click the Input Message tab to display it. The left screen in Figure 4–20 shows the Input Message tab with settings chosen.

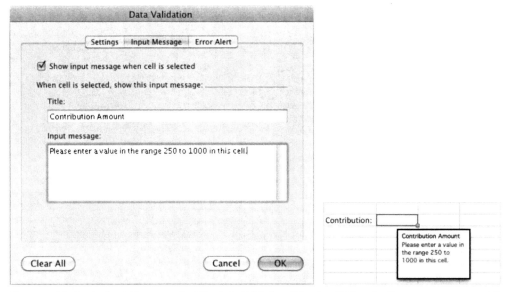

Figure 4–20. *On the Input Message tab of the Data Validation dialog box (left), enter the message you want the user to see when the cell is active (right).*

7. To display a message when the user makes the cell active, select the Show input message when cell is selected check box. Type the title in the Title box and the message in the Input message box. The right screen in Figure 4–20 shows how the message appears.

8. Click the Error Alert tab to bring it to the front. The left screen in Figure 4–21 shows the Error Alert tab with settings chosen; the right screen in Figure 4–21 shows how the error message appears.

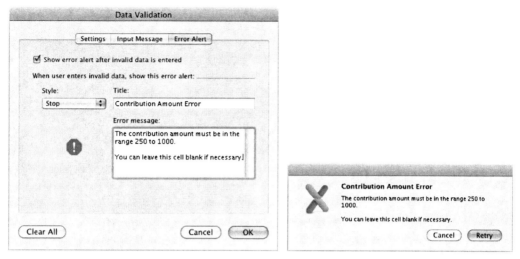

Figure 4–21. *On the Error Alert tab of the Data Validation dialog box (left), set up the error to display when the user enters invalid data in the cell (right).*

9.　Select the Show error alert after invalid data is entered check box if you want Excel to display an error message box when the user enters invalid data. Usually, this is helpful.

10.　In the Style pop-up menu, choose the icon type for the behavior you want:

■　*Stop.* The error dialog box has a Retry button and a Cancel button. If the user clicks the Retry button, Excel selects the entry that failed validation so that the user can change it. If the user clicks the Cancel button, Excel restores the cell's previous entry.

NOTE: On Windows, the Stop, Warning, and Information settings in the Style pop-up menu make the error message box show the different icons that appear under the Style pop-up menu when you make your choice. For example, the Stop style shows the red octagon bearing a white exclamation point that you see on the left in Figure 4–21. On Mac OS X, the error message box displays the same Excel icon (shown on the right in Figure 4–21) for each style, but with different command buttons and behavior.

■　*Warning.* The error dialog box ends with a "Continue?" prompt after your message and has a Yes button, a No button, and a Cancel button. If the user clicks the Yes button, Excel accepts the value, even though it has failed validation. If the user clicks the No button, Excel selects the entry that failed validation so that the user can change it. If the user clicks the Cancel button, Excel restores the cell's previous entry.

■   *Information.* The error dialog box has an OK button and a Cancel button. If the user clicks the OK button, Excel accepts the value, even though it has failed validation. If the user clicks the Cancel button, Excel restores the cell's previous entry.

> **TIP:** To force the user to enter valid data, choose the Stop item in the Style pop-up menu on the Error Alert tab of the Data Validation dialog box. The Warning style and the Information style can be useful for when you're providing gentler guidance on how to use the worksheet and it's not essential that the data conform.

11.   Enter the title and error message for the message box.

12.   Click the OK button to close the Data Validation dialog box. Excel applies the validation.

Formatting Quickly with Table Formatting and Styles

To save you time with formatting, Excel provides preset formatting that you can apply to a table to give it an overall look. And to save you the effort of applying many different types of formatting over and over again to different cells, Excel includes styles— collections of formatting you can apply all at once.

Formatting with Table Formatting

When you need to format a table quickly, see if Excel's preset table formatting will do the trick. Select the table, choose **Tables ➤ Table Styles ➤ Table Styles**, and then click the style you want.

> **NOTE:** See Chapter 10 for instructions on creating and working with Excel tables.

Formatting with Styles

As you've seen earlier in this chapter, you can give any cell exactly the formatting you want by using the controls in the Font group, Alignment group, and Number group of the Home tab of the Ribbon, by using the controls on the Formatting toolbar, or by opening the Format Cells dialog box and working on its six tabs. But applying formatting one aspect at a time—font, font size, alignment, and so on—is slow work, and it's easy to apply formatting inconsistently.

To save time and ensure your formatting is consistent, you can use Excel's styles. Each style is a collection of formatting that you can apply to one or more cells. The style contains six types of formatting, one for each tab of the Format Cells dialog box:

- *Number.* For example, General, Currency, or Percentage.

- *Alignment.* Horizontal alignment (for example, General, Center, or Justify), vertical alignment (for example, Top, Center, or Bottom), and any trimmings (such as wrapping the text to the window).

- *Font.* The font, font size, font color, and so on.

- *Border.* Any borders you've applied to the style, or No Borders if it has no borders.

- *Fill.* Any fill you've applied to the style, or No Shading if it's plain.

- Protection. Locked, Hidden, both, or No Protection.

Most Excel templates contain plenty of styles to get you started, but you can create your own custom styles as well if you need to.

Meeting Excel's Styles

To see which styles are available in a workbook, choose **Home ➤ Format ➤ Styles** and look at the Cell Styles panel (see Figure 4–22). This panel lists the styles in the following categories:

- *Custom.* This category appears only when you have created one or more custom styles in the workbook.

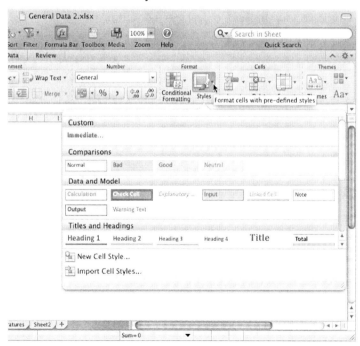

Figure 4–22. *The Styles panel displays your custom styles at the top and Excel's built-in styles in different categories.*

- *Comparisons.* This category has Good, Bad, and Neutral styles that you can use to apply color coding to cells. Here is also where you will find the Normal style that Excel applies to any cell that doesn't have another style.

- *Data and Model.* This category contains the Calculation, Check Cell, Explanatory, Followed Hyperlink, Hyperlink, Input, Linked Cell, Note, Output, and Warning Text styles. Most of these styles are used for data modeling. Excel automatically applies the Hyperlink style to cells containing hyperlinks you have not clicked yet, changing their style to Followed Hyperlink once you have clicked them.

NOTE: The Hyperlink style appears in the Data and Model category in the Styles panel only if the workbook contains hyperlinks. Similarly, the Followed Hyperlink style appears only if the workbook contains hyperlinks you've followed.

- *Titles and Headings.* This category contains four styles for descending levels of headings (Heading 1, Heading 2, Heading 3, and Heading 4), the Title style for giving a worksheet a title, and the Total style for easily formatting cells that contain totals.

- *Themed Cell Styles.* This category contains six Accent styles (Accent 1 through Accent 6) featuring six of the theme colors, with four degrees of shading for each. This category appears only if the workbook's template contains themed cell styles.

Applying a Style

To apply a style, choose **Home ➤ Format ➤ Styles**, and then click the style on the Styles panel. You can also apply the various Number styles (such as the Currency styles, the Percent style, and the Comma style) from the Number group on the Home tab of the Ribbon.

Creating Custom Styles

If none of Excel's styles meets your needs, you can create your own. To create a style, follow these steps:

1. Format a cell with the formatting you want the style to have.

TIP: To jump-start your formatting, apply the existing style that's nearest to the look and formatting you want. Then change the formatting so it looks the way you want.

2. Select the cell you've formatted.

3. Choose Home ➤ Format ➤ Styles ➤ New Cell Style to display the New Cell Style dialog box (shown in Figure 4–23 with settings chosen).

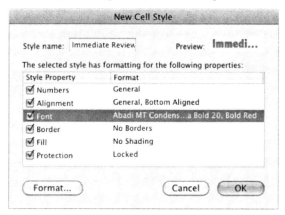

Figure 4–23. *In the New Cell Style dialog box, you can quickly create a new style based on the formatting of the selected cell. You can change the formatting as needed by clicking the Format button and working in the Format Cells dialog box.*

4. In the Style name box, type the name you want to give the style.

5. In the "The selected style has formatting for the following properties" area, clear the check boxes for any formatting the cell has that you want to omit from the style. For example, clear the Protection check box to leave out the Locked or Hidden formatting.

NOTE: If you need to alter the formatting, click the Format button to display the Format Cells dialog box. Make the changes needed, and then click the OK button to return to the New Cell Style dialog box.

6. Click the OK button to close the New Cell Style dialog box and create the style. Excel adds the style to the Custom area at the top of the Styles panel.

TIP: Instead of creating a new style, you can modify one of the built-in styles. Choose **Home ➤ Format ➤ Styles** to display the Styles panel, Ctrl+click or right-click the style you want to change, then click the Modify item on the context menu. In the Modify Cell Style dialog box, select or clear the check boxes in the "The selected style has formatting for the following properties" area or click the Format button to display the Format Cells dialog box, and make the changes you need. When you have finished, click the OK button to return to the Modify Cell Style dialog box, then click the OK button.

Copying Styles from One Workbook to Another

If you have styles in one workbook that you want to use in another workbook, you can copy the styles across. Excel calls this *importing styles*. When you import the styles, the destination workbook receives all the styles from the source workbook—you can't pick and choose (but see the nearby Tip).

To import the styles, follow these steps:

1. Open the source workbook (the workbook that contains the styles) and the destination workbook.

2. Switch to the destination workbook by clicking in it.

3. Choose Home ➤ Format ➤ Styles ➤ Import Cell Styles to display the Import Cell Styles dialog box (see Figure 4–24).

Figure 4–24. *Use the Import Cell Styles dialog box to copy all the styles from one workbook into another workbook.*

4. In the Copy cell styles from an open workbook list box, click the source workbook.

5. Click the OK button to close the import Cell Styles dialog box. Excel copies the styles into the destination workbook and you can then start using them.

TIP: If you need to copy just one style from one workbook to another, apply that style to a cell in the source workbook. Then copy that cell and switch back to the destination workbook. Ctrl+click or right-click a cell you don't mind changing, and then click Paste Special to display the Paste Special dialog box. In the Paste area, select the Formats option button, and then click the OK button. Excel pastes the style onto the cell, and you can then use the style in the workbook.

Deleting Styles You Don't Need

If you no longer need a style, you can delete it. Choose **Home** ➤ **Format** ➤ **Styles**, Ctrl+click or right-click the style in the Cell Styles panel, and then click Delete on |the context menu.

> **NOTE:** Excel prevents you from deleting the Normal style, because it uses this style for any cell that doesn't have another style applied.

Adding Headers and Footers to Your Worksheets

Before distributing a worksheet for viewing on screen, on paper, or as a PDF file, you'll probably want to add headers, footers, or both to identify the pages. Excel gives each worksheet a separate header and footer, which you can fill with either preset text or custom text. Each header and footer area consists of a left section, a center section, and a right section, so you can easily add several different pieces of information.

You can add information to headers and footers either by using the Header/Footer tab of the Page Setup dialog box or by switching to Page Layout view and working directly in the header and footer areas. We'll start with the Page Setup dialog box, which is the easiest way to add canned text.

Adding Headers and Footers Using the Page Setup Dialog Box

To add headers and footers to the active worksheet using the Page Setup dialog box, follow these steps:

1. Choose **Layout** ➤ **Page Setup** ➤ **Header & Footer** from the Ribbon or **View** ➤ **Header and Footer** from the menu bar to display the Header/Footer tab of the Page Setup dialog box. Figure 4–25 shown the Header/Footer tab of the Page Setup dialog box with a preset header chosen.

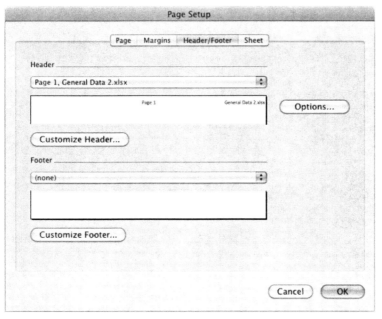

Figure 4–25. *From the Header/Footer tab of the Page Setup dialog box, you can quickly add either preset headers and footers or custom headers and footers to the active worksheet.*

2. If you want to add a preset header or footer, open the Header pop-up menu or the Footer pop-up menu and click the preset. Each pop-up menu has various choices, ranging from just the page number to your name, the page number, and the date. The preset you've chosen appears in the preview box.

3. If you want to create a custom header or footer, click the Customize Header button to display the Header dialog box (see Figure 4–26) or the Customize Footer button to display the Footer dialog box (which is the same apart from the name).

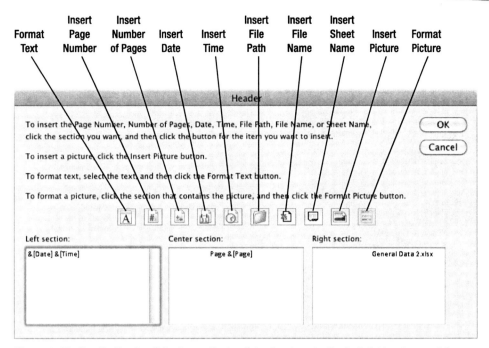

Figure 4–26. *Use the Header dialog box or Footer dialog box to enter the text, field codes, or pictures you want in the left section, center section, and right section of the header or footer.*

4. Click in the Left section box, and then set up the header or footer you need:

   ▧ Click a button on the toolbar in the Header dialog box or Footer dialog box to insert a field code (such as &[Date] for the date), a piece of information (such as the sheet name), or a picture.

   ▧ Type in any text needed. (You can also type in field codes if you know them—but using the buttons is usually easier.)

   ▧ Format the text as needed by selecting it, clicking the Format Text button, and then working in the Font dialog box.

5. Click in the Center section box, and then enter the information needed, using the same techniques as in step 4.

6. Click in the Right section box, and then enter the information needed.

7. Click the OK button to close the Header dialog box or the Footer dialog box. Excel returns you to the Page Setup dialog box, where the Header preview box or the Footer preview box shows the header or footer you just created.

8. If you need to change the paper size or orientation, click the Options button to display the different Page Setup dialog box shown in Figure 4–27. Choose the paper size (for example, US Letter) in the Paper Size pop-up menu, and then click the appropriate button in the Orientation area (the left button gives portrait orientation, the right gives landscape orientation). Then click the OK button.

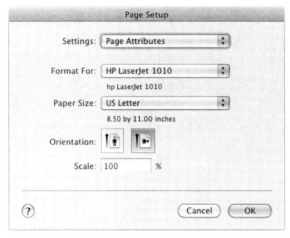

Figure 4–27. *In this smaller Page Setup dialog box, you can choose the paper size and orientation for the worksheet.*

9. When you've finished creating headers and footers, click the OK button to close the Page Setup dialog box.

Adding Headers and Footers Directly on the Worksheet

Instead of using the Page Setup dialog box as described in the previous section, you can add or edit headers and footers directly on the worksheet. To do so, follow these steps:

1. If the worksheet is in Normal view, switch to Page Layout view by clicking the Page Layout View button at the left end of the status bar or choosing **View ➤ Page Layout** from the menu bar.

2. Scroll the page so that you can see the header area or footer area you want to edit.

3. Move the mouse pointer over the header area or footer area so that Excel displays a gray box around it and shows the prompt "Double-click to add header" (see Figure 4–28) or "Double-click to add footer."

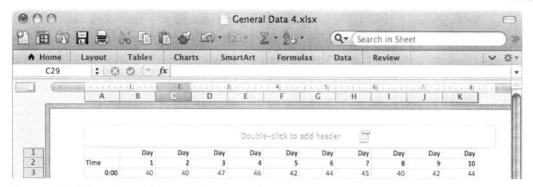

Figure 4–28. *In Page Layout view, move the mouse pointer over the header area or footer area, and then double-click to open the area for editing.*

4. Double-click to open the header area or footer area for editing. Figure 4–29 shows the header area open and editing underway.

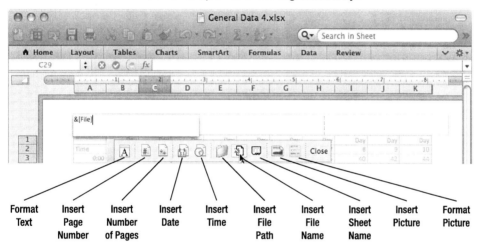

| Format Text | Insert Page Number | Insert Number of Pages | Insert Date | Insert Time | Insert File Path | Insert File Name | Insert Sheet Name | Insert Picture | Format Picture |

Figure 4–29. *When you open the header area or footer area for editing, Excel displays a toolbar of commands for creating headers and footers..*

5. Click in the area you want to change, and then add the header or footer by following these techniques:

    ▤ Click a button on the toolbar to insert a field code (such as &[Date] for the date), a piece of information (such as the sheet name), or a picture.

    ▤ Type in any text needed.

    ▤ Format the text as needed by selecting it, clicking the Format Text button, and then working in the Font dialog box.

6. When you have finished creating or editing the header or footer, click the Close button on the toolbar to close the header or footer. Excel returns you to the worksheet.

Summary

In this chapter, you learned how to apply all of Excel's most useful types of formatting to a worksheet. You know how to manipulate the worksheet's rows and columns to make it fit your data, how to format cells and ranges, and how to save time and worry by using conditional formatting and data validation.

You also saw how to format quickly with table formatting and styles, and learned how to give your worksheets headers and footers to help identify them and their contents easily.

This is the end of the first part of the book. In the second part, I'll show you how to perform calculations and present your data.

Performing Calculations and Presenting Data

In this part of the book, you get up to speed with formulas, functions, charts, and graphical elements such as pictures and sparklines.

In Chapter 5, we go over what formulas and functions are, and what the difference between the two is. This chapter then teaches you how to create your own formulas using Excel's calculation operators, starting with straightforward formulas that use a single calculation operator each, and then moving on to more complex formulas that use multiple calculation operators. You also learn how to override Excel's default order for evaluating operators and how to troubleshoot common problems that occur with formulas.

In Chapter 6, you learn how to insert functions in your worksheets using the various tools that Excel provides, find the functions you want, and point the functions to the data they need for the calculations. The second part of the chapter explains Excel's different categories of functions, such as database functions, logical functions, and math and trigonometric functions, and gives examples of how to use widely used functions.

In Chapter 7, we cover how to present data clearly and persuasively using Excel's wide range of charts. You learn the different ways you can place charts in worksheets, the components of charts, and the types of charts you can use. We then dig into how you create a chart from your data, lay it out the way you want, and give it the look it needs. We also look at ways of reusing the custom charts you create and ways of using Excel charts in Word documents or PowerPoint presentations.

In Chapter 8, we look at how to add visual appeal to your worksheets by using four types of graphical elements that each fit within a single cell. You quickly grasp how to use data bars to compare the values in a range of cells, how to add color scales to adjust the background colors of cells to provide a visual reference to their values, and how to use icon sets to provide quick visual references to performance. And you learn to create miniature charts using sparklines.

In Chapter 9, we look at ways of giving your workbooks visual interest by adding graphics, shapes, SmartArt diagrams, and WordArt items. You learn how to make a picture look as you want it to, how to position graphical objects wherever you need them, how to position graphical items relative to cells, and how to arrange graphical objects to control which ones are visible.

Chapter 5

Performing Custom Calculations with Formulas

To make your worksheets deliver the information you want, you'll probably need to perform calculations with your data. To perform calculations, you enter formulas and functions in cells. You'll learn to use formulas in this chapter and functions in Chapter 6.

We'll start by going over what functions and formulas are so that you're clear on the difference, and then make sure you know how you refer to cells and ranges in Excel.

After that, I'll show you how to create your own formulas using Excel's calculation operators. We'll start with straightforward formulas that use a single calculation operator, and then move on to more complex formulas that use multiple calculation operators.

When you use multiple calculation operators in a formula, you need to make sure Excel evaluates them in the right order—otherwise, you can produce results not only in the wrong ballpark but also in a different league. So you need to know Excel's default order for evaluating operators, and how to change the order when necessary. With this knowledge, you can build complex formulas—but you may want to take the easy route and build them one piece at a time so you can easily detect and fix problems.

At the end of the chapter, I'll introduce you to common problems that occur with formulas and tell you how to troubleshoot them.

Understanding the Difference Between Formulas and Functions

In Excel, you can perform calculations in two main ways, each of which starts with an equal sign:

- *By using a function.* A *function* is a preset calculation that performs a standard calculation. For example, when you need to add several values together, you use the SUM() function—for instance, **=SUM(1,2,3,4,5,6)**, which is simpler than **=1+2+3+4+5+6** but has the same effect.

- *By using a formula.* A *formula* is a custom calculation that you create when none of Excel's functions does what you need. The word *formula* tends to sound imposing, but a formula can be a simple calculation; for example, to subtract 50 from 100, you can type **=100-50** in a cell (the equal sign tells Excel you're starting a formula). Formulas can also be more complex. For example, say you need to add the contents of the cells in the range A1:A6 and then divide them by the contents of cell B1. Excel doesn't have a built-in function for doing this, because it's not a standard calculation. So instead, you create a formula such as this: **=SUM(A1:A6)/B1**. (In this example, **/** is the keyboard equivalent of the ÷ symbol.)

I'll show you how to use formulas in this chapter and functions in the next chapter. But before we start on formulas, let's go over the ways of referring to cells and ranges in formulas and functions.

Referring to Cells and Ranges in Formulas and Functions

To make your formulas and functions work correctly, you need to refer to the cells and ranges you want. This section makes sure you know how to refer to cells and ranges, both when they're on the same worksheet as the formula and when they're on a different worksheet. You can even refer to cells and ranges in another workbook—as long as it will remain in the same place in your Mac's file system.

Referring to a Cell

To refer to a cell on the same worksheet, simply use its column lettering and its row number. For example, use **=A10** to refer to cell A10.

To refer to a cell on a different worksheet, enter the worksheet's name followed by an exclamation point and the cell reference. For example, use **=Supplies!A10** to refer to cell A10 on the worksheet named Supplies. The easiest way to set up such a reference is like this:

1. Start creating the formula. For example, type = in the cell.

2. Click the worksheet tab for the worksheet that contains the cell you want to refer to.

3. Click the cell.

4. Click the Enter button on the formula bar to enter the reference. Excel returns you to the worksheet on which you're creating the formula.

> **NOTE:** Instead of clicking the Enter button on the formula bar in step 4, you can press Return to enter the cell reference. When you do this, Excel moves the active cell to the cell below the formula on the worksheet. You then need to press the up arrow key before taking Step 5.

5. Press Ctrl+U to resume editing the cell. Alternatively, click in the formula bar, and continue editing there.

6. Finish creating the formula as usual.

> **NOTE:** If the worksheet's name contains any spaces, you must put the name inside single quotes; for example, **='Sales Results'!A10** rather than **=Sales Results!A10**. You can also use the single quotes on worksheet names that don't have spaces if you find it easier to be consistent. If you omit the single quotes when they're needed, Excel displays an error message.

To refer to a cell in a different workbook, enter the workbook's path, then the file name in brackets, then the worksheet's name, and then the cell reference. For example, the reference **='Shared:Spreads:[Results.xlsx]Sales!'AB12** refers to cell AB12 on the worksheet named Sales in the workbook Results.xlsx in the Shared:Spreads folder.

Unless you happen to know the path, file name, worksheet name, and cell, it's usually easiest to set up the reference using the mouse. Follow these steps:

1. Open the workbook you want to refer to.

2. In the workbook that will contain the reference, start creating the formula. For example, type = in the cell.

3. Switch to the other workbook.

   - ▓ If you can see the other workbook, click it.

   - ▓ If you can't see the other workbook, open the Window menu on the menu bar, and then click the appropriate window.

4. Navigate to the worksheet that contains the cell, and then click the cell.

5. Switch back to the workbook in which you're creating the reference, and then complete the formula.

When you create a reference to a cell in another workbook, Excel keeps the value of the referring cell updated. If you move or delete the other workbook, Excel displays a dialog box warning you that it can't find the workbook and asking if you want to locate it manually.

Referring to a Range

To refer to a range that consists of a block of cells, give the addresses of the first cell and the last cell, separating them with a colon. For example, to refer to the range from cell P10 to cell Q12, use **=P10:Q12**.

To refer to a range that consists of individual cells, give the address of each cell, separating the addresses with commas. For example, to refer to cell J14, cell K18, and cell Z20, use **=J14,K18,Z20**.

To refer to a range on a different worksheet or in a different workbook, use the techniques explained in the previous section. For example, if you need to refer to the range P10 to Q12 on the worksheet named Stock Listing, use **='Stock Listing'!P10:Q12**.

Making One Row or Column Refer to Another Row or Column

Sometimes you may need to make the contents of one row or column refer to another row or column. For example, say you need to make each cell in row 25 refer to the corresponding cell in row 4, so that cell A25 refers to cell A4, cell B25 to cell B4, and so on.

To do this, click the row heading for row 25, selecting the row. Then type **=4:4** to create the reference to row 4, and press Cmd+Return to enter it in all the cells of the selection. Similarly, you can refer to a whole column by entering its letter designation, a colon, and the letter designation again; for example, **E:E**.

UNDERSTANDING ABSOLUTE REFERENCES, RELATIVE REFERENCES, AND MIXED REFERENCES

Using cell addresses or range addresses is straightforward enough, but when you start using formulas, there's a complication. When you copy a formula and paste it, you need to tell Excel whether the pasted formula should refer to the cells it originally referred to, or the cells in the same relative positions to the cell where the formula now is, or a mixture of the two. (If you move a formula to another cell by using drag and drop or Cut and Paste, Excel keeps the formula as it is.)

To make references clear, Excel uses three types of references:

  - *Absolute reference.* A reference that always refers to the same cell, no matter where you copy it. Excel uses a dollar sign ($) to indicate that each part of the reference is absolute. For example, B3 is an absolute reference to cell B3.

  - *Relative reference.* A reference that refers to the cell by its position relative to the cell that holds the reference. For example, if you select cell A3 and enter **=B5** in it, the reference means "the cell one column to the right and two rows down." So if you copy the formula to cell C4, Excel changes the cell reference to cell D6, which is one column to the right and two rows down from cell C4. To indicate a relative reference, Excel uses a plain reference without any dollar signs; for example, B5.

■   *Mixed reference.* A reference that is absolute for either the column or the row and relative for the other. For example, $B4 is absolute for the column (B) and relative for the row (4), while B$4 is relative for the column and absolute for the row. When you copy and paste a mixed reference, the absolute part stays the same, but the relative part changes to reflect the new location.

If you're typing a reference, you can type the $ signs into the reference to make it absolute or mixed. If you're entering references by selecting cells, click in the reference in cell you're editing or in the Formula bar, and then choose **Formulas ➤ Function ➤ Switch Reference** from the Ribbon. Click the Switch Reference button repeatedly to cycle a reference through its absolute, relative, column-absolute, and row-absolute versions. If a formula refers to multiple cells, you need to alter the reference for each cell separately—you can't change the whole lot in one fell swoop.

Referring to Named Cells and Ranges

To make your references easier to enter and recognize, you can assign a name to any cell or range, as discussed in the section "Identifying Parts with Named Ranges" in Chapter 3. You can then refer to the cell or range by the name, even if it's on another worksheet whose name you've forgotten.

Understanding the Components of Formulas

When you need to perform a custom calculation in a cell, use a formula rather than a function. All you need to do is type in a simple formula using the appropriate calculation operators, such as + signs for addition and – signs for subtraction. In this section, you'll meet the calculation operators, try using them in a worksheet, and learn the order in which Excel applies them—and how to change that order.

Meeting Excel's Calculation Operators

To perform calculations in Excel, you need to know the operators for the different operations—addition, division, comparison, and so on. Table 5–1 explains the full set of calculation operators you can use in your formulas in Excel.

Table 5–1. *Calculation Operators You Can Use in Excel*

Calculation Operator	Operation	Explanation or Example
Arithmetic Operators		
+	Addition	=1+2 adds 2 to 1.
–	Subtraction	=1–2 subtracts 2 from 1.
*	Multiplication	=2*2 multiplies 2 by 2.

Calculation Operator	Operation	Explanation or Example
/	Division	=A1/4 divides the value in cell A1 by 4.
%	Percentage	=B1% returns the value in cell B2 expressed as a percentage. Excel displays the value as a decimal unless you format the cell with the Percentage style.
^	Exponentiation	=B1^2 raises the value in cell B1 to the power 2.

Comparison Operators

=	Equal to	=B2=15000 returns TRUE if cell B2 contains the value 15000. Otherwise, it returns FALSE.
<>	Not equal to	=B2<>15000 returns TRUE if cell B2 does not contain the value 15000. Otherwise, it returns FALSE.
>	Greater than	=B2>15000 returns TRUE if cell B2 contains a value greater than 15000. Otherwise, it returns FALSE.
>=	Greater than or equal to	=B2>=15000 returns TRUE if cell B2 contains a value greater than or equal to 15000. Otherwise, it returns FALSE.
<	Less than	=B2<15000 returns TRUE if cell B2 contains a value less than 15000. Otherwise, it returns FALSE.
<=	Less than or equal to	=B2<=15000 returns TRUE if cell B2 contains a value less than or equal to 15000. Otherwise, it returns FALSE.

Reference Operators

[cell reference]:[cell reference]	The range of cells between the two cell references	A1:G5 returns the range of cells whose upper-left cell is cell A1 and whose lower-right cell is cell G5.
[cell reference],[cell reference]	The range of cells listed	A1,C3,E5 returns three cells: A1, C3, and E5.

Calculation Operator	Operation	Explanation or Example
[cell or range reference] [space][cell or range reference]	The range (or cell) that appears in both cells or ranges given	=A7:G10 B10:B12 returns the cell B10, because this is the only cell that appears in both the ranges given. If more than one cell appears in the range, this returns a #VALUE! error.

Text Operator

&	Concatenation (joining values as text)	=A1&B1 returns the values from cells A1 and B1 joined together as a text string. For example, if A1 contains "New York " (including a trailing space) and B1 contains "Sales", this formula returns "New York Sales." If A1 contains 100 and B1 contains 50, this formula returns 10050.

Creating Straightforward Formulas

Now that you know what the calculation operators are, try the following example of creating a worksheet (see Figure 5–1) with straightforward formulas that use the four most straightforward operators—addition, subtraction, multiplication, and division.

	A	B	C
1	Gross	$84,000.00	
2	Expenses	$30,000.00	
3	Tax Rate	18%	
4	Tax Amount	$15,120.00	
5	Net	$38,880.00	
6	Months	12	
7	Monthly Net	$3,240.00	
8			

Figure 5–1. *Create this simple worksheet to try using Excel's addition, subtraction, multiplication, and division operators.*

To create the worksheet, follow these steps:

1. Create a new workbook. The quickest way to do this is to press Cmd+N.

2. Type the following text in cells A1 through A7:

   ▦ A1. Gross

   ▦ A2. Expenses

   ▦ A3. Tax Rate

   ▦ A4. Tax Amount

   ▦ A5. Net

      ■ A6. Months

      ■ A7. Monthly Net

3. Apply boldface to column A by clicking the column heading and then choosing **Home ➤ Font ➤ Bold**.

4. Apply the Currency format to column B by clicking the column heading and then choosing **Home ➤ Number ➤ Number Format ➤ Currency**.

5. Type the following text in cells B1 through B3:

      ■ B1. 84000

      ■ B2. 30000

      ■ B3. 0.18

6. Apply the Percent style to cell B3 by clicking the cell and then choosing **Home ➤ Number ➤ Number Style ➤ Percent Style**.

> **NOTE:** You can also enter the percentage in step 6 by typing **18%** and pressing Return. Excel automatically changes the number format to Percentage.

7. Now enter the formula **=B1*B3** in cell B4, like this:

    a. Click cell B4 to select it.

    b. Type = to start creating a formula in the cell.

    c. Click cell B1 to enter it in the formula. Excel displays a shimmering dotted blue outline around the cell and adds it to the formula in the cell and to the Formula bar (see Figure 5–2).

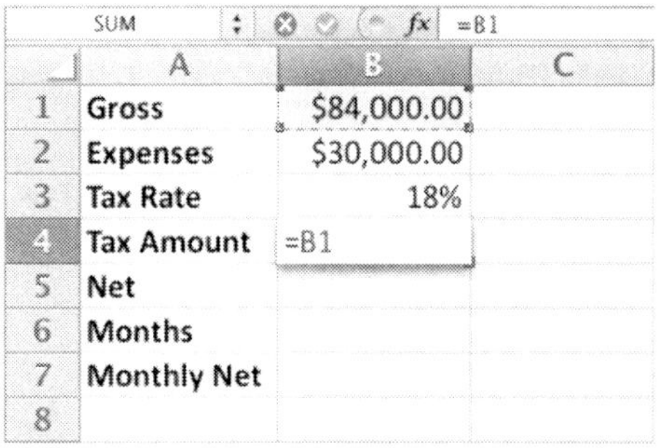

Figure 5–2. *When you click cell B1, Excel adds it to the formula in both the cell and the Formula bar and displays a dotted blue outline around it.*

    d. Type * to tell Excel you want to multiply the value in cell B1. Excel enters the asterisk in the formula and changes the outline around cell B1 to solid blue.

e. Click cell B3 to enter it in the formula. Excel displays a shimmering dotted outline (green this time) around the cell and adds it to the formula in the cell and in the formula bar (see Figure 5–3).

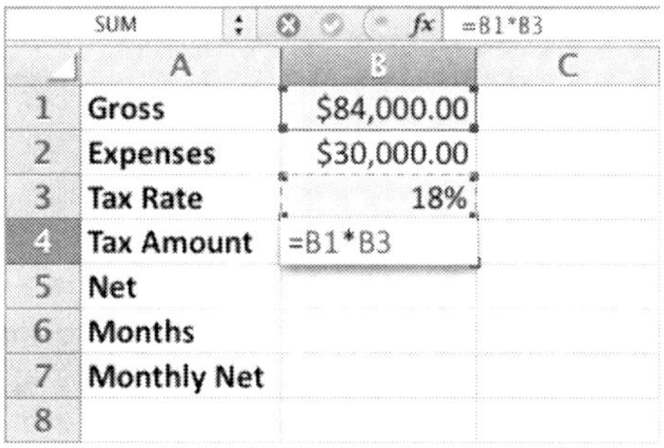

	A	B	C
SUM		*fx* =B1*B3	
1	Gross	$84,000.00	
2	Expenses	$30,000.00	
3	Tax Rate	18%	
4	Tax Amount	=B1*B3	
5	Net		
6	Months		
7	Monthly Net		
8			

Figure 5–3. *Click cell B3 to add it to the formula.*

f. Press Return or click the Enter button (the check-mark button in the Formula bar) to finish entering the formula in cell B4.

8. Enter the formula **=B1-(B2+B4)** in cell B5. Follow these steps:

   a. Click cell B5 to select it. If you pressed Return to enter the previous formula, Excel may have selected this cell already.

   b. Type = to start creating a formula in the cell.

   c. Click cell B1 to add it to the formula.

   d. Type – to enter the subtraction operator.

   e. Type (to start a nested expression. (More on this shortly.)

   f. Click cell B2 to add it to the formula.

   g. Type + to enter the addition operator.

   h. Click cell B4 to add it to the formula.

   i. Type) to end the nested expression.

   j. Click the Enter button to finish entering the formula.

9. Enter **12** in cell B6 and apply General formatting to it. Follow these steps:

   a. Click cell B6.

   b. Choose Home ➤ Number ➤ Number Format ➤ General.

   c. Type **12**.

   d. Press the down arrow to enter the value and move the active cell to cell B7.

10. Enter the formula **=B5/B6** in cell B7. This time, simply type the formula in—lowercase is fine—and then press Return. You'll notice that when you type **B5**, Excel selects cell B5 to let you check visually that you have the right cell.

Now that you've created the worksheet, try changing the figures in cells B1, B2, and B3. You'll see the results of the formulas in cells B4, B5, and B7 change accordingly. Excel recalculates the formulas each time you change a value in a cell, so the formula results remain up to date.

TURNING OFF AUTOMATIC RECALCULATION FOR LARGE WORKBOOKS

If you create a workbook with huge amounts of data, automatic recalculation may make Excel run slowly, especially when one recalculated value causes many other values to need recalculation.

If you find Excel struggling to recalculate a workbook, turn off automatic calculation by choosing **Formulas ➤ Calculation ➤ Settings ➤ Calculate Manually**. If recalculation was the problem, you'll notice the difference immediately.

You can recalculate manually when necessary by choosing **Formulas ➤ Calculation ➤ Recalculate Sheet** (to recalculate just the active worksheet) or choosing **Formulas ➤ Calculation ➤ Recalculate All** to recalculate the whole workbook.

Creating Complex Formulas

As you saw in the previous section, you can quickly create straightforward formulas with a single operator. But often you'll need to create formulas that use multiple operators, as you also did in the previous section. When you do, you must understand the order in which Excel evaluates the operators so that you can get the calculation correct. You also need to know how to tell Excel to evaluate the operators in a different order. And you may want to break a complex formula into multiple steps so you can see exactly what you're doing.

Understanding the Order in Which Excel Evaluates Operators

In the previous example, you entered the formula **=B1-(B2+B4)** in cell B5. The parentheses are necessary because the calculation has two separate stages—one stage of subtraction and one stage of addition—and you need to control the order in which they occur.

Try changing the formula in cell B5 to **=B1-B2+B4** and see what happens. Follow these steps:

1. Click cell B5.

2. Click in the Formula bar to start editing the formula there. (You can also edit in the cell by double-clicking the cell or pressing Ctrl+U, but editing in the Formula bar gives you more space, so it's often easier.)

3. Delete the opening and closing parentheses.

4. Click the Enter button on the Formula bar.

You'll notice that the Net amount (cell B5) jumps substantially. This is because you've changed the meaning of the formula:

- *=B1-(B2+B4).* This formula means "add the value in cell B2 to the value in cell B4, and then subtract the result from the value in cell B1."

- *=B1-B2+B4.* This formula means "subtract the value in cell B2 from the value in cell B1, and then add the value in cell B4 to the result."

Click cell B5 and press Ctrl+U to open the cell for editing. Position the insertion point before **B2** and type **(**; then position the insertion point after **B4** and type **)**. Then press Return to enter the formula in the cell.

> **NOTE:** As you type a closing parenthesis in a formula, you'll see that the opening parenthesis momentarily darkens to make the pairing clear. When a cell has complex contents and contains other nested items, having the corresponding parenthesis darken like this helps you to identify it.

The order in which Excel evaluates the operators is called *operator precedence*, and it can make a huge difference in your formulas—so it's vital to know both how it works and how to override it. Table 5–2 shows you the order in which Excel evaluates the operators in formulas.

Table 5–2. *Excel's Operator Precedence in Descending Order*

Precedence	Operators	Explanation
1	–	Negation
2	%	Percentage
3	^	Exponentiation
4	* *and* /	Multiplication and division
5	+ *and* –	Addition and subtraction
6	&	Concatenation
7	=, <>, <, <=, >, *and* >=	Comparison operators

When two operators are at the same level, Excel performs the operator that appears earlier in the formula first.

Nesting Parts of a Formula to Control Operator Precedence

You can control operator precedence in any formula by nesting one or more parts of the formula in parentheses. For example, as you just saw, using **=B1-(B2+B4)** makes Excel evaluate **B2+B4** before the subtraction.

You can nest parts of the formula several levels deep if necessary. For example, the following formula uses three levels of nesting and returns 180:

=10*(5*(4/(1+1))+8)

Breaking Up a Complex Formula into Separate Steps

A cell can accept more or less as complex a formula as you care to create—and some people enjoy creating formulas that are so complex that it takes an expert to figure them out.

Unless you like to work this way, when you have to create a complex formula, consider breaking it up into separate steps, putting each step in its own cell or row. For example, you could break up that =10*(5*(4/(1+1))+8) formula like this:

- *Cell B1.* =1+1
- *Cell B2.* =4/B1
- *Cell B3.* =5*B2
- *Cell B4.* =B3+8
- *Cell B5.* =10*B4

Broken up like this, each formula is easy to read, and you can easily see if any of the steps gives the wrong result. You can type a text description of each step in the next cell for reference, or (more discreetly) insert a comment describing the step.

When you've checked that the formula works, you have the option of creating a new version of the formula that goes into a single cell. But if you want to keep the worksheet easy to read and easy to audit, leave the formula in its step-by-step form.

Entering Formulas Quickly by Copying and Using AutoFill

In many worksheets, you'll need to enter related formulas in several cells. For example, say you have the worksheet shown in Figure 5–4, which lists a range of products with their prices and sales. Column D needs to show the total revenue derived by multiplying the Units figure by the Price value.

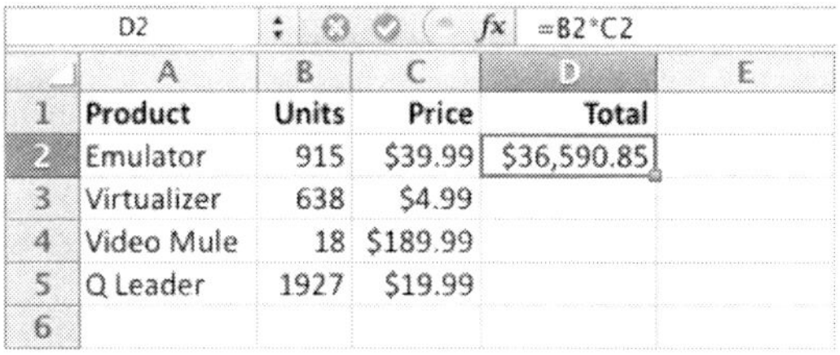

D2 =B2*C2

	A	B	C	D	E
1	Product	Units	Price	Total	
2	Emulator	915	$39.99	$36,590.85	
3	Virtualizer	638	$4.99		
4	Video Mule	18	$189.99		
5	Q Leader	1927	$19.99		
6					

Figure 5–4. *When a worksheet needs similar formulas in a column or row, you can enter one formula manually and then use AutoFill or Copy and Paste to enter it quickly in the other cells.*

Each cell in column D needs a different formula: Cell D2 needs =B2*C2, Cell D3 needs =B3*C3, and so on. Because the formula is the same except for the row number, you can use either AutoFill or Copy and Paste to enter the formula from cell D2 into the other cells as well.

To enter the formula using AutoFill, click the cell that contains the formula (here, cell D2), and then drag the AutoFill handle (the blue square at the lower-right corner of the active cell) down through cell D5. Excel automatically fills in the formulas, adjusting each for the change in row.

To enter the formula using Copy and Paste, click the cell that contains the formula, and then give the Copy command (for example, press Cmd+C). Select the destination cells, and then give the Paste command (for example, press Cmd+V).

> **NOTE:** If you need to copy a formula to a different row or column but have it refer to the original column or row, create the formula using mixed references. If you need to keep the column the same, make the column absolute (for example, **=$B2**); if you need to keep the row the same, make the row absolute (for example, **=B$2**). If you need the formula to refer to the same cell or range always, create it as an absolute reference.

Choosing Preferences for Error Checking

Excel can automatically identify various errors in your formulas. To choose which errors Excel marks, you set the error-checking preferences. Choose **Excel ➤ Preferences** or press Cmd+, (Cmd and the comma key) to display the Excel Preferences dialog box, and then click the Error Checking icon in the Formulas and Lists area to display the Error Checking pane (see Figure 5–5).

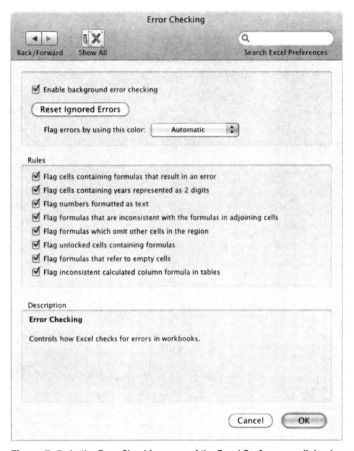

Figure 5–5. *In the Error Checking pane of the Excel Preferences dialog box, choose whether to use background error checking and decide which rules to use.*

You can then choose the following settings in the upper box:

- *Enable background error checking.* Select this check box to turn on error checking in the background. Background error checking is a good idea for small and medium-size workbooks, but you may want to turn it off for larger workbooks because it can slow Excel down. If you do turn off background error checking, be sure to check for errors manually (choose **Formulas ➤ Audit Formulas ➤ Check for Errors**, clicking the main part of the Check for Errors button).

- *Reset Ignored Errors.* Click this button to reset all the errors in the active workbook that you've told Excel to ignore. You may find it helpful to ignore errors when you're building a worksheet and the errors occur because the data isn't in place. When the worksheet is finished, you can click the Reset Ignored Errors button to see any remaining errors.

■ *Flag errors by using this color.* In this pop-up menu, choose the color to use for flagging errors. The default setting is Automatic, which lets Excel choose the color.

In the Rules box, you can select or clear the following check boxes to control which errors (or apparent errors) Excel flags by putting a green triangle at the upper-left corner of the cell:

■ *Flag cells containing formulas that result in an error.* Select this check box to make Excel flag cells whose formulas produce errors. This is normally helpful.

■ *Flag cells containing years represented as 2 digits.* Select this check box to make Excel flag cells that contain years represented by two digits rather than four digits (for example, 11 instead of 2011). Using four-digit years helps avoid confusion in your spreadsheets.

■ *Flag numbers formatted as text.* Select this check box to make Excel flag numbers that have text formatting rather than number formatting or that you've preceded with an apostrophe to force Excel to treat them as text. This option can be helpful, but it's apt to flag cells you've deliberately formatted as text.

■ *Flag formulas that are inconsistent with the formulas in adjoining cells.* Select this check box to make Excel flag formulas that appear wrong because they're different from formulas in adjoining cells. For example, if you have a row of eight cells, and six contain SUM() formulas adding the cells above them but two contain SUM() formulas adding the three cells to their left, this setting makes Excel flag those two cells because they contain formulas different from their neighbors. This can be helpful, but if the two oddball cells are summarizing the fiscal year quarters, you may want the formulas to be different.

■ *Flag formulas which omit other cells in the region.* Select this check box to make Excel flag formulas that are apparently intended to cover a whole region of a worksheet but omit particular cells in it. If these omissions are intentional, you can suppress the flags.

■ *Flag unlocked cells containing formulas.* Select this check box to make Excel flag unlocked cells that contain formulas. This setting can help you track down cells you need to lock to prevent your colleagues taking liberties with your calculations.

■ *Flag formulas that refer to empty cells.* Select this check box to make Excel flag formulas that try to use empty cells. Empty cells can cause plenty of problems in your formulas, including division-by-zero errors, so having Excel identify formulas that use empty cells is usually a good idea.

■ *Flag inconsistent calculated column formula in tables.* Select this check box to make Excel flag formulas in tables that differ from the other formulas in their columns. (Chapter 10 shows you how to create tables.)

When you've finished choosing error-checking preferences, click the OK button to close the Preferences dialog box.

Troubleshooting Common Problems with Formulas

Formulas are great when they work, but a single-letter typo or a wrong reference can prevent a formula from working correctly. This section shows you how to deal with common problems with formulas, starting with solutions to the error messages you're most likely to produce.

> **CAUTION:** This section shows you how to troubleshoot problems that Excel can identify because they prevent your calculations from working. But what can be much more dangerous are mistakes in formulas that *don't* cause errors but instead give the wrong results; because the formulas work correctly, Excel can't detect the errors and so raises no objections, but the values you get aren't what you intend. If having your calculations give the correct results is important to you (as is usually the case), have a competent colleague check your worksheets for mistakes. You may also want to get a book such as *Spreadsheet Check and Control* (O'Beirne, Systems Publishing), which teaches you how to audit Excel worksheets.

Understanding Common Errors—and Resolving Them

Excel includes an impressive arsenal of error messages, but some of them appear far more frequently than others. Table 5–3 shows you eight errors you're likely to encounter, explains what they mean, and tells you how to solve them.

Table 5–3. *How to Solve Excel's Eight Most Common Errors*

Error	What the Problem Is	How to Solve It
#####	The formula result is too wide to fit in the cell.	Make the column wider—for example, double-click the column head's right border to AutoFit the column width.
#NAME?	A function name is misspelled, or the formula refers to a range that doesn't exist.	Check the spelling of all functions; correct any mistakes. If the formula uses a named range, check that the name is right and that you haven't deleted the range.
#NUM!	The function tries to use a value that is not valid for it—for example, returning the square root of a negative number.	Give the function a suitable value.
#VALUE!	The function uses an invalid argument—for example, using =FACT() to return the factorial of text rather than a number.	Give the function the right type of data.
#N/A	The function does not have a valid value available.	Make sure the function's arguments provide values of the right type.
#DIV/0	The function is trying to divide by zero (which is mathematically impossible).	Change the divisor value from zero. Often, you'll find that the function is using a blank cell (which has a zero value) as the argument for the divisor; in this case, enter a value in the cell.
#REF!	The formula uses a cell reference or a range reference that's not valid—for example, because you've deleted a worksheet.	Edit the formula and provide a valid reference.
#NULL!	There is no intersection between the two ranges specified.	Change the ranges to produce an intersection.

CAUTION: The =SUM() function is smart enough to ignore text values that you feed it. For example, if cell A1 contains the value 1 and cell A2 contains the text Dog, the function =SUM(A1:A2) returns 1 even though the formula =A1+A2 returns a #VALUE! error. The =SUM() function's smartness here is a mixed blessing: you get a usable result, which is presumably what you want—but this hides the mistake you've made in trying to add text instead of a numerical value.

Seeing the Details of an Error in a Formula

When Excel identifies an error in a formula, it displays a green triangle at the upper-left corner of the cell that contains the formula. Click the cell to display an action button that you can hold the mouse over to display a ScreenTip explaining the problem (as shown on the left in Figure 5–6) or click to display a menu of actions you can take to resolve the problem (as shown on the right in Figure 5–6).

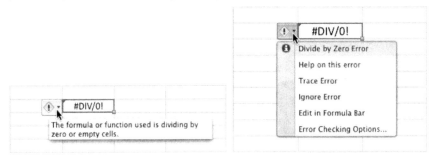

Figure 5–6. *Hold the mouse pointer over the action button for an error cell to display a ScreenTip explaining what's wrong.*

Tracing an Error Back to Its Source

To see which cell is causing an error, click the error cell, then choose **Formulas ➤ Audit Formulas ➤ Check for Errors ➤ Trace Error**. Excel displays an arrow from the cell or cells causing the error to the error cell. The left screen in Figure 5–7 shows a simple example of tracing an error; the more complex the worksheet, the more helpful this feature is. Excel displays a worksheet symbol (see the right screen in Figure 5–7) if the cell reference is on another worksheet or in another workbook.

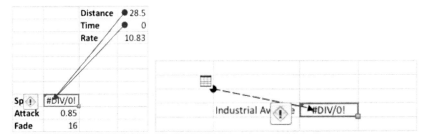

Figure 5–7. *Use the Formulas ➤ Audit Formulas ➤ Check for Errors ➤ Trace Error command to identify the cell or cells causing an error. If the cell reference is on another worksheet or in another workbook, Excel displays a worksheet symbol, as shown on the right.*

NOTE: If you've turned off background error checking in the Error Checking preferences pane, choose **Formulas ➤ Audit Formulas ➤ Check for Errors** (clicking the main part of the Check for Errors button) from the Ribbon or **Tools ➤ Error Checking** from the menu bar to check for errors.

Displaying All the Formulas in a Worksheet

When you need to review or check all the formulas in a worksheet, choose **Formulas ➤ Function ➤ Show ➤ Show Formulas**, placing a check mark next to the Show Formulas item on the Show pop-up menu. Excel displays the formulas and automatically widens the worksheet columns to give you more space (see Figure 5–8).

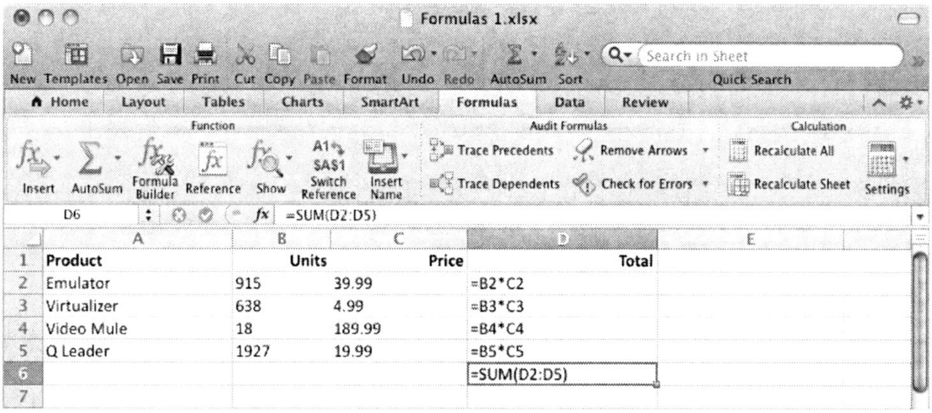

Figure 5–8. *Choose Formulas ➤ Function ➤ Show ➤ Show Formulas when you need to see all the formulas in a worksheet.*

When you've finished viewing the formulas, choose **Formulas ➤ Function ➤ Show ➤ Show Formulas** again, removing the check mark from the Show Formulas menu item. Excel automatically restores the columns to their former widths.

Seeing Which Cells a Formula Uses

To see which cells a formula uses, or to trace errors, click the cell that contains the formula, and then choose **Formulas ➤ Audit Formulas ➤ Trace Precedents**. Excel displays an arrow showing the formula back to its roots. If one of the cells the formula uses contains a formula itself, you can click that cell and click the Trace Precedents button again to display its precedents in turn. Figure 5–9 shows the precedents of cell D6 and one of the cells that it uses, cell D2.

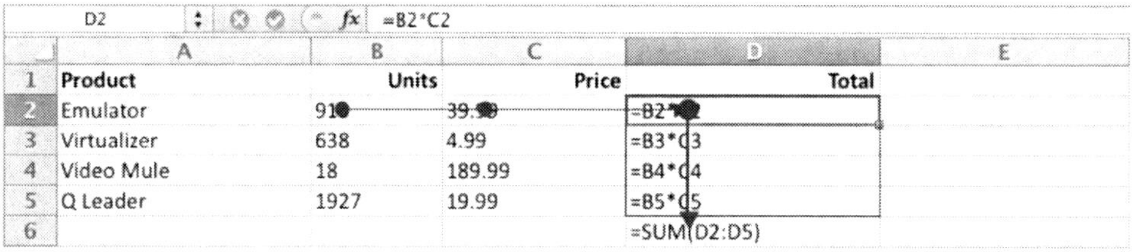

Figure 5–9. *Use the Trace Precedents command to see which cells you're using to produce a formula result. In this example, cells B2 and C2 go to make up the formula in cell D2, which in turn appears in the =SUM(D2:D5) formula in cell D6.*

When you need to look at the problem the other way and see which formulas use a particular cell, click the cell, and then choose **Formulas ➤ Audit Formulas ➤ Trace Dependents**. Again, Excel displays arrows, this time from the cell going to each of the formulas that use it. Figure 5–10 shows an example of tracing dependent cells.

	A	B	C	D	E
1	Gross	$84,000.00		Monthly	$7,000.00
2	Expenses	$30,000.00		Deductions	$1,260.00
3	Tax Rate	18%			
4	Tax Amount	$15,120.00			
5	Net	$38,880.00			
6	Months	12			
7	Monthly Net	$3,240.00			

Figure 5–10. *Use the Trace Dependents command to see which formulas use a particular cell's value to produce their results.*

> **NOTE:** You can use the Trace Precedents command and the Trace Dependents command either with formulas displayed or with formula results displayed, whichever you find most useful.

When you've finished tracing precedents and dependents (or errors), choose **Formulas ➤ Audit Formulas ➤ Remove Arrows** (clicking the main part of the Remove Arrows button) to remove the arrows from the screen. If you want to remove just precedent arrows or dependent arrows, click the Remove Arrows pop-up button, and then click the Remove Precedent Arrows item or the Remove Dependent Arrows item on the pop-up menu.

Removing Circular References

Even if you're careful, it's easy enough to create a *circular reference*—one that refers to itself.

Circular references most often occur when you enter a formula that refers to a cell that itself refers to the cell in which you're entering the formula. For example, say cell A1 contains the formula **=B1**. If you enter the formula **=A1** in cell B1, you've created a circular reference: cell B1 gets its value from cell A1, which gets its value from cell B1, and so on.

You can also enter a circular reference by making a cell refer to itself. For example, if you enter **=A1/B1** in cell A1, you've created a circular reference in that cell, because cell A1 refers to itself. This type of circular reference is usually easier to avoid than the previous type.

Circular references can be useful in some specialized circumstances, such as when you need to perform iterations of a calculation, but normally you don't want them in your worksheets, so Excel helps you to get rid of them.

When you create a circular reference that Excel can't calculate, Excel displays the Excel Cannot Calculate a Formula dialog box shown in Figure 5–11. Click the OK button if you want to open a Help window showing information on how to deal with circular references, or click the Cancel button if you want to go ahead and enter the circular reference in the cell (for example, because you can tell what the problem is and will be able to fix it easily).

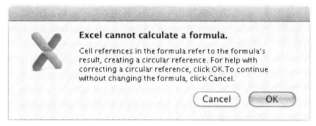

Figure 5–11. *Circular references can cause problems in worksheets, so Excel warns you when you enter one. You can click the Cancel button if you're sure you want to create the circular reference.*

NOTE: If you leave circular references in a worksheet, use the Circular readout on the status bar to identify them. This readout shows the location of the most recent circular reference that Excel has identified. When you've dealt with that circular reference, the Circular readout shows the next one, and so on, until there are none left.

Summary

In this chapter, you learned how to use formulas to perform calculations in your workbooks. You know that a formula is the recipe for a calculation, and you know how to assemble it from its various components—an equal sign, cell or range references, operators, and more. You know how to create the formulas you need and how to troubleshoot them when they go wrong.

In the next chapter, I'll show you how to use Excel's built-in functions, either on their own or in your formulas.

Chapter 6

Using Excel's Built-In Functions

As you saw in the previous chapter, a function is a predefined formula for performing a standard calculation. Excel includes several hundred built-in functions that you can simply insert in a cell and provide with the data they need to deliver the answer. Functions save you from having to create complex formulas from scratch and from getting such formulas wrong, so when you need to perform a standard calculation, check whether Excel has a function for it. There's no point in reinventing the wheel, especially if the result isn't round.

In this chapter, you'll learn how to insert functions into your worksheets using the various tools that Excel provides, how to find the functions you want, and how to point the functions to the data they need for the calculations.

Once you're comfortable with how functions work, we'll review the different categories of functions that Excel provides, such as database functions, logical functions, and math and trigonometric functions. I'll explain the functions you're most likely to find useful, giving examples where they'll be helpful.

Understanding the Components of a Function

In Excel, a function has a name written in capitals followed by a pair of parentheses, which enclose the pieces of data (if any) the function needs. Here are three examples:

- *SUM().* This widely used function adds together two or more values that you specify.

- *COUNT().* This function counts the number of cells that contain numbers (as opposed to text, blanks, or other data types) in the range you specify.

- *TODAY().* This function enters the current date in the cell.

Most functions take *arguments*, pieces of information that tell the function what you want it to work on. Excel prompts you to provide the arguments each function needs. For example, when you enter the function in a cell, Excel displays a ScreenTip showing the arguments needed. Figure 6–1 shows an example using the SUM()function.

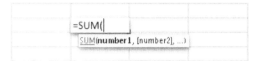

Figure 6–1. *When you enter a function in a cell, Excel prompts you to supply the arguments it needs.*

The ScreenTip shows that the SUM() function has one required argument and one optional argument, and you can add further arguments as needed:

- *Required argument.* Each required argument appears without brackets, like the argument *number1* in the ScreenTip. You separate the arguments with commas, as in the example in the next paragraph. For example, you can use SUM() to add the values of cells in a range: SUM(C1:C10). Here, C1:C10 is a single argument, the required argument.

- *Optional argument.* Each optional argument appears in brackets, like the argument *[number2]* in the ScreenTip. For example, you can use SUM() to add the values of two cells: SUM(C1,C3). Here, C1 is the required argument, and C3 is the first optional argument.

- *Extra arguments.* The ellipsis (…) shows that you can enter extra arguments of the same type. For example, you can use SUM() to add the values of many cells: SUM(C1,C3,D4,D8,E1,XF202). Here, C1 is the required argument, and all the other cell references are optional arguments.

NOTE: A few functions take no arguments. For example, you don't need to tell the TODAY() function which day you're talking about. Similarly, the NOW() function needs no arguments to return the current date and time, and the NA() function simply enters #(N/A) in a cell to indicate that the information is not available. Even when a function takes no arguments, you still need to include the parentheses to make Excel recognize the function.

Entering Functions in Your Worksheets

Excel puts the most widely used functions right at your fingertips, and you can enter even the most specialized functions quickly and easily.

These are the four ways of inserting functions:

- *Use the AutoSum button or AutoSum pop-up menu.* The AutoSum button appears on the Standard toolbar and in the Function group on the Formula tab of the Ribbon and gives quick access to five widely used functions.

- *Use the Insert pop-up menu and the Formula Builder.* The Insert pop-up menu appears in the Function group of the Formulas tab of the Ribbon. When you choose the function you want from the Insert pop-up menu and its submenus, Excel displays the Formula Builder pane in the Toolbox to walk you through inserting the function.

- *Use the Formula Builder pane in the Toolbox.* You can also start working in the Formula Builder pane in the Toolbox without using the Insert pop-up menu first. The easiest way to open the Formula Builder pane is to click the fx button in the formula bar.

- *Type the function in manually.* When you know which function you want, you can type it straight into a cell.

We'll look at the details in the following sections.

Inserting Functions with the AutoSum Pop-up Menu

The quickest and easiest way to enter any of five widely used functions—SUM(), AVERAGE(), COUNT(), MAX(), or MIN()—in your worksheets is to use the AutoSum pop-up menu on the Standard toolbar. Follow these steps:

1. Click the cell you want to enter the function in.

2. If you want to create a SUM() function for the cells immediately above or to the left of the selected cell, click the AutoSum button itself. Otherwise, click the AutoSum pop-up button, and then click the function (see Figure 6–2).

> **NOTE:** You can also use the AutoSum pop-up menu on the Standard toolbar to open the Formula Builder pane in the Toolbox. Just click the More Functions item at the bottom of the pop-up menu.

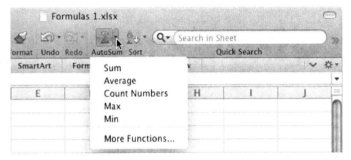

Figure 6–2. *Use the AutoSum pop-up menu on the Standard toolbar when you need to insert the SUM(), AVERAGE(), COUNT(), MAX(), or MIN() function quickly.*

3. Excel inserts the function in the cell you chose and selects the range it thinks you may want to use as the argument. Figure 6–3 shows an example with the AVERAGE() function.

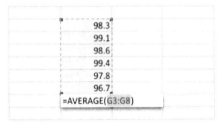

Figure 6–3. *When you insert a function from the AutoSum pop-up menu, Excel selects a range of data it thinks may be suitable.*

4. If you need to change the range, do so in one of these ways:

    ▓ Click and drag to select the right range.

    ▓ Type the range over the range selected within the parentheses.

5. Add another argument to the formula if needed. For example, type a comma, and then click and drag to select another range.

6. When the formula is as you want it, press Return to enter it in the cell. Excel displays the result of the formula.

Inserting Functions with the Formula Builder

When you need to find the right function to insert or when you need to learn about the arguments for a function, use the Formula Builder to insert the function. The Formula Builder is a pane that appears in the Toolbox and provides a complete list of Excel's functions, together with descriptions and details of the arguments they use.

To insert a function with the Formula Builder, follow these steps:

1. Select the cell in which you want to enter the function.

2. Open the Formula Builder in one of these ways:

    ▪ *Formula bar.* Click the fx button.

    ▪ *Standard toolbar.* Click the AutoSum pop-up button, and then click the More Functions item on the pop-up menu.

    ▪ *Menu bar.* Choose **View ➤ Formula Builder**.

    ▪ *Ribbon.* Choose **Formulas ➤ Function ➤ Formula Builder**.

    ▪ *Toolbox.* If the Toolbox is already open, click the Formula Builder tab.

3. If you want to search for a function, click in the Search box at the top, type keywords to search for, and then press Return. The Formula Builder displays a list of results, as shown on the left in Figure 6–4.

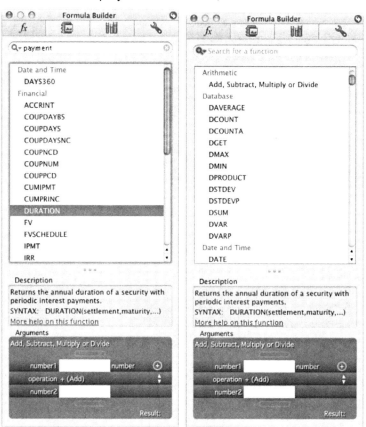

Figure 6–4. *To find a function, type a search term in the Search pane of the Formula Builder and press Return; the Formula Builder shows a list of results (left). Otherwise, browse the full list of functions, and click the function you want to see information on (right).*

4. Otherwise, browse through the list of functions to find the function you need, as shown on the right in Figure 6–4. The Formula Builder breaks the functions up into the following categories, most of which we'll examine in depth later in this chapter:

▪ *Most Recently Used.* This category provides quick access to the functions you've used most recently—so if you're looking for a function you've used before, start by looking here.

> **TIP:** You can make the formula list in the Formula Builder window taller or shorter by dragging the sizing handle—the line of three dots below the list—up or down. The Formula Builder window grows or shrinks to accommodate the list.

▪ *Arithmetic.* This category doesn't actually show functions, just a single entry called "Add, Subtract, Multiply or Divide." When you double-click this item, the Arguments pane at the bottom of the Formula Builder (see the right screen in Figure 6–4) displays controls for helping you set up arithmetic formulas.

▪ *Database.* This category contains functions for working with databases—for example, returning the average of values in a column or list or the count of cells containing numbers in a field.

▪ *Date and Time.* This category contains functions ranging from returning the current date with the TODAY() function to using the WEEKDAY() function to return the day of the week for a particular date.

▪ *Engineering.* This category contains functions including the DEC2HEX() function (for converting a decimal number to hexadecimal, base 16) and the HEX2OCT() function (for converting a hexadecimal number to octal, base 8).

▪ *Financial.* This category contains functions for financial calculations—for example, calculating the payments on your mortgage or the depreciation on an asset.

▪ *Information.* This category contains functions for returning information about data, such as whether it is text or a number.

▪ *Logical.* This category contains functions for performing logical tests—for example, testing whether a particular cell contains an error.

▪ *Lookup and Reference.* This category contains functions for looking up data from other parts of a worksheet or referring to other cells in it.

■ *Math and Trigonometry.* This category contains mathematical functions, such as the SQRT() function for returning a square root, and trigonometric functions, such as the COS() function for calculating a cosine.

■ *Statistical.* This category contains functions for performing statistical calculations, such as working out standard deviations based on a population or a sample.

■ *Text.* This category contains functions for manipulating text, such as the TRIM() function (for trimming off leading and trailing spaces) and the LEFT() function, which returns the leftmost part of the value.

■ *Compatibility.* This category contains functions included for compatibility with Excel 2008 (Mac), Excel 2007 (Windows), and earlier versions. It's best to use these functions only for compatibility with these older versions; if you're developing worksheets for Excel 2011 or Excel 2010 (Windows), use the newer functions that these versions support—for example, use the new POISSON.DIST() function rather than the old POISSON() function.

5.   To learn more about a function, click it. The Formula Builder shows its details at the bottom of the window, as shown on the left in Figure 6–5. From here, you can click the More help on this function link to open a Help window showing detailed information about the function and its arguments.

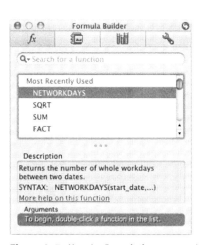
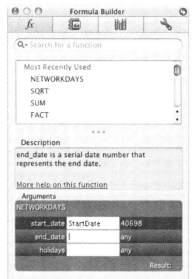

Figure 6–5. *Use the Description area at the bottom of the Formula Builder to identify the function you want (left). When you double-click the function to insert it, the Formula Builder displays the Arguments pane (right).*

6. When you've found the function you want to insert, double-click it. The Formula Builder displays the Arguments pane for the function, as shown on the right in Figure 6–5 (with one argument already entered).

7. Click in the box for the first argument, and then enter the data. You can type in a value or range name, type in a cell reference or range, or use the mouse to choose a cell reference or range in the worksheet (or in another worksheet or workbook).

8. Fill in each of the other arguments for the function. When you have entered all the required arguments, the Result readout in the lower-right corner of the Function Builder window shows the result of the function.

9. Press Return to enter the function in the worksheet.

If you have finished using the Function Builder, close it by clicking its Close button (the button at the left end of its title bar), choosing **View ➤ Formula Builder** from the menu bar, or clicking the Toolbox button on the Standard toolbar.

Inserting Functions with the Insert Pop-up Menu

When you know which function you want to insert, the easiest way to insert it (unless it's one of the five functions on the AutoSum pop-up menu) is to use the Insert pop-up menu. The Insert pop-up menu helps you pick the function by category and inserts it directly in the cell.

To insert a function using the Insert pop-up menu, follow these steps:

1. Select the cell in which you want to enter the function.

2. Choose **Formulas ➤ Function ➤ Insert** to display the Insert pop-up menu. This pop-up menu breaks up the functions into ten categories: Database, Date and Time, Engineering, Financial, Information, Logical, Lookup and Reference, Math and Trigonometry, Statistical, and Text. These categories are similar to those that appear in the Formula Builder, as discussed earlier in this chapter. Each category has a submenu.

3. Click the category of functions you want to insert. Excel displays a submenu containing the functions. Figure 6–6 shows the Date and Time submenu open.

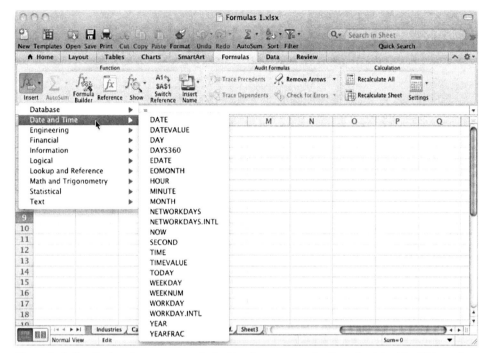

Figure 6–6. *Use the Insert pop-up menu in the Function group on the Formulas tab of the Ribbon when you want to insert a function by category.*

4. Click the function you want to insert. Excel inserts it in the cell.

5. Enter the arguments for the function as usual.

> **TIP:** If you need help providing the function's arguments, click the fx button on the formula bar or choose **Formulas ➤ Function ➤ Formula Builder** from the Ribbon to display the Formula Builder. The Formula Builder shows the details of the function you've just inserted.

6. Press Return or click the Enter button on the Formula bar to enter the formula in the cell.

Inserting Functions by Typing Them into a Worksheet

You can also enter functions in your worksheets by typing them into cells. You'll probably want to use this approach when you're familiar with the function you need and you know its arguments. Follow these general steps:

1. Click the cell to select it.

2. Type = to tell Excel that you're creating a formula.

3. Start typing the function's name. Excel displays a list of matching functions (see Figure 6–7).

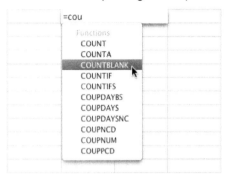

Figure 6–7. *When you start typing a function name into a cell, Excel lists matching functions. Click the function you want to insert, or press the down arrow key (and up arrow key, if necessary) to select the function and press Return.*

NOTE: You can also keep typing until you've typed enough to identify the function uniquely—or type the whole of the function name if you prefer.

4. To enter a function, double-click it, or move the highlight to it by pressing down arrow or up arrow, and then press Return.

5. Specify the arguments for the function. You can either type in a value or a reference or use the mouse to select a cell or range.

NOTE: After entering a function in a cell, you can open the function for editing by double-clicking the cell or by making the cell active and then pressing Ctrl+U. You can edit the function either directly in the cell or in the Formula bar.

Nesting One Function Inside Another Function

When you first start using functions, you'll probably use a single function in a cell. But as you become more experienced with functions, you'll find you sometimes need to use multiple functions to perform the calculations you want.

When you need to use two or more functions together, you can nest one function inside another function. For example, if you need to return the current hour, you can nest the NOW() function (which returns the current date and time) in the HOUR() function (which returns the hour from a given time in 24-hour format; change the cell format if you need the hour in AM/PM format):

```
=HOUR(NOW())
```

As with formulas, you can nest functions many layers deep if you need to. Here's an example with three layers of nesting:

```
=INT(AVERAGE(ROUND(SUM(C1:C6),2),ROUND(SUM(D1:D6),2)))
```

Here's what happens:

- *SUM(C1:C6).* This SUM function adds the values in the range C1:C6. Similarly, SUM(D1:D6) adds the values in the range D1:D6.

- *ROUND(SUM(C1:C6),2).* This ROUND function rounds the result of the SUM(C1:C6) formula to two decimal places. Similarly, ROUND(SUM(D1:D6),2) rounds the result of the SUM(D1:D6) formula to two decimal places.

- *AVERAGE.* This function returns the average of the results returned by the two ROUND functions.

- *INT.* This function returns the integer portion of the result from the AVERAGE function.

> **TIP:** Nesting functions makes for compact spreadsheets and can impress your colleagues. But when you're working out which functions to use, you may find it easier to put each function in a separate cell so that you can see the result each returns—and perhaps add comments explaining what each step does. Once you've got the functions working in separate cells, create the nested version in a single cell, and make sure it gives the same result as the step-by-step version. Again, you may want to add a comment explaining how the nested formula works.

Meeting Excel's Built-in Functions

In this section, I'll introduce you to Excel's ten main categories of built-in functions: Database, Date and Time, Engineering, Financial, Logical, Information, Lookup and Reference, Math and Trigonometry, Statistical, and Text. We'll look at the functions that are most widely useful, with examples where they'll be helpful.

Database Functions

Excel includes 12 database functions you use to identify values in an Excel table that match your specified criteria. (A *table* is a flat-form database you create on a worksheet; Chapter 10 explains how to create tables and gives you examples of using the database functions.) Table 6–1 explains the database functions.

Table 6–1. *Excel's Database Functions*

Database Function	What It Returns
DAVERAGE	The average of the values in a column that match the criteria you specify.
DCOUNT	The count of cells in the database field that match the criteria you specify.
DCOUNTA	The count of nonblank cells in the database field that match the criteria you specify.
DGET	The database record that matches the criteria you specify for a particular field.
DMAX	The largest number in the database field that matches the criteria you specify.
DMIN	The smallest number in the database field that matches the criteria you specify.
DPRODUCT	The result of multiplying the values of the records that match the criteria you specify.
DSTDEV	The standard deviation of the selected database entries from a sample.
DSTDEVP	The standard deviation based on the entire population of the selected entries.
DSUM	The value that results from adding the values in the fields that match the criteria you specify.
DVAR	The variance based on a sample of database entries.
D\VARP	The variance based on the entire population of database entries.

Date and Time Functions

Table 6–2 explains Excel's date and time functions, which you'll find useful in many worksheets.

Table 6–2. *Excel's Date and Time Functions*

Date and Time Function	What It Returns
DATE	The serial number of the specified date. For example, **=DATE(2011,11,18)** returns 40865, the serial date for 18 November 2011. Excel displays this value as a date unless you set the cell format to General.
TIME	The serial number of the specified time. For example, **=TIME(11,59,59)** returns 0.499988426, the serial number for 11:59.59 AM. Excel displays this value as time unless you set the cell format to General.
DATEVALUE	The serial number of the specified date that's formatted as text. For example, **=DATEVALUE("12 December 2011")** returns 40889, the serial date for 12 December 2011.
TIMEVALUE	The serial number of the specified time that's formatted as text. For example, **=TIMEVALUE("3:25.00 PM")** returns 0.502372685, the serial number for 3:25 PM.
DAY	A serial number between 1 and 31, representing the day of the month for the specified serial date. For example, **=DAY(40789)** returns 3, indicating that the date falls on the third day in the month.
MONTH	A serial number between 1 and 12, representing the month in which the specified serial date falls. For example, **=MONTH(40789)** returns 9, indicating that the date is in September.
YEAR	The four-digit number for the specified serial date. For example, **=YEAR(40789)** returns 2011, indicating that the date is in 2011.
YEARFRAC	A number showing how many years are between the specified start date and the specified end date. For example, **=YEARFRAC(DATE(2011,1,1),DATE (2012,3,1))** returns 1.166666667, the number of years between 1 January 2011 and 1 March 2012.
DAYS360	A number showing the number of days between the specified start date and the specified end date, assuming there are 360 days in a year (this is an accounting technique rather than a straightforward denial of conventional timekeeping). For example, **=DAYS360(DATE(2011,1,1),DATE(2012,3,1))** returns 420, the number of days between 1 January 2011 and 1 March 2012 (with that 360-day year).

Date and Time Function	What It Returns
HOUR	A serial number between 0 and 23 representing the hour for the time given. For example, **=HOUR(0.25)** returns 6, representing 6 AM., which is one quarter of the way through the 24 hours in a day.
MINUTE	A serial number between 0 and 59 representing the minute for the time given. For example, **=MINUTE(0.55)** returns 12, being the minutes in 1:12 PM, which is the time 55% through a day.
SECOND	A serial number between 0 and 59 representing the second for the time given. For example, **=SECOND(0.61)** returns 24, being the seconds in 2:38.24 PM, which is the time 61% through a day.
TODAY	The current date in date format. For example, **=TODAY()** returns 6/12/2011 on 12 June 2011.
NOW	The current date and time in date and time format. For example, **=NOW()** returns a date and time such as 6/2/2011 03:15.
WEEKNUM	A serial number between 1 and 52, showing the week of the year the specified date occurs in. For example, **=WEEKNUM(40789)** returns 36, indicating that the date falls in the 36th week of the year.
WEEKDAY	A serial number between 1 (Sunday) and 7 (Saturday) showing the weekday for the specified date. For example, **=WEEKDAY(40789)** returns 7, indicating that the day is a Saturday.
WORKDAY	A serial number giving the date that is the specified number of workdays before or after the specified start date, including the number of holidays specified. For example, **=WORKDAY(DATE(2011,6,12),40,2)** returns 40760, the serial number of 5 August 2011, the workday 40 days after 12 June 2011 if there are two holidays.
NETWORKDAYS	A number giving the net number of work days ("net workdays") between the specified starting date and the specified ending date, minus the number of holidays specified. For example, **=NETWORKDAYS(DATE(2011,6,12),DATE(2011,10,20),2)** returns 94, the net number of workdays between 12 June 2011 and 20 October 2011, assuming that two holidays fall in that period.
EDATE	The serial number of the date that is the specified number of months before or after the given start date. For example, **=EDATE(40789,4)** returns 40911, the serial date four months after the serial date 40789.
EOMONTH	The serial number of the last day of the month that is the specified number of months before or after the given start date. For example, **=EOMONTH(DATE(2011,7,14),6)** returns 40939, the serial number for 31 January 2012, the last day of the month that is six months after 14 July 2011.

Engineering Functions

Table 6–3 explains Excel's engineering functions, which range from calculating Bessel functions to converting numbers to and from binary, octal, and hexadecimal.

Table 6–3. *Excel's Engineering Functions*

Engineering Function	What It Returns
BESSELI	The modified Bessel function In(x), the contour integral. For example, **=BESSELI(1.8,1)** returns 1.31716723.
BESSELJ	The Bessel function Jn(x). This is also called cylindrical harmonics. For example, **=BESSELJ(1.5,2)** returns 0.232087679.
BESSELK	The modified Bessel function Kn(x). This is also called the Basset function or Macdonald function. For example, **=BESSELK(1.8,3)** returns 0.95783635.
BESSELY	The Bessel function Yn(x), also called the Neumann function or the Weber function. For example, **=BESSELY(3.5,1)** returns 0.410188417.
BIN2DEC	The decimal (base 10) equivalent of the specified binary (base 2) number. For example, **=BIN2DEC(1001101)** returns 77. The binary number can be up to 10 characters long; longer numbers cause #NUM! errors.
BIN2HEX	The hexadecimal (base 16) equivalent of the specified binary (base 2) number, optionally specifying the number of characters to use. For example, **=BIN2HEX(111011111)** returns 1DF, while **=BIN2HEX(111011111,4)** returns 01DF. The binary number can be up to 10 characters long; longer numbers cause #NUM! errors.
BIN2OCT	The octal (base 8) equivalent of the specified binary (base 2) number, optionally specifying the number of characters to use. For example, **=BIN2OCT(1011,4)** returns 0013.
COMPLEX	The complex number produced by real and imaginary coefficients. For example, **=COMPLEX(4,5)** returns 4+5i.
CONVERT	The equivalent value in the specified destination measuring system of the value in the specified source measuring system. You can convert Weight and Mass, Distance, Pressure, Force, Energy, Power, Magnetism, Temperature, Liquid, and Metric measurements; see the Help file for details. For example, **=CONVERT(200,"kg","lbm")** converts 200Kg to its equivalent weight in pounds (440.9245244).
DEC2BIN	The binary (base 2) equivalent of the specified decimal (base 10) number, optionally specifying the number of characters to use. For example, **=DEC2BIN(100)** returns 1100100, while **=DEC2BIN(100,10)** returns 0001100100.

Engineering Function	What It Returns
DEC2HEX	The hexadecimal (base 16) equivalent of the specified decimal (base 10) number, optionally specifying the number of characters to use. For example, **=DEC2HEX(-90)** returns FFFFFFFFA6.
DEC2OCT	The octal (base 8) equivalent of the specified decimal (base 10) number, optionally specifying the number of characters to use. For example, **=DEC2OCT(100,6)** returns 000144.
DELTA	1 if the two numbers are equal, 0 if they are not. For example, **=DELTA(B1,B2)** returns 1 if the values in cells B1 and B2 are equal; otherwise, it returns 0.
ERF	The error function integrated between the specified lower limit and specified upper limit. If you omit the upper limit, the error function between zero and the specified lower limit. For example, **=ERF(0.5,2)** returns 0.474822387, the error function integrated between 0.5 and 2.
ERFC	The complementary error function integrated between the specified lower bound and infinity. For example, **=ERFC(2)** returns 0.004677735.
GESTEP	1 if the specified number is greater than or equal to the specified threshold, 0 if it is not. For example, **=GESTEP(5,D1)** returns 1 if 5 is greater than or equal to the value in cell D1; otherwise, it returns 0.
HEX2BIN	The binary (base 2) equivalent of the specified hexadecimal (base 16) number, optionally specifying the number of characters to use. For example, **=HEX2DEC("AF",8)** returns 10101111.
HEX2DEC	The decimal (base 10) equivalent of the specified hexadecimal (base 16) number. For example, **=HEX2DEC("FFFF0000")** returns 4294901760.
HEX2OCT	The octal (base 8) equivalent of the specified hexadecimal (base 16) number, optionally specifying the number of characters to use. For example, **=DEX2OCT("AF00")** returns 127400.
IMABS	The modulus (absolute value) of a complex number. For example, **=IMABS("6+2i")** returns 6.708203932.
IMAGINARY	The imaginary coefficient of a complex number. For example, **=IMAGINARY("8+3i")** returns 3.
IMARGUMENT	The theta argument, an angle expressed in radians, for the specified complex number. For example, **=IMARGUMENT("4+5i")** returns 0.896055385.
IMCONJUGATE	The complex conjugate of the specified complex number. For example, **=IMCONJUGATE("4+5i")** returns 4-5i.

Engineering Function	What It Returns
IMCOS	The cosine of the specified complex number. For example, **=IMCOS(A22)** returns the cosine of the value in cell A22.
IMDIV	The quotient of the specified two complex numbers. For example, **=IMDIV("10+25i","-240+280i")** calculates the quotient of the two numbers given.
IMEXP	The exponential of the specified complex number. For example, **=IMEXP("2+i")** returns 3.99232404844127+6.21767631236797i.
IMLN	The natural logarithm of the specified complex number. For example, **=IMLN("8+10i")** returns 2.5499332139121+0.896055384571344i.
IMLOG10	The base-10 logarithm of the specified complex number. For example, **=IMLOG10("8+10i")** returns 1.10742192402385+0.389151908999031i.
IMLOG2	The base-2 logarithm of the specified complex number. For example, **=IMLOG2("8+10i")** returns 3.67877600230904+1.29273465968293i.
IMPOWER	The specified complex number raised to the specified power. For example, **=IMPOWER("4+2i",3)** returns 16+88i.
IMPRODUCT	The product of the specified complex numbers. For example, **=IMPRODUCT("3+4i","2+3i")** returns -6+17i.
IMREAL	The real coefficient of the specified complex number. For example, **=IMREAL("3+4i")** returns 3.
IMSIN	The sine of the specified complex number. For example, **=IMSIN("3+4i")** returns 3.85373803791938-27.0168132580039i.
IMSQRT	The square root of the specified complex number. For example, **=IMSQRT("3+4i")** returns 2+i.
IMSUB	The difference between the two specified complex numbers. For example, **=IMSUB("3+4i","4+5i")** returns -1-i.
IMSUM	The sum of the specified complex numbers. For example, **=IMSUM("3+4i","4+5i")** returns 7+9i.
OCT2BIN	The binary (base 2) equivalent of the specified octal (base 8) number, optionally specifying the number of characters to use. For example, **=OCT2BIN(45,8)** returns 00100101.
OCT2DEC	The decimal (base 10) equivalent of the specified octal (base 8) number. For example, **=OCT2DEC(45)** returns 37.

Engineering Function	What It Returns
OCT2HEX	The hexadecimal (base 16) equivalent of the specified octal (base 8) number. For example, =**OCT2HEX(45,8)** returns 00000025.

Financial Functions

Table 6–4 introduces you to Excel's financial functions, which cover most common financial calculations and various more specialized calculations.

Table 6–4. *Excel's Financial Functions*

Financial Function	What It Returns
ACCRINT	The interest accrued on a security that pays interest periodically. For example, =**ACCRINT(DATE(2010,8,1),DATE(2010,9,1),DATE(2010,8,15),10%,5000,4)** calculates the interest on a security with an issue date of 1 August 2010, a first interest date of 1 September 2010, a settlement date of 15 August 2010, an interest rate of 10% (I know—dream on), a par value of $5000, and a frequency of four coupon payments per year.
ACCRINTM	The interest accrued on a security that pays interest on maturity rather than along the way. For example, =**ACCRINTM(DATE(2011,1,15),DATE(2012,2,15),10%,10000)** calculates the interest on a security with an issue date of 15 January 2011, a maturity date of 15 February 2012, a rate of 10%, and a par value of $10,000.
AMORDEGRC	An asset's prorated linear depreciation for each accounting period (in the French accounting system). For example, =**AMORDEGRC(5000,DATE(2010,12,3),DATE(2011,3,30),2000,2,12.5%)** calculates the prorated linear depreciation of an asset bought on 3 December 2010 for $5000, putting the end of the first period on 30 March 2011, using a salvage value of $2000, two periods, and a 12.5% depreciation rate.
AMORLINC	An asset's prorated linear depreciation for each accounting period (in the French accounting system). For example, =**AMORLINC(4000,DATE(2010,12,3),DATE(2011,6,30),1500,1,18%)** calculates the prorated linear depreciation of an asset bought on 3 December 2010 for $4000, putting the end of the first and only period on 30 June 2011, using a salvage value of $1500 and an 18% depreciation rate.
COUPDAYBS	The number of days from the coupon period's beginning to the settlement date. For example, =**COUPDAYBS(DATE(2011,2,19),DATE(2013,2,19),4)** returns the number of days for a bond with a settlement date of 19 February 2011, a maturity date of 19 February 2013, and quarterly coupon payments.

Financial Function	What It Returns
COUPDAYS	The number of days in the coupon period containing the settlement date. For example, **=COUPDAYS(DATE(2011,3,1),DATE(2011,12,1),2)** returns the number of days from the start of the coupon period to the settlement date for a bond with a settlement date of 1 March 2011, a maturity date of 1 December 2011, and semiannual coupons.
COUPDAYSNC	The number of days to the next coupon date from the settlement date. For example, **=COUPDAYSNC(DATE(2011,7,4),DATE(2012,4,8),2)** calculates the number of days for a bond with a settlement date of 4 July 2011, a maturity date of 8 April 2012, and semiannual coupons.
COUPNCD	The next coupon date after the settlement date. For example, **=COUPNCD(DATE(2011,11,12), DATE(2012,12,13),4)** returns the next coupon date after the settlement date of 12 November 2011 for a bond with a maturity date of 13 December 2012 and quarterly coupons.
COUPNUM	The number of coupons payable between the settlement date and the maturity date. For example, **=COUPNUM(DATE(2011,1,5),DATE(2013,5,8),2)** returns the number of coupons payable between the settlement date of 5 January 2011 and the maturity date of 8 May 2013 for a bond with a semiannual coupon.
COUPPCD	The previous coupon date before the settlement date. For example, **=COUPPCD(DATE(2011,1,8),DATE(2014,1,8),4)** returns the previous coupon date before the settlement date of 8 January 2011 for a bond with a maturity date of 8 January 2014 and quarterly coupons.
CUMIPMT	The cumulative interest paid between the two periods specified. For example, **=CUMIPMT(1%,60,10000,1,12,1)** calculates the cumulative interest paid at a monthly rate of 1% (making 12% per year), on a loan that uses 60 periods (five years), with a value of $10,000. The function calculates the cumulative interest paid in the periods 1 to 12 (the first year), assuming the payment is at the beginning of the month (the final 1) rather than the end of the month (which would be represented by 0).
CUMPRINC	The cumulative principal paid on a loan between the two periods specified. For example, **=CUMPRINC(0.5%,24,1500,1,6,0)** calculates the cumulative principal paid on a $1500 loan for the first 6 months of a 24-month period. The loan uses a rate of 0.5% a month, and the payments are made at the end of the month (the 0 at the end) rather than at the start of the month (which would be represented by 1).
DB	The depreciation calculated using the fixed-declining balance method. For example, **=DB(1000,250,6,2)** calculates the second-year depreciation on an asset that costs $1000, has a salvage value of $250, and depreciates over six years.

Financial Function	What It Returns
DDB	The depreciation calculated using the double-declining balance method or another method. For example, =DDB(2000,500,8,4,2) calculates the fourth-year depreciation on an asset that costs $2000 and has a salvage value of $500. The asset's value depreciates over eight years using the double-declining balance method (represented by the 2 at the end).
DISC	The discount rate for a security. For example, =DISC(DATE(2011,1,11),DATE(2012,2,20),96.5,100,3) calculates the discount rate for a security with a settlement date of 11 January 2011, a maturity date of 20 January 2012, a price of $96.50 per $100, a redemption rate of $100 per $100 of face value, using the Actual/365 day count basis.
DOLLARDE	The decimal dollar price equivalent of the specified fractional dollar price. For example, =DOLLARDE(1.08,32) calculates the decimal dollar price of 1 dollar and 8/32, returning 1.25.
DOLLARFR	The fractional dollar price equivalent of the specified decimal dollar price. For example, =DOLLARFR(1.25,32) calculates the fractional dollar price equivalent of $1.25 in thirty-seconds, returning 1.08.
DURATION	The annual duration of a security that pays interest periodically. For example, =DURATION(DATE(2011,1,20),DATE(2012,6,12),7%,10%,2) calculates the annual duration of a security with a settlement date of 20 January 2011, a maturity date of 12 June 2011, an annual coupon rate of 7%, and an annual yield of 10%.
EFFECT	The effective annual interest rate. For example, =EFFECT(6%,4) calculates the effective annual interest rate for a 6% interest rate that uses four compounding periods per year.
FV	The future value of an investment. For example, =FV(8%/12,60,-500) calculates the future value of an investment into which you put $500 a month for 60 months and receive 8% interest over 12 months.
FVSCHEDULE	The future value of an investment to which compound interest rates have been applied. For example, =FVSCHEDULE(100,{0.09,0.1,0.11,0.12}) calculates the future value of an investment of $100 that receives 9% interest the first year, 10% interest the second year, 11% interest the third year, and 12 percent interest the fourth year.
INTRATE	The interest rate for a security that is fully vested. For example, =INTRATE(DATE(2011,1,20),DATE(2012,6,15),10000,11000) returns the interest rate on a $10,000 security with a settlement date of 20 January 2011, a maturity date of 15 June 2012, and a redemption value of $11,000.

Financial Function	What It Returns
IPMT	The interest payments for an investment for a specified period. For example, **=IPMT(4%/12,1,24,-1000)** calculates the interest period for the first month of a 24-month investment that has a value of $1000 and that receives a princely 4% divided over 12 months.
IRR	The internal rate of return for cash flows. For example, **=IRR({-50000,10000,12000,19000,28000})** calculates the internal rate of return for a venture than costs $50,000 up front and brings in $10,000 the first year, $12,000 the second year, $19,000 the third year, and $28,000 the fourth year.
ISPMT	The interest paid for an investment over a specified period. For example, **=ISPMT(7%/12,6,5*12,5000)** calculates the payment in the sixth month of a five-year (5*12 months) investment of $5,000 that earns 7% interest divided by 12 months.
MDURATION	The Macauley modified duration for a security that has an assumed par value of $100. For example, **=MDURATION(DATE(2011,2,18), DATE(2014,2,28),7%,9%,2)** calculates the Macauley modified duration for a security that has a settlement date of 18 February 2011, a maturity date of 28 February 2014, a 7% annual coupon rate, a 9% annual yield, and semiannual coupon payments.
MIRR	The modified internal rate of return for cash flows. For example, **=MIRR({-50000,10000,12000,19000,28000},3.5%,9%)** calculates the modified internal rate of return for a business than costs $50,000 to buy and brings in $10,000 the first year, $12,000 the second year, $19,000 the third year, and $28,000 the fourth year. You borrow money at 3.5% interest per year and manage to reinvest your cash flows at 9%.
NOMINAL	The annual nominal interest rate. For example, **=NOMINAL(4.6%,4)** calculates the annual nominal interest rate for an effective interest rate of 4.6% with four compounding periods per year.
NPER	The number of periods for an investment that uses constant payments and a constant rate of interest. For example, **=NPER(6.5%/12,-250,5000)** calculates the number of periods to pay off $5000 at $250 per month, given an interest rate of 6.5% annually (divided by 12 for the months).
NPV	The net present value of an investment. For example, **=NPV(8%/12,{500,750,1000})** calculates the net present value of an investment that brings in $500 in the first period, $750 in the second period, and $1000 in the third period, using an 8% discount rate divided by 12 months.

Financial Function	What It Returns
ODDFPRICE	The price per $100 face value of a security that uses an odd first period. For example, =**ODDFPRICE(DATE(2009,11,9),DATE(2016,4,1),DATE(2009,9,1), DATE(2010,2,1),0.08,0.065,100,2)** calculates the price per $100 face value of a security that has a settlement date of 9 November 2009, a maturity date of 1 April 2016, an issue date of 1 September 2009, and a first coupon date of 1 February 2010. The security has an interest rate of 8%, an annual yield of 0.065, a redemption value of $100 per $100 face value, and 2 coupon payments per year.
ODDFYIELD	The yield of a security that uses an odd first period. For example, =**ODDFYIELD (DATE(2010,10,1),DATE(2021,3,1),DATE(2010,9,15),DATE(2011,3,1),6%,86,100,2 ,0)** calculates the yield of a security that has a settlement date of 1 October 2010, a maturity date of 1 March 2021, an issue date of 15 September 2010, and a first coupon date of 1 March 2011. The security has a 6% interest rate, a price of $86, and a redemption value of $100. The coupon payments are semiannual, and the calculation uses the US 30/360 day count basis.
ODDLPRICE	The price per $100 face value of a security that uses an odd last period. For example, =**ODDLPRICE(DATE(2011,6,6),DATE(2012,8,4),DATE(2011,5,16), 7%,7.25%,100,4,0)** calculates the price per $100 face value of a security that has a settlement date of 6 June 2011, a maturity date of 4 August 2012, and a last interest date of 16 May 2011. The security has an interest rate of 7%, an annual yield of 7.25%, and a redemption value of $100. The coupon frequency is quarterly, with payments made on a 30/360 basis.
ODDLYIELD	The yield of a security that uses an odd last period. For example, =**ODDLYIELD(DATE(2011,7,11),DATE(2012,11,11),DATE(2011,5,4),4.25%,97.5,1 00,2)** calculates the yield on a security that has a settlement date of 11 July 2011, a maturity date of 11 November 2011, and a last interest date of 4 May 2011. The security draws a 4.25% interest rate, has a price of $97.50 and a redemption value of $100, and pays twice a year.
PMT	The payment for a loan that uses constant payments and a fixed interest rate. For example, =**PMT(8%/12,36,-5000)** calculates the monthly payment required to pay off a loan of $5000 in monthly payments over a 36–month period with an interest rate of 8%.
PPMT	The payment for a particular period on the principal for an investment that uses constant payments and a fixed interest rate. For example, =**PPMT(7.5%/12,1,24,- 2000)** calculates the payment for the first month of a 24-month plan on a $2000 investment running at 7.5% interest annually.
PRICE	The price per $100 face value of a security that pays interest periodically. For example, =**PRICE(DATE(2011,3,4),DATE(2012,6,5),6.5%,7.4%,100,4)** calculates the price per $100 face value of a security that has a settlement date of 4 March 2011 and a maturity date of 5 June 2012. The security has a 6.5% interest rate, a 7.4% yield, a $100 redemption value, and quarterly frequency.

Financial Function	What It Returns
PRICEDISC	The price per $100 face value of a discounted security. For example, **=PRICEDISC(DATE(2011,8,4),DATE(2012,9,17),5%,100)** calculates the price per $100 face value of a security with a settlement date of 4 August 2011 and a maturity date of 17 September 2012. The security has a 5% discount rate and a $100 redemption value.
PRICEMAT	The price per $100 face value of a security that pays interest when it reaches maturity. For example, **=PRICEMAT(DATE(2011,8,14),DATE(2013,5,5),DATE (2011,6,15),8.5%,8%)** calculates the price per $100 face value of a security with a settlement date of 14 August 2011, a maturity date of 5 May 2013, and an issue date of 15 June 2011. The security has an interest rate of 8.5% and an annual yield of 8%.
PV	The present value of an investment—how much a series of future payments is worth altogether now. For example, **=PV(10%/12,36,-250)** calculates how much 36 monthly payments of $250 is worth at 10% interest.
RATE	The interest rate per period of an investment. For example, **=RATE(60,-380,14000)** calculates the interest rate per month on a $14,000 investment that receives $380 per month for 60 months.
RECEIVED	The value at maturity of a fully invested security. For example, **=RECEIVED (DATE(2011,7,17),DATE(2013,8,4),10000,4%)** calculates the value at maturity of a security worth $10,000 with a settlement date of 17 July 2011, a maturity date of 4 August 2013, and a discount rate of 4%.
SLN	The straight-line depreciation for an asset over one period. For example, **=SLN(3000,300,3)** calculates the depreciation per period of an asset that costs $3,000 new and has a salvage value of $300 after 3 years. (That's right—it's a high-end computer.)
SYD	The sum-of-years' digits depreciation for an asset over a specified period. For example, **=SYD(3000,300,3,1)** shows how much you lose on the previous example's $3000 computer (with a salvage value of $300 after 3 years) in the first year.
TBILLEQ	A percentage showing the bond-equivalent yield of a treasury bill. For example, **=TBILLEQ(DATE(2011,12,1),DATE(2012,8,1),8.2%)** shows the bond-equivalent yield of a treasury bill with a settlement date of 1 December 2011, a maturity date of 1 August 2012, and an 8.2% discount rate. The maturity date must be one year or less after the settlement date.

Financial Function	What It Returns
TBILLPRICE	A treasury bill's price per $100 face value. For example, **=TBILLPRICE(DATE (2011,9,10),DATE(2012,7,12),7.2%)** calculates the price per $100 face value of a treasury bill with a settlement date of 10 September 2011, a maturity date of 12 July 2012, and a discount rate of 7.2 percent. The maturity date must be one year or less after the settlement date.
TBILLYIELD	A percentage showing a treasury bill's yield. For example, **=TBILLYIELD(DATE (2011,8,20),DATE(2012,8,19),94.25)** calculates the yield for a treasury bill with a settlement date of 20 August 2011, a maturity date of 19 August 2012, and a price per $100 face value of $94.25.
VDB	The depreciation for an asset using the double-declining balance method or a variable declining balance. For example, **=VDB(8000,2000,10,2,3,3)** calculates the depreciation for an asset with an initial cost of $8000 and a salvage value of $2000 after 10 years. The function calculates the depreciation for the second to third year of the asset's life, using a depreciation factor of 3.
XIRR	The internal rate of return (IRR) for a schedule of cash flows with variable dates rather than regular dates. For example, **=XIRR(E43:E46,F43:F46)** calculates the internal rate of return for the cash flows in the range E43:E46 and the dates in the range F43:F46.
XNPV	The net present value (NPV) for cash flows that use a variable schedule (or a periodic schedule—but for periodic cash flows, NPV is usually a better choice). For example, **=XNPV(10%,{1000,900},F43:F44)** calculates the net present value for the cash flows $1000 and $900 and their corresponding dates in the range F43:F44, using a 10% discount rate.
YIELD	The yield on a security that has periodic interest payments, such as a bond. For example, **=YIELD(DATE(2011,8,10),DATE(2014,7,12),7.25%,94.75,100,4)** calculates the yield on a security that has a settlement date of 10 August 2010, a maturity date of 12 July 2014, and an interest rate of 7.25%. The security's price is $94.75, its redemption value is $100, and its frequency is quarterly.
YIELDDISC	A discounted security's annual yield. For example, **=YIELDDISC(DATE (2011,3,15),DATE(2012,9,14),94.5,100)** calculates the annual yield on a security with a settlement date of 15 March 2011, a maturity date of 14 September 2012, a price of $94.50, and a redemption value of $100.
YIELDMAT	The annual yield of a security that pays interest when it matures. For example, **=YIELDMAT(DATE(2011,5,10),DATE(2013,4,30),DATE(2011,3,31),8%,93.2)** calculates the annual yield of a security with a settlement date of 10 May 2011, a maturity date of 30 April 2013, an issue date of 31 March 2011, an interest rate of 8 %, and a price of $93.2 per $100 face value.

NOTE: For a security or investment, the *issue date* is when the seller makes the instrument available. The *settlement date* is when the buyer purchases a coupon for the financial instrument. The *maturity date* is when the instrument comes to term and the coupon expires.

Logical Functions

When you need to evaluate logical conditions, use Excel's logical functions, which you'll find explained in Table 6–5. For many worksheets, after using a logical function to find out the situation, you'll want to use other functions to make Excel take suitable actions.

Table 6–5. *Excel's Logical Functions*

Logical Function	What It Returns
AND	TRUE if all the specified arguments are TRUE; otherwise FALSE. For example, **=AND(C1="Minneapolis",D1=2012)** returns TRUE if cell C1 contains the text "Minneapolis" and D1 contains the value 2012.
FALSE	FALSE. You use this function to generate a FALSE value—for example, for testing. Simply enter **=FALSE()** in the cell that you need to provide a FALSE value.
IF	The first of the specified values if the condition is TRUE, the second of the specified values if the condition is FALSE. For example, **=IF(HOUR(NOW())<12,"AM","PM")** displays "AM" if the current hour is less than 12 and "PM" otherwise.
IFERROR	The specified error value if the expression causes an error; otherwise, the expression itself. For example, **=IFERROR(E4,"Enter a value in cell E3.")** displays the message "Enter a value in cell E3" if cell E4 contains an error.
NOT	FALSE from a TRUE value, or TRUE from a FALSE value. For example, **=NOT(TRUE)** returns FALSE.
OR	TRUE if any of the specified conditions is TRUE; FALSE if all the conditions are FALSE. For example, **=OR(F6="Minneapolis",F6="Little Rock", F6="Sioux Falls")** returns TRUE if one of the three city names appears in cell F6; otherwise, it returns FALSE.
TRUE	TRUE. You use this function to generate a TRUE value—for example, for testing. Simply enter **=TRUE()** in the cell that you need to provide a TRUE value.

Information Functions

When you need to return information about the contents or formatting of a particular cell or range, use the information functions that Table 6–6 explains.

Table 6–6. *Excel's Information Functions*

Information Function	What It Returns
CELL	The details of the contents, location, or formatting of the first cell in the range you specify. You can return various pieces of information. For example, **=CELL("address",Tax_Rate)** returns the address of the cell with the defined name Tax_Rate.
ERROR.TYPE	A number giving the error type the cell contains: 1 for #NULL!, 2 for #DIV/0!, 3 for #VALUE!, 4 for #REF!, 5 for #NAME?, 6 for #NUM!, and 7 for #N/A. For example, **=IF(ERROR.TYPE(F3)=2,"Enter a number other than zero in cell F2.")** displays a message in cell F3 if it contains a divide-by-zero error.
INFO	Information about Excel, the operating system, or the computer. For example, **=INFO("system")** returns "mac" if Excel is running on a Mac or "pcdos" if Excel is running on a PC. **=INFO("release")** returns the version of Excel—for instance, 14.0 for Excel 2011.
ISBLANK	TRUE if the cell is blank; FALSE if it has contents. For example, **=ISBLANK(A24)** returns TRUE if cell A24 is blank.
ISERR	TRUE if the cell contains any error except #N/A; otherwise FALSE. For example, **=ISERR(B3)** returns TRUE if cell B3 contains any error except #N/A.
ISERROR	TRUE if the cell contains any error (including #N/A); otherwise FALSE. For example, **ISERROR(B3)** returns TRUE if cell B3 contains any error.
ISEVEN	TRUE if the cell contains an even number (ignoring any decimal places); otherwise FALSE. For example, **=ISEVEN(4.7)** returns TRUE.
ISLOGICAL	TRUE if the cell contains a logical value; otherwise FALSE. For example, **=ISLOGICAL(B10)** returns TRUE if cell B10 contains the value TRUE or the value FALSE.
ISNA	TRUE if the cell contains #N/A; otherwise FALSE. For example, **=ISNA(C8)** returns TRUE if cell C8 contains #N/A.
ISNONTEXT	TRUE if the cell is blank or contains anything except text, FALSE if the cell contains text. For example, **=ISNONTEXT(B1)** returns FALSE if cell B1 contains text.

Information Function	What It Returns
ISNUMBER	TRUE if the cell contains a number; otherwise FALSE. For example, **=ISNUMBER(B1)** returns TRUE if cell B1 contains a number.
ISODD	TRUE if the cell contains an odd number; otherwise FALSE. For example, **=ISODD(A14)** returns TRUE if cell A14 contains an odd number.
ISREF	TRUE if the value is a valid reference to a cell, range, or defined name; otherwise FALSE. For example, **=ISREF("Gross_Income")** returns TRUE if the workbook contains a range named Gross_Income.
ISTEXT	TRUE if the cell contains text; otherwise FALSE. For example, **ISTEXT(A1)** returns TRUE if cell A1 contains text.
N	A number converted from the specified value. Specifically, a number returns the same number; a date returns the equivalent serial date; TRUE returns 1, and FALSE returns 0; an error returns its error value (explained the ERROR.TYPE entry earlier in this table); and anything else returns 0. Because Excel automatically converts values, you seldom need to use this function; Excel provides it for compatibility with other spreadsheet applications.
NA	#N/A. You use this function to enter the error value deliberately in the cell. For example, enter **=NA()** in cell A1 causes it to show the error value #N/A.
TYPE	A number representing the data type the cell contains: 1 for a number, 2 for text, 4 for a logical value, 16 for an error value, and 64 for an array. For example, **=TYPE(B2)** returns 2 if cell B2 contains text.

Lookup and Reference Functions

For returning information from lists and tables (flat-file databases), Excel includes the lookup and reference functions explained in Table 6–7.

Table 6–7. *Excel's Lookup and Reference Functions*

Lookup and Reference Function	What It Returns
ADDRESS	The cell reference denoted by the row number and the column number.
AREAS	The number of different areas contained in a reference. An area can be either a single cell or a range of contiguous cells (not a range of noncontiguous cells).
CHOOSE	The value (in a set of values) that you specify by index number.
COLUMN	The column number of the reference you provide.
COLUMNS	The number of columns in the reference or array.
GETPIVOTDATA	Data from a PivotTable report.
HLOOKUP	The value from the specified row in the data table. Horizontal lookup matches the field in the top row of the table, then returns the value from the specified row further down the same column.
HYPERLINK	Contains a hyperlink.
INDEX	A value from a table or a reference to such a value.
INDIRECT	A reference specified by a text string in a cell. You can use INDIRECT to change the reference in the cell without changing the formula.
LOOKUP	A value from either a one-column or one-range row or from an array.
MATCH	The position of a matching item in an array (rather than the item's contents).
OFFSET	A reference to the range offset from a specified cell or range by the number of rows and columns you specify.
ROW	The row number of the specified reference.
ROWS	The number of rows in the specified reference or array.
TRANSPOSE	Cells transposed from a vertical range to a horizontal range, or vice versa. You must use TRANSPOSE as an array formula.
VLOOKUP	The value from the specified column in the data table. Vertical lookup matches the field in the first column of the table, then returns the value from the specified column further across the same row.

Mathematical and Trigonometric Functions

Table 6–8 explains the mathematical and trigonometric functions that Excel offers, providing examples only for those that are less straightforward.

Table 6–8. *Excel's Mathematical and Trigonometric Functions*

Mathematical and Trigonometric Function	What It Returns
ABS	The absolute value of the specified number.
ACOS	The arccosine of the specified number.
ACOSH	The inverse hyperbolic cosine of the specified number.
AGGREGATE	An aggregate in the specified list or database.
ASIN	The arcsine of the specified number.
ASINH	The inverse hyperbolic sine of the specified number.
ATAN	The arctangent of the specified number.
ATAN2	The arctangent from the specified x and y coordinates.
CEILING	The specified number rounded to the nearest integer or to the nearest significant multiple.
CEILINGPRECISE	The specified number rounded up to the nearest integer or the nearest significant multiple.
COMBIN	The number of combinations for the specified number of items.
COS	The cosine of the specified angle.
COSH	The hyperbolic cosine of the specified number.
DEGREES	The number of degrees for the specified number of radians.
EVEN	The next integer up from the specified positive number, or the next integer down from the specified negative number.
EXP	e raised to the power of the specified number.
FACT	The factorial of the specified number (for example, 1x2x3x4 if you specify 4).
FACTDOUBLE	The double factorial of the specified number.

Mathematical and Trigonometric Function	What It Returns
FLOOR	The specified number rounded down to the next significant multiple.
FLOOR.PRECISE	The specified number rounded down to the nearest integer or the nearest significant multiple.
GCD	The greatest common divisor for the specified numbers. For example, **=GCD(240,100)** returns 20.
INT	The specified number rounded down to the nearest integer.
LCM	The least common multiple of the specified numbers. For example, **=LCM(3,4)** returns 12.
LN	The natural logarithm of the specified number.
LOG	The logarithm of the specified number to the base you enter. For example, **=LOG(12,2)** returns the logarithm of 12 with base 2.
LOG10	The base-10 logarithm of the specified number.
MDETERM	The matrix determinant of the specified array.
MINVERSE	The inverse matrix for the specified array.
MMULT	The matrix product of the two specified arrays. Each array must have the same number of rows and columns as the other.
MOD	The modulus (remainder) after the specified number is divided by the specified divisor. For example, **=MOD(7,2)** returns 1.
MROUND	The specified number rounded to the specified multiple. For example, **=MROUND(7,3)** returns 6.
MULTINOMIAL	The multinomial of the specified set of numbers.
ODD	The next odd integer above the specified positive number, or the next odd integer below the specified negative number.
PI	The value of Pi to 15 digits (3.14159265358979).
POWER	The specified number raised to the specified power. For example, **=POWER(10,5)** returns 100000.
PRODUCT	The product of the specified numbers. For example, **=PRODUCT(2,3,4)**

Mathematical and Trigonometric Function	What It Returns
	returns 24.
QUOTIENT	The quotient, the integer portion of a division. For example, **=QUOTIENT(25,3)** returns 8.
RADIANS	The number of radians for the specified number of degrees.
RAND	A random number between 0 and 1, inclusive. The number changes each time you recalculate the worksheet. (Technically, the number is pseudo-random rather than truly random; this distinction is important for some purposes.)
RANDBETWEEN	A random number between the specified bottom value and top value. For example, **=RANDBETWEEN(1,10)** returns a random number between 1 and 10, inclusive. The number changes each time you recalculate the worksheet. (Technically, the number is pseudo-random rather than truly random,)
ROMAN	The Roman numeral equivalent of the specified Arabic numeral. For example, **=ROMAN(2011)** returns MMXI.
ROUND	The specified number rounded to the specified number of digits. For example, **=ROUND(3.33333,2)** returns 3.33.
ROUNDDOWN	The specified number rounded down to the specified number of digits. For example, **=ROUNDDOWN(18.57321,2)** returns 18.57.
ROUNDUP	The specified number rounded up to the specified number of digits. For example, **=ROUNDUP(18.57321,2)** returns 18.58.
SERIESSUM	The sum of a power series.
SIGN	Returns 1 if the specified number is positive, 0 if it is zero, or -1 if it is negative.
SIN	The sine of the specified angle.
SINH	The hyperbolic sine of the specified number.
SQRT	The square root of the specified number.
SQRTPI	The square root of the specified number multiplied by Pi.
SUBTOTAL	The subtotal of the specified section of a database.
SUM	The sum of the specified numbers. For example, **=SUM(1,2,3)** returns 6.

Mathematical and Trigonometric Function	What It Returns
SUMIF	The sum of the cells specified by a criterion.
SUMIFS	The sum of the cells specified by multiple criteria.
SUMPRODUCT	The sum of the products in the specified ranges or arrays.
SUMSQ	The sum of the squares of the specified numbers. For example, **=SUMSQ(3,4)** returns 25.
SUMX2MY2	The sum of the differences between the squares of the two specified ranges.
SUMX2PY2	The sum total of the sums of the squares of numbers in the two specified ranges.
SUMXMY2	The sum of the squares of the differences in the two specified ranges.
TAN	The tangent of the specified angle.
TANH	The hyperbolic tangent of the specified number.
TRUNC	The specified number truncated to the specified number of digits. For example, **=TRUNC(24.567,1)** returns 24.5.

Statistical Functions

Excel includes many statistical functions for statistical calculations such as these:

- *Deviations.* These functions include AVEDEV, STDEVA, STDEV, and STDEVP.

- *Distributions.* These functions include BETADIST, CHIDIST, BINOMDIST, EXPONDIST, KURT, POISSON, and WEIBULL

- *Transformations.* These functions include FISHER and FISHERINV.

Many of the statistical functions are too specialized to cover here. Table 6–9 covers the statistical functions that are used for more general business and study purposes. If you work with statistics, look through the full list in the Statistical section of the Formula Builder list to find the other functions you want.

Table 6–9. *Excel's Most Widely Useful Statistical Functions*

Statistical Function	What It Returns
AVERAGE	The average of the specified values, cells, ranges, or arrays. For example, **=AVERAGE(1,2,3)** returns 2, and **=AVERAGE(B1:B6)** returns the average of the range B1:B6.
MEDIAN	The median (the number in the middle of the given set) of the numbers or the values in the specified cells. For example, **=MEDIAN(1,2,2,3,4,4,6)** returns 3.
MODE	The mode, the value that occurs most frequently in the specified values or range of cells. For example, **=MODE(1,1,2,2,2,3,3,4,18)** returns 2.
COUNT	The number of cells in the specified range that either contain numbers or include numbers in their list of arguments. For example, **=COUNT(C1:C8)** returns the number of cells in the range C1:C8 that contain numbers or include numbers.
COUNTBLANK	The number of empty cells in the specified range. For example, **=COUNTBLANK(C1:C8)** returns the number of empty cells in the range C1:C8.
COUNTIF	The number of cells in the specified range that meet the criteria you set. For example, **=COUNTIF(C1:C10,">2")** counts the cells in the range C1:C10 that contain numbers larger than 2.
MAX	The largest value in the specified range. For example, **=MAX(C1:C6)** returns the largest value in the range C1:C6.
MIN	The lowest value in the specified range. For example, **=MIN(C1:C6)** returns the lowest value in the range C1:C6.

Text Functions

When you need to manipulate text in your worksheets, use the text functions explained in Table 6–10. For example, you may need to return only a particular part of a text string, find one string in another string, or change the case of text.

Table 6–10. *Excel's Text Functions*

Text Function	What It Returns
BAHTTEXT	The number converted to Thai text and with the *Baht* suffix.
CHAR	The character represented by the specified character code. For example, **=CHAR(66)** returns a B. Normally, you'd just type the letters you need, but this function can be useful when working with workbooks created using different characters sets.
CLEAN	The specified text string with all nonprintable characters removed. For example, **=CLEAN(A1)** strips all nonprintable characters from the text string in cell A1. This function is sometimes useful when importing files created in other spreadsheet formats.
CODE	The character code for the first character in the specified string. For example, **=CODE("$")** returns 36, the character code for the $ sign.
CONCATENATE	A text string consisting of the specified text strings joined together. For example, **=CONCATENATE("San Francisco ","Depot")** returns the text string "San Francisco Depot." Note that you must include any spaces needed— otherwise, Excel smashes the text together. Instead of using this function, you can simply use the concatenation operator (the & sign).
DOLLAR	The specified number converted to text in the Currency format. For example, **=DOLLAR(9)** returns $9.00.
EXACT	TRUE if the two text strings match exactly, containing the same characters in the same case; otherwise FALSE. For example, **=EXACT("Oakland","OAKLAND")** returns FALSE because the two strings use different case.
FIND	The starting position of one specified text string within another text string. This function is case-sensitive. For example, **=FIND("juve","Bovine Rejuvenation Ointment")** returns 10, because the *j* is the tenth character (including the space).
FIXED	The specified number rounded to the specified number of decimals, with or without commas. For example, **=FIXED("10.8726",2)** returns 10.87.
LEFT	The specified number of characters from the beginning of the text string. For example, **=LEFT("Product Ratings",7)** returns "Product."

Text Function	What It Returns
LEN	The number of characters in the specified text string, including spaces. For example, **=LEN("Product Ratings")** returns 15.
LOWER	The text string converted to lowercase. For example, **=LOWER("OAKLAND WAREHOUSE")** returns "oakland warehouse."
MID	The specified number of characters after the starting point given in the specified text string. For example, **=MID("Human Heart-Rate Monitor",7,10)** returns "Heart-Rate."
PROPER	The text string converted to "proper case" (first letter capitalized, the rest lowercase). For example, **=PROPER("OAKLAND WAREHOUSE")** returns "Oakland Warehouse."
REPLACE	The specified text string with the given replacement string inserted in the location specified. For example, **=REPLACE("Human Heart-Rate Monitor",7,10,"Pulse")** returns "Human Pulse Monitor."
REPT	The specified text string repeated the specified number of times. For example, **=REPT("IMPROVED! ",4)** returns "IMPROVED! IMPROVED! IMPROVED! IMPROVED!"
RIGHT	The specified number of characters from the end of specified text string. For example, **=RIGHT("Product Ratings",7)** returns "Ratings."
SEARCH	The character position at which the specified character is located in the specified string. For example, **=SEARCH("P","Human Pulse Monitor")** returns 7, the position of the letter *P* in the string "Human Pulse Monitor."
SUBSTITUTE	The specified text string with the given new text string substituted for the specified old text string. For example, **=SUBSTITUTE("Make the Most of Excel 2008","Excel 2008","Excel 2011")** replaces the text "Excel 2008" with the text "Excel 2011" in the text string "Make the Most of Excel 2008."
T	The text string for a text value, or empty double quotation marks (a blank string) for a nontext value. For example, **=T(A19)** returns the text string or a blank string for the contents of cell A19. You don't normally need to use the T function, because Excel automatically converts values to text as needed.
TEXT	The text string containing the specified value converted to the format chosen. For example, **="Results for " &TEXT("4 August 2011","mmmm yyyy")** returns "Results for August 2011" because of the format specified in the function.
TRIM	The specified text string with spaces removed from the beginning and ends, and extra spaces between words removed to leave one space between words. For example, **=TRIM(" 4512 Christy Blvd. ")** strips out the superfluous spaces and returns "4512 Christy Blvd."

Text Function	What It Returns
UPPER	The text string converted to uppercase. For example, **=UPPER("don't walk")** returns "DON'T WALK."
VALUE	The value contained in the specified text string. For example, **=VALUE("5")** returns 5. Normally, you seldom need to use this function, because Excel converts values automatically as needed.

Choosing the Right Calculation Preferences for Your Needs

If you create complex worksheets, you may need to change the calculation settings Excel uses—for example, by switching from automatic recalculation to manual recalculation, by limiting the number of iterations Excel performs, or by changing values from full precision to the number of decimal places actually shown in the cells.

To change the calculation settings, open the Calculation preferences pane (see Figure 6–8) like this:

1. Choose Excel ➤Preferences or press Cmd+, (Cmd and the comma key) to display the Excel Preferences dialog box.

2. In the Formulas and Lists area, click the Calculation icon.

> **CAUTION:** In the Calculation preferences pane, the Calculate sheets options and the Iteration options affect all your workbooks, not just the active workbook. The Workbook options affect only the active workbook.

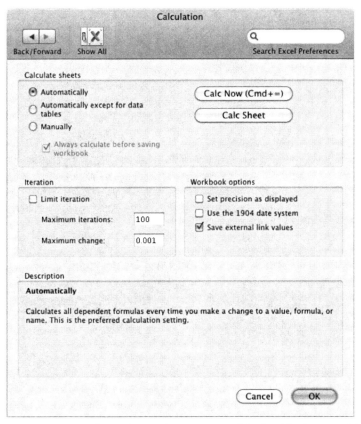

Figure 6–8. *In the Calculations preferences pane of the Excel Preferences dialog box, you can choose when to calculate worksheets, limit iteration, and change workbook-specific options.*

Choosing When to Calculate Worksheets

In the Calculate sheets box, first choose how to recalculate the worksheets by selecting the appropriate option button:

- *Automatically*. Select this option button to have Excel recalculate all dependent formulas every time you change a value. This is the default setting and ensures your worksheets remain up-to-date. Use this setting unless your worksheets are complex and recalculating them becomes slow.

- *Automatically except for data tables*. Select this option button to recalculate all dependent cells except those in data tables each time you change a value. Use this setting when recalculating data tables automatically becomes too slow. You can then recalculate data tables manually as needed.

- *Manually.* Select this option button to turn off automatic recalculation altogether. Use this setting for large and complex worksheets in which automatic recalculation becomes slow enough to be disruptive.

If you select the Manually option button, select the Always calculate before saving workbook check box if you want Excel to recalculate each workbook when you save it. The advantage to doing this is that it ensures that the saved version of the workbook displays the correct values, which is especially important the next time you open the workbook. The disadvantage is that saving the workbook takes much longer.

You can force recalculation of the entire workbook by clicking the Calc Now button in the Calculate sheets box in the Calculation preferences pane, or force recalculation of the active worksheet by clicking the Calc Sheet button. But normally you'll find it easier to recalculate by choosing **Formulas ➤ Calculation ➤ Recalculate** All (or pressing Cmd+=) or **Formulas ➤ Calculation ➤ Recalculate Sheet** from the Ribbon.

> **TIP:** You can quickly switch between automatic recalculation and manual recalculation by choosing **Formulas ➤ Calculation ➤ Settings ➤ Calculate Manually** or **Formulas ➤ Calculation ➤ Settings ➤ Calculate Automatically** from the Ribbon. To open the Calculation preferences pane from the Ribbon, choose **Formulas ➤ Calculation ➤ Settings ➤ Calculation Options**.

Controlling Iteration of Calculations

When Excel runs into a circular reference, it stops automatically either after 100 iterations of the calculation or when all the values change by less than 0.001. These settings work well for general use—especially if your worksheets don't need circular references (as is the case for many worksheets).

If your worksheets do need circular references, **you** can control the iteration of calculations by adjusting the settings in the Iteration box in the Calculation preferences pane. Select the Limit iteration check box, and then adjust the values in the Maximum iterations text box and the Maximum change text box as necessary.

Choosing Workbook Options

In the Workbook options box in the Calculation preferences pane, you can choose three settings that affect only the active workbook:

- *Set precision as displayed.* Select this check box if you want Excel to change the values in the workbook's cells to match the values that are displayed in the cells. Excel stores values using 15 digits, which is called full precision. You can format cells to display only as many decimal places as you want. For example, you may need to see currency amounts with two decimal places (such as $110.28), even though the number Excel is storing has further digits (such as 110.2769821). If you select the Set precision as displayed check box, Excel changes the underlying value to match the displayed value—for example, changing 110.2769821 to 110.28.

CAUTION: Select the Set precision as displayed check box only if you're dead certain you need to change the values—for example, because you're performing a financial operation that requires you to round or truncate a value and then use that rounded or truncated value rather than the underlying value. Normally, you want to keep the underlying precise values even if you format the cells to display only a small number of decimal places (or none).

- *Use the 1904 date system.* Select this check box to use serial dates starting with 2 January 1904 rather than 1 January 1901, the standard start date. Normally, you will need to do this only if you're working with dates in workbooks developed in earlier versions of Excel:Mac.

- *Save external link values.* Select this check box if you want Excel to save values from an external data source in the workbook. This is usually a good idea, but you may need to clear this check box if you're bringing in large amounts of data from an external source, as saving the data in Excel may take a long time or make the workbook large and unwieldy.

When you've finished choosing Calculation preferences, click the OK button to close the Excel Preferences dialog box.

Summary

In this chapter, you learned how to use functions to perform calculations in your workbooks. You know that a function is a preset formula built into Excel, how to insert functions using the various tools Excel provides, and how to furnish functions with the arguments they need to work. You met Excel's main categories of functions and learned about the most useful functions they contain for general use.

In the next chapter, I'll show you how to create clear and persuasive charts.

Chapter 7

Creating Clear and Persuasive Charts

In this chapter, you'll learn how to create powerful charts that present your data clearly and persuasively.

We'll start by going over the essentials of charts, such as the different ways you can place them in your workbooks, which components charts have, and which types of charts you can create. We'll then spend most of the chapter looking in detail at how you create a chart from your data, lay it out the way you want, then give it the look it needs—everything from displaying or hiding components to formatting components for impact.

Once you've created a chart that looks just right, you can reuse your custom chart formatting by either pasting it onto an existing chart or by creating a custom chart template from it.

At the end of the chapter, you'll learn how to use your Excel charts in Word documents or PowerPoint presentations.

Learning the Essentials of Charts in Excel

Before you start creating charts, let's look at the two ways you can place charts in your workbooks, go over what the different components of charts are called and what they show, and get an overview of the many different types of charts that Excel offers you.

Understanding Embedded Charts and Chart Sheets

In Excel, you can place a chart either on a worksheet (for example, with its data) or on its own chart sheet:

■ *Chart on a worksheet.* Excel calls a chart on a worksheet an *embedded chart*—the chart object is embedded in the worksheet. Usually, the worksheet also contains the chart's data, but you can embed a chart on a different worksheet if necessary. Create an embedded chart when you want to look at the chart alongside its data or alongside other information. Figure 7–1 shows an embedded chart.

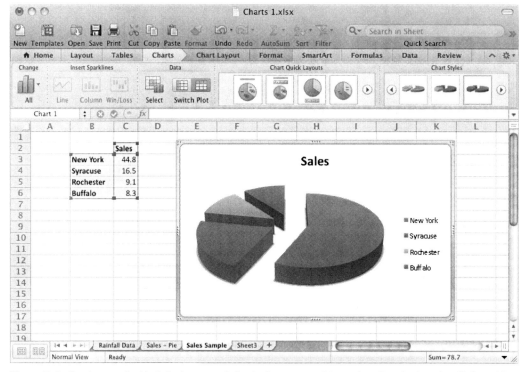

Figure 7–1. *Create an embedded chart on a worksheet when you want to work on the chart or view it alongside its data.*

■ *Chart on chart sheet.* Instead of creating an embedded chart, you can create a chart on a *chart sheet*—a separate sheet in the workbook that contains only a chart. Using a chart sheet gives you more space to lay out the chart and view it. The chart sheet doesn't contain the source data, but you can add a data table showing the source data if you don't mind sacrificing some of the chart sheet's space for the table. Figure 7–2 shows a chart on a chart sheet without a data table.

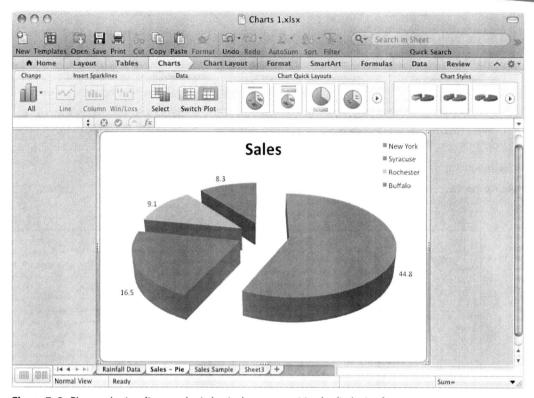

Figure 7–2. *Place a chart on its own chart sheet when you want to give it plenty of space.*

NOTE: You can change an embedded chart to a chart on its own chart sheet, or a chart on a chart sheet to an embedded chart, as needed. I'll show you how to do so a little later in this chapter.

Understanding the Components of a Chart

Excel's charts vary widely in looks and uses, but most of them use the same set of components. Figure 7–3 shows a typical type of chart—a 3-D column chart—of rainfall data for six months for seven weather stations, with the main parts of the chart labeled.

NOTE: If you have some sample data you're ready to turn into a chart, select the data and choose **Charts ➤ Insert Chart ➤ Column**, then click a chart type on the Column panel. This will give you a quick column chart that you can experiment with as we go through the components of charts. If you'd like to create your own version of the Rainfall Data chart used for most of the examples in this chapter, go to the Apress website (www.apress.com), locate this book's support page, and download the workbook named 35217 chart.xlsx.

The following sections discuss the individual components of charts.

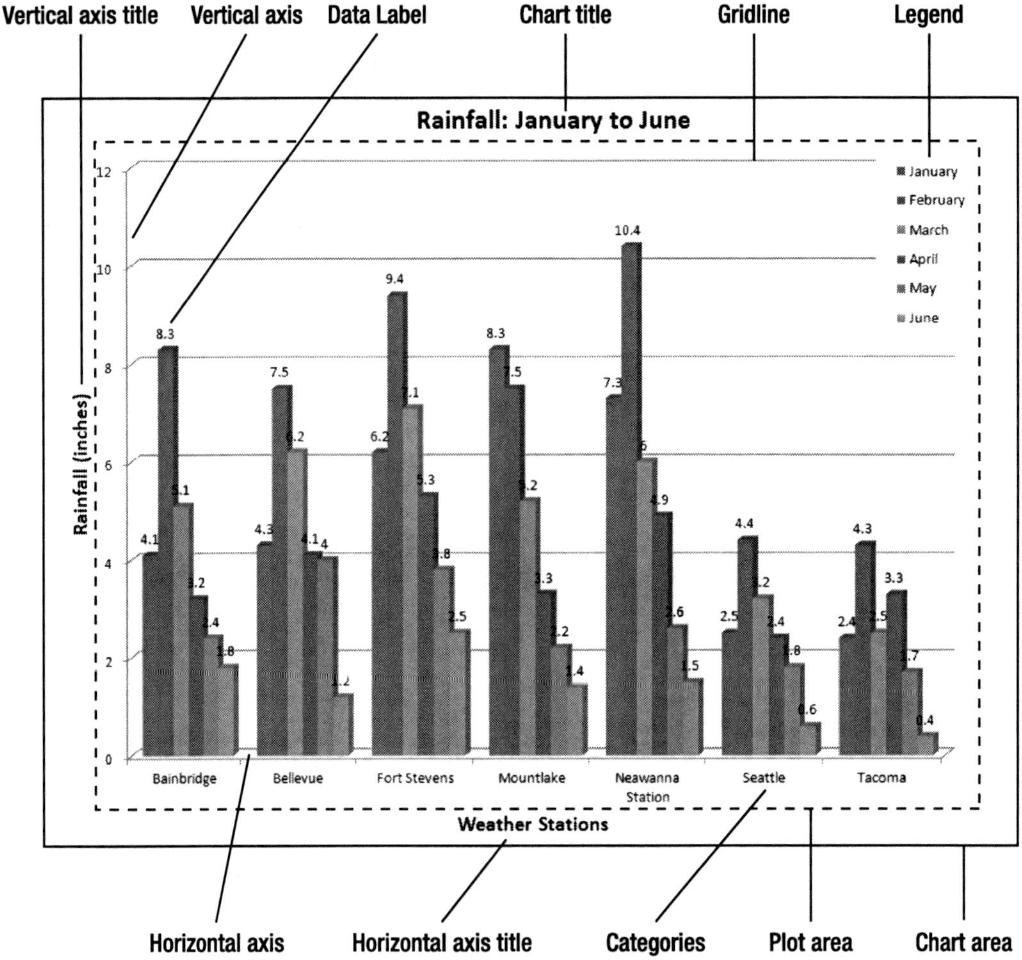

Figure 7–3. *This column chart contains most of the typical elements of Excel charts. The chart area is the whole area occupied by the chart, and the plot area is where the data series are plotted.*

Chart Area and Plot Area

The *chart area* is the whole area occupied by the chart. If the chart has a white background, the easiest way to see the extent of the chart area is to click the chart so that Excel displays a border around it.

The *plot area* is the area of the chart that contains the plotted data—in other words, the main part of the chart area, excluding the areas occupied by the chart title, the axis titles, and the legend (if it appears outside the plot area).

Chart Axes

Most charts have one, two, or three axes:

■ *Horizontal axis.* This is the axis along which the data categories are laid out—for example, the weather stations in the sample chart. This axis is also called the *category axis* or the *x-axis.*

■ *Vertical axis.* This is the axis along which the data series are laid out. This axis is also called the y-*axis.*

■ *Depth axis.* In 3-D charts, this is the axis that provides the third dimension. This axis is also called the z-*axis.*

Each axis has tick marks that show where the values appear on it.

Categories and Data Series

The *categories* are the subdivisions of data that appear on the horizontal axis. For example, in the sample chart, each weather station is a category.

The *data series* are the sets of data used to create the chart. For example, in the sample chart, the data series contain the rainfall measurements.

Chart Title and Axis Titles

The *chart title* is text that identifies the chart as a whole. Normally, you put the chart title at the top of the chart, where the reader will see it immediately, but you can place it elsewhere if you want. For example, you may place the chart title in open space in the chart area so that you can make the chart itself larger.

The *horizontal axis title* is text that explains what is shown on the horizontal axis; for example, the weather stations in the sample chart.

The *vertical axis title* is text that explains what the vertical axis shows; for example, the amount of rainfall in the sample chart.

A 3-D chart can also have a *depth axis title* that explains what the depth axis shows.

NOTE: Chart titles and axis titles are optional, so you can include only those your chart needs. Generally, people viewing your charts will benefit from having clear chart titles and axis titles. But don't feel obliged to include any element that seems to complicate your charts. Remember the adage, "if in doubt, leave it out."

Data Markers, Gridlines, and Data Labels

The *data markers* are the points on the chart that show where each data point appears. Each series typically contains several data markers. Depending on the chart type, the data markers may appear as separate points, or they may be linked together.

To make it easy to see how the data markers relate to the axes, you can add *gridlines* to the chart—lines that run across or up from the data markers.

Data labels are text items that display the exact value of data points. You can display data labels when viewers need to see the exact figure for each data point rather than judging the value from the chart.

Choosing the Best Chart Type for Your Data

Excel enables you to create an impressive variety of different types of charts. Some of the charts are useful for many purposes, whereas others are highly specialized. Table 7–1 describes the types of charts that Excel provides and suggests typical uses for them. The table lists the charts in the same order as Excel's Chart panel, which I'll describe shortly and which puts the most widely used chart types first.

Table 7–1. *Excel's Chart Types and Suggested Uses*

Chart Category	Description	Suggested Uses
Column	Displays data in vertical bars.	Comparing equivalent items (such as sales results) or sets of data that change over time (such as rainfall).
Line	Displays each series in a line.	Showing evenly spaced values that change over time, such as temperatures.
Pie	Displays a single data series as a pie divided up by the contribution of each data point.	Showing how much each item contributes to the whole; for example, breaking down expenses by department.
Bar	Displays data in horizontal bars.	Comparing similar items or indicating progress.

Chart Category	Description	Suggested Uses
Area	Displays data as lines but with the areas between the lines shaded.	Showing how values have changed over time, especially the contribution of different data points in the series.
Scatter	Displays each data point as a point (or cross, or similar marker) on the plot area. Also known as an XY chart.	Showing values sampled at different times or that are not directly related to each other.
Stock	Displays each data series as a vertical line or bar indicating three or more prices or measurements (for example, high, low, and closing prices).	Showing the daily prices of stocks. Also suitable for some scientific data.
Surface	Displays the data points as a three-dimensional surface.	Comparing two sets of data to find a suitable combination of them.
Doughnut	Displays the data series as a sequence of concentric rings.	Showing how much each item contributes to the whole—like a pie chart, but it works with two or more data series.
Bubble	Displays the data points as bubbles of different sizes depending on their values.	Showing the relative importance of each data point.
Radar	Displays the combined values of different data series.	Showing how the combined values of separate data series compare to each other (for example, the sales contributions of several different products over several periods of time).

Creating, Laying Out, and Formatting a Chart

In this section, we'll look at how to create a chart from your data, lay it out with the components and arrangement you want, and apply the most useful types of formatting.

Creating a Chart

To create a chart, you use the commands on the Charts tab of the Ribbon. Follow these steps:

1. Select the data you want to chart, including any row or column headings needed. For example, click the first cell in the data range, then Shift+click the last cell. If you've downloaded the sample workbook, select cells A1:G8 on the Rainfall Data sheet.

TIP: You can create a chart from either a block range or a range of separate cells. To use separate cells, select them as usual—for example, click the first cell, then Cmd+click each of the others. Make sure that the cells contain comparable data, or the resulting chart will be odd and perhaps deceptive.

2. Click the Charts tab of the Ribbon to display its contents, then click the appropriate button in the Insert Chart group: Column, Line, Pie, Bar, Area, Scatter, or Other (which contains the Stock, Surface, Doughnut, Bubble, and Radar chart types). For the sample chart, click the Column button.

NOTE: If the Excel window isn't wide enough to display multiple buttons in the Insert Chart group, a single pop-up button called All appears. Click this button to display a panel that shows all the chart types. You'll need to scroll down the panel to see most of them. When the Excel window is wide enough to display some chart-type buttons, but not all of them, you'll find the missing buttons on the Other pop-up menu.

3. On the panel that opens, click the chart type you want. Figure 7–4 shows the Column panel, which is one of the most widely useful. For the sample chart, click the 3-D Clustered Column chart type.

Excel creates the chart as an embedded chart in the current worksheet, as shown earlier in Figure 7–1. You can then reposition it, resize it, or move it to a chart sheet as follows:

■ *Reposition the chart.* If you want to keep the chart as an embedded chart, move the mouse pointer over the chart border so that it turns to a four-headed arrow, then drag the chart to where you want it.

■ *Resize the chart.* Click to select the chart, then drag one of the handles that appears. Drag a corner handle to resize the chart in both dimensions; you can also Shift+drag to resize the chart proportionally. Drag a side handle to resize the chart in only that dimension; for example, drag the bottom handle to resize the chart only vertically.

■ *Move the chart to a chart sheet.* If you want to move the chart to a chart sheet, follow the instructions in the next section.

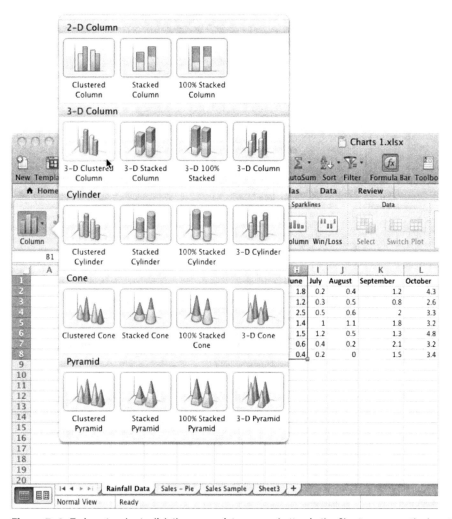

Figure 7–4. *To insert a chart, click the appropriate pop-up button in the Charts group on the Insert tab of the Ribbon, then click the chart type you want.*

Changing a Chart from an Embedded Chart to a Chart Sheet

You can change a chart from being embedded in a worksheet to being on its own chart sheet like this:

1. Click the chart on the worksheet it's embedded in.

2. Choose **Chart ➤ Move Chart** from the menu bar to display the Move Chart dialog box (see Figure 7–5).

TIP: You can also display the Move Chart dialog box by Ctrl+clicking or right-clicking the chart and then clicking Move Chart on the context menu.

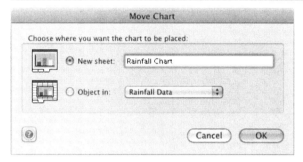

Figure 7–5. *Use the Move Chart dialog box to change a chart from being embedded to being on its own chart sheet.*

3. Select the New sheet option button.

4. Type the name for the new chart sheet in the New sheet text box.

5. Click the OK button. Excel creates the new chart sheet and moves the chart to it. The chart is still attached to its source data, so if you change the data, Excel changes the chart too.

NOTE: You can also use the Move Chart dialog box to move a chart from a chart sheet to an embedded chart on a worksheet or to move an embedded chart from one worksheet to another.

Changing the Chart Type

If you find the chart type you've chosen doesn't work for your data, you can change the chart type easily without having to create the chart again from scratch. Follow these steps:

1. Click the chart to select it.

2. Click the Charts tab of the Ribbon to display its contents.

3. In the Change Chart Type group, open the panel for the chart category, then click the chart type. For example, click the Pie pop-up button to display the Pie panel, then choose your favorite kind of pie from it.

Switching the Rows and Columns in a Chart

When Excel displays the chart, you may realize that the data series are in the wrong place; for example, the chart is displaying months by rainfall instead of rainfall by months.

When this happens, there's a quick fix: switch the rows and columns by choosing **Charts > Data > Switch Plot** from the Ribbon. Excel displays the chart with the series the other way around.

Changing the Source Data for a Chart

Sometimes you may find that your chart doesn't work well with the source data you've chosen. For example, you may have selected so much data that the chart is crowded, or you may have missed a vital row or column.

When this happens, you don't need to delete the chart and start again from scratch. Instead, follow these steps:

1. Choose **Charts > Data > Select** from the Ribbon or **Chart > Source Data** from the menu bar to display the Select Data Source dialog box (see Figure 7–6).

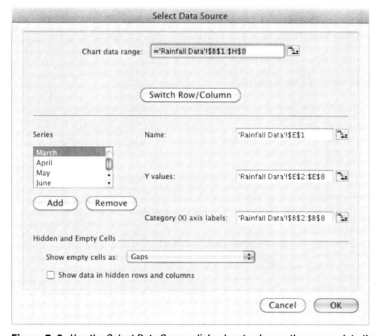

Figure 7–6. *Use the Select Data Source dialog box to change the source data the chart is using.*

2. In the Chart data range box, enter the data range you want to use:

    ▪ Usually, it's easiest to click the Collapse Dialog button to collapse the dialog box, drag on the worksheet to select the right data range, then click the Collapse Dialog button again to restore the dialog box. (If you prefer, you can just work around the Select Data Source dialog box instead.)

    ▪ You can also type the data range in the Chart data range box. This is easy when you just need to change a column letter or row number to fix the data range.

3. If you need to switch the rows and columns as well, click the Switch Row/Column button.

4. If your chart data contains empty cells, open the Show empty cells as pop-up menu and choose how to represent them. Your choices are Gaps (the default setting for most charts) or Zero.

5. Select the Show data in hidden rows and columns check box only if you want the chart to include data in hidden rows and columns within the source range. Normally, you'll want to keep these hidden, but it's sometimes useful to show them.

6. Click the OK button to close the Select Data Source dialog box. Excel applies the changes to the chart.

Choosing the Layout for the Chart

When you've sorted out the chart type and the source data, it's time to choose the layout for the chart. For each chart type, Excel provides various preset layouts that control where the title, legend, and other elements appear. After applying a layout, you can customize it further as needed.

To apply a layout, click the chart and then click the Charts tab of the Ribbon. If a suitable layout appears in the Layouts box in the Chart Quick Layouts group, click it. To see the full range of layouts, hold the mouse pointer over the Layouts box in the Chart Quick Layouts group until the panel button appears, then click the panel button. On the Quick Layout panel that Excel displays (see Figure 7–7), click the layout you want to apply to the chart.

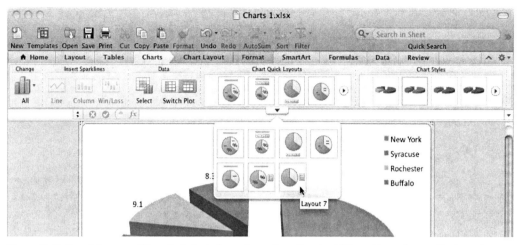

Figure 7–7. *To set the overall layout of chart elements, such as the chart title and legend, open the Layouts panel, then click the layout you want.*

Adding a Separate Data Series to a Chart

Sometimes you may find you need to add to a chart a data series that doesn't appear in the chart's source data—for example, to add projections of future success to your current data.

To add a data series, work from the Select Data Source dialog box. Follow these steps:

1. Click the chart to select it.

2. Choose **Charts ➤ Data ➤ Select** from the Ribbon or **Chart ➤ Source Data** from the menu bar to display the Select Data Source dialog box. You can also Ctrl+click or right-click the chart and then click Select Data on the context menu.

3. Click the Add button below the Series list box. Excel adds a new item to the series box, giving it a default name such as Series3 or Series4.

4. Click in the Name text box, then type the name you want to give the series. If the name appears in a cell on the worksheet, you can click it. When you move the focus out of the Name text box, Excel changes the default name to the name you type.

5. In the Y values text box, type the values for the series inside the braces, putting a comma between the values; for example, **{4.5,8.3,6.2,5.1,4.8,10.2}**. If the values appear in cells on the worksheet, you can enter them by selecting the range.

> **NOTE:** When adding a new data series, you don't normally need to change the contents of the Category (X) axis labels text box. This text box contains the range of cells that provide the labels for the horizontal axis.

6. Click the OK button to close the Select Data Source dialog box.

Applying a Style to a Chart

To control the overall graphical look of a chart, apply one of Excel's styles to it from the Styles box or the Styles panel in the Chart Styles group on the Charts tab of the Ribbon. Click the chart to select it, then click the Charts tab of the Ribbon to display its controls. Either click a style in the Styles box or hold the mouse pointer over the Styles box until the panel button appears, click the panel button to display the Styles panel (see Figure 7–8), then click the style.

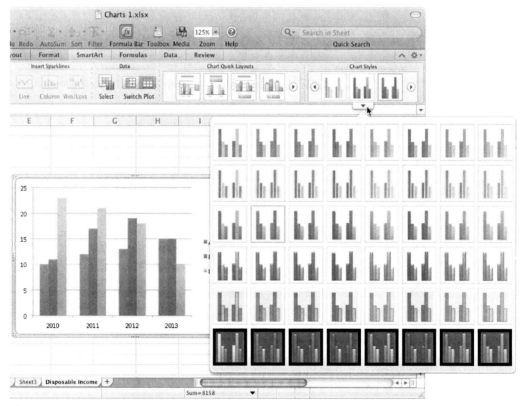

Figure 7–8. *To give the chart an overall graphical look, apply a style from the Styles box or the Styles panel in the Chart Styles group of the Charts tab of the Ribbon.*

Adding a Title to a Chart

To let viewers know what a chart is about, you'll normally want to add a title to it. To do so, follow these steps:

1. Click the chart to select it.

2. Choose **Chart Layout ➤ Labels ➤ Chart Title** from the Ribbon, then choose the title type you want:

    ▪ *No Chart Title.* Choose this item to remove the existing title. You can also click the title and press Delete to delete it.

    ▪ *Title Above Chart.* Choose this item to place the title above the chart, making the chart smaller to provide space for the title. Use this placement when you want to keep the title clearly separated from the chart; for example, because the chart is busy.

    ▪ *Overlap Title at Top.* Choose this item to place the title on the chart, centered over the top. Placing the title on the chart lets you keep the chart as large as possible. If the title lands on top of data, you can click it and drag it to a different position.

3. Triple-click to select the contents of the Chart Title placeholder that Excel adds for you.

4. Type the title for the chart over the default text.

5. If necessary, drag the chart title placeholder to a different position.

6. Click elsewhere to deselect the chart title.

> **TIP:** If you need to format the chart title, double-click the chart title to display the Format Title dialog box.

Adding Axis Titles to the Chart

To make clear what the chart shows, you'll usually want to add titles to the axes. To do so, follow these steps:

1. Click the chart to select it.

2. Choose **Chart Layout ➤ Labels ➤ Axis Titles ➤ Horizontal Axis Title ➤ Title Below Axis** from the Ribbon to insert a title placeholder for the horizontal axis.

3. Triple-click to select the contents of the placeholder.

4. Type the text for the axis title.

5. If necessary, drag the placeholder to a different position.

6. Choose **Chart Layout > Primary Vertical Axis Title** from the Ribbon, then click the placement you want:

  ▪ *Rotated Title.* Click this item to have Excel rotate the axis title 90 degrees counterclockwise so that it runs upward along the axis.

  ▪ *Vertical Title.* Click this item to have the axis title appear vertically, with the letters placed horizontally one above the other.

  ▪ *Horizontal Title.* Click this item to have the axis title appear horizontally. This placement is easiest to read, but it takes up more of the chart's space than the other two placements.

7. Triple-click to select the contents of the placeholder.

8. Type the text for the axis title.

9. If necessary, drag the placeholder to a different position.

> **NOTE:** If the chart has a z-axis, you can add the axis title by choosing **Chart Layout > Labels > Axis Titles > Depth Axis Title** and then clicking the Rotated Title item, the Vertical Title item, or the Horizontal Title item, as needed.

Changing the Scale or Numbering of an Axis

When you insert a chart, Excel automatically numbers the vertical axis to suit the data range. If you need to change the scale or numbering, follow these steps:

1. Double-click the vertical axis, or Ctrl+click or right-click in the vertical axis titles area, then click Format Axis on the context menu to display the Format Axis dialog box. The Scale category appears at the front (see Figure 7–9).

> **NOTE:** You can also open the Format Axis dialog box from the Ribbon. Click the Format tab, go to the Current Selection box, open the pop-up menu, and click Vertical (Value) Axis. Then click the Format Selection button below it. You can also click the vertical axis and choose **Format > Axis** from the menu bar or press Cmd+1.

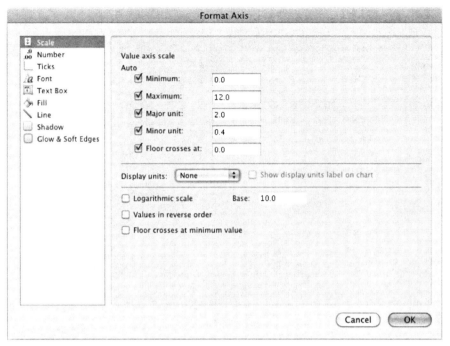

Figure 7–9. *You can format an axis to control its values, major and minor units, and whether the chart shows units (such as thousands). Excel applies the changes as you work in the Axis Options category of the Format Axis dialog box.*

2. Use the controls in the Value axis scale area to set up the values on the axis:

    ■ *Minimum.* To have Excel set the minimum value on the axis, select the Minimum check box. To set it yourself, click in the text box, then type in the value; Excel clears the check box for you.

    ■ *Maximum.* To have Excel set the maximum value that appears on the axis, select the Minimum check box. To set it yourself, click in the text box, then type in the value; Excel clears the check box for you.

    ■ *Major unit.* To have Excel decide the interval between major units on the axis, select the Major unit check box. To set it yourself, click in the text box, then type in the value; Excel clears the check box for you. Depending on how big your chart is, you'll probably want between five and ten major units on the scale you've set by choosing the Minimum value and Maximum value.

■ *Minor unit.* To have Excel decide the interval between minor units on the axis, select the Minor unit check box. To set it yourself, click in the text box, then type in the value; Excel clears the check box for you. You'll normally want between four and ten minor units per major unit, depending on what the chart shows.

3. In the middle section of the Scale pane, choose whether to display the units the chart uses—for example, choose the Hundreds item, the Thousands item, or the Millions item in the Display units pop-up menu. If you choose to display units, make sure the Show display units label on chart check box is selected, making Excel display a label showing the units. If you don't want to show the units, choose None in the Display units pop-up menu.

4. In the lower part of the Scale pane, choose options as needed:

■ *Logarithmic scale.* If you need the chart to use a logarithmic scale rather than an arithmetic scale, select the Logarithmic scale check box, then enter the logarithm base in the Base box. For example, enter 10 to have the scale use the values 1, 10, 100, 1000, 10000, and so on, at regular intervals.

■ *Values in reverse order.* For some charts, it's helpful to have the values run in reverse order—for example, lowest values at the top instead of the highest. When you need this setup, select this check box.

■ *Floor crosses at minimum value.* Select this check box if you want the floor of the chart to cross the vertical axis at the minimum value rather than at zero.

■ *Display units.* If you want the chart to show units—Hundreds, Thousands, Millions, and so on—select the unit in this pop-up menu. Excel reduces the figures shown accordingly; for example, 1000000 appears as 1, with Millions next to the scale. This helps make the axis easier to read.

5. In the left pane, click the Ticks item to display the Ticks pane (see Figure 7–10), then set up the positioning of the tick marks:

■ *Major Tick Mark Type.* In this box, select the Inside option button to have the major tick marks appear inside the chart, the Outside option button to have them appear outside (on the axis side), or the Cross option button to have them appear on both sides. Select the None option button if you do not want major tick marks.

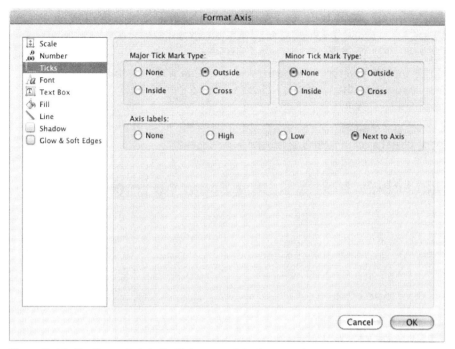

Figure 7–10. *Use the controls in the Ticks pane of the Format Axis dialog box to control how the ticks on the axis appear.*

- *Minor tick mark type.* In this box, select the Inside option button to have the minor tick marks appear inside the chart, the Outside option button to have them appear outside (on the axis side), or the Cross option button to have them appear on both sides. Select the None option button if you do not want minor tick marks.

- *Axis labels.* In this box, select the Next to Axis option button to have the labels appear next to the axis. Select the High option button to have the labels appear on the high side of the chart, or select the Low option button to have them appear on the low side. Select the None option button to suppress the labels.

6. When you're satisfied with the axis, click the Close button to close the Format Axis dialog box.

Adding a Legend to a Chart

Many charts benefit from having a legend that summarizes the colors used for different data series. You can add a legend by selecting the chart, choosing **Chart Layout ➤ Labels ➤ Legend**, then clicking the placement you want: Legend at Right, Legend at Top, Legend at Left, Legend at Bottom, Overlap Legend at Right, or Overlap Legend at Left.

Each of the non-"Overlap" items reduces the chart area to make space for the legend. The two "Overlap" items place the legend on the chart without reducing its size, so they're good for keeping the chart as large as possible.

Whichever placement you use for the legend, you can drag it to a better position as needed. You can also resize the legend by clicking it and then dragging one of the handles that appears around it.

If you need to remove a legend from a chart, either click the legend and then press Delete, or choose Chart Layout ➤ Labels ➤ Legend ➤ No Legend.

Adding Axis Labels from a Range Separate from the Chart Data

Depending on how the worksheet containing the source data is laid out, you may need to add axis labels that are in separate cells from the chart data. To do this, follow these steps:

1. Click the chart to select it.

2. Choose Charts ➤ Data ➤ Select from the Ribbon to display the Select Data Source dialog box.

3. Click the Collapse Dialog button to the right of the Category (X) axis labels text box to collapse the dialog box.

4. Drag through the cells in the work sheet that contain the axis labels. Excel enters them in the Category (X) axis labels text box.

5. Click the Collapse Dialog button again to restore the Select Data Source dialog box.

6. Click the OK button to close the Select Data Source dialog box. Excel applies the labels to the axis.

Adding Data Labels to the Chart

If viewers will need to see the precise value of data points rather than just getting a general idea of their value, add data labels to the chart. To do so, click the chart, then choose Chart Layout ➤ Labels ➤ Data Labels ➤ Value if you want to show the values. The Data Labels pop-up menu offers different options, depending on the chart type. For example, for pie charts, you can choose the Series Name item, the Category Name item, the Percentage item, or the Category Name and Percentage item.

CAUTION: Use data labels sparingly. Only some charts benefit from data labels—other charts may become too busy, or having the details may distract the audience from the overall thrust of the chart.

When you add data labels to a chart, Excel displays a data label for each data marker. If you want to display only some data labels, delete the ones you don't need. To delete a data label, click it once to select all data labels, then click it again to select just the one label. Then either press Delete or Ctrl+click or right-click the selection and click Delete on the context menu.

Choosing Which Gridlines to Display

On many types of charts, you can choose whether to display horizontal and vertical gridlines to help the viewer judge how the data points relate to each other and to the axes.

To control which gridlines appear, follow these steps:

1.   Select the chart.

2.   Choose **Chart Layout ➤ Axes ➤ Gridlines**, then click Horizontal Gridlines, Vertical Gridlines, or Depth Gridlines to display the appropriate submenu.

3.   Click the menu item for the type of gridlines you want to display:

     ▪   *No Gridlines.* Click this item to suppress the display of gridlines.

     ▪   *Major Gridlines.* Click this item to display only gridlines at the major divisions in the data series. For example, if your data is in the range 0–25, major gridlines normally appear at 5, 10, 15, 20, and 25.

TIP: When the viewer needs to see clearly where each value falls, use either data labels or major and minor gridlines. If using minor gridlines (with or without major gridlines) makes the chart look cluttered, use only major gridlines. Normally, it's best not to use both horizontal and vertical minor gridlines, because they tend to make charts look confusingly busy—but sometimes your charts may need them.

     ▪   *Minor Gridlines.* Click this item to display gridlines at the minor divisions in the data series. For example, if your data is in the range 0–25, minor gridlines normally appear at each integer—1, 2, 3, and so on up to 25.

■ *Major and Minor Gridlines.* Click this item to display both major and minor gridlines. The major gridlines appear darker than the minor gridlines so that you can see the difference between them. Having both major and minor gridlines is usually clearer than having only minor gridlines, as you can see in Figure 7–11.

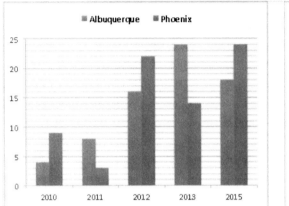 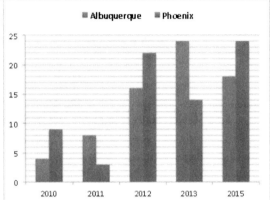

Figure 7–11. *Using both major and minor gridlines (left) usually makes a chart easier to read than using only minor gridlines (right).*

4. Repeat steps 2 and 3 for each set of gridlines the chart needs.

NOTE: To change the values at which the gridlines appear, format the axis, as described in the section "Changing the Scale or Numbering of an Axis" earlier in this chapter.

Formatting a Chart Wall and Chart Floor

Some charts look fine with a plain background, but for 3-D charts, you may want to decorate the chart walls (the areas at the back and the side of the chart) and the chart floor (the area at the bottom of the chart). You can add a solid color, a gradient, a picture, or a texture to the walls, the floor, or both. Figure 7–12 shows a chart that uses a picture for the walls.

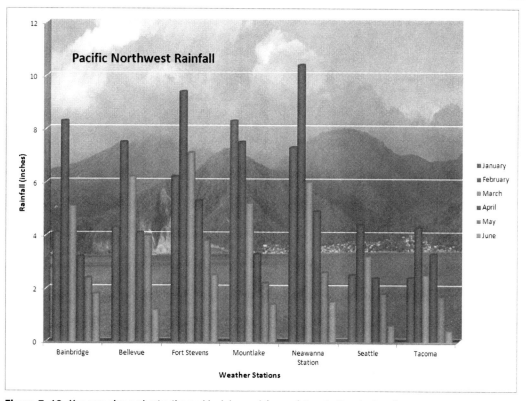

Figure 7–12. *You can give a chart a themed look by applying a picture to the chart walls.*

TIP: Usually, the chart walls and floors are the elements that look best with a custom fill (such as a picture). But you can apply a custom fill to many other chart elements as well. To do so, display the Format dialog box for the element, click the Fill category in the left pane, then make your choices.

To format the chart wall or the chart floor, follow these steps:

1. Click the chart to select it.

2. Choose **Chart Layout ➤ Current Selection ➤ Chart Elements**, then click the item you want to format: Back Wall, Floor, Side Wall, or Walls (to format both the back wall and the side wall).

3. Click the Format Selection button in the Current Selection group to display the Format dialog box for the item you selected. Figure 7–13 shows the Format Walls dialog box with the controls for inserting a picture fill displayed.

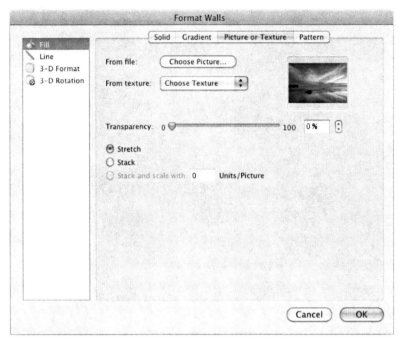

Figure 7–13. *Use the Fill pane in the Format dialog box to apply a picture fill to objects such as the chart walls or floor.*

4.   Make sure the Fill item is selected in the left pane.

5.   In the Fill pane, set up the fill you want:

  ▪ *No fill.* Click the Solid tab to display its contents. Open the Color pop-up menu, then choose the No Fill item if you want the item to be transparent.

  ▪ *Solid fill.* Click the Solid tab to display its contents. Open the Color pop-up menu, then click the color you want. Choose the Automatic item if you want to use the default color. Drag the Transparency slider, or type a value in the text box, to choose how transparent the fill is.

  ▪ *Gradient fill.* Click the Gradient tab to display its contents. Open the Style pop-up menu, then choose the gradient style you want: None, linear, Radial, Rectangular, or Path. Use the Angle knob and Direction pop-up menu to set the angle and direction of the gradient if applicable. Then, in the Color and transparency area of the Gradient tab, choose the gradient, color, and transparency.

- *Picture or texture fill.* Click the Picture or Texture tab to display its contents. To use a picture, click the Choose Picture button, click the picture in the Choose a Picture dialog box, then click the Insert button. To use a texture, choose it from the Texture pop-up palette. Set the degree of transparency by dragging the Transparency slide or entering a percentage in the text box. Then select the Stretch option button if you want to stretch the picture or texture to fill the space, select the Stack option button if you want to tile the picture or texture to occupy the space without distorting it, or select the Stack and scale with *N* Units/Picture option button to tile the picture with the number of units you type in the text box.

- *Pattern fill.* Click the Pattern tab to display its contents. In the Pattern box, click the pattern you want. Then choose the foreground color in the Foreground color pop-up menu and the background color in the Background color pop-up menu.

6. Click the Close button to close the Format dialog box.

Formatting Individual Chart Elements

You can format any of the individual elements of a chart—for example, the legend, the gridlines, or the data labels—by selecting the element and then using its Format dialog box. This dialog box includes the name of the element it affects: the Format Data Labels dialog box, the Format Plot Area dialog box, and so on.

You can display the Format dialog box in either of these ways:

- *Ctrl+click or right-click the element, then click the Format item on the context menu.* This is usually the easiest way of opening the Format dialog box.

- Select the element in the Chart Elements pop-up menu, then click the Format Selection button. If it's hard to Ctrl+click or right-click the element on the chart (for example, because the chart is busy), choose **Chart Layout ➤ Current Selection ➤ Chart Elements** or **Format ➤ Current Selection ➤ Chart Elements**, then click the element you want on the pop-up menu. You can then click the Format Selection button (also in the Current Selection group) to open the Format dialog box for the element.

The contents of the Format dialog box vary depending on the object you've selected, but for most objects, you'll find categories such as these:

- *Fill.* You can fill in a solid shape with a solid color, color gradient, picture, or texture. See the section "Formatting a Chart Wall and Chart Floor" earlier in this chapter for instructions on creating fills.

- *Line.* You can give a shape a color border, gradient border, or no line. You can also choose among different border styles, change the border width, and pick a suitable line type.

- *Shadow.* You can add a shadow to the shape, set its color, and adjust its transparency, width, and other properties.

- *Glow and Soft Edges.* You can make an object stand out by giving it a glow, choosing a color that contrasts with the object's surroundings, and choosing how wide the glow should be. You can also apply soft edges to a shape.

- *3-D Format.* You can apply a 3-D format to different aspects of a shape—for example, setting a different bevel for the top and bottom of the shape.

- 3-D Rotation. You can apply a 3-D rotation to the object.

- *Font.* For objects that use text, you can control how the text looks.

> **TIP:** If the chart element contains text, you can also format it by using the controls on the Home tab of the Ribbon or keyboard shortcuts. For example, to apply boldface to the data labels, click the data labels, then choose **Home** ➤ Font ➤ **Bold** (or press Ctrl+B). This is often easier than using the Font pane in the Format dialog box for the element.

Copying a Chart's Formatting to Another Chart

After you set up a chart with all the formatting you need, you can apply that formatting to another chart by using Copy and Paste. Follow these steps:

1. Click the formatted chart to select its chart area.

2. Right-click the border of the chart, then click Copy on the context menu to copy the chart and its formatting to the Clipboard.

3. Go to the sheet that contains the chart onto which you want to paste the formatting.

4. Choose **Home** ➤ **Clipboard** ➤ **Paste** ➤ **Paste Special** to display the Paste Special dialog box shown in Figure 7–14.

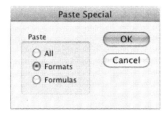

Figure 7–14. *In the Paste Special dialog box, select the Formats option button to paste just the formatting from one chart onto another chart.*

5.   Select the Formats option button.

6.   Click the OK button to close the Paste Special dialog box. Excel applies the formatting to the chart.

Reusing Your Own Designs by Creating Custom Chart Types

If you want to be able to reuse a chart design you've created, you can turn it into a custom chart type. Follow these steps:

1.   Select the formatted chart either on a chart sheet or on a worksheet.

2.   Choose **Charts ➤ Change Chart Type ➤ Other ➤ Save As Template** from the Ribbon or **Chart ➤ Save as Template** from the menu bar to display the Save Chart Template dialog box. This is a standard Save As dialog box.

3.   If you want, change the folder in which to save the chart type. Excel suggests using the `~/Library/Application Support/Microsoft/Office/Chart Templates/` folder (where `~` represents your home folder). This is good for a template only you will use, but if your colleagues will need to use the template too, store it in a shared folder on the network.

4.   Type a descriptive name for the template in the Save As text box.

5.   Click the Save button to close the Save Chart Template dialog box. Excel saves the template in the folder you chose.

To create a chart based on your template, follow these steps:

1.   Select the source data for the chart.

2.   Choose **Charts ➤ Insert Chart ➤ Other** to display the Other pane, then scroll down to the Templates area at the bottom of the pane.

3.   Click the template.

Choosing Chart Preferences

To make your charts appear the way you want, you may need to change the settings in the Chart pane in the Excel Preferences dialog box. The Chart pane contains some settings that affect only the selected chart and other settings that affect all charts.

To open the Chart pane, follow these steps:

1. Click the chart for which you want to change the chart specific settings.

2. Choose Excel ➤ Preferences or press Cmd+, (Cmd and the comma key) to display the Excel Preferences dialog box.

3. Click the Chart icon in the Authoring area. Excel displays the Chart preferences pane (see Figure 7–15).

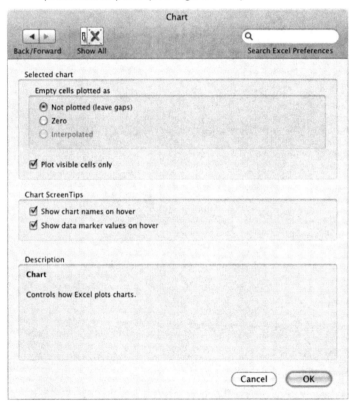

Figure 7–15. *In the Chart pane of the Excel Preferences dialog box, you can choose settings for both the current chart and for all charts.*

In the Empty cells plotted as box within the Selected chart area, choose how to represent empty cells in the chart:

- *Not plotted (leave gaps).* Select this option button to make the chart show a gap where each empty cell appears. This is the best choice for general use.

- *Zero.* Select this option button to make the chart show an empty cell as a zero value. In some chart types, this can help you focus on missing values that you need to supply. In other chart types, having these zero values appear is visually confusing.

- *Interpolated.* Select this option button if you want Excel to fill in missing values for you, basing them on the available values around them. This option button is available only for some chart types.

> **NOTE:** Interpolating missing chart values is useful when you're working with identifiable trends. For example, if you're missing one hour's temperature measurement, and the previous hour's temperature was higher and the next hour's temperature was higher, the interpolated value appears between the two values. On the other hand, if you're missing a day's rainfall data, interpolating the value isn't sensible, because there's usually no linear relationship between one day's rainfall and the next day's.

Select the Plot visible cells only check box if you want to omit any hidden rows or columns within the chart data source from the chart. This is what you'll normally want to do. Clear this check box to make all the data show up, even if it's hidden in the data source.

In the Chart ScreenTips area, select the check boxes for the ScreenTips you want to see:

- *Show chart names on hover.* Select this check box to make Excel display a ScreenTip containing an item's name when you hold the mouse pointer over that item. For example, when you hold the mouse pointer over a data series, a ScreenTip shows the data series' name and details.

- *Show data marker values on hover.* Select this check box to make Excel display a ScreenTip showing the value of a data marker when you hold the mouse pointer over the data marker.

When you've finished choosing Chart preferences, click the OK button to close the Excel Preferences dialog box.

Using Your Charts in Word Documents and PowerPoint Presentations

Excel is Office's application for creating charts, but you will likely also want to use charts to illustrate Word documents and PowerPoint presentations. You can either reuse a chart you've already created in Excel or create a new chart especially for that document or presentation.

Understanding How You Can Add a Chart to a Document or Slide

A chart can be a great way of presenting complex or detailed information in a manner that's instantly clear in a document or on a slide. You can add a chart to a Word document or a PowerPoint presentation in either of these ways:

- *Create a chart on an embedded worksheet.* Click the Charts tab of the Ribbon, then choose the chart type by using the pop-up buttons and panels in the Insert Chart group. Word or PowerPoint then opens Excel for you and creates a new workbook so that you can enter the chart data and create the chart. The workbook is embedded in the Word document or PowerPoint presentation, so it becomes part of that file.

NOTE: In PowerPoint, you can also click the Insert Chart icon in a content placeholder to start creating a chart on an embedded worksheet.

- *Copy a chart from an Excel workbook.* Create your chart in Excel using the techniques described earlier in this chapter, then copy the finished chart and paste it into the Word document or onto the PowerPoint slide. You can choose whether to embed the chart's data in the Word document or PowerPoint presentation or just to insert the chart as a picture or PDF file.

Here's how to choose when to create a new embedded workbook, embed an existing workbook, link back to a workbook, or insert a picture:

- *Create a new embedded workbook.* Do this when you don't yet have the data for the chart in Excel and you need to keep the chart's data with the Word document or PowerPoint presentation. For example, you'll send the presentation to someone else who will need to work on the chart data too.

- *Embed an existing chart and its data.* Do this when you have the data for the chart or the chart itself in a workbook in Excel and you need to keep the chart's data available in the Word document or PowerPoint presentation. After embedding the chart and its data, you can open the chart from Word in Excel and edit it there.

- *Link back to a workbook.* Do this when you want to be able to change the chart or its source data in Excel and then automatically bring those changes into Word or PowerPoint by updating the chart. Linking requires the workbook to stay in the same relative place in the computer's file system to the document or presentation so that Word or PowerPoint can find the updated data. Moving the document or presentation to a different computer breaks the link.

> **CAUTION:** Linking a chart can be great when it works—but links can fail at the most awkward times. Before giving a presentation that includes linked charts, double-check that the links are working. That way, you'll have a chance to fix any problems rather than discovering them when your audience sees them.

- *Insert a picture.* Do this when you don't need to keep the connection between the chart and its source data and you will not need to edit the chart in the document or presentation.

Creating a Chart in a New Embedded Workbook

To create a chart on a worksheet in a new workbook embedded in a Word document or PowerPoint presentation, follow these steps:

1. Open the document in Word or the presentation in PowerPoint.

2. On the document page or slide where you want to create the chart, click the Charts tab of the Ribbon. Word or PowerPoint displays the Charts tab of the Ribbon.

3. In the Insert Chart group, click the pop-up button for the category of chart you want to create. For example, click the Column pop-up button to display the Column panel.

4. On the pop-up panel, click the chart type. Word or PowerPoint creates a chart of that type on the slide and launches Excel, which creates a new workbook, embeds it in the document or presentation, and gives it a name such as Chart in Microsoft Office Word or Chart in Microsoft Office PowerPoint.

5. Change the chart range and the sample data (Figure 7–16 shows an example using PowerPoint) to the data your chart needs. Word or PowerPoint automatically updates the chart to match the data in the Excel worksheet.

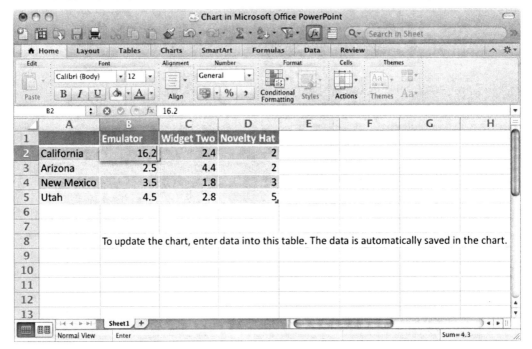

Figure 7–16. *Excel enters sample data on the first worksheet in the embedded workbook. Change this data to create your chart.*

6. When you have finished changing the data, close Excel. For example, click the Close button (the red button at the left end of the title bar) or choose **Excel ➤ Quit** Excel.

> **NOTE:** Excel saves the data in the embedded workbook automatically, so you don't need to save it while you're working in the Excel window.

7. Use the controls on the Charts tab and the Chart Layout tab of the Ribbon to format the chart the way you want it. Figure 7–17 shows a PowerPoint slide containing a chart with formatting under way.

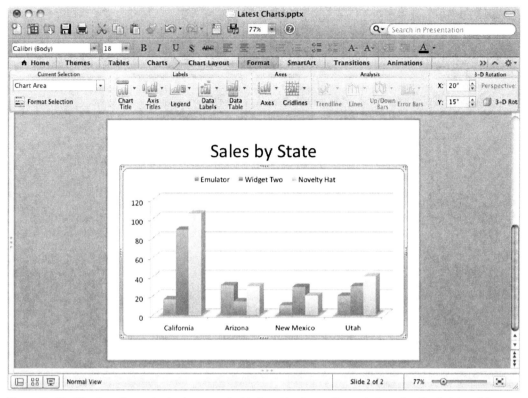

Figure 7–17. *After inserting a chart using an embedded workbook, use the controls on the Charts tab and the Chart Layout tab of the Ribbon in Word or PowerPoint (shown here) to format the chart.*

8. Save your Word document or PowerPoint presentation.

> **NOTE:** To edit the data on your chart again, choose **Charts ➤ Data ➤ Edit** from the Ribbon, clicking the main part of the Edit button. Word or PowerPoint opens Excel, which displays the embedded worksheet.

Pasting a Chart from Excel into a Word Document or PowerPoint Slide

If you have a chart already created in Excel or if you have a workbook containing the data from which you will create the chart, you can paste the chart into Word or PowerPoint. Follow these general steps:

1. Create the chart using the techniques explained earlier in this chapter.

2. Click the chart to select it.

3. Copy the chart to the Clipboard. For example, click the Copy button on the Standard toolbar or press Cmd+C.

4. Switch to Word or PowerPoint, then navigate to the document or slide on which you want to insert the chart.

5. Paste in the chart from the Clipboard. For example, click the Paste button on the Standard toolbar, or press Cmd+V.

6. Click the Paste Options button at the lower-right corner of the chart, then click the appropriate option button in the upper group on the Paste Options pop-up menu (see Figure 7–18):

   ▪ *Chart (linked to Excel data).* Select this option button to link the chart back to the Excel workbook it came from.

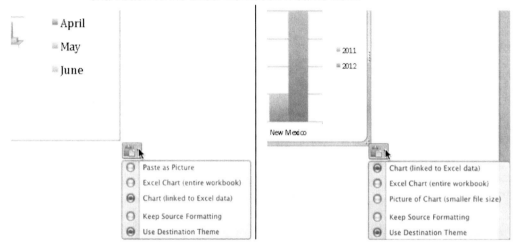

Figure 7–18. *When pasting a chart from Excel into a Word document (left) or PowerPoint slide (right), click the Paste Options button, and use the option buttons on the pop-up menu to choose how to paste the chart.*

   ▪ *Excel Chart (entire workbook).* Select this option button to embed the entire Excel workbook in the PowerPoint presentation.

   ▪ *Paste as Picture (Word) or Picture of Chart (smaller file size) (PowerPoint).* Select this option button to insert a picture of the chart. As the PowerPoint name says, inserting the picture helps keep the presentation file size down, but you can't edit the picture.

7. If you want the chart on the slide or in the document to use the original formatting you gave it in Excel, click the Paste Options button again, then select the Keep Source Formatting option button. Otherwise, leave the Use Destination Theme option button selected, and the chart will pick up the formatting from the document or presentation.

8. Use the controls on the Charts tab or the Chart Layout tab of the Ribbon to format the chart the way you want it. (If you inserted the chart as a picture, use the controls on the Format Picture tab of the Ribbon.)

9. Save the document or presentation.

To edit the data in either an embedded or linked chart, choose Charts ➤ Data ➤ Edit, clicking the main part of the Edit button.

Summary

In this chapter, you learned how to create powerful and persuasive charts from your data. You know what the separate components of charts are called, how to create a chart, and how to position it either on a worksheet or on its own chart sheet. You can also make Excel show the components you want for a chart and format them as needed. To save time and effort, you also learned to reuse your custom chart formatting either by pasting it onto an existing chart or by creating a custom chart template from it.

You now also understand the different ways you can use an Excel chart in a Word document or a PowerPoint presentation; you know which way works best in which circumstances; and you know how to insert the chart, format it, and edit it.

In the next chapter, I'll show you how to enhance your worksheets with data bars, color scales, icon sets, and sparklines. Turn the page when you're ready to get started.

Chapter 8

Using Data Bars, Color Scales, Icon Sets, and Sparklines

In this chapter, we'll look at how you can use four graphical elements to give your worksheets more visual appeal and oomph without using full-scale charts. These four elements are data bars, color scales, icon sets, and sparklines. Each is a graphical element that appears in a single cell.

Data bars, color scales, and icon sets are part of Excel's conditional formatting, which you learned about in Chapter 4. Data bars are like single-cell bar charts that you use to compare the values in a range of cells. Color scales give you an easy way to adjust the background colors of cells to reflect their values—for example, red for poor performance and green for good performance. Icon sets enable you to quickly add an icon that represents how a value compares to the rest of its cohort; for example, you can add up-pointing arrows to good results.

Sparklines are miniature charts that fit in a single cell. You use sparklines much as you would use a tiny chart—to illustrate a series of data. For example, you can create a sparkline that shows a line indicating a stock's price movements over a number of days.

Using Data Bars

A *data bar* is a horizontal bar that appears in a cell to graphically represent the value in a corresponding cell. Normally, you'll use data bars to represent the values of multiple cells so that you can see the relationship among the cells' values.

For example, the worksheet in Figure 8–1 uses data bars to show the sales by five different salespeople for April, May, June, and the second quarter of the year as a whole. Each cell that contains a data bar has the same value as the cell to its left, so the data bar in cell C2 illustrates the value shown in cell B2. Looking at the data bars, you can easily see that although Salesperson Smith had a weak April and a shoddy May, her strong June sales brought her up to a respectable result for the quarter overall.

	A	B	C	D	E	F	G	H	I
1	Salesperson	April		May		June		Q2	
2	Smith	$68,225		$69,038		$161,699		$298,962.00	
3	Jones	$56,523		$160,323		$121,860		$338,706.00	
4	Ramirez	$66,322		$106,892		$139,446		$312,660.00	
5	Lee	$166,383		$79,370		$84,946		$330,699.00	
6	Kim	$100,254		$54,864		$117,269		$272,387.00	

Figure 8–1. *Data bars give a quick graphical representation of the values in the cells. Here, each cell showing a data bar contains the same value as the cell to its left.*

Creating Data Bars

By default, Excel places data bars alongside the data they represent. You can choose to display only the data bars in the cells, or you can display the data bars in separate cells to make the worksheet easier to read.

Creating Data Bars in the Same Cells as Their Data

To create data bars that appear in the same cells as their data, follow these steps:

1. Enter the data from which you'll create the data bars. If the data is already in the worksheet, you're all set.

2. Select the cells that contain the data.

3. Choose Home ➤ Format ➤ Conditional Formatting ➤ Data Bars to display the Data Bars panel (see Figure 8–2).

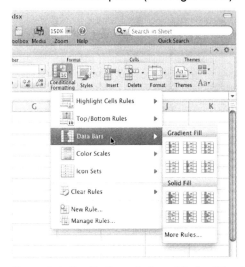

Figure 8–2. *Use the Home ➤ Format ➤ Conditional Formatting ➤ Data Bars command to create data bars in the selected cells. You can choose between a gradient fill and a solid fill.*

4. Click the color and fill type you want in either the Gradient Fill section or the Solid Fill section of the Data Bars panel. Excel creates the data bars in the cell. The left screen in Figure 8–3 shows an example.

> **TIP:** A gradient fill works best for data bars you display in the same cells as their data, because the lighter end of the gradient leaves the text readable. For data bars you display in cells on their own, you may prefer solid fills.

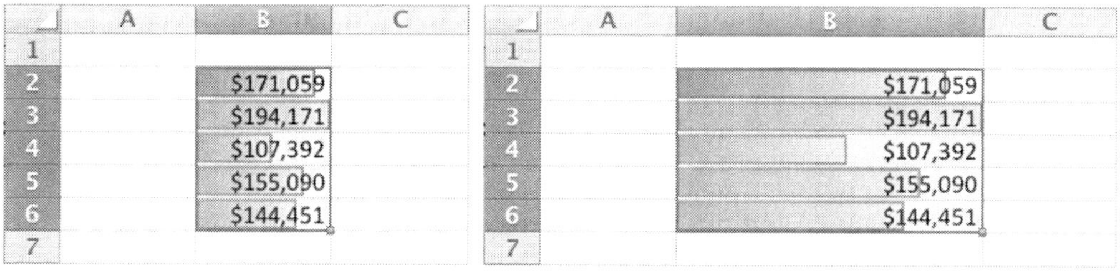

Figure 8–3. *After creating data bars (left), you may need to widen the column to give them more impact (right).*

5. Change the column width if necessary. For example, drag the right border of the cell's column heading to the right to make the column wider and give the data bars more impact, as shown on the right in Figure 8–3.

Creating Data Bars in Different Cells Than Their Data

To make your data bars easy to read, you may want to have them appear in cells on their own, either with the underlying data appearing in cells alongside them (or elsewhere, as needed) or without the data appearing at all. You can make the data bars appear on their own in cells by setting Excel to display only the data bars there. If you want the data for the data bars to be visible, you need to place it in different cells.

To make the data bars appear without their data, follow these steps:

1. Create the data bars as described in the previous section, so that the data bars appear in the same cells as their data.

2. With the cells still selected, choose Home ➤ Format ➤ Conditional Formatting ➤ Manage Rules to display the Manage Rules dialog box (see Figure 8–4).

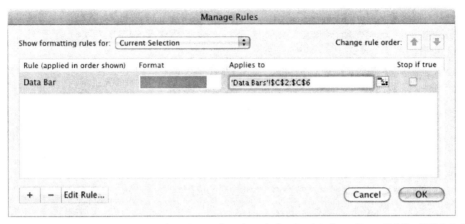

Figure 8–4. *In the Manage Rules dialog box, select the rule for the data bars, then click the Edit Rule button.*

3. Make sure the right rule is selected. If you've applied only one conditional formatting rule to the cells, it will be selected; if you've applied multiple rules, you may need to select the right rule.

4. Click the Edit Rule button to display the Edit Formatting Rule dialog box (see Figure 8–5).

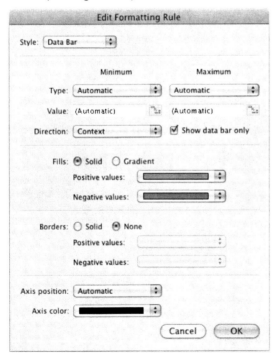

Figure 8–5. *In the Edit Formatting Rule dialog box, select the Show data bar only check box if you want to display the data bars without the values that produced them.*

5. Select the Show data bar only check box.

6. Click the OK button to close the Edit Formatting Rule dialog box.

7. Click the OK button to close the Manage Rules dialog box.

> **TIP:** With the Edit Formatting Rule dialog box open, you can quickly change among data bars, icon sets, and color scales. Just open the Style pop-up menu and choose 2-Color Scale, 3-Color Scale, Data Bar, or Icon Sets, as appropriate.

To create data bars that appear in separate cells from the values that produce them, set up the cells that will contain the data bars with formulas referring to the cells that contain the values. For example, the worksheet shown in Figure 8–6 uses simple formulas such as =B2 to make the cells in column C have the same values as the cells in column B. You can then set up the data bars as described earlier in this chapter in the target cells—in this case, in column C.

	A	B	C
1	Salesperson	April	
2	Smith	65695	=B2
3	Jones	189850	=B3
4	Ramirez	87182	=B4
5	Lee	59653	=B5
6	Kim	109641	=B6

Figure 8–6. *When you need to produce data bars in cells separate from their data, use formulas to give the data-bar cells the same values as the cells that provide the data. For example, cell C2 here contains the formula =B2 and will show the data bar for the value in cell B2.*

Using Color Scales

Color scales are a handy way of showing how the values in a set of cells compare to each other by setting the background color of each cell to represent its value. Excel lets you use either two-color scales or three-color scales. For example, to illustrate a range of temperatures, you could use a two-color scale with blue for the low temperatures and red for the high temperatures, or a three-color scale with blue representing an uncomfortably low temperature, green comfortable, and red uncomfortably warm. Figure 8–7 shows an example of this kind of daily temperature chart for the first half of a year.

	A	B	C	D	E	F	G	H	I	J	K	L	M	N	O	P	Q	R	S	T	U	V	W	X	Y	Z	AA	AB	AC	AD	AE	AF
1	Day	1	2	3	4	5	6	7	8	9	10	11	12	13	14	15	16	17	18	19	20	21	22	23	24	25	26	27	28	29	30	31
2	January	7	4	8	8	-1	7	0	-1	4	6	4	2	-1	4	4	1	3	2	1	4	8	0	5	7	6	1	0	7	6	4	6
3	February	9	4	5	8	3	7	5	10	6	4	7	10	10	10	4	7	9	7	6	10	10	6	2	5	7	4	8	2	5		
4	March	11	6	10	11	12	11	12	8	7	12	12	12	11	6	10	5	7	12	7	11	8	9	7	4	7	9	9	11	10	7	7
5	April	14	11	10	14	10	10	16	18	9	13	9	18	11	11	15	17	8	10	16	11	18	16	18	10	11	16	15	10	16	10	
6	May	22	21	24	25	24	21	24	13	12	16	18	18	16	11	15	11	24	14	10	14	25	22	16	14	10	13	24	25	20	11	20
7	June	26	16	28	28	27	21	23	16	28	21	26	23	23	19	15	16	21	22	28	15	22	21	26	25	24	27	20	24	23	19	

Figure 8–7. *You can add impact and clarity to mundane data such as temperatures by formatting the cells with a color scale. In this worksheet, the shading for much of January, February, and March is blue, indicating colder temperatures. The shading for April, May, and June is red, indicating higher temperatures.*

To create a color scale, follow these steps:

1. Enter the data from which you'll create the color scale.

2. Select the cells that contain the data.

3. Choose **Home ➤ Format ➤ Conditional Formatting ➤ Color Scale** to display the Color Scale panel (see Figure 8–8).

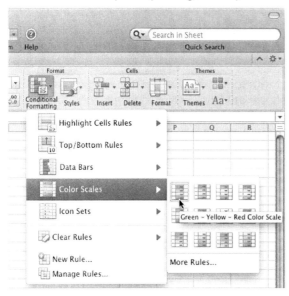

Figure 8–8. *On the Color Scales panel, click the scale type you want. You can change the colors later if you need to.*

4. Click the type of color scale you want. Excel applies it to the cells.

Sometimes the color scale's default settings may suit your needs, but usually you'll need to adjust the color scale to change the points at which each color is used or to change the colors themselves. To adjust a color scale, follow these steps:

1. With the cells still selected, choose **Home ➤ Format ➤ Conditional Formatting ➤ Manage Rules** to display the Manage Rules dialog box (shown in Figure 8–4, earlier in this chapter).

2. Make sure the right rule is selected. If you've applied only one conditional formatting rule to the cells, it will be selected; if you've applied multiple rules, you may need to click the right rule.

3. Click the Edit Rule button to display the Edit Formatting Rule dialog box (see Figure 8–9).

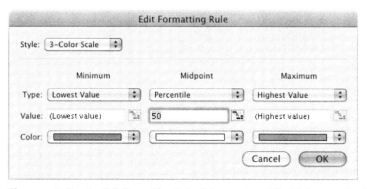

Figure 8–9. *Use the Edit Formatting Rule dialog box to set the Minimum value, Midpoint value, and Maximum value for the scale. You can also change the colors by using the three Color pop-up menus.*

4. If you need to change from a three-color scale to a two-color scale or vice versa, open the Style pop-up menu, then click 3-Color Scale or 2-Color Scale, as appropriate.

5. In the Minimum column, open the Type pop-up menu and choose Lowest Value, Number, Percent, Formula, or Percentile, as needed. Next, enter a suitable value in the Value box, either by typing it in or by clicking the Collapse Dialog button, clicking the appropriate cell in the worksheet, then clicking the Collapse Dialog button again. If necessary, open the Color pop-up menu and choose a different color.

6. For a three-color scale, go to the Midpoint column, then set the type, value, and color.

7. In the Maximum column, set the type, value, and color.

8. Click the OK button to close the Edit Formatting Rule dialog box. Excel returns you to the Manage Rules dialog box.

9. Click the OK button to close the Manage Rules dialog box. Excel applies the changes to the worksheet.

Representing Data Graphically with Icon Sets

Another helpful way of representing data graphically is by using icon sets to indicate the relationship of a set of values to each other. For example, you can apply a set of directional arrows to make Excel show green up arrows on high values, yellow right-pointing arrows on midpoint values, and red down arrows on low values. Figure 8–10 shows this kind of icon set used to track the month-by-month and full-quarter performance of the five salespeople you met earlier in this chapter.

	A	B	C	D	E
1	Salesperson	July	August	September	Q3
2	Smith	⇨ $141,997 ⇨	$94,591 ⇨	$135,099 ⇧	$371,687.00
3	Jones	⇧ $182,651 ⇩	$48,821 ⇩	$94,479 ⇨	$325,951.00
4	Ramirez	⇩ $63,970 ⇨	$86,599 ⇧	$191,580 ⇧	$342,149.00
5	Lee	⇩ $80,014 ⇧	$123,762 ⇩	$118,371 ⇨	$322,147.00
6	Kim	⇩ $96,903 ⇨	$86,933 ⇩	$88,273 ⇩	$272,109.00

Figure 8–10. *Apply an icon set to a range of cells to provide a quick visual reference to their relationship. This worksheet uses four icon sets—one on column B, one on column C, one on column D, and one on column E— rather than a single icon set, which would compare all the values in B2:E6 to each other and show that the third-quarter totals in column E made the monthly values look pretty miserable.*

To apply an icon set to cells, follow these steps:

1. Enter the data that will produce the icon set.

2. Select the cells that contain the data.

3. Choose Home ➤ Format ➤ Conditional Formatting ➤ Icon Sets to display the Icon Sets panel (see Figure 8–11).

Figure 8–11. *On the Icon Sets panel, click the set of icons you want to apply to the selected cells.*

4. Click the icon set you want to apply.

Many icon sets work straight out of the box (as it were), but you may need to adjust others as follows:

1. With the cells still selected, choose Home ➤ Format ➤ Conditional Formatting ➤ Manage Rules to display the Manage Rules dialog box (shown in Figure 8–4, earlier in this chapter).

2. Make sure the right rule is selected. If you've applied only one conditional formatting rule to the cells, it will be; if you've applied multiple rules, you may need to click the right rule.

3. Click the Edit Rule button to display the Edit Formatting Rule dialog box (see Figure 8–12).

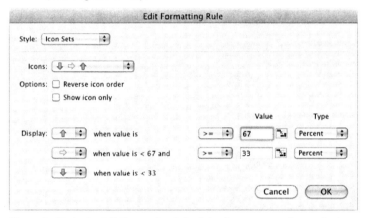

Figure 8–12. *In the Edit Formatting Rule dialog box, you can change the icons, reverse the order, show only the icons, and change the threshold values.*

4. To change the icons used, open the Icons pop-up menu, then click the icon set you want.

5. If you want to show the icons in reverse order, select the Reverse icon order check box.

6. If you want to show the icons without the values that produce them, select the show icon only check box.

TIP: When you want to show each value in one cell and its icon in another cell, set up the icon cells with formulas that refer to the value cells. For example, enter **=B2** in cell C2, then apply an icon set to the icon cells, open the Edit Formatting Rule dialog box, and select the Show icon only check box.

7. In the Display area, choose the icons you want to use and the threshold values for them.

8. Click the OK button to close the Edit Formatting Rule dialog box. Excel returns you to the Manage Rules dialog box.

9. Click the OK button to close the Manage Rules dialog box and return to your worksheet, which shows the changes you made.

Showing Data Trends with Sparklines

As you saw in Chapter 7, charts are great for illustrating medium to large quantities of information, but sometimes you'll want something smaller—a chart that'll fit inside a single cell, giving a quick visual indication of a trend. Excel calls such charts *sparklines*.

Excel provides three kinds of sparklines:

- *Line.* A line sparkline is a straightforward line that runs through the data points, as in the top part of Figure 8–13. A line sparkline is good for showing data that flows from one data point to the next, such as temperatures.

- *Column.* A column sparkline shows the data as a series of columns, as in a column chart. The middle part of Figure 8–13 shows an example. A column sparkline is good for comparing data points that are separate from each other, such as sales results by month.

- *Win/Loss.* A win/loss sparkline shows results as either a win (a positive result) or a loss (a negative result). The lower part of Figure 8–13 shows an example of win/loss sparklines. A win/loss sparkline is good for when you want to take a black-and-white view of results—for example, whether your investments are up or down in a particular month. In a win/loss sparkline, a zero value appears as a blank.

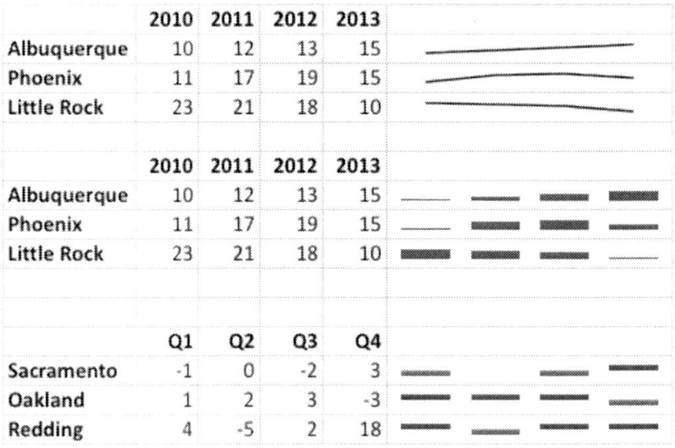

	2010	2011	2012	2013	
Albuquerque	10	12	13	15	
Phoenix	11	17	19	15	
Little Rock	23	21	18	10	

	2010	2011	2012	2013	
Albuquerque	10	12	13	15	
Phoenix	11	17	19	15	
Little Rock	23	21	18	10	

	Q1	Q2	Q3	Q4	
Sacramento	-1	0	-2	3	
Oakland	1	2	3	-3	
Redding	4	-5	2	18	

Figure 8–13. *Sparklines are single-cell charts that you can use to indicate trends or results visually.*

Inserting Sparklines

To insert one or more sparklines in a worksheet, follow these steps:

1. Click the cell or select the range you want to place the sparklines in.

2. Click the Charts tab to display its contents, go to the Insert Sparklines group, then click the Line button, the Column button, or the Win/Loss button, as needed. Whichever button you click, Excel displays the Insert Sparklines dialog box (see Figure 8–14).

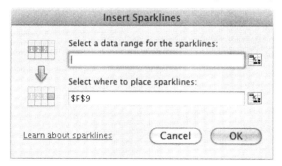

Figure 8–14. *In the Insert Sparklines dialog box, choose the data range for the sparklines and the cells in which to place them.*

3. With the focus in the Select a data range for the sparklines text box (where Excel places it when it displays the Insert Sparklines dialog box), click and drag in the worksheet to enter the range that contains the data for the sparklines.

4. Make sure the Select where to place sparklines text box contains the range in which you want to place the sparklines. If you chose the range before displaying the Insert Sparklines dialog box, it'll be correct. Otherwise, click in this text box, then drag in the worksheet to select the range.

5. Click the OK button to close the Insert Sparklines dialog box. Excel inserts the sparklines in the cells.

Formatting Your Sparklines

After inserting sparklines, you can format them by using the controls on the Sparklines tab of the Ribbon. Click a cell in the sparklines to select the group of sparklines and make Excel add the Sparklines tab to the Ribbon. If Excel doesn't display the Sparklines tab automatically, click the tab to display it (see Figure 8–15).

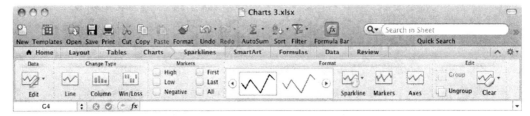

Figure 8–15. *Use the controls on the Sparklines tab of the Ribbon to format sparklines to look the way you want them to.*

These are the main moves for formatting your sparklines:

■ *Change the source data for a group of sparklines.* Click a cell in the group of sparklines, then choose **Sparklines ➤ Data ➤ Edit** from the Ribbon (clicking the main part of the Edit button). Excel displays the Edit Sparklines dialog box, which has the same controls as the Insert Sparklines dialog box.

■ *Change the source data for a single sparkline.* Click the sparkline cell, then choose **Sparklines ➤ Data ➤ Edit ➤ Edit Single Sparkline.** Excel displays the Edit Sparkline dialog box, which works like the Insert Sparklines dialog box, but affects only the cell you chose.

■ *Change a sparkline to a different type.* Click the sparkline cell, then click the Line button, the Column button, or the Win/Loss button in the Change Type group on the Sparklines tab of the Ribbon.

■ *Add markers to the sparklines.* In the Markers group on the Sparklines tab of the Ribbon, select the High check box, the Low check box, the Negative check box, the First check box, or the Last check box as needed—or select the All check box to select all the others. To change the marker color, choose **Sparklines ➤ Format ➤ Markers**, then work in the Markers dialog box (see Figure 8–16).

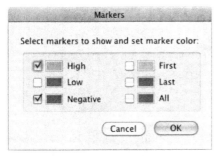

Figure 8–16. *Use the Markers dialog box to change the colors of markers and to choose which ones appear on the sparklines.*

TIP: For many kinds of data, the High marker and Low marker are the most useful. Win/loss sparklines use the Negative marker by default, while line sparklines and column sparklines don't use any markers by default.

■ *Apply a style to the sparklines.* In the Format group on the Sparklines tab of the Ribbon, either click a style in the Styles box or hold the mouse pointer over the Styles box to display the panel button. Next, click the panel button to display the Styles panel, then click the style you want.

■ *Change the color of the sparklines.* Choose **Sparklines ➤ Format ➤ Sparkline** to display the Sparkline panel, then click the color you want.

■ *Change the weight of the sparklines.* Choose **Sparklines ➤ Format ➤ Sparkline ➤ Weight**, then click the line weight.

■ *Change the axes for the sparklines.* Choose **Sparklines ➤ Format ➤ Axes** to display the Axes dialog box (see Figure 8–17), then make your choices in it.

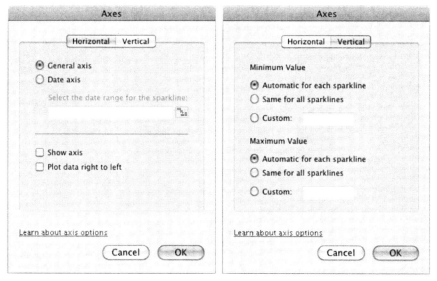

Figure 8–17. *You can use the Axes dialog box to choose settings for the horizontal and vertical axes of the sparklines.*

■ *Group sparklines together.* If you need to format separate sets of sparklines quickly, group them together. Select each set of sparklines, then choose **Sparklines ➤ Edit ➤ Group** from the Ribbon to group them.

■ *Clear sparklines.* When you no longer need sparklines, clear them from the cells. Select the sparkline cells you want to clear, then choose **Sparklines ➤ Edit ➤ Clear**, clicking the main part of the Clear button. You can also click a single cell and then choose **Sparklines ➤ Edit ➤ Clear ➤ Clear Selected Sparkline Groups** to clear all the cells in the group

Summary

In this chapter, you've learned how to illustrate your worksheets by attaching data bars, color scales, and icon sets to conditional formatting. You've also learned how to show data trends with sparklines.

In the next chapter, I'll show you how to illustrate your worksheets further using pictures, clip art, SmartArt diagrams, and shapes.

Chapter 9

Illustrating Your Worksheets with Pictures, SmartArt, and More

To give your workbooks visual interest, you can add graphics, shapes, SmartArt diagrams, and WordArt items to them. Graphics are pictures and images in the various formats that Excel can import, and shapes are Excel's built-in shapes, which include everything from simple arrows and regular shapes (such as circles, squares, and triangles) to complex shapes you create on the fly. SmartArt includes a range of graphics such as organization charts and flowcharts, while WordArt is graphical text that you create to your preferred design.

This chapter shows you how to insert clip art and other pictures, how to insert shapes and format them, and how to position graphical objects where you want them. You'll learn how to make a picture look the way you want it, how to position graphical objects wherever you need them, and how to illustrate your workbooks by adding SmartArt diagrams and WordArt items. Beyond that, I show you how to position graphical items relative to cells and how to arrange graphical objects to control which ones are visible.

Before we start, there's one vital thing you need to know: Even though a worksheet appears to be flat, it actually consists of multiple separate layers. Until you add objects to a layer, the layer is transparent, so you see through the layer to whatever is underneath. One layer contains the worksheet's cells; the other layers contain graphical objects. Having these multiple layers enables you to position graphical objects either in front of the cells or behind them. You can also position a graphical object in front of another graphical object; for example, to superimpose one image on another.

Inserting Clip Art

When you need a quick illustration in a workbook, you can insert a clip art item. Office includes a modest but useful set of clip art pictures that you can use in your workbooks. You can also download other clip art pictures from the Office pages of the Microsoft web site.

Excel gives you two tools for inserting clip art:

- *Clip Art Browser.* The Clip Art Browser is a pane that appears in the Media Browser. It shows a variety of clip art pictures.

- *Clip Gallery application.* The Clip Gallery is a separate application that you can use to manage your clips and insert them in your workbooks. The Clip Gallery has a wider selection of clip art pictures than the Clip Art Browser pane, but some of the items are the same. The Clip Gallery also has more features for helping you locate images.

We'll start with the Clip Art Browser.

Inserting a Clip Art Picture Using the Clip Art Browser

When you need a clip art picture, first see whether the Clip Art Browser contains a suitable picture. To open the Clip Art Browser and insert an item, follow these steps:

1. Choose Insert ➤ Clip Art ➤ Clip Art Browser from the menu bar to display the Clip Art Browser pane in the Media Browser window. Figure 9–1 shows the Clip Art Browser pane.

Figure 9–1. *Use the Clip Art Browser pane in the Media Browser to insert clip art pictures in your workbooks. You can drag the sizing handle at the lower-right corner to resize the Media Browser.*

2. In the pop-up menu at the top, choose All Images if you want to see all the images available, or choose the category of images you want—for example, Animals or Business.

3. If you want to zoom in to see the pictures at a larger size, drag the zoom slider at the bottom to the right. To zoom out, drag the slider to the left.

4. Browse through the clip art items that appear in the Clip Art Browser to find the one you want.

5. To insert an item, click it and drag it to where you want it to appear in the workbook.

Instead of inserting a clip art picture in the workbook, you can Ctrl+click it or right-click it and then click Copy on the context menu to copy it to the Clipboard. You can then use the Paste command (for example, press Cmd+V) to paste the clip art picture where you need it.

Inserting a Clip Art Picture Using the Clip Gallery

If the Clip Art Browser doesn't contain a suitable picture for your workbook, try the Clip Gallery. Follow these steps:

1. Click the cell at which you want to position the upper-left corner of the picture.

2. Choose Insert ➤ Clip Art ➤ Clip Art Gallery from the menu bar to launch the Clip Gallery application (see Figure 9–2).

3. In the Category list box, click the category of pictures you want to display. You can then scroll through the pictures.

4. To search by clip name or keyword, type the search term in the Search box, and then click the Search button. The Clip Gallery adds all matching clips to the Search Results category at the top of the Category list box and displays this category in the main box.

5. Click the clip art item you want to insert in the workbook.

6. Click the Insert button. Excel inserts the clip art item and automatically closes the Clip Gallery.

Figure 9–2. *The Clip Gallery is a tool for managing your clip art and inserting clip art items in workbooks. To see more pictures at once, drag the sizing handle at the lower-right corner down or to the right.*

Managing Your Clip Art Items with the Clip Gallery

To get the most out of the Clip Gallery, you can add your own pictures, motion clips, and sounds to it. You can also download clip art items from the Microsoft Office web site and add them to the Clip Gallery. To keep the Clip Gallery items arranged and make it easy to find the items you need, you can change the categories in the Clip Gallery and tag the items with keywords.

Adding Your Own Pictures to the Clip Gallery

To add your own pictures to the Clip Gallery, follow these steps:

1. Choose Insert ➤ Clip Art ➤ Clip Art Gallery from the menu bar to open the Clip Gallery.

2. Click the Import button to display the Import dialog box (see Figure 9–3).

Figure 9–3. *Use the Import dialog box to add your own pictures or downloaded pictures to the Clip Gallery.*

3. In the Enable pop-up menu, choose the type of items you want to add:

    ▦ *All Clips.* Select this item to import any type of item the Clip Gallery can handle.

    ▦ *Clip Gallery Images.* Select this item to add picture files to the Clip Gallery.

    ▦ *Clip Gallery Movies.* Select this item to add movies.

    ▦ *Clip Gallery Sounds.* Select this item to add sound files.

    ▦ *Clip Gallery Packages.* Select this item to add gallery packages you've downloaded.

    ▦ *Microsoft Office Online Files.* Select this item to add gallery packages you've downloaded in the `.cil` file format from the Microsoft Office web site.

4. Click the file to add to the gallery.

5. In the lower-left corner of the Import dialog box, select the appropriate option button to choose how to add the item to the Clip Gallery:

    ▦ *Copy into Clip Gallery.* Select this option button to make a copy of the clip and add that copy to the Clip Gallery. Take this approach when the clip art item is on a removable drive or a network drive.

- *Move into Clip Gallery.* Select this option button to move the clip from its current folder to the Clip Gallery. Use this option when you've downloaded a file but not for your material that you've organized into folders.

- *Add alias to Clip Gallery.* Select this option button to add an alias to the Clip Gallery. The alias is a file shortcut; it points to the file in its current location. Use this option for material you've organized into folders but want to add to the Clip Gallery.

6. Click the Import button. The Clip Gallery closes the Import dialog box and displays the Properties dialog box for the item (or the first item if you're importing multiple items). Figure 9–4 shows the Description tab of the Properties dialog box for a picture.

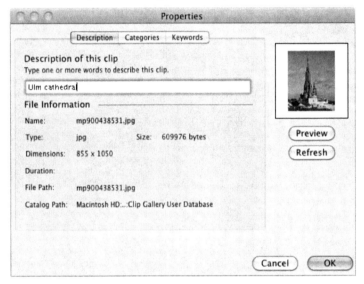

Figure 9–4. *On the Description tab of the Properties dialog box for a clip art item, enter a useful description in place of the file name.*

7. In the Description of this clip box, type a description of what the clip shows. The Clip Gallery suggests the first part of the file name as the description, but you'll often want to improve on this.

8. Click the Categories tab to display its contents (see Figure 9–5).

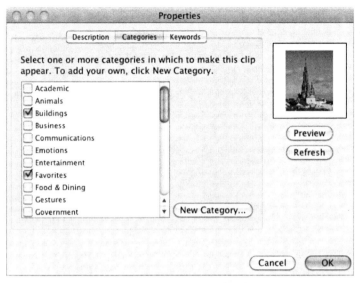

Figure 9–5. *On the Categories tab of the Properties dialog box, select the check box for each category you want to assign the item to. To add a category, click the New Category button.*

9. Select the check box for each category you want the picture to appear in. If no category is suitable, create one by clicking the New Category button, typing the name in the New Category dialog box, and clicking the OK button.

10. Click the Keywords tab to display its contents (see Figure 9–6).

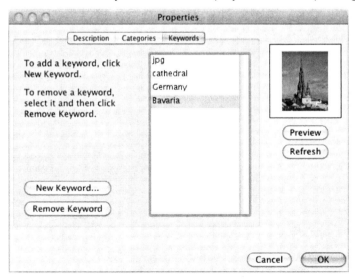

Figure 9–6. *On the Keywords tab of the Properties dialog box, add keywords to the clip art item so that you will be able to search for it.*

11. Mark the clip art item with the keywords it needs. Use these techniques:

- *Add a keyword.* Click the New Keyword button to open the New Keyword dialog box. Type the keyword, and then press the Return key or click the OK button.

- *Remove a keyword.* Click the keyword in the list box, and then click the Remove Keyword button. In the confirmation dialog box that opens, click the OK button.

12. Click the OK button to close the Properties dialog box. The Clip Gallery imports the picture and adds it to the categories you chose.

Downloading Clip Art Items from the Microsoft Office Web Site

The Clip Gallery contains enough items to get you started with clip art, but if you need to use clip art extensively in your workbooks, you'll probably want to download other items from the Microsoft Office web site and add them to the gallery. To do so, follow these steps:

1. Choose Insert ➤ Clip Art ➤ Clip Art Gallery from the menu bar to open the Clip Gallery.

2. Click the Online button to launch or activate your default browser and display the Images page on the Microsoft Office web site.

> **NOTE:** The first time you click the Online button in the Clip Gallery, the Launch Browser dialog box appears, asking your permission for it to launch your default browser. Select the Don't Ask Me Again check box, and then click the Yes button.

3. Browse to find the images you want.

4. Add each image to your basket by moving the mouse pointer over the image, waiting until the details panel pops up, and then clicking the Add to Basket link on it.

5. When you're ready to download the images, move your mouse over the Selection Basket link in the upper-right corner, and then click the Download link.

6. On the web page that appears, click the Download button to download the clip art items in an archive file.

7. Click the Downloads folder on the Dock, and then click the archive file. Its name starts with ClipArt, and it has the file extension .cil, so it should be easy to identify. The Clip Gallery automatically imports the files.

NOTE: If your Dock doesn't contain a Downloads folder, open a Finder window to the Downloads folder in your user account. Then double-click the archive file. Alternatively, click the Import button in the Clip Gallery window, click the file in the Import dialog box, and then click the Import button.

After importing the files, you may want to set their properties and keywords as described in the previous section to make them easier to find.

Organizing the Clip Gallery with Categories

As you saw a little earlier in this chapter, you can create new categories as needed when importing items into the Clip Gallery. You can also create or delete categories by clicking the Categories button in the Clip Gallery and working in the Categories dialog box (see Figure 9–7):

- *Create a category.* Click the New Category button to display the New Category dialog box. Type the name for the category, and then click the OK button.

NOTE: These categories appear only in the Clip Gallery, not in the Clip Art Browser.

- *Delete a category.* Click the category in the list box, and then click the Delete button. In the confirmation dialog box, click the OK button.

Figure 9–7. *Use the Categories dialog box in the Clip Gallery to delete existing categories or create new categories.*

Inserting Pictures in Your Workbooks

Clip art is fine for basic illustrations, but everybody has access to the same collection of pictures. To make your workbooks unique, you can insert your own photos and other pictures, too.

You can insert either pictures you've added to iPhoto or pictures that are in your Mac's file system but not in iPhoto. Because iPhoto is Mac OS X's standard application for importing photos from a digital camera and editing them, you'll probably want to use it much of the time.

Inserting Pictures from iPhoto

To insert a picture from iPhoto, follow these steps:

1. Click the Media button on the Standard toolbar or choose **View ➤ Media Browser** from the menu bar to open the Media Browser.

2. Click the Photos button on the toolbar to display the Photos Browser pane (see Figure 9–8).

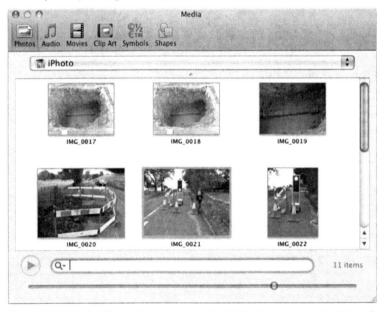

Figure 9–8. *Use the Photos Browser pane in the Media Browser to add a picture from iPhoto to a workbook.*

3. In the pop-up menu, choose the source of the pictures. For example, choose iPhoto to see all pictures in iPhoto, choose Events to see a list of Events you've created in iPhoto, or choose Last Import to see the photos you last imported.

4. Click the photo you want, and then drag it to the workbook window, dropping it where you want it to appear.

5. Leave the Media Browser window open if you want to use it further. Otherwise, click the Close button (the red button in its upper-left corner) to close it.

Inserting Pictures from Your Mac's File System

To insert a picture that's not in iPhoto but is stored in your Mac's file system or on a network drive, follow these steps:

1. Position the insertion point or selection where you want the picture to appear.

2. Choose Insert ➤ Photo ➤ Picture from File from the menu bar to display the Choose a Picture dialog box (see Figure 9–9).

Figure 9–9. *From the Choose a Picture dialog box, you can choose whether to link the picture to the workbook. For some picture types, you can also choose to treat the picture layers as separate objects so that you can manipulate them independently.*

3. Navigate to the folder that contains the file, and then click the file.

4. If you want to link the picture file to the workbook rather than insert it, select the Link to File check box. When you do this, you can select the Save with Document check box to store the latest version of the picture file in the workbook. See the sidebar "Linking a Picture to a Workbook" for advice about linking.

5. If you want to be able to manipulate each layer of the picture separately, select the Treat picture layers as separate objects check box. This feature is available only for some types of pictures, such as JPEGs.

6. Click the Insert button. Excel closes the Choose a Picture dialog box and inserts the picture in the workbook.

> **TIP:** You can also insert a picture file by dragging it from a Finder window to a workbook.

LINKING A PICTURE TO A WORKBOOK

When you add a picture to a workbook from your Mac's file system, you can either insert it or link it. Inserting the picture adds a copy of the picture to the workbook. Excel saves the picture in the workbook, so even if you move the workbook, the picture stays in it.

If you need to keep the workbook's file size down or if you need to be able to update the picture easily, you can link the picture instead. Linking makes Excel add to the workbook a link to the picture file. When you open the workbook, Excel loads the current version of the picture from the file. But if you move the workbook to a different computer, the link no longer works, because Excel can't find the picture file.

To solve the problem of broken links, you can link a picture but also save the latest version of it. To do this, select the Link to File check box and the Save with Document check box in the Choose a Picture dialog box. When you open the workbook, Excel checks to see whether the linked version is available. If so, Excel loads the linked picture; if not, it displays the version saved in the workbook.

Adding and Formatting a Shape

If a workbook needs a drawing, you can create it from scratch by using shapes. Excel provides a wide variety of shapes, from arrows and basic shapes to stars, banners, and callouts.

To insert a shape, follow these steps:

1. Display the area of the workbook where you want to add the shape. When adding a shape, you don't need to position the insertion point or make a selection.

> **NOTE:** You can also insert a shape by choosing **Home ➤ Insert ➤ Shape** from the Ribbon to display the Shape panel, clicking the category of shape (for example, Lines and Connectors), and then clicking the type of shape. But in general the Shape Browser gives you an easier way to access shapes.

2. Click the Media button on the Standard toolbar or choose **View ➤ Media Browser** from the menu bar to display the Media Browser.

3. Click the Shapes button in the toolbar to display the Shapes Browser pane (see Figure 9–10).

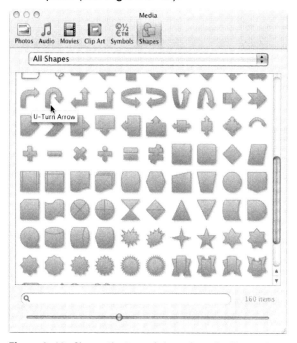

Figure 9–10. *Choose the type of shape from the Shapes Browser pane in the Media Browser. Hold the mouse pointer over a shape to see a ScreenTip showing its description.*

4. In the pop-up menu at the top of the Shapes Browser, click the category of shapes you want to see: All Shapes, Rectangles, Basic Shapes, Lines and Connectors, Block Arrows, Equation Shapes, Flowchart, Stars and Banners, or Callouts.

5. Click the shape you want. Excel changes the mouse pointer to a crosshair.

6. With this crosshair, click where you want to place one corner of the shape, and then drag to the opposite corner (see Figure 9–11). It doesn't matter which corner you place first, because you can drag in any direction, but placing the upper-left corner first is usually easiest.

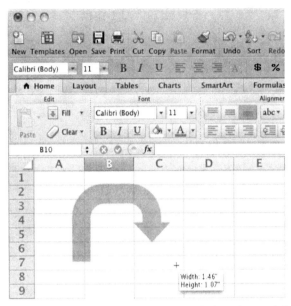

Figure 9–11. *Click and drag with the crosshair to place and size the shape you're inserting.*

When you release the mouse button, the shape appears with selection handles around it, so you can work with it as described in the following sections. When the shape is selected, Excel adds the Format tab to the Ribbon, which provides controls for formatting the shape.

Close the Media Browser window by clicking its Close button (the red button in the upper-left corner) unless you need to insert more shapes or other objects.

Applying a Style to a Shape

After inserting a shape, you can apply a style to it from the Shape Styles box or panel in the Shape Styles group on the Format tab of the Ribbon. If the style you want appears in the Shape Styles box, click it; otherwise, move the mouse pointer over the Shape Styles box so that the panel button appears, and then click the button to display the panel (see Figure 9–12). You can then click the style you want.

To refine the shape, open the Fill panel, the Line panel, or the Effects drop-down panel in the Shape Styles group, and then click the option you want. For example, choose **Format ➤ Shape Styles ➤ Shape Effects ➤ 3-D Rotation**, and then click one of the 3D rotation effects (see Figure 9–13).

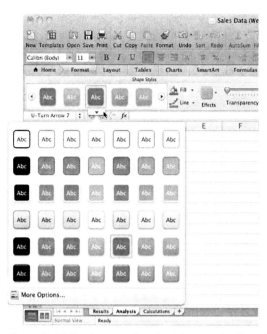

Figure 9–12. *To change a shape's style, open the Shape Styles panel on the Format tab of the Ribbon, and then click the style you want.*

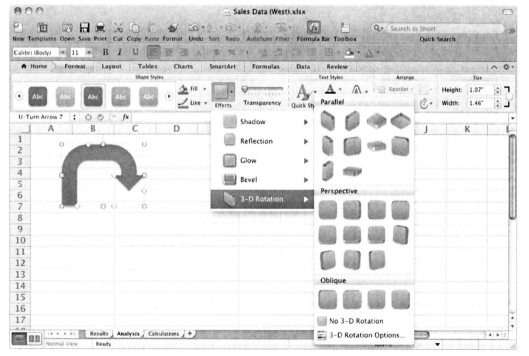

Figure 9–13. *Use the Fill panel, the Line panel, or the Effects panel (shown here) to make the shape look the way you want.*

Rotating a Graphical Object

After inserting a graphical object, you can rotate it as needed. Click to select the object, and then drag the green handle to the left to rotate counterclockwise (see Figure 9–14) or to the right to rotate clockwise.

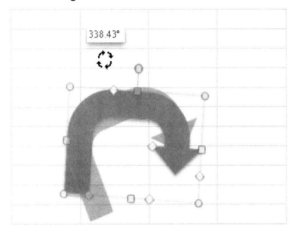

Figure 9–14. *Drag the green rotation handle to the left or right to rotate a graphical object.*

Positioning a Graphical Object

If you don't get a graphical object in precisely the right position when you insert it, you can easily move it afterward.

The quick way to reposition a graphical object is to click it and then drag it to where you want it. This works well most of the time, but for more precision you can also click the object to select it and then press an arrow key (for example, the Left arrow key) to nudge it a small distance in the arrow's direction.

When you need to control exactly where the object appears, Ctrl+click or right-click the object, and then click the Format command on the context menu to display the Format dialog box for the object (for example, click the Format Picture command to display the Format Picture dialog box). In the left pane, click the Size item to display the controls for resizing the object and controlling its placement. Figure 9–15 shows the Size category in the Format Picture dialog box.

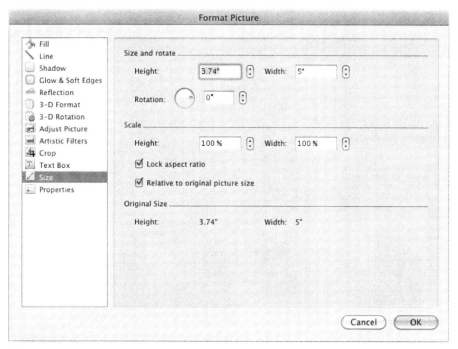

Figure 9–15. *Use the controls in the Size category of the Format dialog box for an object to resize and position the object precisely.*

Making a Picture Look the Way You Want It

After you insert a picture, you can use the controls that appear on the Format Picture tab of the Ribbon to make the picture look the way you want it. You can adjust the picture's colors, apply a picture style to the picture, or crop the picture so that only part of it shows.

Adjusting a Picture's Sharpness, Brightness, Contrast, and Colors

To adjust the sharpness, brightness, or contrast in a picture, click the picture to select it, and then choose **Format Picture ➤ Adjust ➤ Corrections** to open the Corrections panel (see Figure 9–16). Click the color correction you want.

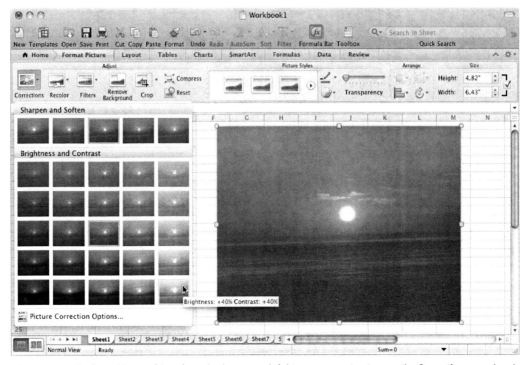

Figure 9–16. *To fix problems with a picture's sharpness, brightness, or contrast, open the Corrections panel and choose the look you want.*

To change the colors in a picture, click it, choose **Format Picture ➤ Adjust ➤ Recolor**, and then click the effect you want. The Color drop-down panel has different sections for Color Saturation, Color Tone, and Recolor (for example, Grayscale or Sepia).

To apply an effect such as paint strokes or a light screen to a picture, click the picture, choose **Format Picture ➤ Adjust ➤ Filters**, and then click the effect you want.

To reset a picture to its original look, choose **Format Picture ➤ Adjust ➤ Reset**.

Applying a Picture Style

To apply a picture style to a picture, click the picture, click the Format Picture tab of the Ribbon to display it, and then click the picture style you want. If the picture style appears in the Quick Styles box in the Picture Styles group, click it there; otherwise, move the mouse pointer over the Quick Styles box so that the panel button appears, click the panel button, and then click the picture style on the panel (see Figure 9–17).

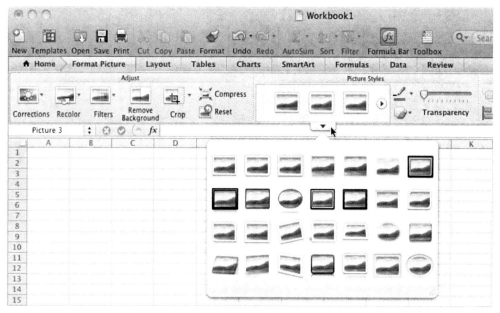

Figure 9–17. *Choose the picture style from the Quick Styles box or panel in the Picture Styles group of the Format Picture tab on the Ribbon.*

Cropping a Picture

If you need the workbook to show only part of a picture rather than the whole picture, you can crop off the parts you don't want.

Excel lets you crop a picture in several ways, but this way is usually the easiest:

1. Click the picture to select it. Excel adds the Format Picture tab to the Ribbon.

2. Click the Format Picture tab if Excel has not displayed it.

3. Choose **Format Picture ➤ Adjust ➤ Crop**, clicking the top part of the Crop button rather than the drop-down button. Excel displays crop handles on the picture (see Figure 9–18).

Figure 9–18. *The quick way of cropping is to drag the crop handles until they encompass the part of the picture you want to keep.*

4.   Drag the crop handles to make the cropping area contain the part of the picture you want to show:

    ▨ Shift+drag to crop the image proportionally.

    ▨ Option+drag to crop the image evenly around its center point.

    ▨ Option+Shift+drag to crop the image proportionally around its center point.

    ▨ Cmd+drag to crop the image in increments of worksheet cells.

> **TIP:** If you make the crop area exactly the size you need, you can click and drag within the crop area to make a different part of the picture appear in it. You move the picture, not the crop area—much as if you were to reach through a window and move the landscape until the window displayed the part you wanted to see.

5.   Click the Crop button again to turn off the Crop tool, or click elsewhere in the workbook to deselect the picture. Excel applies the cropping to the picture.

> **NOTE:** You can also crop a picture to fit into a shape. To do this, choose **Format Picture ➤ Adjust ➤ Crop**, clicking the Crop pop-up arrow button rather than the top part of the button. On the pop-up menu that appears, choose Mask to Shape, and then click the shape you want.

Saving Space by Compressing Pictures

When you insert pictures in a workbook (rather than linking them, as discussed earlier in this chapter), Excel saves a copy of each picture in the workbook. This can greatly increase the file size of the workbook.

To keep the workbook's file size down, you can compress the pictures and delete the cropped areas of them. To do so, follow these steps:

1. Click a picture to make Excel add the Format Picture tab to the Ribbon.

2. Choose **Format Picture ➤ Adjust ➤ Compress** to display the Reduce File Size dialog box (see Figure 9–19).

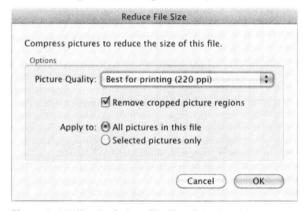

Figure 9–19. *Use the Reduce File Size dialog box when you want to reduce the file size of one or more pictures or when you want to delete the cropped areas of pictures.*

3. In the Picture Quality pop-up menu, select the picture quality you want:

   ■ *Best for printing (220 ppi).* Compresses the pictures only a little, leaving them high enough quality for most purposes.

   ■ *Best for viewing on screen (150 ppi).* Compresses the pictures a bit further but leaves them looking good enough for use on the screen.

   ■ *Best for sending in e-mail (96 ppi).* Compresses the pictures to the extent that they start to look bad but are OK for viewing on the screen at small sizes.

   ■ *Keep current resolution.* Keeps the pictures at their current resolution. You'd use this setting for removing the cropped parts of pictures without changing the resolution.

4. In the Apply to area, select the Selected Pictures Only option button if you want to affect only the picture you've selected. Normally, you'll want to select the All Pictures In This File option button to make Excel compress all the pictures in the workbook.

5. Select the Remove Cropped Picture Regions check box if you want to get rid of the areas you've cropped off. This is a good idea once you're sure you won't need to adjust the cropping of any pictures in the workbook to reveal more.

NOTE: Removing the cropped picture regions not only reduces the file size, but it can save embarrassment if the cropped areas contain sensitive information.

6. Click the OK button. Excel closes the Reduce File Size dialog box and changes the quality or cropping as you specified.

Inserting SmartArt Diagrams

When you need to create an illustration such as an organization chart, a flow chart, or a Venn diagram, use the SmartArt feature. Follow these steps:

1. Position the insertion point or the selection where you want to insert the SmartArt object.

2. Click the SmartArt tab on the Ribbon to display its contents. You can also display this tab by choosing Insert ➤ SmartArt Graphic from the menu bar.

3. In the Insert SmartArt Graphic box, click the button for the category of SmartArt graphic you want to create: List, Process, Cycle, Hierarchy, Relationship, Picture, or Other. A panel opens, showing the available types. Figure 9–20 shows the Hierarchy panel, which includes various kinds of organization charts.

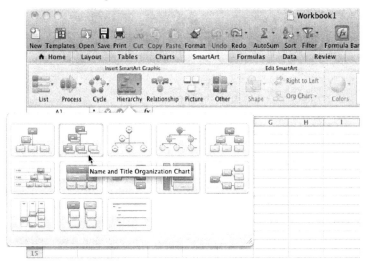

Figure 9–20. *Open the panel for the category of SmartArt graphics you want, and then click the type of graphic.*

4. Click the type of graphic you want. Excel inserts it in the workbook and displays the Text Pane (see Figure 9–21).

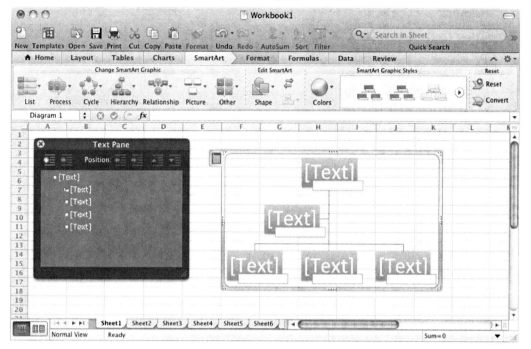

Figure 9–21. *When you insert a SmartArt graphic, Excel displays the Text Pane next to it so that you can enter text.*

NOTE: If Excel doesn't display the Text Pane, click the Text Pane button at the upper-left corner of the SmartArt graphic to display the Text Pane. You can also click this button to hide the Text Pane when you don't need it.

5. In the Text Pane, type the text for each item. As you do, Excel adds the text to the SmartArt graphic (see Figure 9–22).

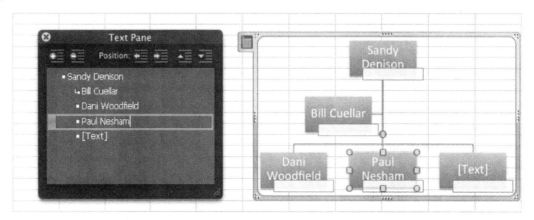

Figure 9–22. *Add the text to the SmartArt graphic by typing in the Text Pane.*

6. Add any other items the SmartArt graphic needs. For example, to add the titles to the org chart shown, click in each title placeholder, and then type the title.

7. Resize the SmartArt graphic to suit the workbook best. For example, you may need to make it the right size to go alongside related data.

8. If you need to change the layout of the SmartArt graphic, choose another layout from the Change SmartArt Graphic group on the SmartArt tab of the Ribbon.

9. Apply a style to the SmartArt graphic by choosing a style from the Quick Styles box or the panel in the SmartArt Graphic Styles group on the SmartArt tab.

When you have finished creating the SmartArt graphic, save the workbook as usual.

Adding Decorative Text with WordArt

If you need to add a design touch to a workbook, you can add a WordArt item. WordArt gives you an easy way to turn text into graphical items—for example, for your company logo.

To create a WordArt item, follow these steps:

1. Choose Insert ➤ WordArt from the menu bar to add a WordArt item and to add the Format tab to the Ribbon.

2. Type your text over the placeholder text ("Your Text Here") in the WordArt box (see Figure 9–23).

Figure 9–23. *Type your text in the WordArt container and drag it to where you want it in the worksheet.*

3. Drag the WordArt item to where you want it. Move the mouse pointer over the item's border, and then drag.

4. Resize the WordArt item as needed. You can either drag a side or corner handle or change the values in the Height box and Width box in the Size group on the Format tab. Select the check box on the right size of the Size group if you want to preserve the aspect ratio of the WordArt item (so that Excel automatically adjusts the width when you change the height, and vice versa).

5. Format the WordArt item so it looks the way you want it:

   ▦ Move the mouse pointer over the Shape Styles box, click the panel button that appears, and then click the style you want to use.

   ▦ To change the WordArt item's fill, choose **Format ➤ Shape Styles ➤ Fill**, and then click the fill you want.

   ▦ To change the WordArt item's line color, weight, or type, choose **Format ➤ Shape Styles ➤ Line**, and then choose suitable options.

   ▦ To apply an effect, choose **Format ➤ Shape Styles ➤ Effects**, and then choose the effect you want. For example, click the 3-D Rotation submenu, and then choose a rotation effect.

   ▦ To change the text style, work with the controls in the Text Styles group on the Format tab.

Positioning Graphical Objects Relative to Cells

As you've seen earlier in this chapter, you can drag a graphical object to wherever in the worksheet you need it to appear. But you can also connect the graphical object to the cells over which it appears, so that when you move the cells, the object moves too. This setting is handy when you need to keep the graphical object with particular cells. You can also have Excel resize the object when you resize the cells.

To control whether a graphical object moves and changes size with cells, follow these steps:

1. Ctrl+click or right-click the graphical object, and then click the Properties command on the context menu to display the Format dialog box. For example, Ctrl+click or right-click a picture, and then click the Format Picture command to display the Format Picture dialog box.

2. In the left pane, click the Properties item to display the Properties pane (see Figure 9–24).

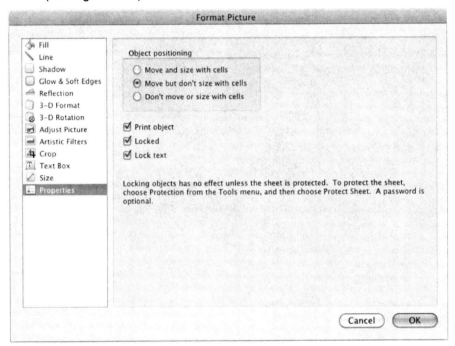

Figure 9–24. *In the Properties pane of the Format dialog box, choose whether to move and resize the graphical object with cells. You can also choose whether to print the object, lock it, or lock its text.*

3. In the Object positioning box, select the Move And Size With Cells option button, the Move But Don't Size With Cells option button, or the Don't Move Or Size With Cells option button, as appropriate.

NOTE: In the Properties pane of the Format dialog box, you can also clear the Print object check box if you want to avoid printing the graphical object. You can also select the Locked check box to lock the object, or the Lock text check box to lock the object's text; these settings take effect only when you protect the worksheet against changes.

4. Click the OK button to close the Format dialog box. Excel applies your choices to the graphical object.

Arranging Graphical Objects to Control Which Is Visible

When you have placed multiple graphical objects in the same area of a workbook, you may need to arrange the order in which they appear in the workbook's layers to control how they appear in relation to each other. For example, you may need to move a particular object to the front of the stack of layers, so that it appears on top of the other objects, or move another object back so that it appears behind one of its companion objects.

To change where an object appears in the layers, Ctrl+click or right-click the object, click or highlight the Arrange submenu, and then click the appropriate command:

- *Bring to Front.* Click this command to bring the item to the very front of the stack.

- *Send to Back.* Click this command to send the item right to the back of the stack.

- *Bring Forward.* Click this command to bring the object forward by one layer. Give the command again as many times as necessary to bring the object up the stack to where you need it.

- *Send Backward*. Click this command to send the object backward by one layer. As with the Bring Forward command, you may need to give this command multiple times to get the object to where you need it.

Summary

In this chapter, you learned how to work with graphical objects in Excel. You now know how to insert clip art and how to manage clip art items using Office's Clip Gallery application. You know how to insert your own pictures from iPhoto or your Mac's file system, how to insert shapes and format them, and how to position graphical objects where you want them. You also learned how to recolor, crop, and compress pictures; how to create SmartArt graphics and WordArt items to illustrate your workbooks; and how to position graphical objects relative to cells and arrange graphical objects to control which is visible.

This is the end of Part II of the book. In Part III, I show you how to analyze your data, how to share your workbooks with your colleagues, and how to automate your workbooks.

Part

Analyzing Data and Sharing and Automating Workbooks

In this part of the book, you learn to analyze, manipulate, and share the workbooks you've built.

In Chapter 10, we look at how to use Excel's tables to create databases for storing information, sorting it, and filtering it to find the records you need. You also learn how to put Excel's database functions to work with tables.

In Chapter 11, we cover how to analyze your data using four powerful tools. You learn to use data tables to assess the impact of one or two variables on a calculation and scenarios to experiment with different sets of values without changing your core data. You also learn to use Goal Seek to solve single-variable problems and Solver to crack multi-variable problems.

In Chapter 12, we go through what PivotTables are and how you can use them to examine the data in your worksheets and find the secrets it contains. You learn how to create PivotTables either using Excel's automated tool or by placing fields manually where you need them, how to change the PivotTable once you've created it, and how to sort and filter the data it contains.

In Chapter 13, we talk about ways to share your workbooks with others. We start by covering how to print worksheets, create PDF files from them, and export data to comma-separated values files. We then move on to sharing workbooks so that multiple people can work on them at the same time, and how to track the changes if necessary so that you can review them later. We finish by looking at how to merge changes from separate copies of the same workbook into one workbook and how to consolidate multiple worksheets into a single worksheet.

In Chapter 14, we explore how to record macros to eliminate the drudgery of performing the same task over and over again. You learn how to run macros using the menus or toolbars, by creating keyboard shortcuts, or even by assigning macros to worksheet objects such as command buttons. You also meet the Visual Basic Editor and learn how to edit a macro to change what it does.

Chapter 10

Creating Databases Using Tables

Packed with more than 16,000 columns and more than 1 million rows, each Excel worksheet has enough space to contain serious amounts of data—so it's great for creating a database to store information and quickly find the items you need.

In this chapter, you'll learn to use Excel's tables to create databases for storing information, sorting it, and filtering it to show the information you need. You'll also learn how to put Excel's database functions to work with tables.

Creating Databases in Excel

When you need to store a lot of the same type of information in a worksheet, you can create a database in a table. For example, if you run a business, you can make a database of your customers and their orders.

The first step is to set up the table and to tell Excel that you're creating a table rather than a regular worksheet. The next step is to add your data to the table, either by typing it into the cells as usual or by using a data-entry form.

Once the data is in the table, you can sort the table to reveal different aspects of its contents or filter it to identify items that match the criteria you specify.

Understanding What You Can and Can't Do with Excel Tables

Before you start creating a table in Excel, it's important to be clear about what you can and can't do with Excel tables.

As you know, an Excel worksheet consists of rows and columns. To create a table on a worksheet, you make each row into a *record*—an item that holds all the details of a single entry. For example, in a table that records your sales to customers, a record would contain the details of a purchase. You make each column a *field* in the table—a column for the purchase number, a column for the date, a column for the customer's last name, and so on. Figure 10–1 shows part of an Excel table for tracking sales to customers.

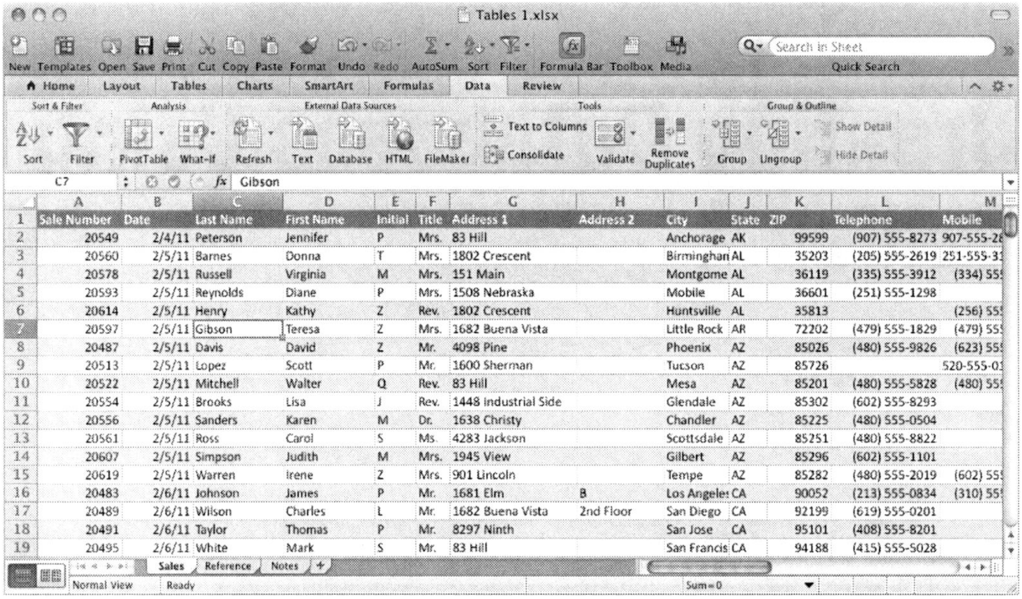

	A	B	C	D	E	F	G	H	I	J	K	L	M
1	Sale Number	Date	Last Name	First Name	Initial	Title	Address 1	Address 2	City	State	ZIP	Telephone	Mobile
2	20549	2/4/11	Peterson	Jennifer	P	Mrs.	83 Hill		Anchorage	AK	99599	(907) 555-8273	907-555-28
3	20560	2/5/11	Barnes	Donna	T	Mrs.	1802 Crescent		Birminghan	AL	35203	(205) 555-2619	251-555-31
4	20578	2/5/11	Russell	Virginia	M	Mrs.	151 Main		Montgome	AL	36119	(335) 555-3912	(334) 555
5	20593	2/5/11	Reynolds	Diane	P	Mrs.	1508 Nebraska		Mobile	AL	36601	(251) 555-1298	
6	20614	2/5/11	Henry	Kathy	Z	Rev.	1802 Crescent		Huntsville	AL	35813		(256) 555
7	20597	2/5/11	Gibson	Teresa	Z	Mrs.	1682 Buena Vista		Little Rock	AR	72202	(479) 555-1829	(479) 555
8	20487	2/5/11	Davis	David	Z	Mr.	4098 Pine		Phoenix	AZ	85026	(480) 555-9826	(623) 555
9	20513	2/5/11	Lopez	Scott	P	Mr.	1600 Sherman		Tucson	AZ	85726		520-555-01
10	20522	2/5/11	Mitchell	Walter	Q	Rev.	83 Hill		Mesa	AZ	85201	(480) 555-5828	(480) 555
11	20554	2/5/11	Brooks	Lisa	J	Rev.	1448 Industrial Side		Glendale	AZ	85302	(602) 555-8293	
12	20556	2/5/11	Sanders	Karen	M	Dr.	1638 Christy		Chandler	AZ	85225	(480) 555-0504	
13	20561	2/5/11	Ross	Carol	S	Ms.	4283 Jackson		Scottsdale	AZ	85251	(480) 555-8822	
14	20607	2/5/11	Simpson	Judith	M	Mrs.	1945 View		Gilbert	AZ	85296	(602) 555-1101	
15	20619	2/5/11	Warren	Irene	Z	Mrs.	901 Lincoln		Tempe	AZ	85282	(480) 555-2019	(602) 555
16	20483	2/6/11	Johnson	James	P	Mr.	1681 Elm	B	Los Angele:	CA	90052	(213) 555-0834	(310) 555
17	20489	2/6/11	Wilson	Charles	L	Mr.	1682 Buena Vista	2nd Floor	San Diego	CA	92199	(619) 555-0201	
18	20491	2/6/11	Taylor	Thomas	P	Mr.	8297 Ninth		San Jose	CA	95101	(408) 555-8201	
19	20495	2/6/11	White	Mark	S	Mr.	83 Hill		San Francis	CA	94188	(415) 555-5028	

Figure 10–1. *An Excel database consists of a table, with each row forming a record and each column containing a field.*

This is what's called a *flat-file* database: all the data in the database is stored in a single table rather than in separate tables that are linked to each other.

This means you can use Excel to create any database for which you can store all the data for a record in a single row. Because you have a million rows at your disposal, you can create large databases if necessary, but they may make Excel run slowly.

What you can't do with Excel is create *relational databases*—ones that store the data in linked tables. A relational database is the kind of database you create with full-bore database applications such as FileMaker, Microsoft Access (on Windows), Oracle (on various operating systems), or SQL Server (on Windows). In a relational database, every record has a unique ID number or field that the application uses to link the data in the different tables.

Creating a Table and Entering Data

In this section, you'll look at how to create a table and enter data in it either by using standard Excel methods or by using a data-entry form.

Creating a Table

To create a table, follow these steps:

1. Create a workbook as usual. For example, you can:

    ▓ Create a new blank workbook. Press Cmd+N or choose **File ➤ New Workbook** from the menu bar.

    ▓ Create a workbook based on a template or an existing workbook. Press Cmd+Shift+P or choose **File ➤ New from Template**, then make your choices in the Excel Workbook Gallery dialog box.

2. Name the worksheet on which you'll create the table. Double-click the worksheet tab, type the name you want (up to 31 characters, including spaces), then press Return to apply the name.

3. Type the headings for the table. For example, if the table will contain customer names and addresses, you'd type fields such as Last Name, First Name, Middle Initial, Title, Address 1, and so on. Try to get all the fields in place at this point; you can add columns to the table later, but you'll then need to add extra data to the existing records.

> **NOTE:** Usually, it's easiest to put the headings in the first row of the worksheet, but if you need to have information appear above the table, leave rows free for it.

4. Format the headings differently from the rows below them. For example, click the row header for the heading row, then press Cmd+B to apply boldface.

5. Select the headings and at least one row below them.

6. Choose **Tables ➤ Table Options ➤ New** from the Ribbon, clicking the main part of the New button rather than the pop-up button. Excel makes the following changes:

    ▓ Creates the table.

    ▓ Gives the table a default name, such as Table1 or Table2.

    ▓ Turns the header row into headers with pop-up buttons.

> **NOTE:** If your headings have the same formatting as the data rows, choose **Tables ➤ Table Options ➤ New ➤ Insert Table with Headers** rather than **Tables ➤ Table Options ➤ New**. Otherwise, Excel inserts a new row containing headers above your heading row. If your table doesn't have headers, choose **Tables ➤ Table Options ➤ New ➤ Insert Table without Headers**.

■ Applies a table style with shading based on the workbook's theme. You can change the style later as needed.

7. Rename your table by following these steps:

   a. Click the Name pop-up menu at the left end of the Formula bar, then click the table name. Excel selects the table if it's not still selected.

   b. Click in the Name text box to select the table name.

   c. Type the new name for the table. As with chart names, the table name must be unique in the workbook, must start with a letter or an underscore, and cannot contain spaces or symbols.

   d. Press Return to apply the table name.

Customizing the Table's Looks

At this point, you can start entering data in the table (as discussed next)—but before you do, you may want to change the way it looks. To do so, follow these steps:

1. Click anywhere in the table.

2. Click the Tables tab of the Ribbon if it's not already displayed.

3. If a suitable style appears in the Table Styles box on the Ribbon, click it. If not, hold the mouse pointer over the Table Styles box to display the panel button, then click the panel button to display the Table Styles panel (see Figure 10–2). Click the style you want to apply.

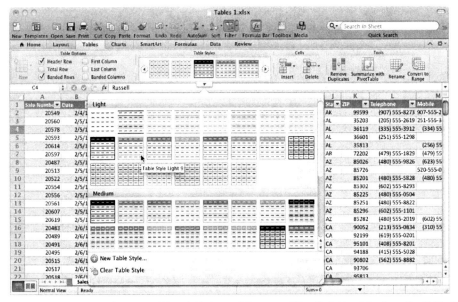

Figure 10–2. *You can format a table quickly by applying one of Excel's table styles from the Table Styles panel on the Tables tab of the Ribbon. Scroll down the panel to see the other styles.*

4. In the Table Options group on the Tables tab of the Ribbon, select the check box for each table style option you want to use:

    ■ *Header Row.* Select this check box to display the header row. This is almost always useful.

    ■ *Total Row.* Select this check box to add a row labeled Total immediately after the table's last row. This is useful when you need to add a total formula or another formula in the last row. To add a formula, click a cell in the Total row, click the pop-up button that appears, then click the formula you want on the pop-up menu (see Figure 10–3).

	Sale Numbe	Date	Last Name	First Name	Initial	Title	Address 1
153	20622		Reyes	Rachel	M	Rev.	4098 Pine
154	20503	11/8/10	Rodriguez	Anthony	O	Mr.	1482 Business Loop
155	20564		Jenkins	Michelle	N	Dr.	1681 Elm
156	Total						
157			✓ None				
158			Average				
159			Count				
160			Count Numbers				
161			Max				
162			Min				
163			Sum				
164			StdDev				
165			Var				
166			More Functions...				

Figure 10–3. *Adding a Total row to a table lets you quickly insert functions in the row's cells. Excel changes the header row to column labels when you scroll down the worksheet.*

TIP: The pop-up menu in the Total row of a table gives you instant access to the most widely used functions in databases—Average, Count, Count Numbers, Max, Min, Sum, StdDev (Standard Deviation), or Var (calculating variance based on a sample). You can also click the More Functions item at the bottom of the pop-up menu to display the Formula Builder, from which you can access the full range of Excel's functions. For example, you can insert the COUNTBLANK() function to count the number of blank cells in a column. You might do this to ensure that a column of essential data contains no blanks.

■ *Banded Rows.* Select this check box to apply a band of color to every other row. This helps you read the rows of data without your eyes wandering to another row. Some table styles apply banding to the rows automatically.

■ *First Column.* Select this check box if you want the first column to have different formatting. You may want to do this if the first column contains the main field for identifying each record (for example, a unique number).

- *Last Column*: Select this check box if you want the last column to have different formatting. Usually, you'll want this only if the last column contains data that is more important in some way than the data in the other columns.

- *Banded Columns.* Select this check box to apply a band of color to every other column. This is sometimes helpful but usually less helpful than banded rows. (Don't use both—the effect is seldom useful.)

When you've finished choosing a style and options for the table, save your work as usual.

Entering Data in a Table

You can enter data in a table either by typing it in directly or by using a data-entry form. In most cases, the data-entry form is the easier option, as you'll see in a moment. You can also connect a table to an external data source, as discussed in the following section.

Entering Data Directly in the Table

A table is essentially an Excel worksheet at heart, so you can enter data in the table by using the standard techniques you've learned in the past few chapters. For example, click a cell, then type data into it; or, if you have the data in another worksheet, copy it and paste it in.

When you enter data in the row immediately after the last row in the table, Excel automatically expands the table to include that row. To add a row within the table, click a cell in the row above which you want to add the new row, then choose Insert ➤ Rows from the menu bar. Again, Excel automatically expands the table to include the new row.

To insert a column in the table, click a cell in the column before which you want to add the new column, then choose Insert ➤ Columns from the menu bar. Once more, Excel automatically expands the table.

> **TIP:** You can quickly select a row, a column, or an entire table with the mouse. To select a row, move the mouse pointer to the left part of a cell in the table's leftmost column, then click with the horizontal arrow that appears. To select a column, move the mouse pointer over a column heading, then click with the downward arrow that appears. To select the whole table, move the mouse pointer over the upper-left cell in the table, then click with the diagonal arrow that appears.

Entering Data Using a Data-Entry Form

Typing directly into the table tends to be awkward, especially when the table contains too many columns to fit in the Excel window with the whole content of each column displayed. When your database has grown beyond a few rows, you can usually enter data more easily by using a data-entry form—a dialog box that Excel automatically tailors to suit your table.

Choose **Data ➤ Form** to display the data-entry form dialog box. Figure 10–4 shows this dialog box, whose title bar shows the name of the worksheet you're using (here, Sales) rather than the word *Form*.

Figure 10–4. *The Form dialog box bears the name of the worksheet your table is on (here, Sales) and shows all fields in the order they appear in the header row.*

To use the data form, you move to the record you want in one of these ways:

- *Create a new record.* Click the New button to create a new record in the database. When you type the data in the fields, Excel adds the new record after the last current record in the database.

- *Move forward or backward through the records.* Click the Find Next button to display the next record, or click the Find Prev button to display the previous record.

- *Scroll through the records.* Drag the scroll box up or down the scroll bar to move quickly through the records. Click the scroll arrows to move in smaller increments.

- *Search for a record.* Follow these steps:

    1. Click the Criteria button to switch to the criteria view of the form. Excel clears any data in the fields.

    2. Type your search term in the field by which you want to search. For example, to search for your customers in Arizona, type **AZ** in the State field (assuming your database has this field).

    3. Click the Find Next button to find the next instance, or click the Find Prev button to find the previous instance.

Excel automatically switches the dialog box back to Form view when you search. If you decide you don't need to search after all, click the Form button (which replaces the Criteria button) to return to Form view.

Once you've created or located the record you want to change, type or edit the data in the fields in the data-entry form dialog box. Excel enters it in the columns for you.

When you've finished using the Form dialog box, click the Close button to close it.

Connecting a Table to an External Data Source

If you have your data in an external data source, such as a relational database, you can import the data into an Excel table to work with it. You can then refresh the data in the Excel table with the latest data from the database.

Connecting to a Database

To connect to a relational database, such as a Microsoft Access database or an Oracle database, you need to install an Open Database Connectivity (ODBC) driver for Excel. You can then establish the connection, import the data, and refresh it as needed.

Getting and Installing an ODBC Driver

Before you can import data into a table in Excel, you must install an Open Database Connectivity (ODBC) driver. This is a piece of software that enables Excel to connect to the database and pull data out of it.

Microsoft doesn't provide ODBC drivers for Excel for Mac, so you need to get one from a third-party vendor. To find the latest list of compatible ODBC drivers, open your web browser, go to http://www.microsoft.com/mac/, then search for **ODBC Excel**. At this writing, there are two providers:

- OpenLink Software (http://www.openlinksw.com/)
- actualtechnologies LLC (http://www.actualtech.com/)

Each offers several different ODBC drivers for different types of database, so make sure you get the right one. Normally, you'll want to start by getting the trial version to make sure it does what you need, then pay for the full version. Some trial versions are limited by time; others are limited by the amount of data they'll return. Either way, you'll eventually need to buy the full version.

Establishing a Connection to a Database

To establish a connection to a database, position the active cell on the appropriate worksheet in the workbook you want to use, then choose **Data ➤ External Data Sources ➤ Database** to open the dialog box for setting up the connection. Figure 10.5 shows the iODBC Data Source Chooser dialog box, which you use to establish a connection using OpenLink Software's ODBC driver.

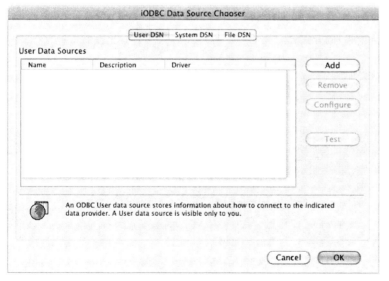

Figure 10–5. *Choose your database in the dialog box for the ODBC driver you installed. This screen shows the iODBC Data Source Chooser dialog box.*

Use the controls in the dialog box to specify the connection to the data source. The specifics depend on the ODBC driver you're using.

When you have set up the connection, click the Return Data button. Excel displays the Returning External Data to Microsoft Excel dialog box (see Figure 10–6). In this dialog box, you can choose where to place the data that the connection returns:

■ *Existing sheet.* To put the data on an existing worksheet, select this option button, then click the cell you want to use as the upper-left corner of the range. You can click the Collapse Dialog button to get the Returning External Data to Microsoft Excel dialog box out of the way if necessary, but usually it's easy enough just to work around it.

■ *New sheet.* Select this option button if you want to put the data on a new sheet. Excel creates this sheet for you and starts inserting the data at cell A1.

■ *PivotTable.* Select this option button if you want to create a PivotTable from the data. This option button is available only for some types of database connections. (PivotTables are discussed in Chapter 12.)

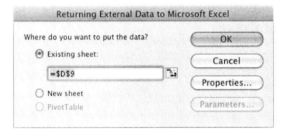

Figure 10–6. *In the Returning External Data to Microsoft Excel dialog box, choose whether to put the data on an existing worksheet, on a new worksheet, or in a PivotTable. You can click the Properties button to set the properties for the data returned from the database.*

If you need to choose options for how Excel returns the data, click the Properties button in the Returning External Data to Microsoft Excel dialog box to display the External Data Range Properties dialog box (see Figure 10–7). Here you can choose the following options:

■ *Name.* In this text box, type the name you want to give to the external data range. This name is to help you identify the data range; it becomes more important when you use multiple data ranges.

■ *Query definition.* In this box, select the Save query definition check box if you want to save the query; normally, you'll want to do this so you don't have to set it up again. If the query uses a password, you can select the Save password check box to store the password too; you may prefer (or be forced) to enter the password each time for security.

- *Refresh control.* In this box, select the Prompt for file name on refresh check box if you want Excel to prompt you to enter the file name when you refresh the data. Select the Refresh data on file open check box if you want Excel to refresh the data automatically each time you open the workbook; this is usually helpful if you normally want to work with the latest data. Select the Remove external data from worksheet before saving check box if you want Excel to remove the external data from the workbook when you save it—for example, because you're using the workbook to manipulate data you don't want others to see in it.

- *Data layout.* In the top part of this box, select the Include field names check box and the Include Row Numbers check box if you want to include these items, as is usually helpful. Select the Adjust column width check box if you want Excel to adjust the column width to fit the data. Select the Import HTML table(s) only check box if you want to import only tables when importing from an HTML data source.

- *If the number of rows in the data range changes upon refresh.* In this area of the Data layout box, select the appropriate option button: "Insert cells for new data, delete unused cells," "Insert entire rows for new data, clear unused cells," or "Overwrite existing cells with new data, clear unused cells." Normally, the "Insert cells for new data, delete unused cells" option button is the best choice.

- *Fill down formulas in columns adjacent to data.* Select this check box if you want Excel to automatically fill in formulas down the cells of columns next to the data—for example, to continue a SUM formula you've entered.

- *Use Table.* Select this check box to have Excel put the external data in a table. This is what you'll usually want.

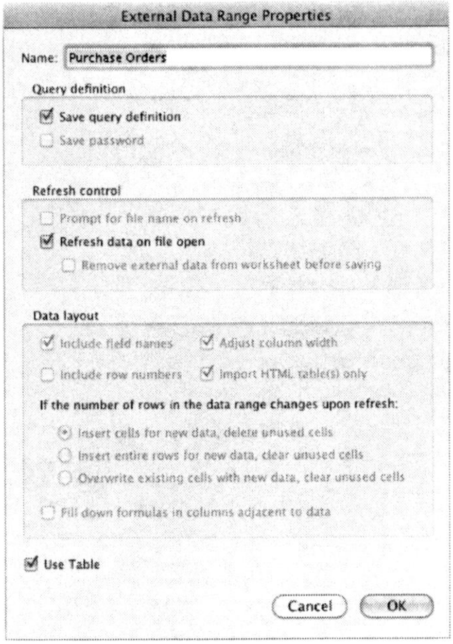

Figure 10–7. *In the External Data Range Properties dialog box, name the connection, choose whether to save the query definition, decide when to refresh the data, and choose the layout to use.*

> **NOTE:** Some of the options in the External Data Range Properties dialog box are available only for certain types of connections.

When you've finished choosing options in the External Data Range Properties dialog box, click the OK button to close it and return to the Returning External Data to Microsoft Excel dialog box. Then click the OK button to close this dialog box. Excel brings in the data from the data source.

Refreshing the Data from a Database

If you've set the table to update the data from the database automatically at intervals or when you open the workbook, Excel takes care of the refreshing. If you've set the table for manual refreshing, or if you need to pull the latest data into the table right this moment, you can refresh the table manually by using the commands on the Data ➤ External Data Sources ➤ Refresh menu. Click the Refresh All command to refresh all the tables, or click the Refresh Data command to refresh just the data in the current table.

If a refresh seems to be taking too long, choose Data ➤ External Data Sources ➤ Refresh ➤ Cancel Refresh to cancel it.

Importing Data from a FileMaker Pro Database

If you need to pull data from a FileMaker Pro database into a table, choose **Data ➤ External Data Sources ➤ FileMaker** to launch the FileMaker Pro Import Wizard. Follow through the steps of this Wizard as discussed in the section "Importing Data from a FileMaker Pro Database" in Chapter 1.

NOTE: To import data from a FileMaker Pro database, you must have FileMaker Pro installed on the Mac you're running Excel on.

Resizing a Table

When you've created a table, Excel normally resizes it for you automatically when you add or delete rows or columns. For example, when you add a record by using the Form dialog box, Excel expands the table to include it.

Excel also expands the table automatically if you add data to the row after the current last row in a table that doesn't have a Total row. Excel calls this feature Table AutoExpansion. If you don't want Excel to do this, click the AutoCorrect actions button that appears below and to the right of the first cell in the added row, then click Undo Table AutoExpansion (see Figure 10–8). Click the actions button again, then click Stop Automatically Expanding Tables.

NOTE: When you add a new row to a table using Table AutoExpansion, Excel makes the change only when you start typing data in the row. When you do, Excel applies the style to the row, and you can see that it's part of the table. But until you start typing, it's just another plain row.

	Sale Numbe	Date	Last Name	First Name	Initia
155	20564		Jenkins	Michelle	N
156	20700				
157					
158					
159		Undo Table AutoExpansion			
160		Stop Automatically Expanding Tables			
161		Control Table AutoExpansion Options...			
162					

Figure 10–8. *You can use the AutoCorrect actions button both to undo Table AutoExpansion and to turn it off.*

NOTE: To turn Table AutoExpansion back on, choose **Excel ➤ Preferences** or press Cmd+, (Cmd and the comma key). In the Excel Preferences dialog box, click the Tables icon in the Formulas and Lists area to display the Tables preferences pane. Select the Automatically Expand Tables As I Type check box, then click the OK button.

Sorting a Table by One or More Fields

When you need to examine the data in your table, it's often useful to sort it. Excel lets you sort a table either quickly by a single field or by using multiple fields.

> **TIP:** If you need to be able to return a table to its original order, include a column with sequential numbers in it. These numbers may be part of your records (for example, sequential sales numbers for transactions) or simply ID numbers for the records. In either case, you can use AutoFill to enter them quickly. To return the table to its original order, you can then sort it by this column.

Sorting Quickly by a Single Field

To sort a table by a single field, click any cell in the column you want to sort by, then choose **Data ➤ Sort & Filter ➤ Sort**, clicking the main part of the Sort button. This produces a sort in ascending order (A to Z, low values to high values, early dates to later dates, and so on). To reverse the sort to descending order, click the main part of the Sort button again.

> **NOTE:** You can also sort by choosing **Data ➤ Sort & Filter ➤ Sort ➤ Ascending**, **Data ➤ Sort & Filter ➤ Sort ➤ Descending**, or by one of the other items on the Sort pop-up menu: Cell Color on Top, Font Color on Top, or Icon on Top. Usually, ascending and descending are the most useful kinds of sorting for a table. (You normally use sorting by Cell Color on Top, Font Color on Top, or Icon on Top for sorting cells that have conditional formatting applied.)

After you sort, the table remains sorted that way until you change it.

Sorting a Table by Multiple Fields

Often, it's useful to sort your table by two or more fields at the same time. For example, in a customer database, you may need to sort your customers first by state and then by city within the state.

To sort by multiple fields, follow these steps:

1. Choose **Data ➤ Sort & Filter ➤ Sort ➤ Custom Sort** to display the Sort dialog box. Figure 10–9 shows the Sort dialog box with two criteria entered and a third criterion under way.

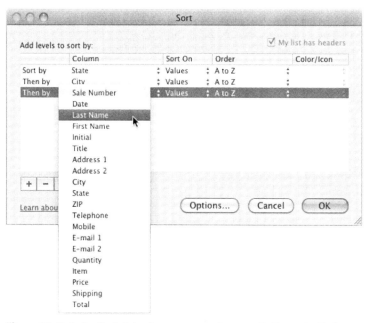

Figure 10–9. *In the Sort dialog box, you can set up exactly the sort criteria you need to identify data in your database.*

2. Set up your first sort criterion using the controls on the first row of the main part of the Sort dialog box. Follow these steps:

    a. Open the Column pop-up menu in the Sort by row, then click the column you want to sort by first. For example, click the State column.

    b. Open the Sort On pop-up menu in the same row, then click what you want to sort by: Values, Cell Color, Font Color, or Cell Icon. In most cases, you'll want to use Values, but the other three items are useful for tables to which you've applied conditional formatting.

    c. Open the Order pop-up menu on the same row, then click the sort order you want. If you choose Values in the Sort On pop-up menu, you can choose A to Z for an ascending sort, Z to A for a descending sort, or Custom List. Choosing Custom List opens the Custom List dialog box, which you can use to choose a custom list by which to sort the results. For example, you could use a custom list of your company's products or offices to sort the database into a custom order rather than being restricted to ascending or descending order.

d. If you need the sort to be case sensitive (so that "smith" appears before "Smith," and so on), click the Options button. In the Sort Options dialog box (see Figure 10–10), select the Case Sensitive check box, then click the OK button.

Figure 10–10. *Select the Case sensitive check box in the Sort Options dialog box if you want to treat lowercase letters differently than their uppercase versions.*

3. Click the Add (+) button to add a second line of controls to the main part of the Sort dialog box.

4. Set up the criterion for the second-level sort on the Then By line using the same technique. For example, set up a second-level sort using the City column in the database.

5. Set up any other criteria needed by repeating steps 3 and 4.

6. Click the OK button to close the Sort dialog box. Excel sorts the data using the criteria you specified.

NOTE: When you're sorting data that's not in a table, there are two main differences. First, the My Data Has Headers check box in the Sort dialog box is available, and you must select it if the data range you're sorting includes a header row. (Otherwise, Excel sorts the headers into the data range.) Second, you can select the Sort left to right option button in the Sort Options dialog box to sort columns rather than rows, a choice that's not available in a data table.

Identifying and Removing Duplicate Records in a Table

When you've created a large table, you may need to check it for duplicate records and remove those you find. Excel provides a Remove Duplicates feature that saves you having to comb the records by hand.

CAUTION: Two warnings before removing duplicate values: First, make sure you have a backup copy of your database workbook—for example, use Finder to copy the current version of a file to a safe location. Second, be certain you know which fields in the table should contain unique values and which can contain duplicate values. For example, a customer ID number field must be unique, because each customer has a different ID number; but a customer last name field can't reasonably be unique, because many customers will likely share last names. Most databases need a unique ID number or code of this type.

To remove duplicate records from a table, follow these steps:

1. Click any cell in the table.

2. Choose **Tables ➤ Tools ➤ Remove Duplicates** from the Ribbon or **Data ➤ Table Tools ➤ Remove Duplicates** from the menu bar to display the window shown in Figure 10–11.

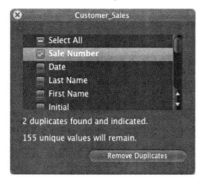

Figure 10–11. *Use this window to locate duplicate values in columns that should contain only unique values. The window's title bar shows the name of the data table.*

3. If the Select All check box contains a check mark, click the check box to remove the check mark, and clear all the check boxes in the Columns box.

4. Select the check box for each column you want to check for duplicates. The readout at the bottom of the dialog box shows the number of duplicates.

TIP: Normally, it's best to check a single column at a time for duplicate values. Make sure that the column is one that must contain a unique value.

5. Click the Remove Duplicates button if you want to remove the duplicates.

6. Repeat the process with another field if necessary.

7. When you have finished removing duplicates, click the × button at the left end of the title bar to close the window.

Filtering a Table

When you need to find records in a table that match the terms you specify, you can *filter* it. Filtering makes Excel display only the records that match your search terms, hiding all the other records.

> **NOTE:** You can also search for records by using Excel's Find feature. Choose **Edit ➤ Find** from the menu bar or press Cmd+F to display the Find dialog box, type your search term in the Find What box, then click the Find Next button. Filtering displays all the matching records together rather than spread out in the table, so it's often more convenient than using Find.

To make filtering easy, Excel provides a feature named AutoFilter. To use AutoFilter, follow these steps:

1. Click a cell in the table.

2. Click the Data tab of the Ribbon to display its contents.

3. In the Sort & Filter group, make sure that the Filter button is selected so that it looks pushed in; if not, click the main part of the button. Excel normally selects the Filter button when you create a table, so this button should be pushed in unless you've turned filtering off. Selecting this button makes Excel display a pop-up button on each column heading in the table.

4. On the column you want to use for filtering, click the pop-up button to display the AutoFilter window (shown on the left in Figure 10–12). The AutoFilter window's title bar shows the name of the field you clicked.

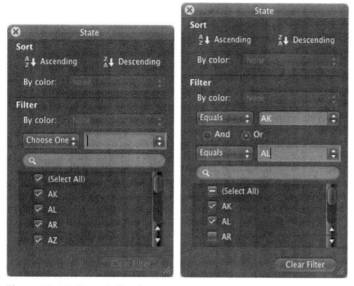

Figure 10–12. *To apply filtering, click the pop-up arrow on a column heading to display the AutoFilter window (left). In the Filter area, open the first pop-up menu, and choose the comparison you want (right). You can then add further comparisons as needed.*

5. Click the type of sorting or filtering you want to apply:

    ▨ *Sort.* Click the type of sort you want to apply. Normally, you'll want to click either the Ascending button or the Descending button. But if your data table uses colors, you can sort by color instead—just choose the color in the By color pop-up menu in the Sort area.

    ▨ *Filter.* If you want to filter the table by color, choose the color in the By color pop-up menu. Otherwise, open the pop-up menu that appears as Choose One in the left part of Figure 10–12, then choose the comparison from it. For example, choose Equals to set a filter that picks particular states, or choose Begins With to set a filter that selects cities that start with text you specify. Use the fields in the Custom AutoFilter window to set up the rest of the comparison; the right screen in Figure 10–12 shows an example that filters by Equals AK or Equals AL, returning the records that have the state AK or the state AL.

NOTE: The filter comparisons depend on the contents of the column you selected in the table. For example, if the column contains numbers, the comparisons include the mathematical comparisons Greater Than, Greater Than or Equal To, Less Than, Less Than or Equal To, Between, Top 10, Bottom 10, Above Average, and Below Average. If the column contains dates, the comparisons include Before, After, Between, Tomorrow, Next Week, Next Month, and Next Year.

When you've specified the details of the filter, Excel applies it to the table and reduces the display to those rows that match the filter. Excel displays a filter symbol in place of the drop-down button on the column that contains the filtering (as on the State column heading in Figure 10–13).

City	State	ZIP	Telephone
Montgome	AL	36119	(335) 555-3912
Huntsville	AL	35813	
Anchorage	AK	99599	(907) 555-8273
Birminghan	AL	35203	(205) 555-2619
Mobile	AL	36601	(251) 555-1298

Figure 10–13. *The filter symbol (shown on the State column heading here) indicates that you're filtering the table by that column.*

To remove filtering from a single column, click the filter symbol on the column heading, then click the Clear Filter button in the AutoFilter window.

To remove filtering from the table as a whole, choose Data ➤ Sort & Filter ➤ Filter, deselecting the Filter button in the Sort & Filter group.

Using Database Functions with Tables

As you saw in Chapter 6, Excel contains 12 database functions for use with tables. Each of these functions requires three arguments:

- *database.* This argument tells the function which database or table to use. You can specify *database* as either a range (for example, A1:F4) or by the table's name (for example, "Customer_Sales").

- *field.* This argument tells the function which field in the database you're interested in. For example, you could specify "State" to use the field named State.

- *criteria.* This argument tells the function the range in which to find the criteria for the comparison. The range must have at least one column label and at least one cell under the column label; this is where you specify the condition.

NOTE: Usually it's best to place the criteria range above the table rather than below it, because placing the range below the table can prevent the Table AutoExpansion feature from working. Placing the criteria range above the table also helps make sure that it doesn't overlap the table's own range. Placing the criteria range to the side of the table also works, but it makes the range hard to view unless the table is relatively narrow.

Figure 10–14 shows an example of using a database function. As you'll remember from Chapter 6, the DAVERAGE() function returns the average value of the cells in the specified field that match your criteria. Here, the DAVERAGE(A4:C8,"Satisfaction",A1:C2) function in cell C9 works like this:

- **A4:C8** specifies the range of the table. (Yes, it's unrealistically small.)

- **"Satisfaction"** tells the function to use the Satisfaction field (in column C).

- **A1:C2** tells the function to look for the criteria in the range A1:C2. Cell B2 gives the criterion to use: the number in the Staff column must be less than 20 (Staff>20).

- Given this information, the DAVERAGE() function takes the Satisfaction values of the two rows for which Staff>20 is true (San Francisco and Oakland) and averages them, returning 8.4.

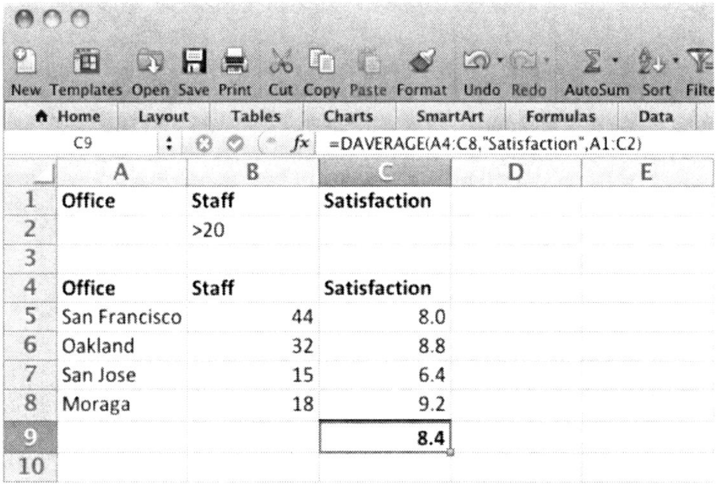

Figure 10–14. *To use a database function such as DAVERAGE(), you must set up a criteria range in the worksheet. The best place for the criteria range is above the table.*

Summary

In this chapter, you learned how to use Excel's tables to create a database in which you can store information, sort it, and apply filtering to find the records you need. You also learned how to use Excel's database functions with tables.

In the next chapter, I'll show you how to solve business questions using what-if analysis, the Goal Seek feature, and the Solver add-in. Turn the page when you're ready to start.

Chapter 11

Solving Business Questions with What-If Analysis, Goal Seek, and Solver

For much of your work with Excel, you'll probably want to manipulate the hard data you already have, as you've been doing so far in the book. But at other times, you'll need to ask questions of your data—for example, by how much do you need to raise prices to boost your revenue by a certain amount, or what will happen if you cut 10 percent off your manufacturing costs?

In this chapter, we'll look at four tools Excel gives you for performing what-if analysis:

- *Data tables.* Use a data table when you want to assess the impact of one or two variables on a calculation.

- *Scenarios.* Use scenarios when you want to experiment with different data in your worksheet without changing the core data that you already have.

- *Goal Seek.* Use Goal Seek when you need to make one cell's value reach a particular figure by changing one other value.

- *Solver.* Use the add-in Solver application when you need to make one cell's value reach a particular figure by changing two or more other values.

Assessing the Impact of Variables Using Data Tables

A *data table* is a tool you can use to calculate how one or two variables change the result of a calculation. Use a data table when you want to see the range of results in a worksheet rather than seeing a single result at a time.

Creating a Data Table with One Variable

When you need to see how only one variable changes the result of a calculation, you can quickly create a data table. You place the input values—the values you want to test—in either a row or a column, and then tell Excel where to find them.

Creating a data table seems odd at first, but you'll quickly get the hang of it. Try this example of putting together a data table that uses one variable.

First, create a new worksheet and set up the straightforward =FV() formula shown in Figure 11–1 to calculate the future value of an investment that pays 10% interest over 12 months, has a period of 60 months, and takes $600 out of your pay packet every month. Follow these steps:

1. Enter these data labels in the following cells:

    ▓ A1. Interest Rate

    ▓ A2. Months

    ▓ A3. Payment

    ▓ A4. Future Value

B4		$\cdot$ ⊗ ◯ (⌃ fx =FV(B1,B2,B3)	
	A	B	C
1	Interest Rate	0.83%	
2	Months	60	
3	Payment	-$600.00	
4	Future Value	$46,462.24	
5			

Figure 11–1. *The example calculation for the data table uses the FV() function to calculate the future value of a $600-a-month investment.*

2. Enter the formula **=10%/12** in cell B1. Apply the Percentage number format to this cell and make the cell show two decimal places so that you see 0.83% rather than the 1% that Excel typically displays (which makes the calculation visually confusing).

3. Enter the value **60** in cell B2.

4. Enter the value **-600** in cell B3. Apply the Currency number format to make its meaning visually clear.

5. Enter the FV function in cell B4: **=FV(B1,B2,B3)**.

So far, so good. Now set up the input values for the data table. Follow these steps:

1. Enter the label **Months** in cell A6.

2. Enter the values for the data table in cells A7:A10:

   - A7. 48

   - A8. 60

   - A9. 72

   - A10. 84

TIP: It's easy enough to type in the input values for this small data table, but if you want to extend the sequence, try entering 48 in cell A7 and 60 in cell A8, selecting the cells, and then dragging the AutoFill handle to fill in the remaining cells.

Your worksheet should now look like the one in Figure 11–2.

	A	B
1	Interest Rate	0.83%
2	Months	60
3	Payment	-$600.00
4	Future Value	$46,462.24
5		
6	Months	
7	48	
8	60	
9	72	
10	84	

Figure 11–2. *Enter the input values for the data table in cells A7:A10.*

Now you can enter the formula that uses the data table. For the data table to work, you need to place the formula in the cell where Excel expects to find it:

- *Column-oriented data table.* Enter the formula in the row above the first input value, and in the next column to the right. In the example, this is cell B6.

- *Row-oriented data table.* Enter the formula in the column to the left of the first input value and in the next row down.

In this case, we're creating a column-oriented data table, so we need to enter the formula in cell B6. Enter the formula =**FV(B1,A5,B3)**, as shown in Figure 11–3—in other words, the same formula as in cell B4, but using cell A5 instead of cell B2 to supply the number of months.

FV		$\otimes$ $\oslash$ $\frown$ fx	=fv(b1,a5,B3)	
	A	B	C	D
1	Interest Rate	0.83%		
2	Months	60		
3	Payment	-$600.00		
4	Future Value	$46,462.24		
5				
6	Months	=fv(b1,a5,B3)		
7		48		
8		60		
9		72		
10		84		

Figure 11–3. *Enter the formula in the cell above and to the right of the input values.*

NOTE: When you enter the formula for the data table, Excel usually displays either a value that's clearly wrong or an error value. In this example, the formula cell displays the result $0.00, because cell A5 is blank and so is supplying a zero value for the Months argument. In other formulas, a zero value produces an error value. This isn't a problem, as you'll see in a moment.

Now you're ready to set up the data table. Follow these steps:

1. Select the range of cells that contains the input values and the formula. In this example, select the range A6:B10.

2. Choose **Data ➤ Analysis ➤ What-If ➤ Data Table** from the Ribbon or **Data ➤ Data Table** from the menu bar to display the Data Table dialog box (see Figure 11–4).

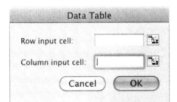

Figure 11–4. *In the Data Table dialog box, enter the row input cell or the column input cell for the data table you're creating.*

3. Click in the Column Input Cell box, and then click the cell you used as the input value—in this case, cell A5. Excel enters an absolute reference, A5.

NOTE: When you're creating a row-oriented data table, click in the Row Input Cell box in the Data Table dialog box, and then click the cell you used for the input value.

4. Click the OK button to close the Data Table dialog box. Excel enters the array formula {=TABLE(,A5)} in each cell alongside a cell containing an input value.

5. Apply the Currency number format to the results cells so that the results appear as dollar values.

Figure 11–5 shows the data table with the results in place.

	A	B	C
1	Interest Rate	0.83%	
2	Months	60	
3	Payment	-$600.00	
4	Future Value	$46,462.24	
5			
6	Months	$0.00	
7		48	$35,233.50
8		60	$46,462.24
9		72	$58,866.79
10		84	$72,570.25

Figure 11–5. *After you create the data table, the results appear alongside the input values.*

Creating a Data Table with Two Variables

When you need to analyze what happens when two pieces of information used in a calculation change, create a data table with two variables. For example, when calculating an investment with the FV() function, you may need to look at not only different numbers of months for the period but also different payments.

To create a two-variable data table, you place one set of input data down a column to the left of the table and the other set of input data across a row above the table. For example, Figure 11–6 shows a two-variable data table that uses the FV() function to calculate the future value of an investment:

- The range D6:D11 contains the input values for the Period argument (48, 60, 72, 84, 96, or 108 months).

- The range E5:I5 contains the input values for the Payment argument (-$500.00, $550.00, –$600.00, -$650.00, or -$700.00). These cells are formatted with the Currency number format.

- Cell A7 is the row input cell, and cell A9 is the column input cell. When you create the data table by choosing **Data ➤ Analysis ➤ What-If ➤ Data Table** from the Ribbon or **Data ➤ Data Table** from the menu bar, you specify both the row input cell and the column input cell in the Data Table dialog box.

- Cell D5 contains the formula for the data table: =FV(B1,A9,A7).

- Each results cell contains the formula {=TABLE(A7,A9)}.

E6				$f\!x$	{=TABLE(A7,A9)}				
	A	B	C	D	E	F	G	H	I	J
1	Interest Rate	0.83%								
2	Months	60								
3	Payment	-$600.00								
4	Future Value	$46,462.24			PAYMENT VALUES					
5				$0.00	-$500.00	-$550.00	-$600.00	-$650.00	-$700.00	
6	Row Input		M	48	$29,361.25	$32,297.37	$35,233.50	$38,169.62	$41,105.74	
7			O	60	$38,718.54	$42,590.39	$46,462.24	$50,334.10	$54,205.95	
8	Column Input		N	72	$49,055.66	$53,961.22	$58,866.79	$63,772.35	$68,677.92	
9			T	84	$60,475.21	$66,522.73	$72,570.25	$78,617.77	$84,665.29	
10			H	96	$73,090.54	$80,399.59	$87,708.65	$95,017.70	$102,326.75	
11			S	108	$87,026.86	$95,729.54	$104,432.23	$113,134.91	$121,837.60	
12										

Figure 11–6. *In a two-variable data table, you enter one set of input values down a column (here, column D) and the other set of input values in a row (here, row 5). The formula goes in the cell where the column and row intersect (here, cell D5).*

NOTE: When you no longer need a data table, select the table, and then press Delete or choose Home ➤ Edit ➤ Clear ➤ Clear All.

Examining Different Scenarios in a Worksheet

Often, when you've built a worksheet, you'll want to experiment with different data in it. For example, if you're setting budgets, you may need to play around with different figures for the different departments to get the overall balance you require.

You can experiment with different data by changing the values directly in your worksheet—but then you may need to restore your original values afterward. Another approach is to create multiple copies of the worksheet (or of the workbook) and then change the values in the copies, leaving the original untouched. This works fine, but if you then need to change the original worksheet (for example, adding another column of data), the changes quickly become messy.

Instead of working in these awkward ways, you can use Excel's scenarios. A *scenario* is a way of entering different values into a set of cells without changing the underlying values. You can switch from one scenario to another as needed, and you can merge scenarios from different versions of the same worksheet into a single worksheet.

Creating the Worksheet for Your Scenarios

Start by creating the workbook and worksheet you'll use for your scenarios. If you have an existing workbook with the data in it, open it up. Set up the data and formulas in your worksheet as usual.

TIP: To make your scenarios easy to set up and adjust, define a name for each cell that you will change in the scenario. Click the cell, choose **Insert ➤ Name ➤ Define** to display the Define Name dialog box, and then work as described in the "Assigning a Name to a Cell or Range" section in Chapter 3. For example, type the name in the Names In workbook text box, and then click the Add button to add the name and leave the dialog box open so that you can click another cell and define a name for it, too.

Figure 11–7 shows the sample worksheet this section uses as an example. The worksheet summarizes the financial returns from a modest portfolio of rental properties.

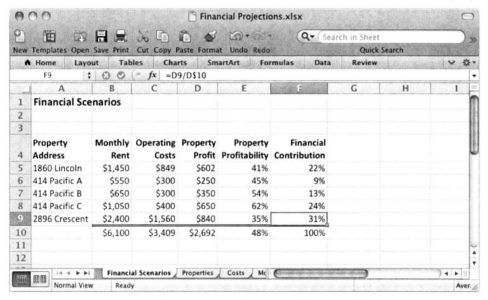

Figure 11–7. *To start using scenarios, create a worksheet containing your existing data and the formulas needed.*

Here's what you see on the worksheet:

- The Property Address column shows each property's address.

- The Monthly Rent column shows each property's monthly rent. Cell B10 contains a SUM() formula to produce the total rent. Each of the cells here has a name to make it easy to recognize—Rent_Lincoln, Rent_Pacific_A, and so on.

- The Operating Costs column shows the monthly operating cost for each property, including all mortgage costs and other financial horrors. Cell C10 uses a SUM() formula to produce the total running cost. The numbers in this column are rounded. Each of these cells has a name: Costs_Lincoln, Costs_Pacific_A, and so on. Again, this is so that we can refer to the cells easily and clearly.

■ The Property Profit column shows how much profit each rental unit returns after subtracting the operating cost from the rent (for example, cell D5 contains the sum =B5-C5). The numbers in this column are rounded; that's why cell D5 appears to contain a math error but is in fact correct. Cell D10 uses a SUM() formula to return the total profit.

■ The Property Profitability column shows the property's profitability as a percentage. To produce the profitability figure, we divide the Property Profit value by the Monthly Rent value—for example, cell E5 contains the formula = D5/B5. At the bottom of the column, cell E10 uses an AVERAGE() formula to show the average profitability of the properties.

■ The Financial Contribution column shows each property's contribution to the total profit as a percentage. To produce the contribution figure, we divide each property's profit by the total profit in cell D10. For example, cell F9 contains the formula =D9/D$10, using a mixed reference to keep the row absolute when copying the formula. Cell F10 contains a SUM() formula that adds the percentages, letting us see that they total 100%.

Times are bad, and the total profit is too low. So, we'll use scenarios to see how we can improve matters by raising rents and shaving costs.

Opening the Scenario Manager Dialog Box

When you're ready to start working with scenarios, choose Data ➤ Analysis ➤ What-If ➤ Scenario Manager from the Ribbon or Tools ➤ Scenarios from the menu bar to display the Scenario Manager dialog box. At first, when the workbook contains no scenarios, the Scenario Manager dialog box appears as shown in Figure 11–8.

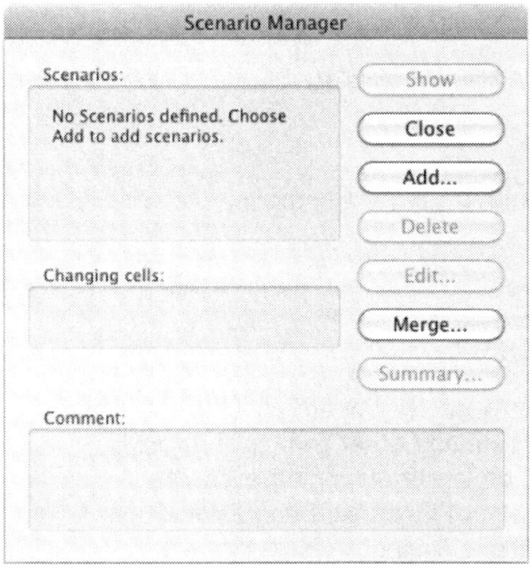

Figure 11–8. *At first, the Scenario Manager dialog box contains nothing but a prompt telling you to click the Add button. Do so.*

Creating Scenarios

After opening the Scenario Manager dialog box, you can create your scenarios.

> **TIP:** First, create a scenario containing your original data. This gives you an easy way to go back to the original data when you've finished testing scenarios.

To create a scenario, follow these steps:

1. From the Scenario Manager dialog box, click the Add button to display the Add Scenario dialog box (see Figure 11–9).

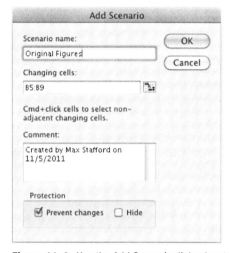

Figure 11–9. *Use the Add Scenario dialog box to set up each scenario. First create a scenario for your original data so that you can easily return to it.*

2. In the Scenario name text box, type a descriptive name for the scenario.

3. Click in the Changing Cells text box, and then enter the details of the cells that users of the scenario are allowed to change. For the original scenario, we're not making changes; but for a scenario that involves changing the rent, the range is cells B5:B9.

    ▧ Click and drag in the worksheet to select a range of contiguous cells. If you need to select noncontiguous cells, click the first one, and then Cmd+click each other cell.

> **NOTE:** When you enter a cell or a range of cells in the Changing Cells text box by clicking in the worksheet, Excel changes the name of the dialog box from Add Scenario to Edit Scenario. Odd though this seems, it's normal.

- You can also type the name of a range into the Changing cells text box.

- There's a Collapse Dialog button to the right of the Changing Cells text box, but you don't need to use it, because Excel automatically collapses the Add Scenario dialog box when you click in the worksheet. After you've selected the changing cells, Excel expands the dialog box again.

4. In the Comment text box, type a comment that explains what the scenario is and how to use it. Excel creates a default comment of *Created by*, your user name (as set in the Office applications), and the date, but a descriptive comment is usually more helpful.

5. Choose settings as needed in the Protection area at the bottom of the dialog box:

   - *Prevent changes.* Select this check box when you need to prevent changes to the scenario. To make the protection take effect, you'll need to protect the worksheet as described in the next section.

   - *Hide.* Select this check box when you need to prevent others from seeing this scenario—for example, because you want them to experiment with their own figures rather than looking at yours. Again, you need to protect the worksheet.

6. Click the OK button to close the Add Scenario dialog box or Edit Scenario dialog box. Excel displays the Scenario Values dialog box (see Figure 11–10). This dialog box shows a text box for each of the changing cells in the scenario. Here's where you see the benefit of naming the changing cells—each text box is easy to identify. If you haven't named the changing cells, the cell addresses appear, and you may need to refer to the worksheet to see which cell is which.

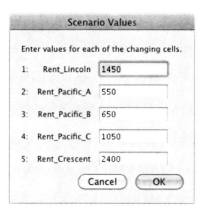

Figure 11–10. *In the Scenario Values dialog box, enter the values to use for the new scenario you're creating. The cell names produce the labels (Rent_Lincoln and so on), which are much easier to refer to than cell addresses (for example, B5).*

7. Change the values as needed for the scenario.

> **TIP:** You can type formulas into the text boxes in the Scenario Values dialog box. For example, to increase the Rent_Lincoln value in Figure 11–10 by 25 percent, you could change the 1450 value to the formula =1.25*1450. After you enter formulas like this, Excel displays the dialog box shown in Figure 11–11 when you close the Scenario Values dialog box, telling you that it has converted names and results of formulas to values. Click the OK button.

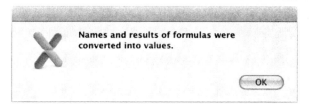

Figure 11–11. *After you enter formulas in the Scenario Values dialog box, Excel automatically converts them to values for you.*

8. Click the OK button to close the Scenario Values dialog box. Excel returns you to the Scenario Manager dialog box, where the scenario now appears in the Scenarios list box.

To add another scenario, click the Add button in the Scenario Manager dialog box, and then repeat the previous process.

Applying Protection to Your Scenarios

If you selected either the Prevent Changes check box or the Hide check box in the Protection area of the Add Scenario dialog box or the Edit Scenario dialog box, you need to protect the worksheet to make the protection take effect.

To protect the worksheet, follow these steps:

1. If the Scenario Manager dialog box is open, click the Close button to close it.

2. Choose **Tools ➤ Protection ➤ Sheet** from the Ribbon or **Tools ➤ Protection ➤ Protect Sheet** from the menu bar to display the Protect the sheet and contents of locked cells dialog box.

3. Type a password in the Password text box and again in the Verify text box.

4. In the Allow users of this sheet to box, make sure the Edit Scenarios check box is cleared.

5. Click the OK button to close the dialog box. Excel applies the protection.

6. Save the workbook. For example, press Cmd+S or click the Save button on the Standard toolbar.

After protecting the scenarios in the worksheet like this, you'll need to turn off the protection before you can edit the scenarios. To turn off the protection, choose **Tools ➤ Protection ➤ Sheet** from the Ribbon or **Tools ➤ Protection ➤ Unprotect Sheet** from the menu bar, type the password in the dialog box that Excel displays, and then click the OK button.

Editing and Deleting Scenarios

From the Scenario Manager dialog box, you can quickly edit a scenario by clicking it in the Scenarios list box, clicking the Edit button, and then working in the Edit Scenario dialog box. Excel automatically updates the scenario's comment for you with details of the modification (for example, "Modified by Jack Cunningham on 02/18/2011"), but you'll often want to type in more details, such as what you're trying to make the scenario show.

When you no longer need a scenario, delete it by clicking the scenario in the Scenarios list box and clicking the Delete button. Excel doesn't confirm the deletion; but if you delete a scenario by mistake, and recovering it is more important than losing any other changes you've made since you last saved the workbook, you can recover the scenario by closing the workbook without saving changes (assuming the scenario was already saved in the workbook).

Switching Among Your Scenarios

Once you've created multiple scenarios for the same worksheet, you can switch among them by clicking the scenario you want in the Scenarios list box in the Scenario Manager dialog box (see Figure 11–12) and then clicking the Show button. Excel displays the scenario's figures in the worksheet's cells. The Scenario Manager dialog box stays open, so you can quickly switch to another scenario.

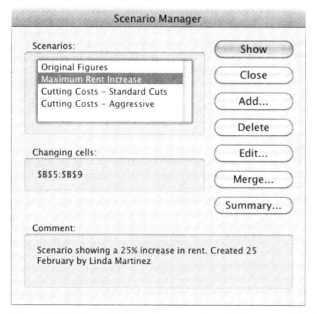

Figure 11–12. *To switch to another scenario, click the scenario in the Scenarios list box in the Scenario Manager dialog box, and then click the Show button.*

TIP: If you need to be able to switch quickly among scenarios, add the Scenario pop-up menu to the Standard toolbar or another convenient toolbar. To customize the toolbar, use the technique described in the "Customizing the Toolbars with the Commands You Need" section in Chapter 2. On the Commands tab of the Customize Toolbars and Menus dialog box, click the Tools item in the Categories list, and then scroll down the Commands list box to find the Scenario pop-up menu.

Merging Scenarios into a Single Worksheet

If you develop and share your scenarios in a single workbook, you can keep them all together. But sometimes you may need to develop your scenarios in separate workbooks and then combine them. You can do this easily by using the Merge command in the Scenario Manager dialog box.

To merge scenarios, follow these steps:

1. Open all the workbooks containing the scenarios you will merge.

2. Make active the workbook and worksheet you will merge the scenarios into.

3. Choose **Data** ➤ **Analysis** ➤ **What-If** ➤ **Scenario Manager** from the Ribbon or **Tools** ➤ **Scenarios** from the menu bar to display the Scenario Manager dialog box.

4. Click the Merge button to display the Merge Scenarios dialog box (see Figure 11–13).

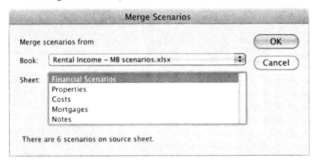

Figure 11–13. *In the Merge Scenarios dialog box, choose the workbook and worksheet that contain the scenarios you want to merge into the active workbook.*

5. Open the Book pop-up menu, and choose the open workbook that contains the scenarios you want to merge in. The Sheet list box shows a list of the worksheets in the workbook.

6. In the Sheet list box, click the worksheet that contains the scenarios. The readout at the bottom of the Merge Scenarios dialog box shows how many scenarios the worksheet contains, which helps you pick the right worksheet.

7. Click the OK button. Excel closes the Merge Scenarios dialog box, merges the scenarios, and then displays the Scenario Manager dialog box again.

NOTE: If any scenario you merge into the active worksheet has the same name as an existing scenario in the worksheet, Excel adds the current date to the incoming scenario to distinguish it.

Creating Reports from Your Scenarios

Sometimes you can make the decisions you need by simply creating scenarios and looking at them in the worksheet. At other times, it's helpful to create a report from the scenarios so that you can compare them. Excel gives you an easy way to create either a summary report or a PivotTable report straight from the Scenario Manager dialog box.

To create a report from your scenarios, follow these steps:

1. Choose **Data ➤ Analysis ➤ What-If ➤ Scenario Manager** from the Ribbon or **Tools ➤ Scenarios** from the menu bar to display the Scenario Manager dialog box.

2. Click the Summary button to display the Scenario Summary dialog box (see Figure 11–14).

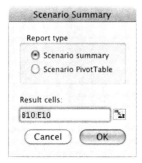

Figure 11–14. *In the Scenario Summary dialog box, choose between a scenario summary and a scenario PivotTable, and then select the result cells for the summary.*

3. In the Report type box, select the Scenario summary option button if you want to create a summary worksheet. If you want to create a scenario PivotTable, select the Scenario PivotTable option button.

4. Click in the Result cells text box, and then enter the addresses of the cells whose results you want the report or PivotTable to show. You can type in addresses or range names or select the appropriate cells in the worksheet.

5. Click the OK button to close the Scenario Summary dialog box. Excel creates the report or PivotTable. Figure 11–15 shows a sample of a summary report, which Excel places on a new worksheet named Scenario Summary at the beginning of the workbook.

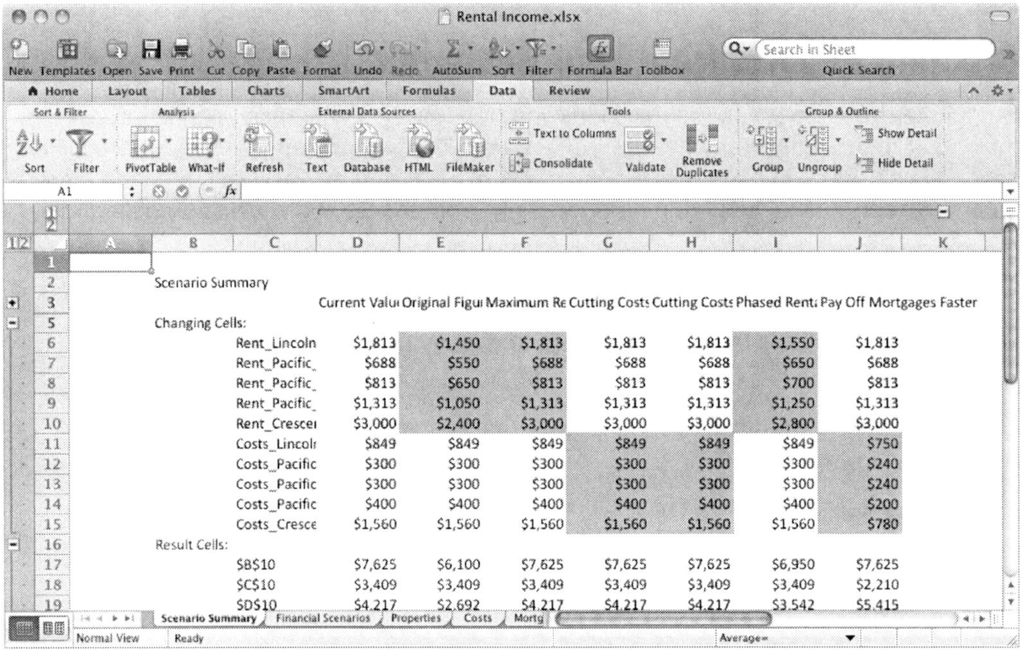

Figure 11–15. *Excel places a summary report on a new worksheet named Scenario Summary at the beginning of the workbook.*

Using Goal Seek

When you're planning or forecasting, you'll often need to work backward from your target to derive the figures you need. For example, when planning your next financial year, you may need to find out how much you need to raise the selling price for your widgets to make an extra $30,000 a year.

To work this out, you can try increasing the unit price for the widgets until your revenue figure is $30,000 higher. But you can save time and effort by using Excel's Goal Seek feature to derive the required price automatically by working backward from the revenue figure.

To derive values using Goal Seek, follow these steps:

1. Open the workbook that contains the data, and navigate to the worksheet that contains the calculation.

2. Make active the cell that contains the formula.

3. Choose **Tools ➤ Goal Seek** from the menu bar to display the Goal Seek dialog box (shown in Figure 11–16 with settings chosen).

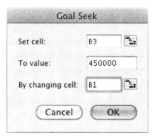

Figure 11–16. *Use the Goal Seek dialog box to work backward from your desired result to the figure you need.*

4. Make sure the Set cell text box contains the right cell. (If you selected the cell in Step 2, it will.) If necessary, change the cell either by typing the correct reference or by double-clicking the current contents of the Set cell text box (to select it) and then clicking the right cell in the worksheet. (You can also click the Collapse Dialog button to collapse the Goal Seek dialog box, but the dialog box is so small anyway that it's usually easier to work around it.)

5. In the To Value text box, type the value you want to get.

6. In the By Changing Cell text box, enter the cell whose value you want to change—in the example, the cell containing the price of the widgets. Again, you can type the cell reference or simply click the cell in the worksheet.

7. Click the OK button. Goal Seek calculates the answer, enters it in the worksheet, and then displays the Goal Seek Status dialog box (see Figure 11–17).

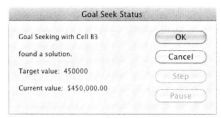

Figure 11–17. *When Excel displays the Goal Seek Status dialog box, look at the value in the target cell in the worksheet. Click the OK button if you want to keep the value. Click the Cancel button if you want to revert to the previous value.*

> **NOTE:** If the calculation is straightforward, Goal Seek finds a solution quickly. But if the calculation is more complex, Goal Seek may take a while. If this happens, you can click the Pause button to pause the calculation to see which value Goal Seek is trying at the moment. If you want to follow the individual values Goal Seek is trying, click the Step button to display the next value but keep the calculation paused; keep clicking the Step button as needed to see further values. Click the Resume button when you want Goal Seek to resume the calculation at full speed.

8. Look at the value in the target cell. Click the OK button if you want to keep it. Click the Cancel button if you want to go back to the previous value.

Solving Multiple-Variable Problems with Solver

If you find Goal Seek useful, but you need more power, you'll want to download and use Solver for Excel for Mac 2011. Solver is a free add-in that lets you change multiple variables, which enables you to ask more complex questions of your data.

Downloading and Installing Solver

To download and install Solver for Excel for Mac 2011, follow these steps:

1. Open your Web browser and go to the Solver for Macintosh Excel 2011 web site (`http://www.solver.com/mac/`).

2. Follow the link for downloading Solver. You need to register using an e-mail address.

3. Double-click the `Solver.pkg` file you downloaded to launch the Install Solver application, and then follow through its steps. Install Solver uses a standard installation routine, in which you need to provide an administrator password for your Mac.

4. In Excel, choose **Tools ➤ Add-Ins** from the menu bar to display the Add-Ins dialog box (see Figure 11–18).

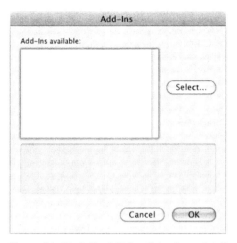

Figure 11–18. *In the Add-Ins dialog box, click the Select button to display the Choose an Add-In dialog box.*

5. Click the Select button to display the Choose an Add-In dialog box, which is a renamed version of the standard Open dialog box.

6. Navigate to the `/Applications/Solver/` folder, and then click the `Solver.xlam` item.

7. Click the Open button. Excel closes the Choose an Add-In dialog box and returns you to the Add-Ins dialog box, which now shows the `Solver.Xlam` item in the Add-ins available list box.

8. Make sure the check box for the `Solver.Xlam` item is selected.

9. Click the OK button to close the Add-Ins dialog box. Excel loads Solver.

Using Solver

You can now use Solver like this:

1. Open the workbook and activate the worksheet that contains the data.

2. Make active the cell that contains the formula you want to analyze.

3. Choose **Tools ➤ Solver** from the menu bar to display the Solver Parameters dialog box (see Figure 11–19).

Figure 11–19. *In the Solver Parameters dialog box, set the parameters for the problem you want Solver to solve.*

4. Make sure the Set Objective box shows the cell you want to analyze. (This box shows the cell you selected in step 2.) If it's the wrong cell, click in the Set Objective box, and then click the right cell.

- You can click the Collapse Dialog button at the right end of the Set Objective box if you want to collapse the Solver Parameters dialog box out of the way.

- You can also type the cell reference or cell name in the Set Objective box.

5. In the To area, select the Max option button, the Min option button, or the Value Of option button. If you select the Value Of option button, type the value in the box to its right.

6. In the By Changing Cells box, enter the references or names of the cells you want Solver to change. You can click the cells in the worksheet (either collapsing the Solver Parameters dialog box or working around it) or type in the references or names.

7. If you want to constrain what Solver can do with the cell values, work with the controls to the right of the Subject to the Constraints box:

    a. Click the Add button to display the Add Constraint dialog box (see Figure 11–20).

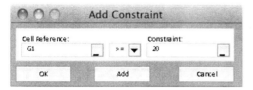

Figure 11–20. *Use the Add Constraint dialog box to set up any constraints needed for the calculation.*

    b. Enter a cell reference or name in the Cell Reference box.

    c. Choose the comparison in the pop-up menu in the middle.

    d. Enter the constraint in the Constraint box. You can enter a value or the reference or name of the cell in which you'll enter the value.

    e. Click the Add button if you want to add another constraint. Otherwise, click the OK button to close the Add Constraint dialog box. The constraints you added appear in the Subject to the Constraints list box.

8. Select the Make Unconstrained Variables Non-Negative check box if you want Solver to use only non-negative (positive or zero) values for variables you haven't constrained.

9. In the Select a Solving Method pop-up menu, choose GRG Nonlinear, Simplex LP, or Evolutionary, as needed. If you're not familiar with different solving methods, start with GRG Nonlinear.

NOTE: Solver uses the Simplex method to solve linear problems (ones in which the change between two related quantities is directly proportional) and the Generalized Reduced Gradient (GRG) Nonlinear method to solve nonlinear problems (ones in which the change between the related quantities isn't directly proportional). The Evolutionary method uses genetic algorithms.

10. If you need to control how Solver performs the calculation, click the Options button, and then choose options on the three tabs of the Options dialog box (shown in Figure 11–21).

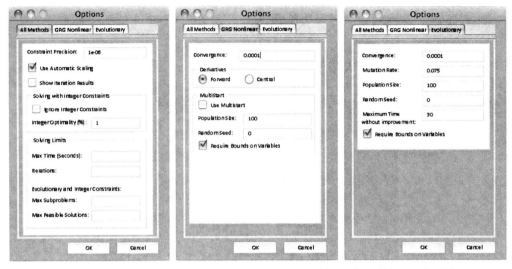

Figure 11–21. *You can choose advanced options on the three tabs of the Options dialog box for Solver.*

11. Click the Solve button to set Solver analyzing the problem. If Solver
finds a solution, it displays the Solver Results dialog box with the
message "Solver found a solution" (see Figure 11–22).

Figure 11–22. *From the Solver Results dialog box, you can choose whether to keep Solver's solution or restore
the original solution.*

NOTE: If Solver can't find a solution to the problem, select the Return to Solver Parameters
Dialog check box in the Solver Results dialog box, and then click the OK button. In the Solver
Parameters dialog box, change the parameters, and try solving the problem again.

12. Select the Keep Solver solution option button if you want to keep the
solution Solver found. Otherwise, select the Restore Original option
button.

13. Click the OK button to close the Solver Results dialog box.

Summary

In this chapter, you've learned how to use data tables to assess the impact of one or two variables on a calculation, how to use scenarios to experiment with different data, and how to solve straightforward problems with Goal Seek. You've also learned how to download, install, and use Solver to crack harder problems.

In the next chapter, I'll show you how to use Excel's powerful PivotTables feature.

Chapter 12

Analyzing Data with PivotTables

In this chapter, we'll look at how you can use PivotTables to analyze the data in your worksheets and draw conclusions from it. PivotTables are great for asking questions of your data and looking at the data in different ways without having to enter it multiple times in separate worksheets.

We'll start by going over what PivotTables are and what you can do with them. After that, I'll show you how to create a PivotTable either by using Excel's automated tool, which can give the PivotTable a jump-start, or by placing the fields on the PivotTable framework manually, which gives you total control.

After you build a PivotTable, you'll often need to change it so that it shows different data or shows the same data differently. I'll show you several examples of the types of changes you can make easily to a PivotTable once you've constructed it.

When the PivotTable is arranged the way you need it, you can format the PivotTable and choose options to control how it appears. And you can sort and filter the data within the PivotTable to show only the information you're after.

Understanding What PivotTables Are and What You Can Do with Them

A PivotTable is a special kind of report that rearranges the fields and records in a table into a different order so that you can examine their relationships. You *pivot* (in other words, rotate) the columns in a PivotTable to display the data summarized in a different way.

For example, take a look at the worksheet shown in Figure 12–1. This worksheet contains a data table that tracks sales made by a company with four product lines: Hardware, Software, Services, and Supplies. The table uses the following columns:

- *Sale.* A unique sequential number used to identify each sale.

- *Year, Month, and Day.* The year, month, and day of the sale. Having these items in separate columns makes it easier to filter by time—for example, to compare one month against another or to see which salesperson sold what in January.

- *Salesperson.* The name of the sales rep who executed the sale.

- *Line.* The product line of the product sold.

- *Product.* The name of the product sold.

Figure 12–1. *The sample table we'll use for creating PivotTables in this chapter*

- *Quantity.* The quantity of the product sold.

- *Price.* The unit price of the product sold.

- *Total Price.* The total price of the products sold (Quantity multiplied by Price).

- *Customer.* The name of the company or organization that bought the products.

This is all straightforward, and you can use a data-entry form to add the data to the data table or edit existing records. You can also easily see your sum total of sales (for example, by adding the figures in the Total Price column). But when you need to dig into the details, you need a different tool.

This is where PivotTables come in. By creating a PivotTable from a data table such as this, you can quickly find the answers to questions such as these:

- Which is your best-selling product line? And your best-selling product?

- How do this year's sales compare to last year's?

- Who was your star salesperson for March? And does another salesperson need some encouragement—or a pink slip?

- Which are your key customers? Which of them needs more one-on-one attention to bring sales up to where they were last year?

In the following sections, we'll put together a PivotTable with the data in the data table, then manipulate it to see what it shows.

> **NOTE:** If you want to work through the examples in this chapter, you'll need a database table like the one shown in the screens. You can either create one yourself or (much easier) download the sample workbook from the book's page on the Apress Web site (www.apress.com).

Creating and Laying Out a PivotTable

You can create a PivotTable either from a database table or from a range of data. If you have a database table already, as in the example, you can create the PivotTable from that. Otherwise, create the database table you'll use, or enter the data in a worksheet as usual without creating a database table.

Once your data is ready, you can create a PivotTable either automatically or manually. Which works best depends on your data and what you're trying to do with it, but often you can save time by creating a PivotTable automatically and then adjusting it as necessary. If an automatic PivotTable turns out not to be what you need, you can create the PivotTable manually from scratch instead.

Creating a PivotTable Automatically

To create a PivotTable automatically, follow these steps:

1. Open the workbook and display the worksheet that contains the table or data you'll use in the PivotTable.

2. Click in the table that you'll use for the PivotTable. If you'll use a range rather than a named table, select the range.

3. Choose Data ➤ Analysis ➤ PivotTable from the Ribbon, clicking the main part of the PivotTable button. You can also click the PivotTable pop-up button, then click Create Automatic PivotTable on the pop-up menu, but there's no advantage to doing so. Excel then does the following:

- Inserts an automatic PivotTable on a new worksheet

- Gives the new worksheet a default name such as Sheet5

- Displays the PivotTable Builder window

- Adds the PivotTable tab to the Ribbon and displays it

- Displays some information about PivotTables the first time you create one

Figure 12–2 shows the automatic PivotTable produced from the sample data table, with the PivotTable Builder window positioned in front of the worksheet.

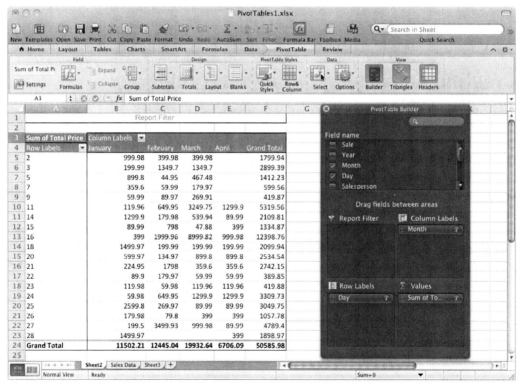

Figure 12–2. *The quickest way to create a PivotTable is to have Excel create it automatically. You will usually need to adjust the PivotTable using the PivotTable Builder window to make the PivotTable show the information you want. Depending on the data you're using, the PivotTable may look substantially different from this one.*

After creating a PivotTable automatically, you'll normally need to adjust it. This is because Excel seldom guesses exactly which information you need where.

To adjust a PivotTable, use the techniques you'll learn in the next section, which shows you how to build a PivotTable from scratch.

Creating a PivotTable Manually

If creating an automatic PivotTable doesn't give a useful result or if you prefer to do things by hand, you can build the PivotTable manually using the PivotTable Builder.

To create a PivotTable manually, follow these steps:

1. Open the workbook, and display the worksheet that contains the table or data you'll use in the PivotTable.

2. Click in the table that you'll use for the PivotTable. If you'll use a range rather than a named table, select the range.

3. Choose Data ➤ Analysis ➤ PivotTable ➤ Create Manual PivotTable from the Ribbon or Data ➤ PivotTable from the menu bar to display the Create PivotTable dialog box (see Figure 12–3). If you're using a named table, you can also choose **Tables ➤ Tools ➤ Summarize with PivotTable** from the Ribbon; if you're using a range, this command isn't available.

Figure 12–3. *In the Create PivotTable dialog box, choose the table or range of data from which to create the PivotTable. Then choose between putting the PivotTable on a new worksheet or an existing worksheet.*

4. In the Choose the data that you want to analyze area at the top of the Create PivotTable dialog box, select the Use a table or a range in this workbook option button.

NOTE: Instead of creating a PivotTable from data in a worksheet, you can create a PivotTable from an external data source such as a FileMaker database or Access database. To do so, you select the Use an external data source option button in the Choose the data that you want to analyze area of the Create PivotTable dialog box, click the Get Data button, then choose the data source. Before you can do this, you must install an Open Database Connectivity (ODBC) driver to enable Excel to connect to the data source, as discussed in Chapter 10.

5. Make sure the Location text box shows the table or range you want to use. If you clicked in the table or selected the range in step 2, you'll be all set. If not, type in the table name or click and drag in the worksheet to select the range (click the Collapse Dialog button first to get the Create PivotTable dialog box out of the way first if necessary).

6. In the Choose where to place the PivotTable area of the Create PivotTable dialog box, choose the appropriate option button:

    ▪ *New worksheet.* Select this option button if you want to place the PivotTable on a new worksheet. This is often clearest, because it gives you plenty of room for the PivotTable.

    ▪ *Existing worksheet.* Select this option button if you want to place the PivotTable on an existing worksheet. Click in the Location text box, click the worksheet's tab, then click and drag in the worksheet to enter the location.

7. Click the OK button to close the Create PivotTable dialog box. Excel positions a PivotTable framework on a new worksheet or the existing worksheet you chose and displays the PivotTable Builder window. Figure 12–4 shows the PivotTable framework on a new worksheet named Sheet4.

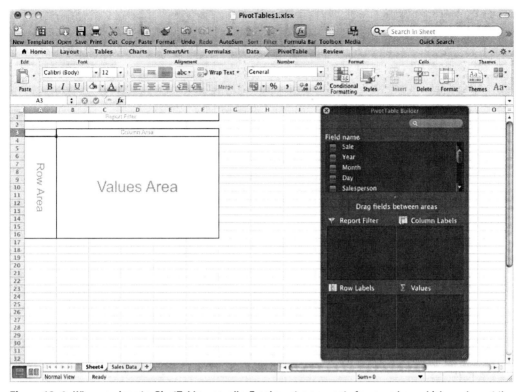

Figure 12–4. *When you insert a PivotTable manually, Excel creates an empty framework on which you lay out the PivotTable the way you need it.*

Now that you've inserted the framework for the PivotTable, you can add fields to it from the Field name list box in the PivotTable Builder window.

Understanding How the PivotTable Framework and PivotTable Builder Window Work

Take a moment to look at the PivotTable framework and the PivotTable Builder window. You use the PivotTable Builder window to arrange the fields on the PivotTable framework.

Here are the essentials you need to know:

- *Field name list box.* This list box in the PivotTable Builder window contains an entry for each of the fields that Excel found in the data table or range you chose. Each item in the list has a check box that you can select to add the field to the PivotTable. The PivotTable framework has no matching area for the Field name list box, because the fields go into the various areas of the PivotTable when you use them.

NOTE: Excel automatically parses the fields in the Field name list box and decides which part of the PivotTable they belong to. Given that Excel has no understanding of what your data table or range contains beyond being able to identify items such as dates, currency, and text, it's pretty smart about this. But you'll often need to move a field from one part of the PivotTable to another by dragging it from one area of the PivotTable Builder window to another.

- *Report Filter.* This area at the top of the PivotTable acts as a filter for the PivotTable as a whole, narrowing down the rest of the table to only the data that matches your filter. For example, if you put the Salespeople field in the Report Filter area by dragging it to the Report Filter box in the PivotTable Builder window, you get a pop-up menu of your salespeople from which you choose whose data you want to show. As you'll see later in this chapter, you can filter by one field, two fields, or more.

- *Row Area.* This area at the left of the PivotTable shows the row headings. You designate those headings by dragging the appropriate field or fields to the Row Labels box in the PivotTable Builder window.

- *Column Area.* This area at the top of the PivotTable shows the column headings. You choose those headings by dragging the appropriate field or fields to the Column Labels box in the PivotTable Builder window.

- *Values Area.* This area in the body of the PivotTable—in most cases the main part of the PivotTable—contains the values. You specify the values by dragging the appropriate field or fields to the Values box in the PivotTable Builder window.

If this is hard to grasp, don't worry. You'll see how PivotTables work in just a moment.

Adding the Fields to the PivotTable Framework

To create the PivotTable, you add fields to the PivotTable framework by dragging fields to the Report Filter box, the Row Labels box, the Column Labels box, and the Values box in the PivotTable Builder window.

NOTE: You can also add fields by selecting their check boxes in the Field name list box. When you select a field, Excel places it automatically depending on what its contents appear to be. Because Excel doesn't know what your data represents and what you're trying to show, it often puts the field in the wrong place. So it's usually best to place the fields yourself by dragging them.

Which fields you need to drag where depends on your data source and what you're trying to make it show. Here's a walk-through using the fields in the data source. If you're using the sample data source, your results should look similar; if your data source is different, they'll look different, but the PivotTable will work in much the same way.

In the Field name list box in the PivotTable Builder window, click the Year field and drag it to the Report Filter box. Excel selects the Year check box, enters Year in cell A1, and creates a pop-up menu for selecting the years in cell B1 (see Figure 12–5).

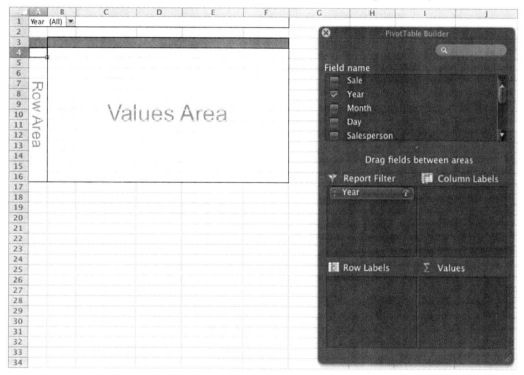

Figure 12–5. *Drag the Year button from the Field name box in the PivotTable Builder window to the Report Filter box to create the Year pop-up menu shown in cell B1 here. Excel selects the (All) item in the pop-up menu at first, making the PivotTable show all the years.*

1. In the Field Name list box, click the Salesperson field and drag it to the Row Labels box. Excel selects the Salesperson check box and creates a row label for each salesperson's name (see Figure 12–6).

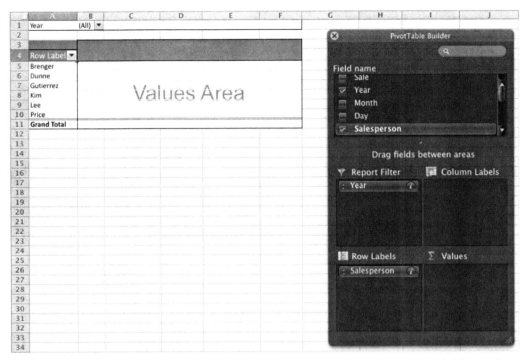

Figure 12–6. *Moving the Salesperson button to the Row Labels box makes Excel create a row label from each salesperson's name.*

2. Drag the Line field from the Field name list box in the PivotTable Builder window to the Column Labels box. Excel selects the Line check box in the Field name list box and adds the product lines as column labels (see Figure 12–7).

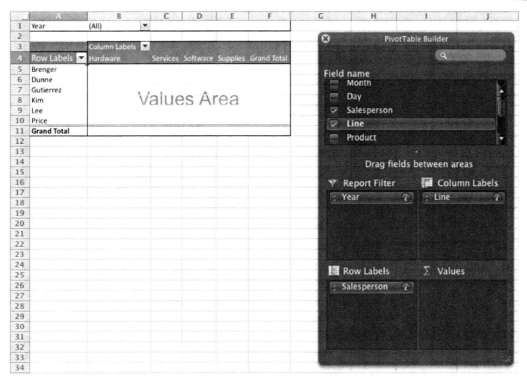

Figure 12–7. *Drag the Line item from the Field name list box in the PivotTable Builder window to the Column Labels area. Excel adds the product lines as column labels and selects the Line check box for you.*

3. Now click the Total Price field in the Field name list box, and drag it to the Values box in the PivotTable Builder window. Excel adds to the PivotTable the values of the items the salespeople sold (see Figure 12–8).

Figure 12–8. *Drag the Total Price field from the Field name list box to the Values box in the PivotTable Builder window to add the totals of each salesperson's sales to the PivotTable.*

This gives us a PivotTable that shows how much of each product line each salesperson sold. At first, the PivotTable shows (All) in the Year pop-up menu in the Report Filter area. To see a breakdown by a year, open the Year pop-up menu, then click the year you want.

This is useful—but it's just the start of what you can do with the PivotTable.

Changing the PivotTable to Show Different Data

The great thing about PivotTables is how easy they are to change to show different data. You can change a PivotTable by adding different fields to it, removing fields it's currently using, or rearranging the fields among the Report Filter box, the Column Labels box, the Row Labels box, and the Values box in the PivotTable Builder window.

Here are four examples of how you can change the basic PivotTable created earlier in this chapter. These examples work as a sequence, so you'll need to make each change in turn if you want to work through them.

- In the Field name list box, click the Product field, then drag it to the Row Labels box in the PivotTable Builder window. Excel adds a list of the product names of the products each salesperson has sold (see Figure 12–9).

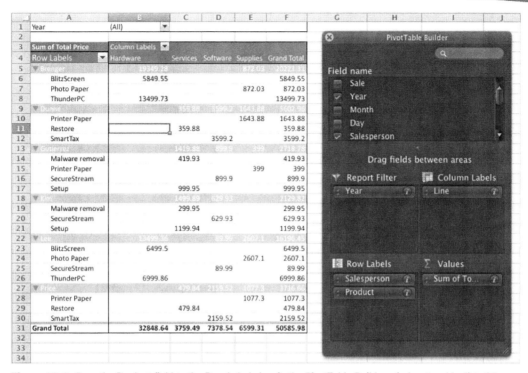

Figure 12–9. *Drag the Product field to the Row Labels box in the PivotTable Builder window to add a list of the products each salesperson has sold. You can collapse any list by clicking the disclosure triangle to the left of the salesperson's name.*

- In the Row Labels box in the PivotTable Builder window, drag the Salesperson field below the Product field. The PivotTable then shows each product with a collapsible list of the salespeople who have been selling it (see Figure 12–10).

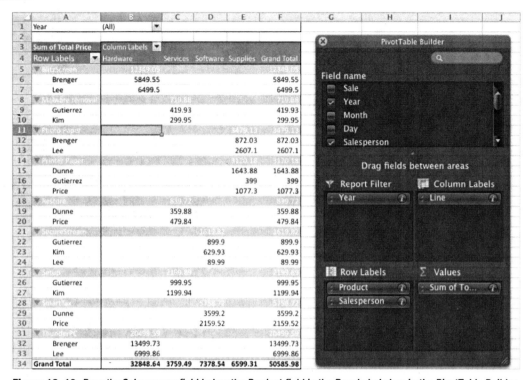

Figure 12–10. *Drag the Salesperson field below the Product field in the Row Labels box in the PivotTable Builder window to produce a list of products showing the salespeople who have been selling them.*

▪ Drag the Product field from the Row Labels box in the PivotTable Builder window to the Column Labels box. Then drag the Line field from the Column Labels box outside the PivotTable Builder window and drop it, making it disappear from the PivotTable. (You can also clear the Line check box in the Field name list box.) These changes produce a PivotTable showing the salespeople by row and what they've sold of the products in columns (see Figure 12–11).

Row Labels	BlitzScreen	Malware removal	Photo Paper	Printer Paper	Restore	SecureStream	Setup	SmartTax	ThunderPC	Grand Total
Brenger	5849.55		872.03						13499.73	20221.31
Dunne				1643.88	359.88			3599.2		5602.96
Gutierrez		419.93		399		899.9	999.95			2718.78
Kim		299.95				629.93	1199.94			2129.82
Lee	6499.5		2607.1			89.99			6999.86	16196.45
Price				1077.3	479.84			2159.52		3716.66
Grand Total	12349.05	719.88	3479.13	3120.18	839.72	1619.82	2199.89	5758.72	20499.59	50585.98

(Year (All); Sum of Total Price; Column Labels)

Figure 12–11. *Removing the product lines and making column labels of the products produces this PivotTable that shows how much each salesperson has sold of each product.*

▪ Make the following changes to see which of your product lines each of your customers bought in a specific period:

1. Drag the Month field from the Field name list box in the PivotTable Builder window to the Report Filter box, placing it below the Year field. You can now filter by month as well as by field. For example, you can choose 2011 as the Year filter, then choose January as the Month filter to see only your January 2011 results.

2. In the Field name list box, clear the Salesperson check box to remove the Salesperson field from the Row Labels area. Then drag the Customer field from the Field name list box to the Row Labels box instead, making the PivotTable show one customer in each row.

3. In the Field name list box, clear the Product check box to remove the Product field from the Column Labels area. Then drag the Line field to the Column Labels box to make the PivotTable show the product lines in the columns. Figure 12–12 shows the resulting PivotTable.

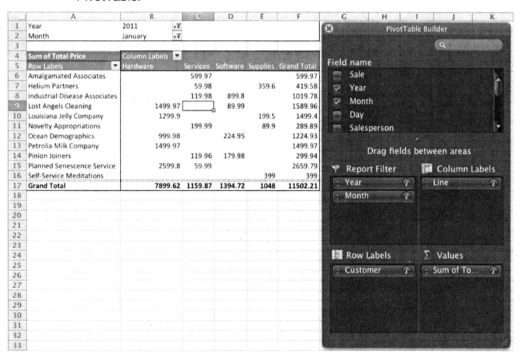

Figure 12–12. *You can add the Month field to the Report Filter box, putting it below the Year field, to filter your PivotTable by first the year (here, 2011) and then the month (here, January). This PivotTable shows how much customers bought from each product line in January 2011.*

When you've finished working with the PivotTable Builder window, you can close it by clicking the Close (×) button at the left end of its title bar or by choosing PivotTable ➤ View ➤ Builder from the Ribbon.

If you need to open the PivotTable Builder window again, choose **PivotTable** ➤ **View** ➤ **Builder** from the Ribbon.

Changing the Function Used to Summarize a Field

When you add values to a PivotTable, Excel tries to automatically use the right function for the calculation that type of data needs. For example, when you add a field that shows prices, Excel uses the SUM() function on the assumption that you want to add the values. And if you use nonnumeric data such as names, Excel uses the COUNT() function, giving you the number of different items.

If you need to change a field to a different function, follow these steps:

Click the field, or click a cell containing data that the field produces.

> **TIP:** You can also open the PivotTable Field dialog box for a field by clicking the i button to the right of the field's name in the PivotTable Builder window.

1. Choose **PivotTable** ➤ **Field** ➤ **Settings** from the Ribbon to display the PivotTable Field dialog box (see Figure 12–13).

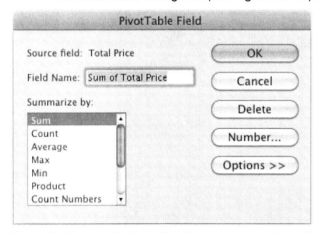

Figure 12–13. *In the PivotTable Field dialog box, you can change the formula used to summarize the field's data.*

2. In the Summarize by list box, click the function you want to use. For example, click the Average function if you want the field to show an average instead of a sum. Excel automatically changes the contents of the Field Name text box to reflect the function you chose—for example, changing the text from Sum of Total Price to Average of Total Price.

TIP: If you need to present the data in a different format (for example, as the amount of difference from a base value), click the Options button in the PivotTable Field dialog box to expand the dialog box and reveal more options. In the Show data as pop-up menu, choose the format you want—for example, Difference From. Then select the base field in the Base field list box and the base item in the Base item list box.

3. If you want to change the field name, type the change in the Field Name text box.

4. Click the OK button to close the PivotTable Field dialog box.

Controlling the Design of a PivotTable

After setting up the framework for your PivotTable, you can use the tools in the Design group of the PivotTable tab of the Ribbon to choose where to display subtotals and grand totals, choose among the PivotTable layouts that Excel offers, and decide whether to insert blank rows between items to make the PivotTable more readable.

The Design group contains four pop-up menus:

- *Subtotals.* In this pop-up menu, click to place a check mark next to the Show at Bottom item if you want to place the subtotals at the bottom of each group (on a line marked Totals). If you prefer to have the subtotals appear at the top of the group, on the same line as the group's label, click to place a check mark next to the Show at Top item instead. Placing a check mark next to one item removes the check mark from the other item—they're alternatives, even though the interface doesn't make this obvious.

- *Totals.* In this pop-up menu, click to place a check mark next to the Show for Rows item if you want to show totals for rows. Click to place a check mark next to the Show for Columns item if you want to show totals for columns. If you don't want the totals, click to remove the check mark. These two items work independently— they're not alternatives.

- *Layout.* In this pop-up menu, click to place a check mark next to the layout you want: Compact Layout (the default, shown at the top of Figure 12–14), Outline Layout (shown in the middle of Figure 12–14), or Tabular Layout (shown at the bottom of Figure 12–14).

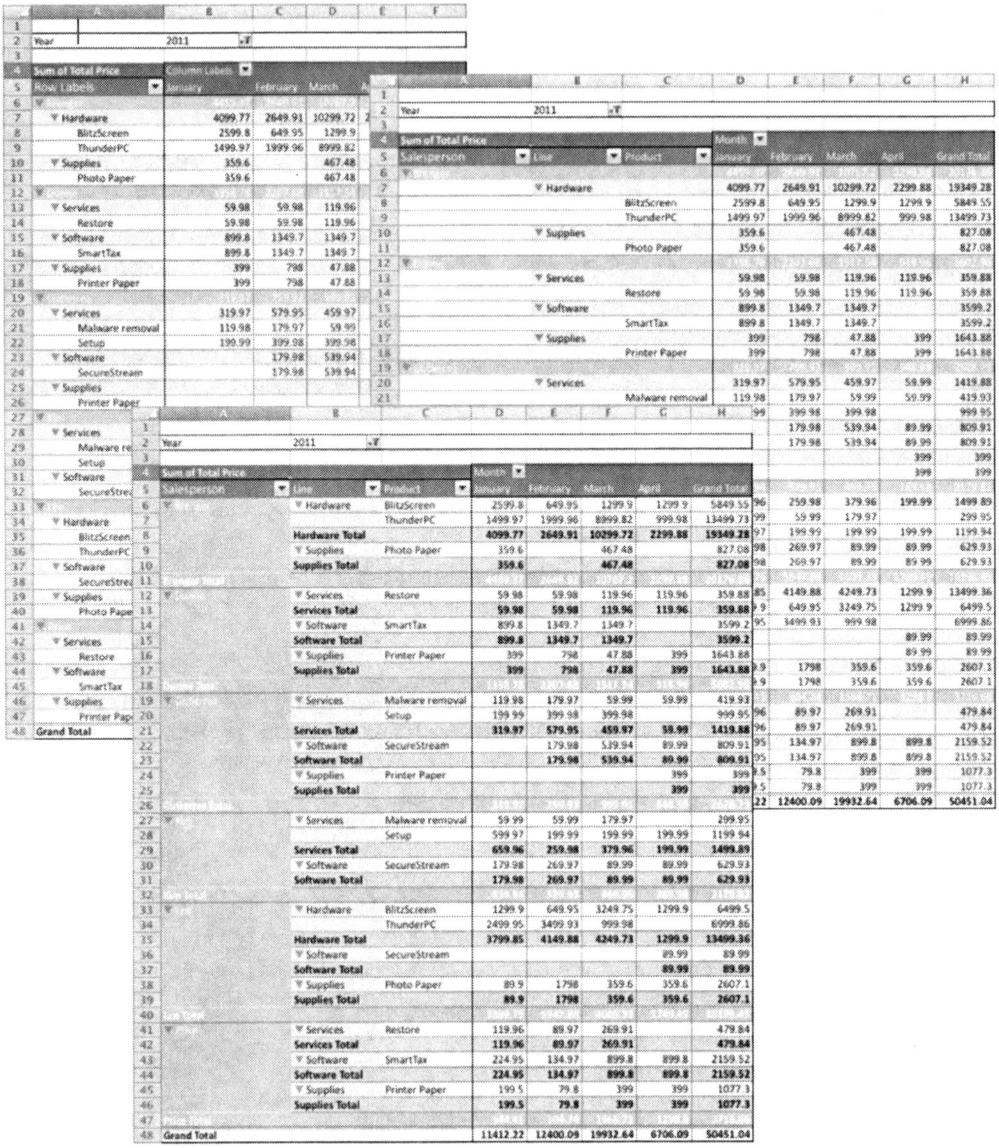

Figure 12–14. *You can choose among three layouts for your PivotTables. Compact Layout (left) is good for presenting data in a small space. Outline Layout (right) and Tabular Layout (bottom) take up more space but make the data easier to read.*

■ *Blanks.* In this pop-up menu, place a check mark next to the item called Insert Blank Line After Each Item if you want to have a blank line appear after each item in the PivotTable. Blank lines make the PivotTable take up much more space but can make it far easier to read. If you don't want blank lines, click to place a check mark next to the item called Remove Blank Line After Each Item. (These two controls are opposites; placing a check mark next to one removes the check mark from the other.)

Formatting a PivotTable

To make a PivotTable look good and convey its contents effectively, you can format it. You can apply the formatting at any point, but usually it's best to lay out the framework and fields of the PivotTable first so that you have a fair idea of how it will appear.

Applying a PivotTable Style

As you've seen in the examples so far in this chapter, Excel applies a style to a PivotTable when you create it. The style helps you distinguish the different areas of the PivotTable visually.

To change the way a PivotTable looks, apply a different style to it from the PivotTable Styles group on the PivotTable tab of the Ribbon. You can either click one of the styles in the Quick Styles box or hold the mouse pointer over the Quick Styles box, click the panel button that appears, then click the PivotTable style you want on the Quick Styles panel.

> **NOTE:** You can also create your own PivotTable styles. To do so, choose **PivotTable ➤ PivotTable Styles ➤ Quick Styles ➤ New PivotTable Style**, then work in the New PivotTable Quick Style dialog box that Excel displays. Briefly, you give the style a name in the Name text box, then click an element in the Table element list box, click the Format button, and choose the formatting you want for the element. After you create a new style, you can apply it from the Custom section at the top of the Quick Styles panel.

Choosing Options for a PivotTable Style

After applying a PivotTable style, you can choose options for it by selecting **PivotTable ➤ PivotTable Styles ➤ Row & Column** and then placing check marks next to the items you want on the Row & Column pop-up menu:

■ *Row Headers.* Place a check mark next to this item to use the style's formatting on the row headers.

- *Column Headers.* Place a check mark next to this item to use the style's formatting on the column headers.

- *Banded Rows.* Place a check mark next to this item to make lines or shaded bands (depending on the style) appear along the rows.

- *Banded Columns.* Place a check mark next to this item to make lines or shaded bands (depending on the style) appear up and down the columns.

Naming a PivotTable and Setting Options for It

When you insert a PivotTable, Excel gives it an automatic name (such as PivotTable1 or PivotTable2) and sets default display options, layout options, and data options. To rename the PivotTable or to choose different options, choose **PivotTable ➤ Data ➤ Options** to display the PivotTable Options dialog box, then work with its controls. (If the Excel window is too narrow for the Ribbon to fit, the command is **PivotTable ➤ Data ➤ Options ➤ PivotTable Options**.)

Figure 12–15 shows the PivotTable Options dialog box with its Display tab at the front.

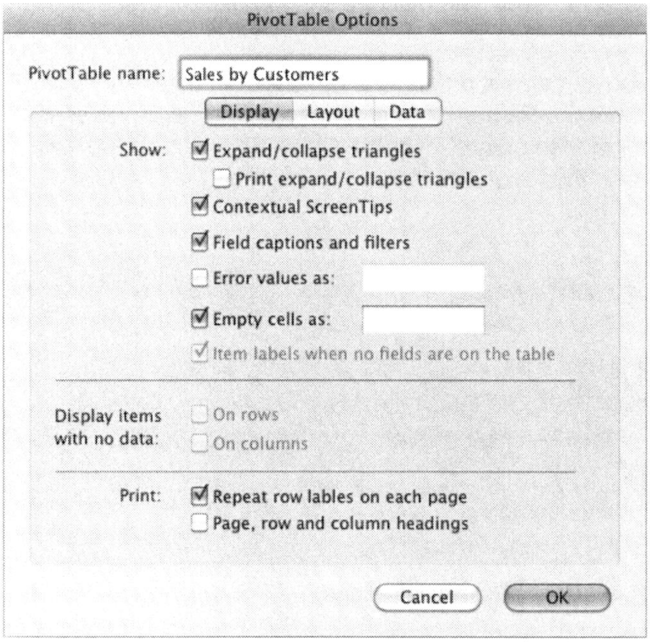

Figure 12–15. *On the Display tab of the PivotTable Options dialog box, choose whether to show items such as expand/collapse triangles and ScreenTips on the PivotTable and whether to print headings and row labels.*

Renaming a PivotTable

To rename a PivotTable, type the new name over the existing name in the PivotTable name text box at the top of the PivotTable Options dialog box. PivotTable names can include spaces, so you can make them descriptive and readable.

> **NOTE:** When you create a PivotTable on its own worksheet, you'll normally want to rename the worksheet from its default name (for example, Sheet5) to a descriptive name (for example, Sales PivotTable). Double-click the current name on the worksheet tab, type the new name, then press Return to apply it.

Choosing Display Options for a PivotTable

To control how Excel displays a PivotTable, click the Display tab in the PivotTable Options dialog box to display its controls (shown in Figure 12–15), then choose the options you want.

These are the options you can choose in the Show area:

- *Expand/collapse triangles.* Select this check box if you want to display the disclosure triangles you click to expand or collapse row labels or column labels. Usually it's useful to display these disclosure triangles, but you can clear this check box if you want to hide them to prevent others from changing the display of a PivotTable.

- *Print expand/collapse triangles.* Select this check box if you want to print the disclosure triangles on printouts of the PivotTables. Printing the disclosure triangles is often useful for PivotTables you print for your own consumption, but you may prefer not to print the triangles on printouts you produce for other people.

- *Contextual ScreenTips.* Select this check box if you want the PivotTable to display ScreenTips for fields and for values when you hold the mouse pointer over a cell. This option is usually helpful.

- *Field captions and filters.* Select this check box if you want captions to appear at the top of the PivotTable and filter pop-up buttons on column labels and row labels. These are usually helpful too.

- *Error values as.* If you want to display standard text in cells that contain errors rather than displaying error messages, select this check box and type the text in the text box.

- *Empty cells as.* If you want to display standard text in empty cells instead of having them simply be empty, select this check box and type the text in the text box.

- *Item labels when no fields are on the table.* This check box is normally selected but dimmed and unavailable, because it applies only to PivotTables created in Excel 2004 (Mac), Excel 2003 (Windows), or earlier versions of Excel. If the check box is available, selecting it makes the PivotTable display item labels even when the Value Area contains no fields.

The Display items with no data area contains two settings that are available only for PivotTables that use an OLAP (Online Analytical Processing) data source:

- *On rows.* Select this check box to display row items that have no values.

- *On columns.* Select this check box to display column items that have no values.

The Print area contains two options for controlling which items print along with the PivotTable:

- *Repeat row labels on each page.* Select this check box to make Excel print the row labels on each page the PivotTable occupies rather than just on the first page. Repeating the row labels makes the PivotTable easier to read, so it's usually a good idea.

- *Page, row and column headings.* Select this check box to repeat the page headings, row headings, and column headings. This too is usually helpful.

Choosing Layout Options for a PivotTable

To control the layout of a PivotTable, click the Layout tab in the PivotTable Options dialog box to display its controls (see Figure 12–16), then choose the settings you want.

These are the settings you can choose in the Layout area of the Layout tab:

- *Allow multiple filters per field.* Select this check box if you want to be able to filter the PivotTable by two or more filters on a single field rather than by just one filter.

- *AutoFit column widths on update.* Select this check box to make Excel automatically resize the column widths to accommodate the data with which you've refreshed the PivotTable. AutoFit is usually helpful.

- *Preserve cell formatting on update.* Select this check box to make Excel retain cell formatting you've applied directly to cells when you update the information in the PivotTable. This option too is usually helpful.

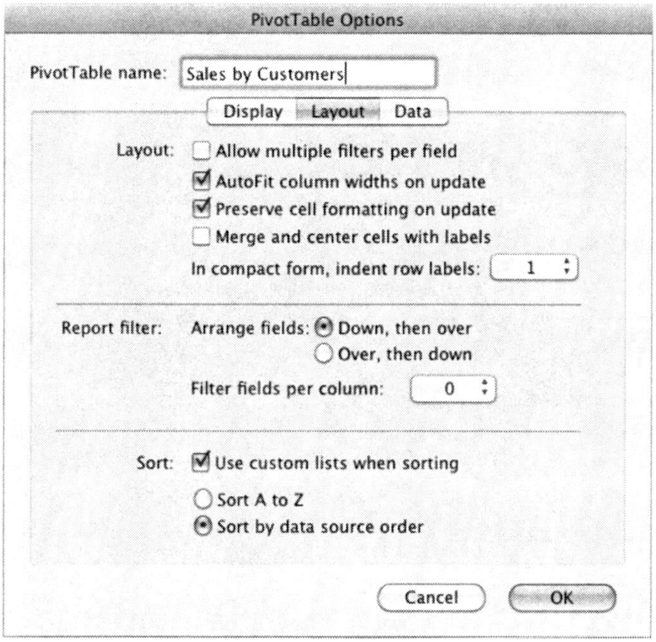

Figure 12–16. *On the Layout tab of the PivotTable Options dialog box, you can set options for the layout, for the report filter, and for sorting.*

- *Merge and center cells with labels.* Select this check box if you want Excel to merge a label cell with a blank cell next to it and center the label across the cells. Try this look to see whether you prefer it to the regular look.

- *In compact form, indent row labels.* In this pop-up menu, choose the number of spaces by which you want to indent row labels when using the Compact Layout for a PivotTable.

These are the settings you can choose in the Report filter area of the Layout tab:

- *Arrange fields option buttons.* Select the "Down, then over" option button to have Excel arrange the fields downward first and then across to the right. Select the "Over, then down" option button if you prefer to arrange the fields first to the right and then downward.

- *Filter fields per column.* In this pop-up menu, choose the number of fields to display in the report filter before moving to another column or row.

These are the settings you can choose in the Sort area of the Layout tab:

- *Use custom lists when sorting.* Select this check box if you want Excel to sort by your custom lists when it encounters the data in them. For example, if you've created a custom list of your company's offices, select this check box to make Excel sort the PivotTable by the order in that list rather than in ascending order or another standard sort order.

- *Sort A to Z.* Select this option button if you want to sort in ascending order. The alternative is the Sort by data source order option button.

- *Sort by data source order.* Select this option button if you want to sort the PivotTable in the same order as the data source. This is the default setting and is useful if you've laid out the data source in your preferred order. If not, select the Sort A to Z option button instead.

Choosing Data Options for a PivotTable

The Data tab of the PivotTable Options dialog box (see Figure 12–17) lets you control how Excel stores the PivotTable's data from an external connection and whether Excel refreshes the data automatically. For a PivotTable connected to an external data source, you can also choose whether to save the connection password with the Excel workbook and whether to run queries in the background.

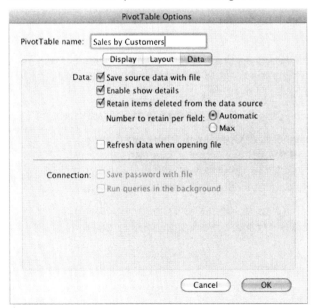

Figure 12–17. *On the Data tab of the PivotTable Options dialog box, choose how to handle the PivotTable's data and connection.*

In the Data area of the Data tab, you can choose the following options:

- *Save source data with file.* Select this check box if you want to store the source data from an external data source in the workbook that contains the PivotTable. This setting has no effect on a PivotTable that contains data drawn from its own workbook, because that workbook contains the data already.

- *Enable show details.* Select this check box if you want to be able to drill down in the PivotTable to show details from the data source.

- *Retain items deleted from the data source.* Select this check box if you want Excel to store data that has been deleted from the data source. Storing the data is useful if you are working with older data in a data source that's being updated.

- *Number to retain per field.* Select the Automatic option button to have Excel store the default number of items for each field of data. Select the Max option button to store as many items as possible for each field of data.

- *Refresh data when opening file.* Select this check box if you want Excel to automatically refresh the data in the PivotTable when you open the workbook. Automatic refreshing is useful when you need to make sure you're working with the latest figures.

In the Connection area, you can choose these two options:

- *Save password with file.* For an external connection, select this check box to save the connection's password in the workbook. Saving the password means you don't need to enter it manually on each refresh, so you'll usually want to do this unless security dictates otherwise.

- *Run queries in the background.* For an external connection, select this check box to run queries in the background rather than in the foreground. Running queries in the background typically makes the queries take longer but allows Excel to remain more responsive while a query is running.

When you've finished choosing options in the PivotTable Options dialog box, click the OK button to close the dialog box.

Refreshing the Data in a PivotTable

Even when you create a PivotTable from a data source in the same workbook, the data in a PivotTable remains static rather than updating automatically the way most other Excel objects do.

When you want to make sure your PivotTable contains the latest data from the data source, choose **PivotTable ➤ Data ➤ Refresh ➤ Refresh**.

To refresh all the PivotTables in a workbook, choose **PivotTable ➤ Data ➤ Refresh ➤ Refresh All**.

If your PivotTable uses an external data source, and you find the refresh operation is taking too long, choose **PivotTable ➤ Data ➤ Refresh ➤ Cancel Refresh** to cancel the operation.

Changing the Source of a PivotTable

Sometimes, after building a PivotTable, you may find you need to change its source data. You can do this without deleting the PivotTable and starting again, which is good news.

To change the source data of a PivotTable, follow these steps:

1. From the Ribbon, choose **PivotTable ➤ Data ➤ Change Source** to display the Change PivotTable Data Source dialog box (see Figure 12–18). If the Ribbon is squashed, you need to choose **PivotTable ➤ Data ➤ Options ➤ Change Source**.

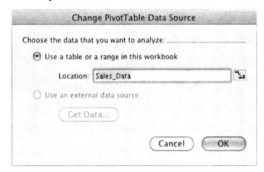

Figure 12–18. *Use the Change PivotTable Data Source dialog box when you need to switch the PivotTable to a different data source.*

2. In the Location text box, enter the range you want to use instead of the current range. You can type in a table name or a range name; type in a range reference; or click the Collapse Dialog button, select the range in the worksheet, then click the Collapse Dialog button again.

3. Click the OK button to close the Change PivotTable Data Source dialog box. Excel updates the PivotTable with data from the new data source.

Sorting and Filtering a PivotTable

To make a PivotTable show the data you require, you may need to sort it or filter it.

To sort a PivotTable, click the pop-up button of the field by which you want to sort. Excel displays the sorting and filtering window for that field. The window bears the field's name, as you can see in Figure 12–19, which shows the sorting and filtering window for the Product field. You can then click the Ascending button to produce an ascending sort (from A to Z, from small numbers to large numbers, and from early dates and times to later ones) or the Descending button to produce a descending sort (the opposite).

Figure 12–19. *To sort or filter a PivotTable, open the sorting and filtering window for the field, then choose options in the Sort area or the Filter area. The sorting and filtering window's title bar shows the field's name (here, Product).*

NOTE: To control how Excel sorts a PivotTable, choose sorting options in the Sort area of the Layout tab of the PivotTable Options dialog box, as discussed earlier in this chapter.

When you apply sorting to a field, the field name pop-up button changes to show an arrow indicating the direction of the sort. For example, in Figure 12–20, you can see an upward arrow indicating a descending sort on the Salesperson field and a downward arrow indicating an ascending sort on the Product field. The Line field shows the regular pop-up button.

4	Sum of Total Price		Line ▼	
5	Salesperson ▼↑	Product ▼↓	Hardware	Services
6	Price	Printer Paper		
7		Restore		479.84
8		SmartTax		

Figure 12–20. *When you sort a PivotTable, the field's pop-up button shows an upward arrow for a descending an sort (as on the Salesperson field here) or a downward arrow for ascending sort (as on the Product field here).*

To filter the PivotTable, click the pop-up button next to the field's name to display the sorting and filtering window, then choose the filtering criteria in the Filter area. Here are some examples:

- *Filter by label.* To filter by label, open the By label pop-up menu, choose the comparison type, then specify the data required. For example, choose the Contains comparison to find labels that match the text string you type in the text box that appears, as shown on the left in Figure 12–21.

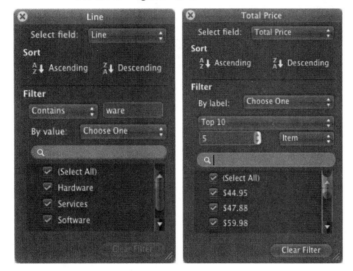

Figure 12–21. *You can filter a field by its label (as shown on the left here) or by its value. You can also search in the Search box or clear the check boxes of items you want to exclude.*

- *Filter by value.* To filter by value, open the By value pop-up menu, then choose the comparison you want. For example, choose the Top 10 item to create a top-however-many-you-choose filter, then set the number of items in the left of the two pop-up menus that appear below the By value pop-up menu when it's showing Top 10 (see the right screen in Figure 12–21). In the right of the two pop-up menus, choose Item, Percentage, or Sum as needed for the filtering.

- *Filter by individual values.* To filter by individual values, clear the (Select All) check box in the lower part of the Filter area, then select the check box for each item you want to use in the filter. To find only particular items so that you can select or clear their check boxes, click in the Search box, then type the search term.

When you apply a filter, the field's pop-up button displays a funnel-like filter symbol, as you can see on the Line field in Figure 12–22.

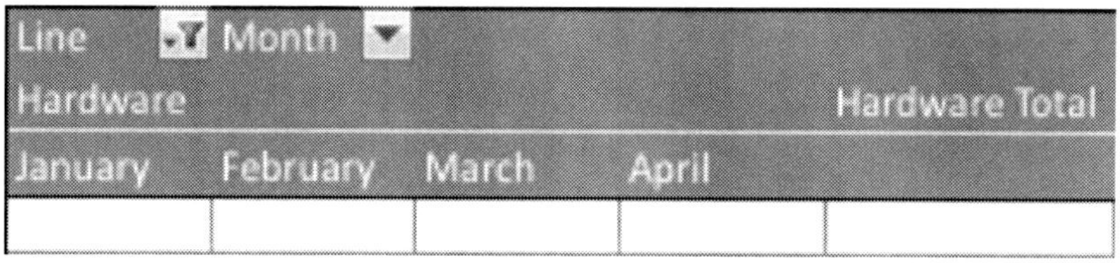

Line	▼	Month	▼		
Hardware				Hardware Total	
January	February	March	April		

Figure 12–22. *Excel displays a funnel-like filter on a field's pop-up button to indicate that you've applied filtering to that field.*

To remove filtering, open the sorting and filtering window again, then click the Clear Filter button at the bottom.

Summary

In this chapter, you learned what PivotTables are and how to create them from your existing tables or other data sources. You know how to start a PivotTable automatically or build it manually, how to rearrange its fields to change the information it displays and the way it displays the information, and how to design and format the PivotTable. Lastly, you learned how to sort and filter PivotTables to make them show the information you need.

In the next chapter, I'll show you how to share your workbooks with your colleagues.

Chapter 13

Collaborating and Sharing with Macs and Windows PCs

In this chapter, I'll show you how to work with other people on your workbooks.

You can give others your workbooks the old-fashioned way—by printing the worksheets and distributing them on paper—or you can take the more modern approach and create PDF files that you can share on a network or via the Internet. You can also export data to a comma-separated values format to make it compatible with many programs.

You can share your workbooks with your colleagues so that two or more of you can work on the same workbook at the same time, and you can track the changes people make to your workbooks so that you can review them closely. These features work on both Mac OS X and Windows, so it doesn't matter which platform your colleagues use. Better still, Excel provides an automated tool for merging the changes in separate copies of the same workbook together, allowing you to easily collate the changes, track them, and review them.

At the end of the chapter, I'll show you how to consolidate multiple worksheets into a single worksheet. This is great when you need to pull together information quickly from related worksheets.

Making Your Worksheets Print Correctly

To print from Excel, you use the Print dialog box. But before you print, you need to tell Excel which part of the workbook to print. You may also want to check the page setup to make sure the page breaks fall where you want them to fall.

Telling Excel Which Part of the Worksheet to Print

Given that each worksheet contains billions of cells, you seldom need to print the whole of a worksheet—you want to print only the range of cells you've used, or perhaps only a small subset of that range. So when you're printing, the first thing to do is tell Excel which part of the worksheet you want to print. Excel calls this setting the print area. You can set a separate print area for each worksheet.

> **CAUTION:** Until you set the print area, Excel assumes you want to print all the cells you've used on the worksheet—even if there are huge amounts of blank space between them. So, it's a good idea always to set the print area before printing.

To set the print area, follow these steps:

1. Click the worksheet whose print area you want to set.

2. Select the range of cells you want to print.

3. Choose **File ➤ Print Area ➤ Set Print Area**. Excel displays a dotted blue line around the print area to indicate that it is set.

4. If you need to add a new area to the existing print area, select the range of cells you want to add, then choose **File ➤ Print Area ➤ Add to Print Area**.

> **NOTE:** When you create a print area that consists of multiple ranges of cells, the ranges don't need to be contiguous. Excel prints each separate range on a separate page.

If you need to change the print area altogether, select a new range of cells, then give the **File ➤ Print Area ➤ Set Print Area** command again.

If you need to clear the print area so that the worksheet has no print area set, click the worksheet, then choose **File ➤ Print Area ➤ Clear Print Area**.

Checking the Page Layout and Where the Page Breaks Fall

When printing a large worksheet, check the page layout of the worksheet and adjust it as needed. Follow these steps:

1. Switch to Page Layout view by clicking the Page Layout View button at the left end of the status bar, choosing **Layout ➤ View ➤ Page Layout** from the Ribbon, or choosing **View ➤ Page Layout** from the menu bar.

2. Click the Layout tab of the Ribbon to show its controls. Figure 13–1 shows a worksheet in Page Layout view with the Layout tab displayed.

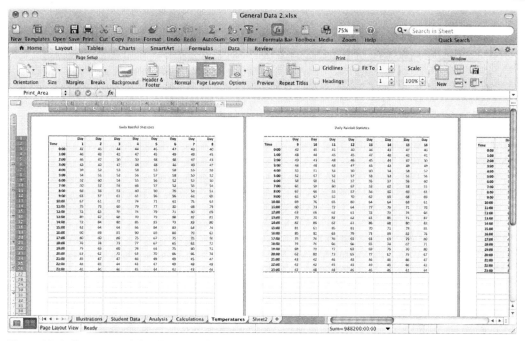

Figure 13–1. *To see a worksheet's pages laid out, switch to Page Layout view. You can then use the controls on the Layout tab of the Ribbon to refine the layout.*

3. Use the controls in the Page Setup group to change the page setup as needed:

    ▨ *Change the margins.* Open the Margins pop-up menu, then click Normal, Wide, or Narrow. For greater control, click Custom Margins, work on the Margins tab of the Page Setup dialog box, then click the OK button.

> **NOTE:** If you prefer to work in Normal view, you can still adjust the page breaks—drag the dotted lines that represent them, or use the controls in the Page Setup group.

    ▨ *Change the orientation.* Open the Orientation pop-up menu, then click Portrait or Landscape.

    ▨ *Change the paper size.* Open the Size pop-up menu, then click the paper size.

    ▨ *Insert a page break.* Click the column before which you want to insert a manual page break. Open the Breaks pop-up menu, then click Insert Page Break.

NOTE: If you put a page break in the wrong place, click the column after it, then choose **Layout > Page Setup > Breaks > Remove Page Break** from the Ribbon. To restore all page breaks to where Excel had placed them, choose **Layout > Page Setup > Breaks > Reset All Page Breaks.**

When you have finished laying out the pages, it's a good idea to save the workbook—for example, click the Save button on the Standard toolbar, or press Cmd+S—to store the print settings.

TIP: To see a full preview of the printout, click the Preview button. Excel creates a preview and displays it in the Preview application, where you can see clearly what will print and how the pages will flow. When you've finished previewing the printout, click the Print button to print it.

Printing a Worksheet or Workbook

After you've set the print area for each worksheet you want to print, you can print a worksheet or workbook like this:

1. If you want to print anything less than a whole workbook, choose what you want to print:

   ■ *Print a worksheet.* Make that worksheet active. For example, click its worksheet tab.

   ■ *Print multiple worksheets.* Make all those worksheets active by selecting their worksheet tabs.

   ■ *Print a selection of cells.* Select the cells.

TIP: When you've set up a worksheet to print exactly the way you want it, you can print it quickly by clicking the Print button on the Standard toolbar. Clicking the Print button sends the print job straight to the printer without displaying the Print dialog box.

2. Choose **File > Print** or press Cmd+P to display the Print dialog box. If the Print dialog box opens at its smaller size, click the down-arrow button to the right of the Printer pop-up menu to expand the dialog box to its larger size.

3. Make sure the Copies & Pages item is selected in the pop-up menu under the Presets pop-up menu. Figure 13–2 shows the Print dialog box with the Copies & Pages item selected.

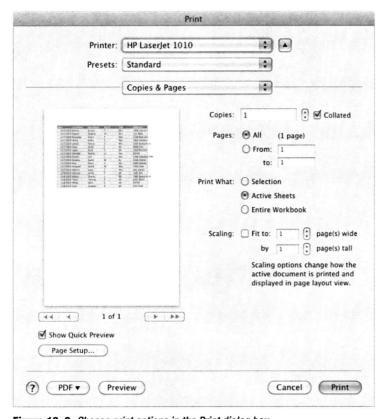

Figure 13–2. *Choose print options in the Print dialog box.*

4. In the Print What area, choose what to print:

    ▪ *Selection.* Select this option button to print only the cells you've selected. This option is useful for printing smaller amounts without resetting the print area.

    ▪ *Active Sheets.* Select this option button to print the active worksheet (if you've selected only one) or active worksheets (if you selected more than one).

    ▪ *Entire Workbook.* Select this option button to print every worksheet in the workbook. Normally, you'll use this option only for small workbooks.

5. Check that the preview of the printout looks right. If you need to change the scaling to make the printout fit the paper better, select the Scaling check box, then set the number of pages in the Fit to *N* page(s) wide box and the by *N* page(s) tall box. For example, you might choose Fit to 1 page(s) wide by 2 page(s) tall.

6. Click the Print button to print the worksheets.

Sharing Your Worksheets as PDFs

If you want to share your worksheets electronically so that other people can view them easily but not edit them—at least, not without going to some trouble—you can create files in the widely used Portable Document Format (PDF).

To create PDFs from a worksheet, follow these steps:

1. Select the range of cells you want to create the PDF from.

2. Choose **File ➤ Print** or press Cmd+P to display the Print dialog box. If the Print dialog box opens at its smaller size, click the down-arrow button to the right of the Printer pop-up menu to expand the dialog box to its larger size.

3. Click the PDF button to display the PDF pop-up menu, then click Save as PDF. Excel displays the Save dialog box (see Figure 13–3).

Figure 13–3. *In the Save dialog box, you can add a title, author, subject, and any keywords needed to a PDF file you're creating from an Excel worksheet.*

4. Enter the file name in the Save As box.

5. Specify the destination folder either in the Where pop-up menu or in the navigation pane.

6. In the lower half of the dialog box, enter any metadata the document needs: the title, author, subject, and keywords. Type a comma or press the Return key after each keyword to create a keyword button.

7. If you want to secure the PDF with a password for opening or printing it, click the Security Options button, then work in the PDF Security Options dialog box (see Figure 13–4). For example, you can select the Require password to open document check box and type a password if you want anybody who tries to open the PDF to provide a password. Click the OK button when you've finished choosing security options.

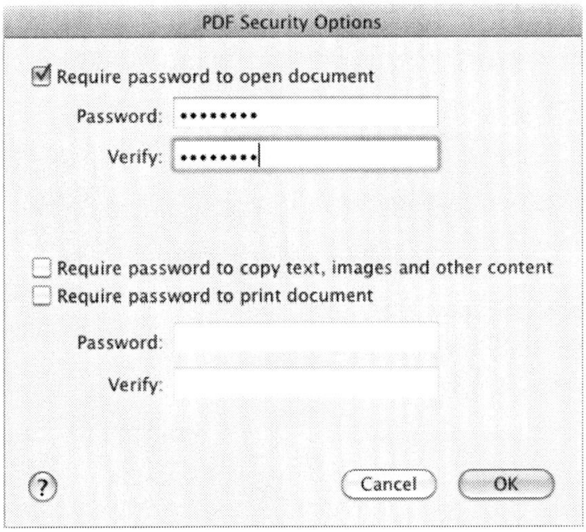

Figure 13–4. *Use the PDF Security Options dialog box to apply a password to open the document or a password to print the document. You can also require a password for copying content from the PDF file.*

8. Click the Save button. Excel closes the Print dialog box and saves the PDF.

TIP: If you just need to e-mail a PDF version of the document without adding metadata or applying a password, you can save a step by choosing the Mail PDF command from the PDF pop-up menu in the Print dialog box. The application creates a new message in your default e-mail application (for example, Outlook) and attaches a PDF file of the document to the message. Depending on the other applications installed on your Mac, you may have other PDF options—for example, saving to Evernote, Yojimbo, or Scrivener.

Exporting Data to CSV Files

When you need to share only the data from an Excel worksheet, you can export it to a comma-separated values (CSV) file. CSV is a very widely used standard for data exchange and consists of text with commas separating the contents of each cell. So when you export a worksheet to a CSV file, you export only the text—Excel strips out all formatting and nontext objects, such as charts or pictures.

To export a worksheet to a CSV file, follow these steps:

1. If the workbook contains any unsaved changes, save it.

2. Make active the worksheet you want to export.

3. Choose File ➤ Save As from the menu bar to display the Save As dialog box.

4. Specify the filename and choose the folder as usual.

5. In the Format pop-up menu, choose Comma Separated Values (.csv).

6. Click the Save button. If the workbook contains more than one worksheet, Excel displays the dialog box shown in Figure 13–5, which warns you that it can't save the workbook in CSV format because it contains multiple worksheets.

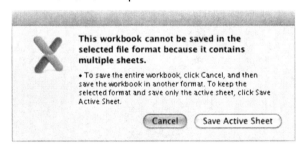

Figure 13–5. *Click the Save Active Sheet button in this dialog box to export only the active worksheet to a CSV file.*

7. Click the Save Active Sheet button to proceed with exporting just the active worksheet. If the worksheet contains any nontext items that Excel will need to strip out to create the CSV file, Excel displays the dialog box shown in Figure 13–6, warning you that it will remove some features. Most worksheets contain items that Excel will need to remove, so you'll usually see this dialog box.

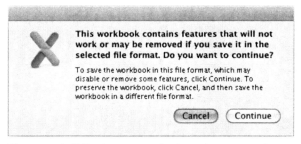

Figure 13-6. *If Excel warns you that it needs to remove features to create the CSV file, click the Continue button.*

8. Click the Continue button. Excel ceases its protests and saves the worksheet as a CSV file.

CAUTION: After you save a worksheet as a CSV file, Excel changes the workbook's window name to that of the CSV file but continues to display the full workbook with all the nontext objects and other worksheets that the CSV conversion has stripped out. Don't work in this workbook, because you're not seeing the CSV file as it actually is. Instead, click the Close button or choose File ➤ Close to close the workbook. When Excel prompts you to save the changes you made to the workbook, click the Don't Save button—there aren't any changes you can save in this format. Then choose File ➤ Open Recent and click the CSV file on the Open Recent submenu. You'll then see the CSV file as it actually is.

Documenting Your Workbooks

When you're creating a workbook and entering data in it, you'll probably be clear about which data is which, why you're laying the data out in the way you've chosen, and why you've used particular types of charts or decided to construct formulas in an idiosyncratic way.

But someone else who opens your workbooks may not intuitively grasp how you've done things. So when you create a workbook you plan to share with others, or when you prepare a workbook for sharing, it's a good idea to document the workbook. This can save you time, bewilderment, and any number of infuriating questions in the days, weeks, or months to come.

Excel provides three main tools for documenting your workbooks:

■ Text in cells

■ Comments attached to cells

■ Data-validation tools

We'll look at each of these tools in turn.

Adding Explanatory Text to Workbooks

The most straightforward way to document a workbook is to enter text in the cells. You already know how to do this, so the only issue is what text to enter and how vigorously to format it so that nobody can miss it.

As a general rule, you'll save yourself grief by explaining more than seems strictly necessary. For example, it should perhaps be obvious that the worksheet named Western Region Sales 2011 contains sales results for the Western Region in 2011—but you should probably put that information in a cell at the top of the worksheet as well for anyone who doesn't look at the worksheet tab. Similarly, even if the formulas you've used are standard and straightforward, it's a good idea to make clear how the figures they show are derived. For this, you can either use text in nearby cells or attach comments to the cells themselves (as discussed in the next section).

> **TIP:** For a complex workbook that contains many worksheets, add a Summary worksheet or Introduction worksheet at the beginning. On this worksheet, state the workbook's purpose and enter a list of the worksheets and what they contain. You may also want to note who's supposed—or permitted—to do what with the workbook. For example, managers must fill in their budget figures, while VPs are to look at the Executive Overview worksheet and approve the figures there but not mess with any other worksheets. You can add macro buttons to the Summary worksheet to display particular worksheets, providing an easy way to navigate the workbook. (See Chapter 14 for coverage of macros.)

Adding Comments to Cells

Entering explanatory text directly in cells makes it easy to see, but you may also want to add information using comments. A comment is text attached to a cell. Excel displays a comment indicator in the cell to indicate a comment is attached; when you hold the mouse pointer over the cell, the comment appears in a balloon. You can also display all the comment balloons on a worksheet, and rearrange them if they overlap.

Adding a Comment

To add a comment to a cell, follow these steps:

1. Make active the cell to which you want to add the comment.

2. Choose **Review ➤ Comments ➤ New** from the Ribbon or **Insert ➤ New Comment** from the menu bar. Excel displays the comment marker and a red triangle in the upper-right corner of the cell, opens a comment balloon, and enters your user name in the balloon in boldface.

TIP: Excel enters your user name (as set in Excel's General preferences pane) in each comment for you, but you can edit the name if necessary, or simply delete it. To make your comments more readable or dramatic, you can apply text formatting to them. For example, click the Bold button or press Cmd+B to make selected text bold.

3.   Type the text of the comment. Figure 13–7 shows an example.

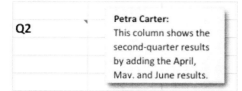

Figure 13–7. *The red triangle at the upper-right corner of the Q2 cell here is the comment marker. Type or paste the text for the comment in the comment balloon.*

4.   When you have finished creating the comment, click anywhere in the worksheet to move the focus from the comment.

NOTE: If the comment indicator doesn't appear in the cell, Excel is set to hide comments and indicators. Choose **Review ➤ Comments ➤ Show All** from the Ribbon to turn on the display of comments.

TIP: When you're working with multiple versions of the same worksheet, you may need to paste comments from one worksheet to another. You can do this easily by using the Paste Special command. Select the range that contains the comments, then copy it to the Clipboard as usual (for example, press Cmd+C). Next click the cell at the upper-left corner of the destination range, choose **Home ➤ Edit ➤ Paste ➤ Paste Special**, select the Comments option button in the Paste area, then click the OK button.

Viewing Comments

Normally, Excel displays only the comment markers in a worksheet. To view a comment, you hold the mouse pointer over a cell that contains a comment, and Excel displays the comment in a balloon. You can also click the cell and then choose **Review ➤ Comments ➤ Show** from the Ribbon to display a comment and keep it displayed while you move to other parts of the worksheet.

If you want to display all the comments, choose **Review ➤ Comments ➤ Show All** from the Ribbon or **View ➤ Comments** from the menu bar.

To select the next comment, choose **Review ➤ Comments ➤ Next**. To select the previous comment, choose **Review ➤ Comments ➤ Previous**.

Deleting Comments

To delete a comment, follow these steps:

1. Select the comment. You can either click the cell that contains the comment or choose **Review ➤ Comments ➤ Next** or **Review ➤ Comments ➤ Previous** to select the comment.

2. Give the Delete command. Either press the Delete key or choose **Review ➤ Comments ➤ Delete**.

> **TIP:** You can edit a comment by Ctrl-clicking or right-clicking a commented cell and then clicking Edit Comment. Similarly, you can delete a comment by Ctrl-clicking or right-clicking a commented cell, and then clicking Delete Comment.

Adding Information with Data Validation

As you saw in the section "Checking Input with Data Validation" in Chapter 4, you can apply data-validation formatting to a cell to make sure that the value the user enters in it meets your requirements. For example, you can use data validation to ensure that the value the user enters is between 250 and 1000 (inclusive) and to display an error alert message box if it's not.

You can use data validation to add information to your worksheets in two ways:

- *Display an input message.* On the Input Message tab of the Data Validation dialog box, select the Show input message when cell is selected check box, then type the title in the Title text box and the message in the Input message text box. When the user selects the cell, Excel displays a balloon containing the input message. This works like an automated comment and can be a great way of providing focused guidance on how to use a workbook.

- *Display an error alert.* On the Error Alert tab of the Data Validation dialog box, select the Show error alert after invalid data is entered check box, then specify the title and error message to include in the dialog box. You can also use this feature to provide detailed instructions for users of your workbooks.

Sharing Your Workbooks with Your Colleagues

You may create some workbooks on your own, but for others, you'll probably need to work with colleagues to collect, enter, and analyze data. You can either share a workbook on the network so that one person can work on it at a time or turn on Excel's sharing features that enable you and your colleagues to work on the workbook at the same time.

Before sharing a workbook, you may choose to protect it with a password or to allow your colleagues to make only some types of changes to it.

Protecting a Workbook or Some of Its Worksheets

Before sharing a workbook with your colleagues for editing individually on a network, you may want to restrict the changes your colleagues can make in the workbook or on some of its worksheets. Excel calls this *protecting* the workbook or worksheets.

Protecting a Workbook

To protect a workbook, follow these steps:

1. Choose **Review ➤ Protection ➤ Workbook** from the Ribbon or **Tools ➤ Protection ➤ Workbook** from the menu bar to display the dialog box shown in Figure 13–8.

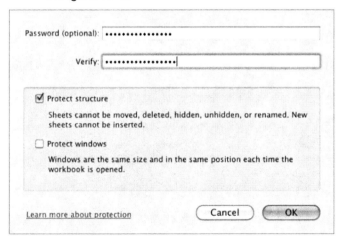

Figure 13–8. *When protecting a workbook, you'll normally want to protect the structure but not the windows.*

2. Select the Protect structure check box to prevent your colleagues from inserting, deleting, or otherwise changing whole worksheets.

3. Select the Protect windows check box only if you need to prevent your colleagues from changing the number or sizes of windows that you're using for the workbook. Normally, you don't need to do this if your colleagues will work conventionally in the workbook.

4. Type a password in the Password text box and in the Verify text box.

5. Click the OK button to close the dialog box.

6. Save the workbook. For example, click the Save button on the Standard toolbar or press Cmd+S.

> **NOTE:** To unprotect a workbook, choose **Review ➤ Protection ➤ Workbook**. Excel displays a dialog box prompting you for the password. Type it, click the OK button, then save the changes to the workbook.

Protecting a Worksheet

When you need to limit the changes your colleagues can make to a particular worksheet, apply protection to it. Follow these steps:

1. Click the worksheet to activate it.

2. Choose **Review ➤ Protection ➤ Sheet** to display the Protect the sheet and contents of locked cells dialog box (shown in Figure 13–9 with settings chosen).

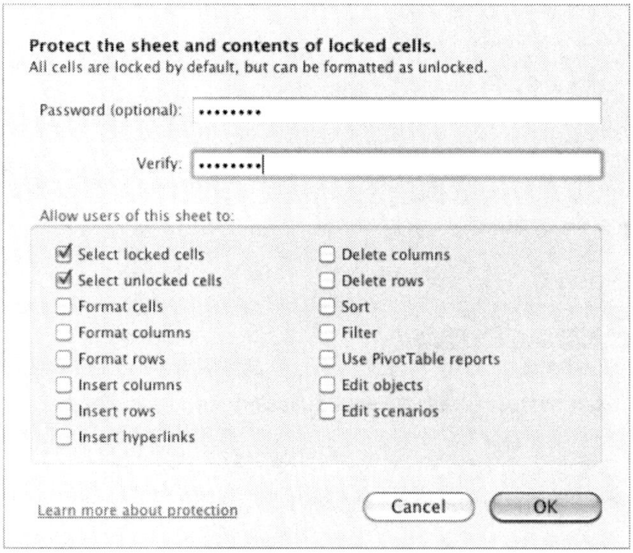

Figure 13–9. *Protect a worksheet when you need to prevent your colleagues from making specific types of changes to it.*

3. Type a password in the Password text box and the Verify text box.

4. In the Allow users of this sheet to box, select each check box for actions you want your colleagues to be able to take. Clear the other check boxes.

5. Click the OK button. Excel closes the dialog box and applies the protection

6. Save the workbook. For example, press Cmd+S or click the Save button on the Standard toolbar.

Tracking Changes to a Workbook

When you share a workbook with other people, you may need to track the changes they make to it so that you can easily review them without having to compare old and new versions of the worksheet. To track the changes, you turn on the Track Changes feature. When you turn on Track Changes, Excel automatically shares the workbook for you.

To turn on Track Changes and share a workbook, follow these steps:

1. Choose Review ➤ Share ➤ Track Changes ➤ Highlight Changes from the Ribbon or Tools ➤ Track Changes ➤ Highlight Changes from the menu bar to display the Highlight Changes dialog box (see Figure 13–10).

Figure 13–10. *In the Highlight Changes dialog box, select the Track changes while editing check box, then choose which changes to save and whether to highlight them on screen.*

2. Select the Track changes while editing check box. Excel then enables the other controls in the dialog box.

3. To specify the time period over which to track the changes, select the When check box, open the pop-up menu, then click the appropriate item:

- *Since I last saved.* Select this item to track only the changes since you last saved the workbook. If you save the workbook only after reviewing the changes, this can be a good way of keeping the number of changes down to a manageable level.

- *All.* Select this item to track all the changes.

- *Not yet reviewed.* Select this item to track changes only until you review them. This is another approach to keeping down the number of changes that remain in the workbook.

- *Since date.* Select this item if you want to specify the date at which to begin tracking the changes. Excel suggests the current date, but you can change it as needed.

4. To choose whose changes Excel tracks, select the Who check box, open the pop-up menu, then click the Everyone item or the Everyone but me item, as needed. (The idea is that you may not need to see the changes you yourself have made.)

5. To specify the range for which to track the changes, select the Where check box, then drag through the range in the worksheet to enter it in the text box. If you need to get the Highlight Changes dialog box out of the way, click the Collapse Dialog button, but usually it's easier just to work around it.

6. Select the Highlight changes on screen check box if you want Excel to highlight the changes on screen. This is usually helpful.

7. Select the List changes on a new sheet check box if you want Excel to create a new worksheet and put a list of the changes on it. Creating this list can be a handy way of reviewing the changes, as you can add comments next to them if you need to.

> **NOTE:** Excel makes the List changes on a new sheet check box available only when you've turned on Track Changes and the workbook contains at least one tracked change. This means that you'll need to close the Highlight Changes dialog box, make some tracked changes, then open the dialog box again before you can select the List changes on a new sheet check box.

8. Click the OK button to close the Highlight Changes dialog box. Excel prompts you to save the workbook (see Figure 13–11).

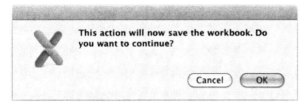

Figure 13–11. *After turning on Track Changes, Excel prompts you to save the workbook. Click the OK button.*

9. Click the OK button. Excel saves the workbook and shares it.

After sharing a workbook by turning on Track Changes, you may need to adjust the sharing. To do so, follow the instructions in the next section.

Sharing a Workbook So That Your Colleagues Can Edit It

When you need to be able to work on a workbook with your colleagues, turn on sharing. Follow these steps:

1. Open the workbook.

2. Choose Review ➤ Share ➤ Share Workbook ➤ Share Workbook from the Ribbon to display the Share Workbook dialog box. The left screen in Figure 13–12 shows the Editing tab of the Share Workbook dialog box, which is where you start the sharing process.

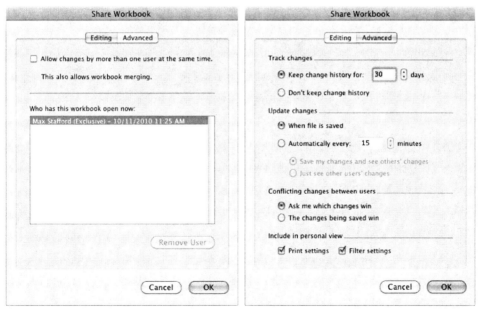

Figure 13–12. *On the Editing tab (left) of the Share Workbook dialog box, select the Allow changes by more than one user at the same time check box. You can then choose options on the Advanced tab (right).*

3. Select the Allow changes by more than one user at the same time check box on the Editing tab.

4. Check the Who has this workbook open now list box. It should show only your name and should include the word Exclusive to indicate that you've got sole access to the workbook.

5. Click the Advanced tab to display its contents (shown on the right in Figure 13–12).

6. In the Track Changes area, choose how long to keep the change history for the workbook:

   ▪ Normally, you'll want to select the Keep change history for option button and set the number of days in the days box.

   ▪ The default setting is 30 days, but if you develop your workbooks quickly, you may want to reduce the interval to 7 days or 14 days to prevent Excel from keeping large amounts of history you don't need.

   ▪ The alternative is to select the Don't keep change history option button, but usually it's best to keep change history so that you can unravel any mysterious changes.

7. In the Update changes area, choose when to update the changes to the workbook:

   ▪ The default setting is the When file is saved option button, which generally works pretty well.

   ▪ The alternative is to select the Automatically every option button and set the number of minutes in the minutes box. The default setting is 15 minutes; if you work fast, you may want to shorten the interval to 5 or 10 minutes.

   ▪ If you select the Automatically every option button, you can choose between the Save my changes and see others' changes option button (usually the better choice) and the Just see other users' changes option button.

8. In the Conflicting changes between users area, choose how to handle conflicting changes to the workbook. Normally, you'll want to select the Ask me which changes win option button so that you can decide which of the conflicting changes to keep. The alternative is to select the option button called The changes being saved win, which tells Excel to overwrite the conflicting changes with the latest changes.

9. In the Include in personal view area, select the Print settings check box if you want to include print settings in your view of the workbook. Select the Filter settings check box if you want to include filter settings. (See Chapter 10 for instructions on filtering an Excel database table.)

10. Click the OK button to close the Share Workbook dialog box. Excel then displays a dialog box telling you that it will save the workbook.

11. Click the OK button. Excel sets up the sharing and adds "[Shared]" to the workbook's title bar so that you can easily see it's shared.

> **TIP:** When you store workbooks in a shared folder, either on your Mac or on a network, you may need to protect them with passwords so that only authorized people can open them. To apply a password to open or a password to modify, use the procedure described in the section "Protecting a Workbook with Automatic Backups and Passwords" in Chapter 3.

Working in a Shared Workbook

Once you've shared a workbook or someone else has shared it, you can perform basic editing in it much as normal. You can enter data and formulas in cells or edit their existing contents, format cells, and use both drag and drop and cut, copy, and paste. You can also insert rows, columns, and even whole worksheets.

Beyond these basics, Excel prevents you from making changes that may cause problems with the sharing. These are the main restrictions:

- *Apply conditional formatting.* If your workbook needs conditional formatting, apply it before sharing the workbook.

- *Insert objects.* You can't insert pictures, SmartArt, charts, hyperlinks, or various other objects.

- *Insert or delete blocks of cells.* You can insert or delete a whole row or column, but you can't insert or delete a block of cells. You also can't merge cells together.

- *Delete a worksheet.* You can't delete a worksheet from the shared workbook.

- *Protect a sheet with a password.* Any protection you've applied before sharing the workbook remains in force, but you can't apply protection to a sheet in a shared workbook.

- *Outline the workbook.* You can't create an outline in a shared workbook. See the section "Creating a Collapsible Worksheet by Outlining It" in Chapter 3 for information on outlining a workbook.

Resolving Conflicts in a Shared Workbook

If you choose the Ask me which changes win option button when sharing the workbook, Excel prompts you to deal with conflicts that arise between the changes you're saving and the changes that your colleagues have already saved. The Resolve Conflicts dialog box (see Figure 13–13) takes you through each of the changes in turn, showing the change you made and the conflicting change.

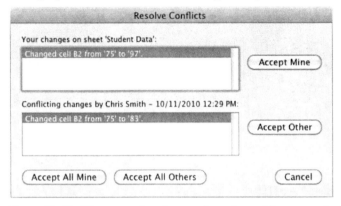

Figure 13–13. *When you and another user have changed the same cells, the Resolve Conflicts dialog box walks you through each change in turn. You can accept all your changes, all your colleagues' changes, or some of each.*

For each change, you can click the Accept Mine button to accept your change or click the Accept Other button to accept your colleague's change. To clear all the changes at once, click the Accept All Mine button or the Accept All Others button. Excel closes the Resolve Conflicts dialog box automatically when you've finished reviewing the conflicts.

Reviewing Tracked Changes in a Shared Workbook

When you've tracked changes in a shared workbook, you can review them, accepting the changes you want to keep and rejecting the other changes.

To review the tracked changes, follow these steps:

1. Open the shared workbook if it's not already open.

2. Choose **Review ➤ Share ➤ Track Changes ➤ Accept or Reject Changes** from the Ribbon or **Tools ➤ Track Changes ➤ Accept or Reject Changes** from the menu bar to display the Select Changes to Accept or Reject dialog box (see Figure 13–14).

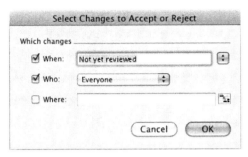

Figure 13–14. *In the Select Changes to Accept or Reject dialog box, choose which changes you want to review, then click the OK button.*

3. Use the controls in the Which changes area to choose which changes Excel presents for your review:

   ■ *When.* Select this check box to specify a date range. Then open the pop-up menu and choose the Not yet reviewed item if you want to review all the changes you haven't yet reviewed, or select the Since date item and enter the date in the text box.

   ■ *Who.* Select this check box if you want to specify whose changes you'll review. Then open the pop-up menu and choose Everyone, Everyone but Me, or a user name.

   ■ *Where.* Select this check box if you want to see the changes in only part of the workbook. Then click in the text box and drag through the range in the worksheet.

4. Click the OK button to close the Select Changes to Accept or Reject dialog box. Excel displays the Accept or Reject Changes dialog box (see Figure 13–15), which shows the number of changes and the details of the first change.

Accept or Reject Changes

Change 1 of 33 made to this document:

Petra Carter, 2/2/2011 1:41 PM:

Changed cell A1 from '<blank>' to '1'.

(Accept) (Reject) (Accept All) (Reject All) (Close)

Figure 13–15. *Use the Accept or Reject Changes dialog box to work your way through the tracked changes in a shared workbook.*

5. Work through the changes using the Accept button and the Reject button. You can also take the nuclear option and click the Accept All button if you decide all the changes are worthwhile or the Reject All button if you decide they're worthless; if you click either button, Excel closes the Accept or Reject Changes dialog box for you.

6. When you've worked your way through the changes, click the Close button to close the Accept or Reject Changes dialog box.

Merging Multiple Workbooks into a Single Workbook

When you have multiple versions of a workbook that you've shared with Track Changes on, you can merge them into a single workbook.

> **NOTE:** You must turn on the Track Changes feature, as discussed earlier in this chapter, before you can merge workbooks. Until Track Changes is on, the Merge Workbooks command is unavailable.

To merge the workbooks, follow these steps:

1. Open the workbook into which you want to merge the changes.

2. Choose **Tools ➤ Merge Workbooks** to display the Select File to Merge into Current Workbook dialog box. Despite its long name, this is a standard dialog box for selecting files, like the Open dialog box.

3. Navigate to the workbook, then select it.

4. Click the OK button to merge the workbooks. Excel marks the cells that have changes.

You can then review the changes as described in the previous section.

Consolidating Multiple Worksheets into a Single Worksheet

When you work with many worksheets, you may need to consolidate worksheets of the same type into a single worksheet. For example, if you have a year's worth of weekly spreadsheets containing sales figures, you may want to consolidate them to get yearly figures.

Excel enables you to consolidate worksheets that have the same layout or worksheets that have different layouts but the same row labels or column labels. You can consolidate up to 255 source worksheets into the destination worksheet, either linking the destination worksheet to the source worksheets or copying the data from the source worksheets to the destination worksheet but not creating a link.

Preparing to Consolidate Worksheets

To consolidate worksheets, you need to open the destination worksheet so that you can enter information in it.

When you're consolidating just a few workbooks, you'll usually also want to open the source workbooks so that you can create references to them easily; while you can create the references without opening the source worksheets, it's more work, because you need to type in the references. When you're consolidating dozens of workbooks, having them all open at once tends to be awkward, and you will usually find it easier to create the references using a single source workbook, then copy the references and edit them for the other workbooks.

Consolidating Worksheets by Their Position

When the worksheets you want to consolidate have the same layout, you can consolidate them by position. Consolidating by position essentially means getting data from the same cell address in each of the source worksheets.

> **CAUTION:** For consolidating by position to work, the worksheets must have identical layouts. If any of the worksheets has a different layout, it won't work—even if the difference is as little as a single row or column having been added or deleted.

To consolidate worksheets by their position, follow these steps:

1. Open the workbooks that contain the source worksheets. If you're consolidating source worksheets that are in the destination workbook, skip this step.

2. Open the destination workbook and activate the destination worksheet. If necessary, add a worksheet that will become the destination worksheet.

3. Make active the upper-left cell of the range you want to put the consolidated data in.

4. Choose Data ➤ Tools ➤ Consolidate to display the Consolidate dialog box (shown in Figure 13–16 with settings chosen).

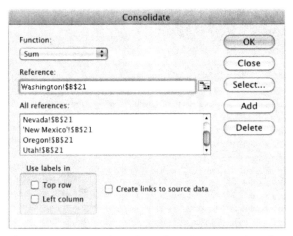

Figure 13–16. *In the Consolidate dialog box, set up the references to the source worksheets you want to consolidate into the destination worksheet.*

5. Open the Function pop-up menu and choose the function to use for the consolidation:

    ■   *Sum.* This function adds the numbers. This is the default function for consolidation.

    ■   *Count.* This function counts the number of items.

    ■   *Average.* This function returns the average of the values.

    ■   *Max.* This function returns the largest value.

    ■   *Min.* This function returns the smallest value.

    ■   *Product.* This function returns the product of multiplying the numbers.

    ■   *Count Numbers.* This function returns the count of numerical values.

    ■   *StdDev.* This function returns the standard deviation of the values.

    ■   *StdDevp.* This function returns the standard deviation based on an entire population.

    ■   *Var.* This function returns the variance based on a sample.

    ■   *Varp.* This function returns the variance based on an entire population.

6. Add the references to the All references list box. Follow these steps:

    a.   Click in the Reference box to place the focus there.

    b. If you need to move the Consolidate dialog box out of the way, click the Collapse Dialog button. If you've got space to work around the dialog box, you don't need to collapse it.

    c. If the source worksheet is in another workbook, activate that workbook. For example, click its window or use the Window menu to switch to it.

> **NOTE:** If you need to open a workbook to add its reference, click the Select button in the Consolidate dialog box to display the Choose a Workbook dialog box. Click the workbook, and then click the OK button.

    d. Click the source worksheet's tab to display the source worksheet.

    e. Select the cell or range on the worksheet.

    f. If you collapsed the Consolidate dialog box, restore it by clicking the Collapse Dialog button.

    g. Click the Add button to add the cell or range address to the All references list box.

    h. Repeat these steps to add further references. On the assumption that you're consolidating worksheets by position, Excel automatically suggests the same cell or range in each worksheet, so you don't have to select the cell or range.

7. In the Use labels in area at the bottom of the Consolidate dialog box, clear the Top row check box and Left column check box.

8. Select the Create links to source data check box if you want Excel to create links to the source worksheets.

9. Click the OK button to close the Consolidate dialog box. Excel consolidates the data into the cell.

Consolidating Worksheets by Category

If the worksheets you want to consolidate don't have identical layouts, but do have the same labels, you can use the labels to consolidate by category.

For example, look at the two months of production results shown in Figure 13–17. The names in the Staff column appear in a different order in each, so you can't consolidate by position. But because the labels are the same, you can consolidate by category. In effect, you're telling Excel "give me the Week 1 result for Cheung's row, whichever row that is" rather than "give me cell B1."

	A	B	C	D	E
1	Staff	Week 1	Week 2	Week 3	Week 4
2	Cheung	69	57	70	71
3	Smith	86	64	51	45
4	Olafsson	74	60	54	53
5	Jones	86	64	48	79
6	Lee	63	57	68	48

	A	B	C	D	E
1	Staff	Week 1	Week 2	Week 3	Week 4
2	Jones	54	46	73	83
3	Cheung	58	67	62	86
4	Olafsson	87	69	82	49
5	Lee	50	64	80	71
6	Smith	73	61	46	82

Figure 13–17. *When the source worksheets have consistent labels but a different layout, you can consolidate the worksheets by category.*

To consolidate worksheets by category, follow these steps:

1. Open the workbooks that contain the source worksheets. If you're consolidating source worksheets that are in the destination workbook, skip this step.

2. Open the destination workbook and activate the destination worksheet. If necessary, add a worksheet that will become the destination worksheet.

3. Make active the upper-left cell of the range you want to put the consolidated data in.

4. Choose **Data ➤ Tools ➤ Consolidate** to display the Consolidate dialog box (shown in Figure 13–16, earlier in this chapter).

5. In the Use labels in area, select the Top row check box if the labels are in the top row. Select the Left column check box if the labels are in the left column, as in the example.

6. Open the Function pop-up menu and choose the function. In this example, you'd select the Sum function, which is the default function.

7. Click in the Reference box to place the focus there.

8. Add the references using the method explained in step 7 of the list in the previous section. Select the consolidation range manually on each source worksheet.

9. Select the Create links to source data check box if you want Excel to create links to the source worksheets.

10. Click the OK button to close the Consolidate dialog box. Excel consolidates the data into the cell.

> **TIP:** To update a consolidation, select the range that contains it, choose **Data ➤ Tools ➤ Consolidate** to display the Consolidate dialog box, then click the OK button. Excel updates the consolidation.

Summary

In this chapter, you learned how to use Excel's features for sharing your workbooks and collaborating with others.

You've learned how to make your worksheets print correctly by setting the print area and checking the page layout and breaks, and you know how to share your worksheets as PDF files or by exporting data to CSV files. You're aware of the three main ways of documenting your workbooks, and you know how to implement sharing, tracking changes along the way. You've also learned how to merge multiple workbooks into a single workbook and how to consolidate multiple worksheets into a single worksheet.

Chapter 14

Automating Tasks with Macros and VBA

So far in this book, you've learned about the many things you can do with Excel when working manually—everything from creating new workbooks to entering data in them to creating charts from that data.

Whatever kind of work you do in Excel, chances are good that you'll need to perform some tasks repeatedly. You can continue to perform them manually if you choose, but you may be able to save any amount of time and effort by automating them.

In this chapter, we'll look at how you can automate tasks by using macros and Visual Basic for Applications (VBA), the programming language included in Excel 2011 and the other Office 2011 applications. We'll look at how to record macros in general, then go through an example of recording a macro that you can open in the Visual Basic Editor and improve. I'll show you how to run the macros you record and create, and how to delete them when you no longer need them.

Macros and VBA are a huge topic, and in this chapter we have space only to scratch the surface. If you want to save as much time and effort as possible, you'll probably want to get a book that covers macros and VBA in detail. You'll find that macros and VBA enable you to automate almost any task you can perform when working interactively (in other words, normally) in Excel—and some tasks you can't perform when working interactively.

Along the way, I'll also mention a couple of other means of automating tasks in Excel and Mac OS X, and I'll show you how to add the Developer tab to the Ribbon so that you can give Visual Basic–related commands quickly.

Understanding Your Options for Automating Tasks

With Excel 2011 on Mac OS X, you can automate tasks in several ways

■ *Create macros.* A *macro* is a sequence of commands that you can run all at once. The easy way to create a macro is to record it by turning on the Macro Recorder and performing the actions you want the macro to repeat; when you turn the Macro Recorder off, you have a macro that you can run again. You can also write macros from scratch by working in the Visual Basic Editor application. Or you can record macros and then use the Visual Basic Editor to edit out unwanted commands or to add other commands. This chapter shows you how to record macros and edit them in the Visual Basic Editor.

■ *Use Automator.* The Automator application, which you'll find in the Applications folder, lets you assemble workflows consisting of actions. If you have the Home & Business Edition of Office, you can include Excel actions in workflows. (If you have Office 2011 Home & Student Edition, you can't use Excel with Automator.) This chapter doesn't cover Automator.

■ *Use AppleScript.* AppleScript is a scripting language in which you can write scripts using the AppleScript Editor utility, which you'll find in the Applications/Utilities folder. (A *script* is essentially a small application.) This chapter doesn't cover AppleScript either.

TIP: When you're getting started automating tasks in Excel, VBA is usually the best place to start. VBA works from within Excel, so you run your macros from Excel. By contrast, an AppleScript runs outside the applications it manipulates. The advantage to using AppleScript is that you can easily manipulate multiple applications rather than just Excel. For example, you can make the Finder take an action, make Excel take an action, then make iTunes dance—all in the same script. You can also share macros with Windows users, whereas AppleScript and Automator run only on Mac OS X.

ADDING THE DEVELOPER TAB TO THE RIBBON

If you need to work extensively with macros, add the Developer tab to the Ribbon to give yourself easy access to essential commands.

To add the Developer tab to the Ribbon, follow these steps:

1. Choose **Excel ➤ Preferences** or press Cmd+, (Cmd and the comma key) to display the Excel Preferences dialog box.

2. In the Sharing and Privacy area, click the Ribbon icon to display the Ribbon preferences pane.

3. Scroll down to the bottom of the "Show or hide tabs, or drag them into the order you prefer" list box, then select the Developer check box.

4. Click the OK button to close the Ribbon Preferences dialog box.

The Developer tab then appears as shown in Figure 14-1, and you can use the four buttons in the Visual Basic group:

- *Editor.* Click this button to launch or switch to the Visual Basic Editor.

- *Macros.* Click this button to display the Macro dialog box.

- *Record.* Click this button to display the Record Macro dialog box.

- *Relative Reference.* Click this button to make the Macro Recorder record relative references in a macro rather than absolute references.

Figure 14-1. *Add the Developer tab to Excel's Ribbon to give yourself easy access to essential commands for working with macros and VBA.*

Recording Macros

When you need to quickly automate a task, you can record a macro using the Macro Recorder. Follow these steps:

1. Plan the actions you'll take in the macro. You may find it helpful to write them down so that you can perform them in the right sequence when recording the macro.

2. Launch Excel if it's not running, or activate it if it is running.

3. Set up a workbook with the conditions you need to perform the actions in the macro. For example, if the macro will move some data from one worksheet to another, enter some sample data to move, and make sure that the workbook contains a worksheet you can use as the destination.

4. Choose **Developer** ➤ **Visual Basic** ➤ **Record** from the Ribbon or **Tools** ➤ **Macro** ➤ **Record New Macro** from the menu bar to display the Record Macro dialog box (shown in Figure 14-2 with settings chosen for recording a macro).

Figure 14-2. *In the Record Macro dialog box, name the macro, choose where to store it, and give it a helpful description. You can also create a keyboard shortcut for running the macro.*

5. In the Macro name text box, type the name for the macro. The Macro Recorder suggests a default name, such as Macro1 or Macro2, but it's better to give the macro a descriptive name that will help you identify it. Follow these naming rules:

   ▪ The first character must be a letter.

   ▪ The remaining characters can be letters, numbers, or underscores in whatever combination you find most helpful. You can use uppercase and lowercase letters. You can't use symbols, spaces, or punctuation marks.

   ▪ The name can be up to 80 characters long, but it's better to keep names much shorter so that they appear in full in the Macro dialog box. Otherwise, the names can be hard to read.

TIP: To make your macro names easy to read, start each main word with a capital letter, and separate words with underscores. For example, Format_Workbook is easier to read than FormatWorkbook, which in turn is clearer than formatworkbook.

6. If you want to create a keyboard shortcut for running the macro, click in the Shortcut key box, then press the key you want to use. Excel creates the shortcut using Cmd+Option, so if you press **w**, the keyboard shortcut is Cmd+Option+W. If you want to add Shift to the keyboard shortcut, hold down Shift as you press the key. You'll see the shifted version of the character in the Shortcut key box, and Excel creates the keyboard shortcut using Cmd+Option+Shift—for example, Cmd+Option+Shift+W.

NOTE: If you plan to create just a few macros, creating a keyboard shortcut for each one you need to run frequently is useful. But if you plan to create many macros, you may need to move them from the default location that the Macro Recorder puts them in. When you move a macro, you break its existing keyboard shortcut—so in this case, it's better not to create keyboard shortcuts when you record your macros, but create them later when you have put the macros where you intend to keep them.

7. In the Store macro in pop-up menu, choose where to store the macro. You have three choices:

- *Personal Macro Workbook.* The Personal Macro Workbook is a special workbook that Excel uses for storing macros. Any macro you store in the Personal Macro Workbook is available all the time Excel is running, so this is the best place to store general-purpose macros. If you open a workbook on another computer, these macros aren't available.

- *This workbook.* Select this item to store the macro in the active workbook, making the macro available only when this workbook is open. This is good for macros you create in a macro-enabled workbook that you will share with your colleagues—even if you transfer the workbook to a different computer, the macro is available.

- *New workbook.* Select this item to create a new workbook and store the macro in it. You can then save the workbook and use it to distribute the macro as needed. This approach tends to be less useful than using the Personal Macro Workbook or the active workbook.

8. In the Description text box, type a description of what the macro does. The description helps you and other people identify the macro afterward, so it's worth spending a few seconds putting together a clear description.

9. Click the OK button. When you do so, you may see the dialog box shown in Figure 14-3, telling you that the operating system has reserved the keyboard shortcut you've chosen. If this happens, click the OK button to return to the Record Macro dialog box, choose a different keyboard shortcut, then click the OK button again.

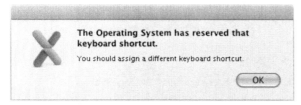

Figure 14-3. *If this dialog box appears, click the OK button to return to the Record Macro dialog box, then choose another keyboard shortcut for running the macro.*

10. After you close the Record Macro dialog box, Excel starts the Macro Recorder, which records the macro. Excel displays a Recording readout on the status bar, and if you've added the Developer tab to the Ribbon, you'll see that the Record button appears as a black square denoting "Stop" rather than the red circle meaning "Record." But apart from these visual cues, the Excel window appears as normal, and it's easy enough to forget you're recording a macro, especially if someone distracts you.

11. Take the actions you want to record into the macro. We'll look at a specific example in a moment, but these are the general rules to follow:

- You can give commands using the Ribbon, toolbars, or menu bar as usual.

- To select cells and ranges, you can use the mouse or the keyboard.

- To switch between recording absolute references and recording relative references, choose **Developer ➤ Visual Basic ➤ Relative Reference**. When the Relative Reference button appears to be pushed in, the Macro Recorder records relative references; when the button has its normal, undifferentiated look, the Macro Recorder records absolute references.

12. To stop recording the macro, choose **Developer ➤ Visual Basic ➤ Record** from the Ribbon or **Tools ➤ Macro ➤ Stop Recording** from the menu bar.

Recording an Example Macro

The previous section described the general steps for recording a macro. This section shows you a step-by-step example of recording a short macro that we'll open and edit in the Visual Basic Editor later in the chapter.

The macro simply copies the active worksheet to an archive workbook so that you have a reference copy of the worksheet. To copy the worksheet, the macro takes five actions:

- Opens the archive workbook.
- Activates the previous workbook.
- Copies the worksheet to the archive workbook.
- Saves the archive workbook.
- Closes the archive workbook.

To record the example macro, follow these steps:

1. Create a workbook named Archive.xlsx, then close it. For example:

   a. Press Cmd+N to create a new blank workbook.

   b. Press Cmd+S to display the Save As dialog box.

   c. Choose the folder in which you want to save the workbook.

   d. Type the name **Archive**.

   e. Click the Save button.

   f. Press Cmd+W to close the workbook.

2. Open a workbook that contains a worksheet you'd like to copy to the archive workbook. Make that worksheet active.

3. Choose **Developer ➤ Visual Basic ➤ Record** from the Ribbon or **Tools ➤ Macro ➤ Record New Macro** to display the Record Macro dialog box.

4. In the Macro name text box, type the name **Copy_Active_Worksheet_to_Archive_Workbook**.

5. Click in the Shortcut key text box and press Shift+C to enter a capital C, which will create the keyboard shortcut Cmd+Option+Shift+C for the macro.

6. In the Store macro in pop-up menu, select Personal Macro Workbook.

7. In the Description text box, type the description for the macro: **Copies the active worksheet to the Archive.xlsx workbook.**

8. Click the OK button to close the Record Macro dialog box. The Macro Recorder starts recording the macro, and the Recording readout appears in the status bar.

9. Record the action for opening the archive workbook:

   a. Press Cmd+O to display the Open: Microsoft Excel dialog box.

   b. Navigate to and select the Archive.xlsx workbook.

   c. Click the Open button. The workbook opens as usual and becomes the active workbook.

10. Press the Cmd+Shift+F6 keyboard shortcut to switch to the previous workbook—the one that contains the worksheet you want to copy.

11. Record the action for copying the worksheet to the archive workbook:

    a. Ctrl-click or right-click the active worksheet's tab, then click Move or Copy on the context menu to display the Move or Copy dialog box.

    b. Open the To book pop-up menu, then click Archive.xlsx.

    c. In the Before sheet list box, click the "(move to end)" item.

    d. Select the Create a copy check box.

    e. Click the OK button to close the Move or Copy dialog box. Excel copies the worksheet to the archive workbook and makes that workbook active.

12. Press Cmd+S to save the archive workbook.

13. Press Cmd+W to close the archive workbook.

14. Choose **Developer ➤ Visual Basic ➤ Record** from the Ribbon or **Tools ➤ Macro ➤ Stop Recording** to stop the Macro Recorder.

> **CAUTION:** At this point, the Macro Recorder has faithfully recorded the commands for copying the exact worksheet you chose from the specific workbook you opened. To make the macro suitable for general use, you need to edit it. See the end of this chapter for details.

Running a Macro

After you record a macro (or create it from scratch, as described later in this chapter), you can run it as needed by pressing its keyboard shortcut, adding it to a toolbar or menu, or by attaching it to an object in a worksheet.

For you to be able to run the macro, the workbook that contains it must be open. If you stored the macro in the Personal Macro Workbook, you can run it at any time, because, after you create the Personal Macro Workbook, Excel keeps the Personal Macro Workbook open in the background whenever you run Excel. If you stored the macro in a workbook, you must open that workbook before you can run the macro.

Running a Macro from the Macro dialog Box

You can run any macro from the Macro dialog box. This is useful for macros that you haven't assigned a means of running and for macros whose keyboard shortcut or menu command you've forgotten.

To run a macro from the Macro dialog box, follow these steps:

1. Choose **Developer** ➤ **Visual Basic** ➤ **Macros** from the Ribbon or **Tools** ➤ **Macro** ➤ **Macro** from the menu bar to display the Macro dialog box (see Figure 14-4).

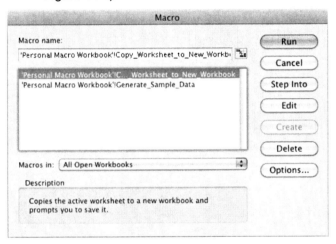

Figure 14-4. *From the Macro dialog box, you can run any macro. You can also open a macro for editing, delete it, or open the Options dialog box.*

2. Open the Macros in pop-up menu and choose which workbooks you want to see the macros for:

    ■ *All Open Workbooks.* Choose this item to see the macros in the Personal Macro Workbook and all the workbooks you've opened. When you have only a few macros, this is the best choice. When you have more macros, seeing all available macros can make it hard to find the macro you need.

    ■ *Personal Macro Workbook.* Choose this item to see only the macros in the Personal Macro Workbook.

> ■ *An open workbook.* Click the name of the open workbook whose macros you want to see.

3. In the Macro name list box, click the macro you want to run.

4. Click the Run button. Excel closes the Macro dialog box and runs the macro.

Running a Macro Using Its Keyboard Shortcut

If you assigned a keyboard shortcut to a macro you recorded, you can run the macro by pressing that keyboard shortcut.

If you didn't assign a keyboard shortcut, you can create one. Follow these steps:

1. As described in the previous section, open the Macro dialog box.

2. Choose the workbook or workbooks in the Macros in pop-up menu.

3. Click the macro in the Macro name list box.

4. Click the Options button to display the Macro Options dialog box (see Figure 14-5).

Figure 14-5. *Use the Macro Options dialog box to assign a keyboard shortcut to a macro or to edit its description.*

5. Click in the Shortcut key box, then press the letter you want.

   ■ Excel creates the shortcut using Cmd+Option, so if you press **n**, the keyboard shortcut is Cmd+Option+N.

   ■ If you want to add Shift to the keyboard shortcut, hold down Shift as you press the key. You'll see the shifted version of the character in the Shortcut key box, and Excel creates the keyboard shortcut using Cmd+Option+Shift—for example, Cmd+Option+Shift+N.

6. If you want to edit the description of the macro, do so in the Description box.

7. Click the OK button to close the Macro Options dialog box.

8. Click the Cancel button to close the Macro dialog box.

Running a Macro from a Toolbar Button or Menu Item

To make a macro easy to run, you can create a toolbar button or a menu item for it. Follow these steps:

1. Ctrl-click or right-click a toolbar, then click Customize Toolbars and Menus on the context menu to display the Customize Toolbars and Menus dialog box. Alternatively, choose **View ➤ Toolbars ➤ Customize Toolbars and Menus** from the menu bar.

2. If you want to create a toolbar button, and the toolbar on which you want to put it isn't displayed, click the Toolbars and Menus tab to display its contents. Select the toolbar's check box in the Show column to display the toolbar.

> **TIP:** If you want to create a new toolbar to add the macro button to, click the New button, type the toolbar name in the Add a Toolbar dialog box, then click the OK button.

3. Click the Commands tab to display its contents.

4. In the Categories list box on the left, scroll down, then click the Macros item. Rather than display a list of the macros in the Commands list box on the right, Excel displays two items—one called Custom Menu Item and the other called Custom Button.

5. Drag the Custom Menu Item object to a menu, or drag the Custom Button object to a toolbar.

6. If you created a toolbar button, click the OK button to close the Customize Toolbars and Menus dialog box. If you created a menu item, leave the dialog box open.

7. Ctrl-click or right-click the toolbar button or menu item, then click Assign Macro on the context menu. Excel displays the Assign Macro dialog box (see Figure 14-6).

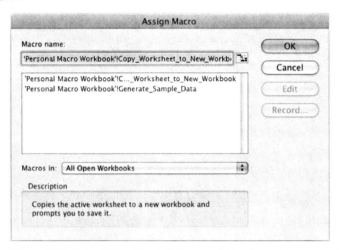

Figure 14-6. *In the Assign Macro dialog box, choose the macro you want to assign to the toolbar button or menu item you created.*

8. In the Macro name list box, click the macro you want to assign to the toolbar button or menu item. If necessary, open the Macros in pop-up menu and choose which workbook or workbooks you want to see the macros for—All Open Workbooks, Personal Macro Workbook, or a particular open workbook.

9. Click the OK button to close the Assign Macro dialog box.

10. Ctrl-click or right-click the toolbar button or menu item again, then click Properties on the context menu to display the Command Properties dialog box (see Figure 14-7).

Figure 14-7. *In the Command Properties dialog box, type the name for the command, then choose an icon to represent it graphically.*

11. In the Name text box, type the name you want to display for the menu item or toolbar button.

12. In the View pop-up menu, choose how you want the toolbar button or menu item to appear:

   - *Default Style.* Choose this item to make a toolbar button appear using the default style you've set for toolbars. (If you've chosen to show icons and text, the button appears as an icon with text beside it; if you've chosen to show only icons, just the icon appears.) A menu item appears as text with an icon if the command has an associated icon.

   - *Text Only (Always).* Choose this item to make the toolbar button or menu item appear as text without an icon.

   - *Text Only (in Menus).* Choose this item to make a menu item appear only as text.

   - *Image and Text.* Choose this item to make the toolbar button or menu item appear as an icon with text beside it.

13. If you want to change the icon, click the arrow button to the left of the Name box, then click the icon you want on the pop-up menu.

14. Select the Begin a group check box if you want to place a divider line before the item. This is useful when you want to put different groups of items in different sections of the menu or toolbar.

15. Click the OK button to close the Command Properties dialog box.

16. If you just created a menu item, click the OK button to close the Customize Toolbars and Menus dialog box unless you want to customize further items.

Running a Macro from an Object in a Worksheet

Toolbar buttons, menu items, and keyboard shortcuts are all easy ways to run macros, but Excel also gives you another way: you can assign a macro to a worksheet object such as a button or a shape. When a user clicks the object, the macro runs.

Assigning a macro to an object can be a great way of making macros easily available to users who might not find them otherwise. For example, if you create a large, friendly button named Recalculate Total (as in Figure 14-8) and put it right next to the cells the user will be looking at, they'll have to work hard to miss it, whereas missing it on a toolbar or menu is easier than falling off a log.

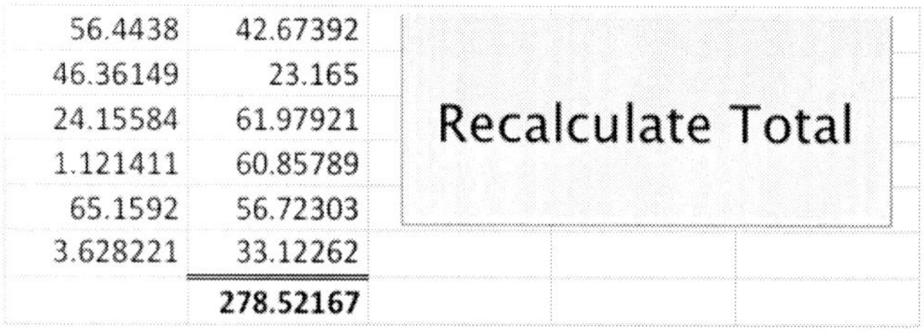

56.4438	42.67392
46.36149	23.165
24.15584	61.97921
1.121411	60.85789
65.1592	56.72303
3.628221	33.12262
	278.52167

Recalculate Total

Figure 14-8. *You can assign a macro to a worksheet object, such as the button shown here, to give users an easy way to run the macro.*

To assign a macro to an object in a worksheet, follow these steps:

1. Place the object in the worksheet. For example, choose **Developer ➤ Form Controls ➤ Button**, then click and drag in the worksheet to create the button. Select the button's default name, then type the name you want (for example, Recalculate Total).

2. Ctrl-click or right-click the object, then click Assign Macro on the context menu to display the Assign Macro dialog box (shown in Figure 14-6, earlier in this chapter).

3. If necessary, open the Macros in pop-up menu and choose which workbook or workbooks you want to see the macros for—All Open Workbooks, Personal Macro Workbook, or a particular open workbook.

4. Click the macro you want to assign.

5. Click the OK button.

You can now click the button in the worksheet to run the macro.

Deleting a Macro

When you no longer need a macro, delete it. Follow these steps:

1. Choose **Developer ➤ Visual Basic ➤ Macros** from the Ribbon or **Tools ➤ Macro ➤ Macro** from the menu bar to display the Macro dialog box.

2. If necessary, choose the appropriate workbook or workbooks in the Macros in pop-up menu.

3. Click the macro in the Macro name list box.

4. Click the Delete button. Excel displays a confirmation dialog box (see Figure 14-9).

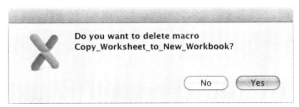

Figure 14-9. *Excel prompts you to confirm that you want to delete a macro.*

5. Click the Yes button.

Editing Macros in the Visual Basic Editor

After recording a macro as described earlier in this chapter, you can simply run it as needed. But if you need to change the macro, you can open it in the Visual Basic Editor and edit it there, deleting or changing actions you've recorded or writing VBA code for taking other actions. In this section, we'll glance very briefly at the Visual Basic Editor and make one small improvement to the recorded macro.

Opening the Sample Macro in the Visual Basic Editor

You can open a macro in the Visual Basic Editor in several ways, but the easiest is by using the Macro dialog box. But if the macro is one you've stored in the Personal Macro Workbook, you must unhide the Personal Macro Workbook so that you can open the macro for editing.

To unhide the Personal Macro Workbook, follow these steps:

1. Choose **Windows ➤ Unhide** from the menu bar to display the Unhide dialog box.

2. In the Unhide workbook list box, click the Personal Macro Workbook item.

3. Click the OK button.

Now open the Macro dialog box, click the macro, then click the Edit button. Excel opens the macro for editing in the Visual Basic Editor.

Meeting the Visual Basic Editor's Interface

Figure 14-10 shows the Visual Basic Editor open with its key components labeled.

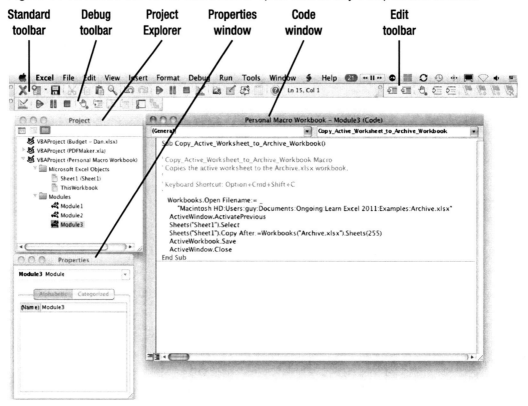

Figure 14-10. *The Visual Basic Editor consists of three main windows—the Project Explorer, the Properties window, and the Code window (in which you create and edit VBA code).*

These are the six main components of the Visual Basic Editor that you see in Figure 14-10:

- *Project Explorer.* This window shows a collapsible tree for each open project—each regular workbook, each add-in (such as the PDFMaker.xla add-in that you can see in Figure 14-10), and the Personal Macro Workbook (if you've unhidden it). In Figure 14-10, the Personal Macro Workbook's tree is expanded, and the code module named Module3 is selected. This module's code appears in the Code window.

- *Properties window.* This window shows the properties for the object that's currently selected. In Figure 14-10, that object is the code module named Module3, which has only one property—the Name property. You could change the code module's name by selecting the contents of the box to the right of the (Name) box and typing a new name.

- *Code window.* This window shows the code for the selected code module or for the code sheet attached to a userform (a custom dialog box that you create). You can open multiple Code windows at once when you need to.

- *Standard toolbar.* This toolbar contains commands for standard operations such as switching to Excel, saving your work, and Cut, Copy, and Paste.

> **NOTE:** If any of the Visual Basic Editor's toolbars isn't visible, choose **View ➤ Toolbars** from the menu bar, then click the toolbar's name on the Toolbars submenu.

- *Edit toolbar.* This toolbar contains commands for editing code—for example, setting a breakpoint (a point at which code automatically stops running so that you can proceed one command at a time and see what happens).

- *Debug toolbar.* This toolbar contains commands for debugging code—going through it step by step, removing errors or otherwise improving it.

Examining the Sample Macro

Now look at the code for the sample macro. It should look like this, with minor variations for file locations and worksheet names:

```
Sub Copy_Active_Worksheet_to_Archive_Workbook()
'
' Copy_Active_Worksheet_to_Archive_Workbook Macro
' Copies the active worksheet to the Archive.xlsx workbook.
'
' Keyboard Shortcut: Option+Cmd+Shift+C
'
    Workbooks.Open Filename:= _
        "Macintosh HD:Users:guy:Documents:Ongoing:Learn Excel 2011:Examples:↵
Archive.xlsx"
    ActiveWindow.ActivatePrevious
    Sheets("Sheet1").Select
    Sheets("Sheet1").Copy After:=Workbooks("Archive.xlsx").Sheets(255)
    ActiveWorkbook.Save
    ActiveWindow.Close
End Sub
```

Here's a quick breakdown:

- The macro begins with the Sub keyword, which indicates that it's a subroutine or subprocedure (in other words, a macro), followed by the macro's name and a pair of empty parentheses.

- The next six lines are comment lines. A comment begins with a straight single quote character (') and is text intended for the human reader rather than the computer. The first, fourth, and sixth comment lines are spacers, empty lines that make the code easier to read. The second line gives the macro's name; the third gives the description; and the fifth gives the keyboard shortcut. This information helps you identify the macro and what it's supposed to do.

- The Workbooks.Open Filename:= statement opens the workbook whose path and filename appear in the string of text inside double quotation marks. Technically, this statement uses the Open method (a command) to add the workbook to the Workbooks collection of Workbook objects.

> **NOTE:** You can break a single code statement to another line by putting a space followed by an underscore at the end of the broken line. You can see an example of this in the Workbooks.Open statement.

- The ActiveWindow.ActivatePrevious statement tells VBA to activate the previous window from the active window.

- The Sheets("Sheet1").Select statement uses the Select command on the Sheets collection to select the worksheet you chose. The Sheets collection contains Sheet objects that represent the worksheets.

- The Sheets("Sheet1").Copy statement uses the Copy command on the Sheets collection to copy the worksheet specified by its name. The After:= argument tells VBA where to place the copied worksheet—in this case, after Sheet 255 in the archive workbook.

- The ActiveWorkbook.Save statement uses the Save method on the ActiveWorkbook object to save the active workbook.

- Similarly, the ActiveWorkbook.Close statement uses the Close method on the ActiveWorkbook object to close the active workbook.

- The macro ends with the End Sub line.

Editing the Sample Macro

Looking at the code and the explanation, you can probably see two problems that we need to fix:

- The macro specifies the sheet to copy by name—Sheet1. We want to copy the active worksheet instead.

- The macro specifies the sheet after which to place the copy by its number—255. We want to place the copy after the last sheet, whatever its number may be.

To fix the first problem, select Sheets("Sheet1") and type **activesheet** over it. Press the up arrow key to move to the previous statement, and you'll see that the Visual Basic Editor changes the capitalization to ActiveSheet. The Visual Basic Editor checks your code as you enter it, helping you to catch errors while you're creating the code rather than waiting until you run it.

To fix the second problem, select the 255 in Sheets(255) and type this instead:

```
Workbooks("Archive.xlsx").Sheets.Count
```

The statement you've changed should look like this:

```
ActiveSheet.Copy After:=Workbooks("Archive.xlsx").Sheets(Workbooks↵
("Archive.xlsx").Sheets.Count)
```

What the code now means is "copy the active worksheet to the workbook Archive.xlsx, putting it after the last of the existing sheets."

Testing the Macro

Now test the macro by stepping through it—going through it one statement at a time. Click the workbook that contains the worksheet you want to copy, then press Cmd+Shift+I repeatedly to step through the macro. You'll see the Visual Basic Editor highlight each line of code in turn as it executes it, and you'll see the Excel windows open, switch, and close.

Saving the Changes

Save the changes you've made to the macro. You can either press Cmd+S in the Visual Basic Editor, just as in most Mac applications, or click the Save button on the Standard toolbar.

Returning from the Visual Basic Editor to Excel

To return from the Visual Basic Editor to Excel, choose Excel ➤ Close and Return to Microsoft Excel from the menu bar with the Visual Basic Editor active. Alternatively, press Cmd+Q.

Hiding the Personal Macro Workbook

Now that you've finished editing the macro, hide the Personal Macro Workbook from view again. With the Personal Macro Workbook active, choose **Window ➤ Hide** from the menu bar.

Summary

In this chapter, you learned how to record macros using the Macro Recorder to automate repetitive tasks. You now know how to run the macros in several convenient ways and how to open macros in the Visual Basic Editor so that you can edit them. You also learned about other ways than VBA of automating tasks in Excel.

This is the end of the book—apart from the index, which you've probably met by now. I hope you've found the book useful and that you're now equipped to tackle your daily work in Excel confidently and efficiently.

Index

Special Characters & Numbers

A

B

CPSIA information can be obtained at www.ICGtesting.com
Printed in the USA
241465LV00007B/8/P